My
iPhone®
for Seniors

Brad Miser

800 East 96th Street,
Indianapolis, Indiana 46240 USA

My iPhone® for Seniors

Copyright © 2015 by Pearson Education, Inc.

ISBN-13: 978-0-7897-5361-8

ISBN-10: 0-7897-5361-8

Library of Congress Control Number: 2014949420

Printed in the United States of America

Third Printing: May 2015

Trademarks

Warning and Disclaimer

Special Sales

For information about buying this title in bulk quantities, or for special sales opportunities (which may include electronic versions; custom cover designs; and content particular to your business, training goals, marketing focus, or branding interests), please contact our corporate sales department at corpsales@pearsoned.com or (800) 382-3419.

For government sales inquiries, please contact governmentsales@pearsoned.com.

For questions about sales outside the U.S., please contact international@pearsoned.com.

Editor-in-Chief
Greg Wiegand

Senior Acquisitions Editor
Laura Norman

Development Editor
Laura Norman

Marketing
Dan Powell

Director AARP Books
Jodi Lipson

Managing Editor
Sandra Schroeder

Project Editor
Mandie Frank

Senior Indexer
Cheryl Lenser

Proofreader
Debbie Williams

Content Editor
Bill Baker

Editorial Assistant
Cindy Teeters

Designer
Mark Shirar

Compositor
Trina Wurst

Contents at a Glance

Register your book at quepublishing.com/register for access to the online chapter.

Find Chapter 17, a guide to starting with your iPhone and iTunes, and other helpful information on this book's website at quepublishing.com/title/9780789753618.

Table of Contents

16 Using Other Cool iPhone Apps and Features   637

Index   664

17 Maintaining and Protecting Your iPhone and Solving Problems   ONLINE

About the Author

Brad Miser has written extensively about technology, with his favorite topics being the amazing "i" devices, especially the iPhone, that make it possible to take our lives with us while we are on the move. In addition to *My iPhone for Seniors*, Brad has written many other books, including *My iPhone*, 8th Edition; *iTunes and iCloud for iPhone, iPad, & iPod touch Absolute Beginner's Guide*; and *Sams Teach Yourself iCloud in 10 Minutes*, 2nd Edition. He has also been an author, development editor, or technical editor for more than 50 other titles.

Brad is or has been a sales support specialist, the director of product and customer services, and the manager of education and support services for several software development companies. Previously, he was the lead proposal specialist for an aircraft engine manufacturer, a development editor for a computer book publisher, and a civilian aviation test officer/engineer for the United States Army. Brad holds a bachelor of science degree in mechanical engineering from California Polytechnic State University at San Luis Obispo and has received advanced education in maintainability engineering, business, and other topics.

Brad would love to hear about your experiences with this book (the good, the bad, and the ugly). You can write to him at bradmiser@icloud.com.

About AARP and AARP TEK

AARP is a nonprofit, nonpartisan organization, with a membership of nearly 38 million, that helps people turn their goals and dreams into real possibilities™, strengthens communities, and fights for the issues that matter most to families such as healthcare, employment and income security, retirement planning, affordable utilities, and protection from financial abuse. Learn more at aarp.org.

The AARP TEK (Technology Education & Knowledge) program aims to accelerate AARP's mission of turning dreams into real possibilities™ by providing step-by-step lessons in a variety of formats to accommodate different learning styles, levels of experience, and interests. Expertly guided hands-on workshops delivered in communities nationwide help instill confidence and enrich lives of people 50+ by equipping them with skills for staying connected to the people and passions in their lives. Lessons are taught on touchscreen tablets and smartphones—common tools for connection, education, entertainment, and productivity. For self-paced lessons, videos, articles, and other resources, visit aarptek.org.

Dedication

To those who have given the last full measure of devotion so that the rest of us can be free.

Acknowledgments

To the following people on the *My iPhone for Seniors* project team, my sincere appreciation for your hard work on this book:

Laura Norman, my acquisitions and development editor, who envisioned the original concept for *My iPhone* and works very difficult and long hours to ensure the success of each edition. Laura and I have worked on many books together, and I appreciate her professional and effective approach to these projects. Thanks for putting up with me yet one more time! Frankly, I have no idea how she does all the things she does and manages to be so great to work with, given the incredible work and pressure books like this one involve!

Bill Baker, my content editor, who made numerous suggestions to help make this book more useful for seniors.

Mandie Frank, my project editor, who skillfully managed the hundreds of files and production process that it took to make this book. Imagine keeping dozens of plates spinning on top of poles and you get a glimpse into Mandie's daily life! (And no plates have been broken in the production of this book!)

Mark Shirar, for the interior design and cover of the book.

Que's production and sales team for printing the book and getting it into your hands.

We Want to Hear from You!

As the reader of this book, *you* are our most important critic and commentator. We value your opinion and want to know what we're doing right, what we could do better, what areas you'd like to see us publish in, and any other words of wisdom you're willing to pass our way.

We welcome your comments. You can email or write to let us know what you did or didn't like about this book—as well as what we can do to make our books better.

Please note that we cannot help you with technical problems related to the topic of this book.

When you write, please be sure to include this book's title and author as well as your name and email address. We will carefully review your comments and share them with the author and editors who worked on the book.

Email: feedback@quepublishing.com

Mail: Que Publishing
         ATTN: Reader Feedback
         800 East 96th Street
         Indianapolis, IN 46240 USA

Reader Services

Visit our website and register this book at quepublishing.com/register for convenient access to any updates, downloads, or errata that might be available for this book.

Using This Book

This book has been designed to help you transform an iPhone into *your* iPhone by helping you learn to use it easily and quickly. As you can tell, the book relies heavily on pictures to show you how an iPhone works. It is also task-focused so that you can quickly learn the specific steps to follow to do lots of cool things with your iPhone.

Using an iPhone involves lots of touching its screen with your fingers. When you need to tap part of the screen, such as a button or keyboard, you see a callout with the step number pointing to where you need to tap. When you need to swipe your finger along the screen, such as to browse lists, you see the following icons:

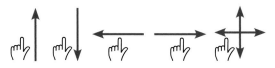

The directions in which you should slide your finger on the screen are indicated with arrows. When the arrow points both ways, you can move your finger in either direction. When the arrows point in all four directions, you can move your finger in any direction on the screen.

To zoom in on the screen, unpinch your figures by placing them together on the center of the screen and then sliding them apart while still touching the screen. To zoom out on screens, place your fingers a little apart on the screen, and then pinch them together. These motions are indicated by the following icons:

When you need to tap once or twice, such as to zoom out or in, you see the following icons matching the number of times you need to tap:

When you can rotate your iPhone, you see this icon:

Occasionally, you shake the iPhone to activate a control. When you do, you see this icon:

As you can see on its cover, this book provides information about a number of iPhone models, which are the iPhone 4s, iPhone 5, iPhone 5c and 5s, iPhone 6, and iPhone 6 Plus. Each of these models has specific features and capabilities that vary slightly from the others. Additionally, they have different screen sizes with the 4s being the smallest and the iPhone 6 Plus being the largest.

Because of the variations between the models, the figures you see in this book may be slightly different than the screens you see on your iPhone. For example, the iPhone 6 has settings that aren't on the iPhone 5s while the 5s and later models support Touch ID (fingerprint recognition) while the 4s and 5/5c don't. In most cases, you can follow the steps as they are written with any of these models even if there are minor differences between the figures and your screens.

When the model you are using doesn't support a feature being described, such as the Display Zoom that is on the iPhone 6 and 6 Plus but not on previous models, you can skip the information or read it to help you decide if you want to upgrade to a newer model.

If you have used an iPhone before running an earlier version of its software, you will notice that there are many changes in iOS 8, some are significant and still others are entirely new. In the case of those features that have changed significantly, or are completely new, we have added an indicator to the text and table of contents to help you easily locate them. When you see **New!** be sure to check out those tasks to quickly get up to speed on what's new in iOS 8.

Getting Started

Learning to use new technology can be intimidating. Don't worry, with this book as your guide, you'll be working your iPhone like you've been using it all your life in no time at all.

I've assumed you have an iPhone in your hands. That's a good thing, because this book is designed for you to read and do at the same time. The tasks explained in this book contain step-by-step instructions that guide you; to get the most benefit from the information, perform the steps as you read them. This book helps you learn by doing!

As you can see, this book has quite a few chapters. However, there are only a few that you definitely should read as a group as you get started. You can read the rest of them as the topics are of interest to you. Most of the chapters are designed so that they can be read individually as you move into new areas of your iPhone. For example, when you want to learn how to send messages, read Chapter 10, "Sending, Receiving, and Managing Texts and iMessages."

After you've finished reading this front matter, I recommend you read and work through Chapter 1, "Getting Started with Your iPhone;" Chapter 2, "Connecting Your iPhone to the Internet, Bluetooth Devices, and iPhones/iPods/iPads;" and Chapter 3, "Setting Up and Using iCloud and Other Online Accounts" in their entirety. These chapters give you a good overview of your iPhone and help you set up the basics you use throughout the rest of the book.

From there, read the parts of Chapter 4, "Configuring an iPhone to Suit Your Preferences," that are of interest to you (for example, you might want to change the wallpaper image that you see in the background of the Home and Lock screens). Tasks covering how to protect your iPhone with a passcode and how to have your iPhone recognize your fingerprints to unlock it and to make purchases from the iTunes Store should be high on your priority list. Chapter 4 is a good reference whenever you need to make changes to how your iPhone is configured.

After you've finished these core chapters, you're ready to explore the rest of the book in any order you'd like. For example, when you want to learn how to use your iPhone's camera and work with the photos you take, see Chapter 15, "Working with Photos and Video You Take with Your iPhone."

Activating Your iPhone

If you've received your iPhone without it being activated for you when you purchased it and you are using an existing number (such as when you upgrade your iPhone), you need to activate it to start using it. (If you can make a phone call with your iPhone, it is already activated and you can skip to Chapter 1.) Activate your iPhone by performing the following steps:

(1) Locate the documentation that came with your phone. This includes information about a phone number you can call or a website you can visit to activate your phone. These details depend on the specific provider you use. These steps describe AT&T's activation process. Other providers use a similar process that is described in the documentation that came with your iPhone.

(2) Using another phone, call the activation phone number shown in the documentation.

(3) Follow the prompts in the automated system to activate your account. You need to provide the phone number you are moving to the new iPhone and your identification information (such as zip code or last four of your social security number).

(4) When you have provided all of the activation information, you can hang up.

(5) On your iPhone, press and hold on the Sleep/Wake button until you see the slide to power off slider.

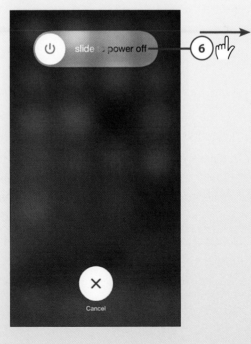

(6) Swipe to the right on the slider to shut down your iPhone.

7 Wait the amount of time you were instructed to when you called for activation; typically this is five minutes.

8 Press and hold the Sleep/Wake button until you see the Apple logo on your iPhone's screen. Your iPhone restarts and the Lock screen appears.

9 Swipe to the right on the slider at the bottom of the screen to unlock the iPhone.

10 Enter your passcode to unlock the phone. When you move to the Home screen, you should see your cell provider's name and at least one dot at the top of the screen. If you see No Service instead, that means your iPhone has not been activated. Shut it down again and wait several more minutes, and then repeat steps 8 and 9. If you still see No Service at the top of the screen, contact your cell provider for help.

Your cell phone provider and signal strength

11   Tap the Phone icon to open the Phone app. (Using your iPhone to makes calls is covered in detail in Chapter 8, "Communicating with the Phone and FaceTime Apps.")

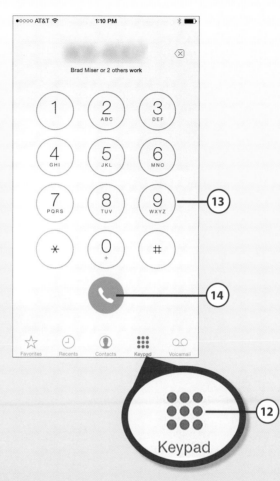

12) Tap the Keypad button.

13) Tap the numbers you want to dial.

14) Tap the receiver button to place the call. If the call is placed successfully, your iPhone is activated and ready to use. If the call fails or can't be placed, go back to step 2 and try again. If the steps don't work a second time, contact the cell phone provider for help.

Help Getting Started with iTunes and Your iPhone

For help getting started with iTunes and if your iPhone is not an upgrade (you got a number number with your phone), see "Getting Started with iTunes" on this book's website.

You'll soon wonder how you ever got along without one!

In this chapter, you get introduced to the amazing iPhone! Topics include the following:

→ Getting to know your iPhone's external features
→ Getting to know your iPhone's software

1

Getting Started with Your iPhone

Your iPhone is one of the most amazing handheld devices ever because of how well it is designed. It has only a few external features you need to understand. For most of the things you do, you just use your fingers on your iPhone's screen, and the iPhone's consistent interface enables you to accomplish most tasks with similar steps.

Getting to Know Your iPhone's External Features

Take a quick look at the iPhone's physical attributes. It doesn't have many physical buttons or controls because you mostly use software to control it.

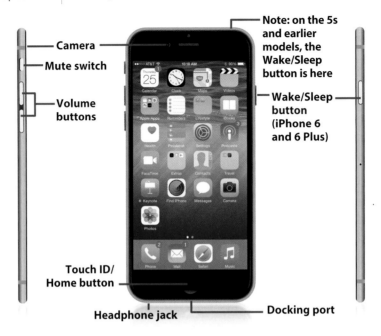

Camera

Mute switch

Volume buttons

Touch ID/ Home button

Headphone jack

Note: on the 5s and earlier models, the Wake/Sleep button is here

Wake/Sleep button (iPhone 6 and 6 Plus)

Docking port

- **Cameras**—One of the iPhone's camera lenses is located on its backside near the top-left corner; the other is on the front at the top at the center of the phone. When you take photos or video, you can choose which camera to use. The flash is located near the camera on the backside (there's no flash when you use the camera on the front).

- **Wake/Sleep button**—Press this to lock the iPhone's controls and put it to sleep. Press it again to wake the iPhone from Sleep mode. You also use this button to shut down the iPhone and to power it up.

- **Mute switch**—This switch determines whether the iPhone makes sounds, such as ringing when a call comes in or making the alert noise for a notification, such as an event on a calendar. Slide it toward the front of the iPhone to hear sounds. Slide it toward the back of the iPhone to mute all sound. When muted, you see orange in the switch.

- **Headphone jack**—Plug the iPhone's EarPods, other types of headphones, or self-powered, external speakers into this jack.

- **Volume**—Press the upper button to increase volume; press the lower button to decrease volume. This is contextual; for example, when you are listening to music, it controls the music's volume, but when you aren't, it controls the ringer volume. When you are using the Camera app, pressing either button takes a photo.

- **Docking port**—Use this port, located on the bottom side of the iPhone, to connect it to a computer or power adapter using the included USB cable. There are also accessories that connect to this port. iPhone 5s, 5c, 6, and 6 Plus have the Lightning port, which uses a flat, thin plug. It doesn't matter which side is up when you plug something into this port. iPhone 4s uses the 30 pin port, which is much larger and has to be inserted "top side up."

- **Touch ID/Home button (iPhone 5s, 6, and 6 Plus)**—This serves two functions. The Touch ID sensor recognizes your fingerprint, so you can simply touch it to unlock your iPhone, sign into the iTunes Store, use Apple Pay, and for many other situations in which you need to confirm your information to complete a transaction. It also functions just like the Home button described in the following bullet.

- **Home button (iPhone 5c, 5, and 4s)**— When the iPhone is asleep, press it to wake up the iPhone. When the iPhone is awake and unlocked, press this button to move to the all-important Home screens; press it twice quickly to open the App Switcher. Press and hold the Home button to activate Siri to speak to your iPhone.

So Many iPhones, So Few Pages

The iPhone is now in its eighth generation. Each successive generation has added features and capabilities to the previous version. All iPhones run the iOS operating system. This book is based on the current version of this operating system, iOS 8. The iPhone 4s and newer can run this version of the software. If you have a version of the iPhone older than the 4s, this book helps you see why it is time to upgrade, but most of the information contained herein won't apply to your iPhone.

There are also differences even among the models of iPhones that can run iOS 8. For example, the iPhone 5s, 6, and 6 Plus models have Touch ID that uses your fingerprint to unlock your iPhone, to sign in to your Apple ID, and for other purposes (such as Apple Pay). The iPhone 4s, 5, and 5c do not have this capability.

This book is primarily based on the latest generation of iPhones: the iPhone 6 and 6 Plus. If you use one of the other models that can run iOS 8, there might be some differences between the details you read in this book and your phone. Those differences aren't significant and shouldn't stop you from accomplishing the tasks as described in this book.

Getting to Know Your iPhone's Software

You might not suspect it based on the iPhone's simple and elegant exterior, but this powerhouse runs very sophisticated software that enables you to do all sorts of great things. The beauty of the iPhone's software is that it is both very powerful and also easy to use—once you get used to its User Interface (UI for the more technical among you). The iPhone's UI is so well designed that after a few minutes, you may wish everything worked so well and was so easy to use.

Using Your Fingers to Control Your iPhone

Apple designed the iPhone to be touched. Most of the time, you control your iPhone by using your fingers on its screen to tap buttons, select items, swipe on the screen, zoom, and type text. This method of interacting with software is called the multi-touch interface.

Going Home

Almost all iPhone activities start at the Home screen. You get to the Home screen by pressing the Touch ID/Home button. Along the bottom of the Home screen is the Home screen toolbar, which is always visible when you move through the Home screen's pages. This gives you easy access to the icons it contains (more on the Home screens shortly); up to four icons can be placed on this toolbar. Above the toolbar are apps that do all sorts of cool things. As you install apps, the number of icons increases. You can also create bookmarks for websites and store them as icons on the Home screens. As more icons are added, you have multiple pages on the Home screen, so there's always room for what you need to store on them. You can organize the icons on the pages of the Home screens in any way you like, and you can place icons into folders to keep your Home screens tidy and so that accessing the icons you use most frequently is convenient. At the top of the screen are status icons that provide you with important information, such as whether you are connected to a Wi-Fi network and the current charge of your iPhone's battery.

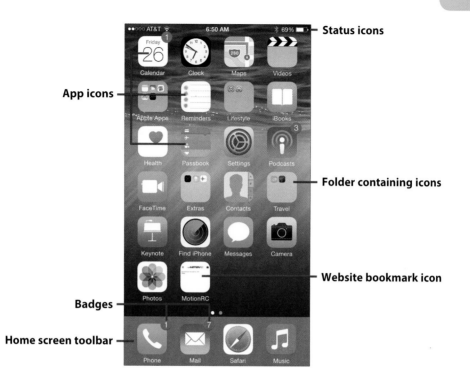

Touching the iPhone's Screen

The following figures highlight the major ways you control an iPhone. A tap is just what it sounds like—you briefly touch a finger to the iPhone's screen over the item you want to control and then lift your finger again. For example, to work with an app, you tap its icon. Sometimes, you double-tap, which is also exactly what it sounds like: you simply tap twice. To swipe, touch the screen at any location and slide your finger in one direction, such as to the left to move to the next screen, which might show the next photo in an album you are viewing. To drag, tap and hold an object and move your finger across the screen without lifting it up; the faster you move your finger, the faster the resulting action happens. (You don't need to apply pressure on the screen, just make contact with your finger on the screen.) To pinch or unpinch, place two fingers on the screen and drag them together or move them apart; the faster and more you pinch or unpinch, the "more" the action happens (such as a zoom in). You can rotate the iPhone to change the screen's orientation.

Tap an app's icon to launch it

Swipe your finger up and down to browse lists

Tap a letter in the index to jump to it

Tap an item to work with it

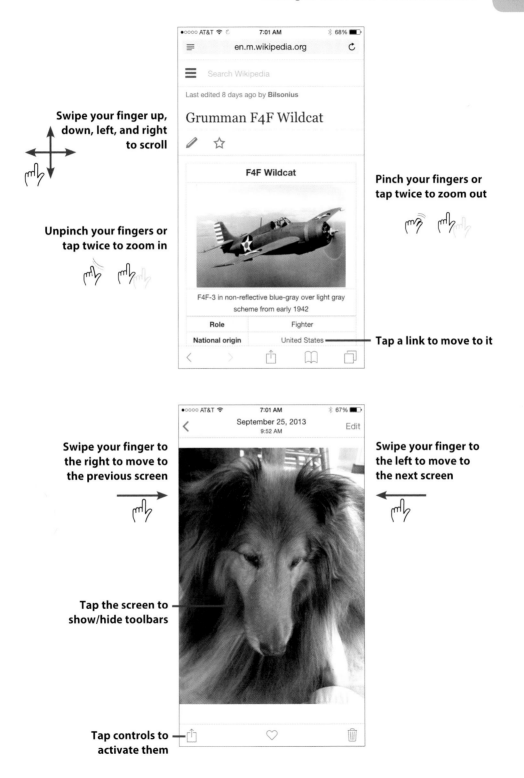

Swipe your finger up, down, left, and right to scroll

Unpinch your fingers or tap twice to zoom in

Pinch your fingers or tap twice to zoom out

Tap a link to move to it

Swipe your finger to the right to move to the previous screen

Swipe your finger to the left to move to the next screen

Tap the screen to show/hide toolbars

Tap controls to activate them

Rotate the iPhone to change the screen's orientation

Working with iPhone Apps

One of the best things about an iPhone is that it can run all sorts of applications, or in iPhone lingo, *apps*. It includes a number of preinstalled apps, such as Mail, Safari, and Music, but you can download and use thousands of other apps through the App Store. You learn about many of the iPhone's preinstalled apps as you read through this book. And as you learned earlier, to launch an app, you simply tap its icon. The app launches and fills the iPhone's screen.

When you tap an app's icon, it opens and fills the iPhone's screen (this is the iBooks app)

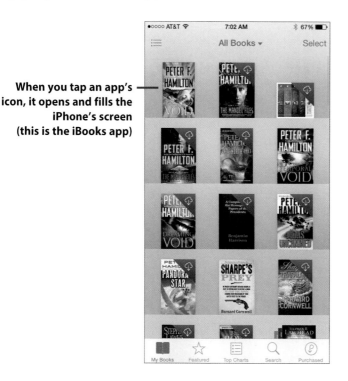

In Chapter 4, "Configuring an iPhone to Suit Your Preferences," you learn how you can organize icons in folders to keep your Home screens tidy and make getting to icons faster and easier. To access an icon that is in a folder, tap the folder. It opens and takes over the screen. Under its name is a box showing the apps or website bookmarks it contains. Like the Home screens, folders can have multiple pages. To move between a folder's pages, swipe to the left to move to the next screen or to the right to move to the previous one. Each time you "flip" a page, you see another set of icons.

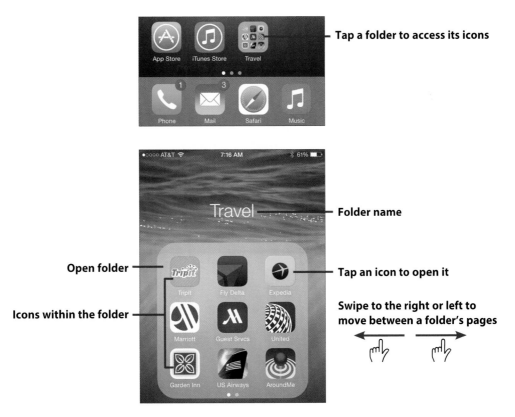

Tap a folder to access its icons

Folder name

Open folder

Tap an icon to open it

Icons within the folder

Swipe to the right or left to move between a folder's pages

To launch an app or open a website bookmark within a folder, tap its icon.

When you are done using an app, press the Home button. You return to the Home screen you were most recently using.

Because the iPhone multitasks, when you move out of an app by pressing the Home button, the app moves into the background but doesn't stop running (although you can control whether or not apps are allowed to work in the background, as you learn in a later section). So, if the app has a task to complete, such as uploading photos or playing audio, it continues to work behind-the-scenes. In some cases, most notably games, the app becomes suspended at the point you move it into the background by switching to a different app or moving to a Home screen. In addition to the benefit of completing tasks when you move into another app, the iPhone's capability to multitask means that you can run multiple apps at the same time. For example, you can run an Internet radio app to listen to music while you switch over to the Mail app to work on your email.

You can control apps by using the App Switcher. To see this, quickly press the Touch ID/Home button twice. The App Switcher appears.

At the top of the App Switcher, you see your Favorites and Recents list. The Favorites list contains people whom you have designated as a Favorite; this makes it very easy to call them, message them, or contact them via FaceTime . The Recents list contains people you have recently contacted via the phone, FaceTime, Messages, or in a number of ways. You can use your Recents list to get back in contact with anyone you see on it. (You learn how to use this part of the App Switcher in Chapter 8, "Communicating with the Phone and FaceTime Apps.")

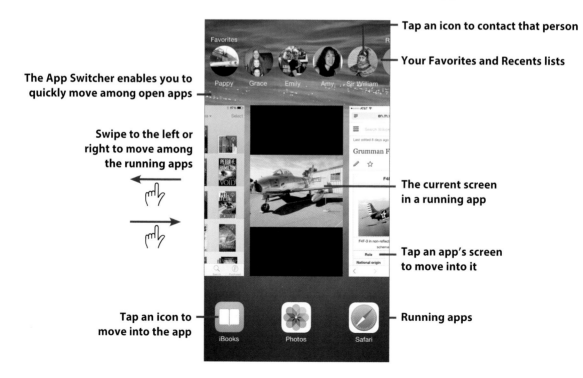

Tap an icon to contact that person

Your Favorites and Recents lists

The App Switcher enables you to quickly move among open apps

Swipe to the left or right to move among the running apps

The current screen in a running app

Tap an app's screen to move into it

Tap an icon to move into the app

Running apps

In the center of the screen, you see thumbnails for the apps that are currently open; in the thumbnail, you see the screen currently open in that app. You can swipe to the left or right to move among the apps you see. You can tap an app to move it to the front so you can use it.

At the bottom of this screen, you see the icons of all the apps that are currently running. Just like the screens in the center of the App Switcher, you can swipe to the left or right on the icons to move among the running apps or tap an icon to bring the app to the front so you can work with it.

When you tap an app's thumbnail or icon, that app takes over the screen, and you can work with it, picking up right where you left off the last time you used it.

To close the App Switcher without moving into a different app, press the Home button once. You move back into the app or Home screen you were most recently using.

Swipe up on an app's screen to force it to close

In some cases (such as when it's using up your battery too quickly or it has stopped responding to you), you might want to force an app to quit. To do this, open the App Switcher by quickly pressing the Touch ID/Home button twice. Swipe up on the app you want to stop. The app is forced to quit, its icon and screen disappear, and you remain in the App Switcher. You should be careful about this, though, because if the app has unsaved data, that data is lost when you force the app to quit. The app is not deleted from the iPhone—it is just shut down until you open it again (which you can do by returning to the Home screen and tapping the app's icon).

Using the Home Screens

Previously in this chapter, you read that the Home screen is the jumping-off point for many of the things you do with your iPhone because that is where you access the icons you tap to launch things such as apps or website bookmarks you've saved there.

The Home screen has multiple pages. To change the page you are viewing, swipe to the left to move to later pages or to the right to move to earlier pages. The dots above the toolbar represent the pages of the Home screen. The white dot represents the page being displayed. You can also change the page by tapping to the left of the white dot to move to the previous page or to the right of it to move to the next page.

Swipe to the left or right to move between pages of your Home screen

Tap to the left or right of the current page (white dot) to move to the previous or the next page

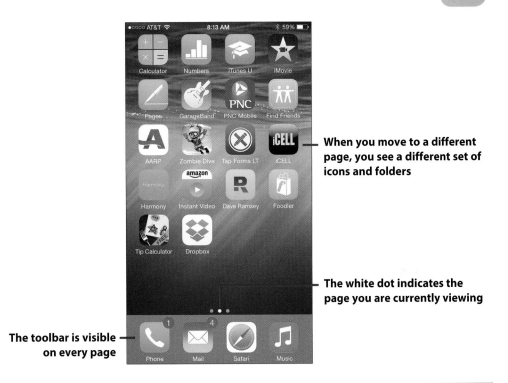

When you move to a different page, you see a different set of icons and folders

The white dot indicates the page you are currently viewing

The toolbar is visible on every page

Home Rotation

As of this writing, when you hold the iPhone 6 Plus horizontally, the Home screens change orientation and the toolbar is reoriented so it is vertical along the right side of the screen. The iPhone 6, 5s, 5c, 5, and 4s do not currently have this capability. Future releases of iOS 8 might enable this on the 6 model, but not likely for the other models due to the smaller screen format.

Searching on Your iPhone

You can use the Spotlight Search tool to search your iPhone. To open this tool, swipe down from the center part of the screen. (Be careful not to swipe down from the very top of the screen because that opens the Notification Center instead.) The Search bar appears at the top of the screen and the keyboard opens.

To perform a search, tap in the Search bar and type the search term using the onscreen keyboard. As you type, items that meet your search are shown on the list below the Search bar. When you finish typing the search term, tap Search.

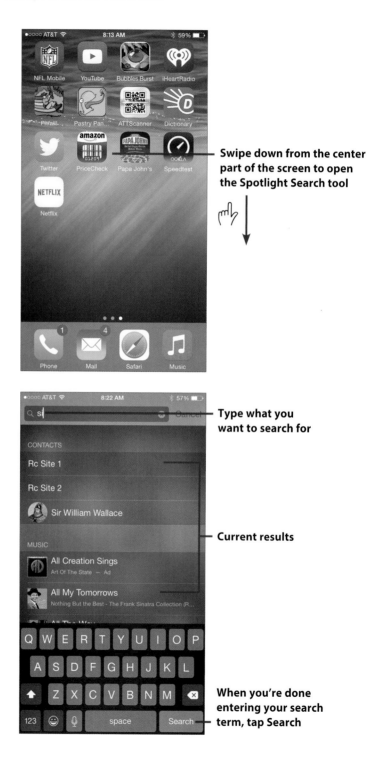

Swipe down from the center part of the screen to open the Spotlight Search tool

Type what you want to search for

Current results

When you're done entering your search term, tap Search

Tap to close the Spotlight tool without moving to a result

Tap to clear the search term

Contacts you found

To work with a result, tap it

Music related to your search term

Search results

The results are organized into sections, each of which is labeled by the type of object it is, such as CONTACTS, MAIL, MUSIC or REMINDERS. To work with an item you find, such as to view contact information you found, tap it; you move into the associated app and see the search result that you tapped. The results remain in the Spotlight Search tool. Move back to the Home screen and open the Spotlight tool again. The results of the most recent search are still listed. To clear the search term, tap the Clear button (x). To close the Spotlight tool without going to one of the results, tap Cancel.

Working with the Control Center

The Control Center provides quick access to a number of very useful controls. To access it, swipe up from the bottom of the screen. If your iPhone is asleep/locked, press the Sleep/Wake or Touch ID/Home button to wake up the phone and then swipe up from the bottom of the screen from the area of the horizontal line. Sometimes when you are using an app, the place you swipe up on is marked with an upward-facing arrow. Regardless of the screen you are on, when you swipe up, the Control Center opens and gives you quick access to a number of controls.

On the Home screen or when you are using apps, swipe up from the bottom of the screen to open the Control Center

On the Lock screen, the place you swipe up on to open the Control Center is marked with a line

On some app screens, where you swipe up to open the Control Center is indicated by an upward-facing arrow

Control Center Tip

Some apps have a toolbar at the bottom of the screen. When you are using such an app, make sure you don't touch a button on the toolbar when you are trying to open the Control Center because you'll do whatever the button is for instead. Just swipe up on an empty area of the toolbar and the Control Center opens.

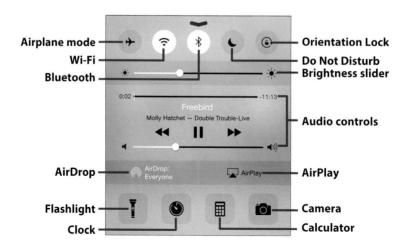

Airplane mode — Orientation Lock
Wi-Fi — Do Not Disturb
Bluetooth — Brightness slider

Audio controls

AirDrop — AirPlay

Flashlight — Camera
Clock — Calculator

At the top of the Control Center are buttons you can use to turn on or turn off important functions. To activate a function, tap the button, which becomes white to show the function is active. To disable a function, tap the button so that it becomes dark to show you it is inactive. For example, to lock the orientation of the iPhone's screen in its current position, tap the Orientation Lock button so it becomes white. Your iPhone screen's orientation no longer changes when you rotate the phone. To make the orientation change when you rotate the phone again, turn off the Orientation Lock button. You learn about Airplane mode and Do No Disturb later in this chapter. Wi-Fi and Bluetooth are explained in Chapter 2, "Connecting Your iPhone to the Internet, Bluetooth Devices, and iPhones/iPods/iPads."

Below the top function buttons is the Brightness slider. Drag the slider to the right to make the screen brighter or to the left to make it dimmer.

In the center of the Control Center are the audio controls you can use with whatever audio is playing, such as music from the Music app or podcasts from the Podcasts app. The Music and Podcasts apps are covered in Chapter 14, "Finding and Listening to Music," and Chapter 16, "Using Other Cool iPhone Apps and Features," respectively.

The AirDrop button enables you to share content with other iOS device users in the same vicinity; this is covered in Chapter 2. The AirPlay button enables you to stream your iPhone's music, podcasts, photos, and video onto other devices, such as a TV to which an Apple TV is connected; using AirPlay is covered in Chapters 14 and 15, "Working with Photos and Video You Take with Your iPhone."

At the bottom of the Control Center are four app icons; tap an icon to open the app, just as you do on the Home screens. The Flashlight app uses your iPhone's flash as a flashlight. The Clock app provides you with a number of time-related functions, which are world clocks, alarms, timer, and stopwatch. The Calculator does just what it sounds like it does; when you hold the iPhone vertically, you see a simple calculator, while if you rotate the iPhone to horizontal, the calculator becomes more powerful. The Camera app enables you to capture photos and video (this is covered in Chapter 15).

Working with Notifications and the Notification Center

Your iPhone has a lot of activity going on, from new emails to reminders to calendar events. The iOS notification system keeps you informed of these happenings through a number of means. Visual notifications include alerts, banners, and badges. Alert sounds can also let you know something has happened, and vibrations make you feel the new activity. You have all sorts of notification options for each app. You learn how to customize the notifications your iPhone uses in Chapter 4.

Working with visual notifications is pretty straightforward.

When a banner appears, you can do one of several things. You can view and then ignore it (it rotates off the screen after displaying for a few seconds). You can tap it to move into the app to take some action, such as to read an email. You can swipe up from the bottom to close it. For some apps, such as Messages, you can swipe down on the banner to respond directly in the notification.

When an alert appears, you must either take action, such as listening to a voice message, tap the Options button to take one of a number of actions, or tap the Dismiss/Close/Ignore button to close the alert and keep doing what you were doing.

Badges appear on an app's or a folder's icon to let you know something has changed, such as a reminder alert.

Badges are purely informational as are sounds and vibrations; you can't take any action on these directly. They inform you about an event so that you can take action, such as to download and install an update to your iPhone's iOS software.

Notifications on the Lock Screen

Notifications can appear on the Lock screen. This is useful because you can see them when your iPhone is locked and awake. If your phone is asleep, you can press the Wake/Sleep button or the Touch/ID Home button to see your notifications without unlocking the iPhone. You can swipe up or down the screen to browse the notifications on the Lock screen or swipe to the right on them to move to the related app, too (if you have configured a passcode for your phone, you need to enter it to move into the associated app).

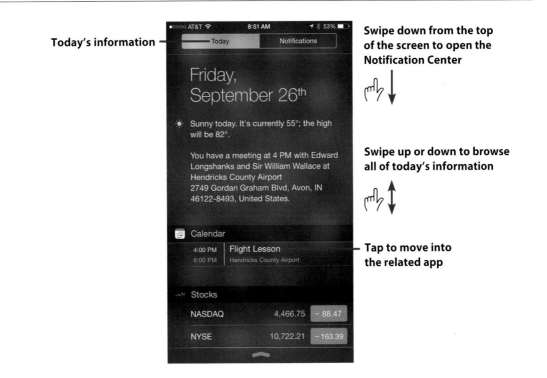

Today's information

Swipe down from the top of the screen to open the Notification Center

Swipe up or down to browse all of today's information

Tap to move into the related app

The Notification Center organizes and displays a variety of information for you. To open the Notification Center, swipe down from the top of the iPhone's screen; if your iPhone is currently asleep/locked, press the Sleep/Wake button and then swipe down from the top of the screen.

Tap the Today tab to see the day and date along with weather information. Under that, you see any information that impacts your day; this information is organized in sections based on its type, such as Reminders, Calendar events, etc. If you swipe up far enough, you see the Tomorrow section that presents information about tomorrow's activities, too.

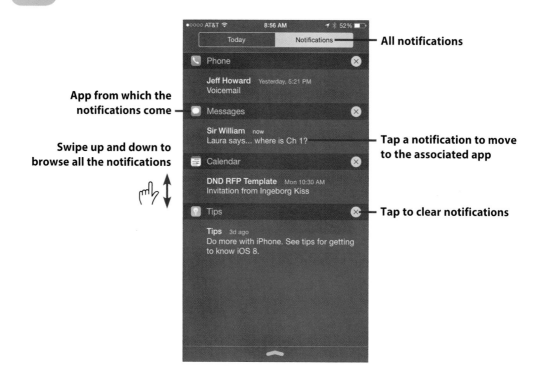

All notifications

App from which the notifications come

Swipe up and down to browse all the notifications

Tap a notification to move to the associated app

Tap to clear notifications

Tap the Notifications tab to see all your current notifications, such as for new email or text messages. These are organized by the app from which they come. Like the Today tab, you can swipe up and down to browse all the notifications or tap a notification to move to the related app. To remove all the notifications for an app, tap its Clear button (x) and then tap Clear.

Active Notifications

Some of the notifications can show more information than can fit on the screen (examples include the Weather and Stocks apps). Swipe to the left or right on these notifications to see more information. Some notifications have links that take you to the Web to get more detailed information.

Using the Do Not Disturb Mode

All the notifications you read about in the previous section are useful, but at times, they can be annoying or distracting. When you put your iPhone in Do Not Disturb mode, its visual, audible, and vibration notifications are disabled so that they won't bother you. It won't ring if someone calls you, either.

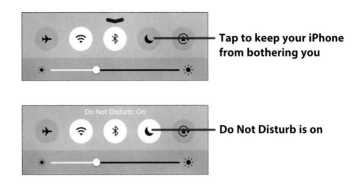

Tap to keep your iPhone from bothering you

Do Not Disturb is on

To put your iPhone in Do Not Disturb mode, open the Control Center and tap the Do Not Disturb button. It becomes white and the Do Not Disturb: On status flashes at the top of the Control Center. Your iPhone stops its notifications and does not ring if someone calls. To make your notifications active again, tap the Do Not Disturb button so it is black; your iPhone resumes trying to get your attention when it is needed.

In Chapter 4, you learn how to set a schedule for Do Not Disturb so that your iPhone goes into this mode automatically at certain times, such as from 10 p.m. to 6 a.m. You can also configure certain exceptions, including whose calls come in even when your iPhone is in this mode.

Using the iPhone 6 Plus' Split-Screen

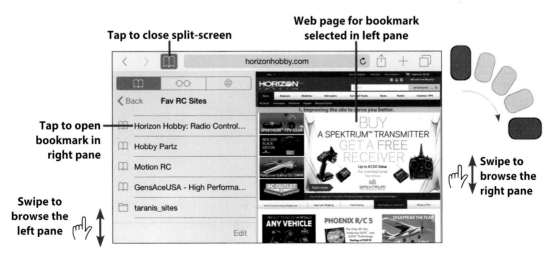

Tap to close split-screen

Web page for bookmark selected in left pane

Tap to open bookmark in right pane

Swipe to browse the left pane

Swipe to browse the right pane

When you hold an iPhone 6 Plus in the horizontal orientation, you can take advantage of the iPhone 6 Plus' Split-screen feature in many apps (not all apps support this). In Split-screen mode, the screen has two panes. The left pane is for navigation while the right pane shows the content selected in the left pane. The two panes are independent, so you can swipe up and down on one side without affecting the other. For example, when you are using Safari to browse the Web, you can select bookmarks in the left pane and see the associated web pages in the right pane; tap the Bookmark button to close the left pane and tap it again to show the pane.

Apps that support this functionality include Settings, Mail, Safari, and Messages; you see examples showing how Split-screen works for some of these apps later in this book. You should hold the iPhone 6 Plus horizontally when using your favorite apps to see if they support this feature.

When you hold the iPhone 6 Plus horizontally and move to the Home screen, the toolbar moves to the right side of the screen and you see the Home screen's pages in the left part of the window. Though this looks a bit different, it works the same as when you hold an iPhone vertically.

Working with Text

You can do lots of things with an iPhone that require you to provide text input. There are a couple of ways you can do this, the most obvious of which is by typing. The iPhone's keyboard is quite amazing. Whenever you need it, whether it's for emailing, entering a website URL, performing a search, or any other typing function, it pops up automatically.

To type, just tap the keys. As you tap each key, you hear audio feedback (you can disable this sound if you want to). The keyboard includes all the standard keys, plus a few for special uses. To change from letters to numbers and special characters, just tap the 123 key. Tap the #+= key to see more special characters. Tap the 123 key to move back to the numbers and special characters or the ABC key to return to letters. The keyboard also has contextual keys that appear when you need them. For example, when you enter a website address, the .com key appears so you can enter these four characters with a single tap.

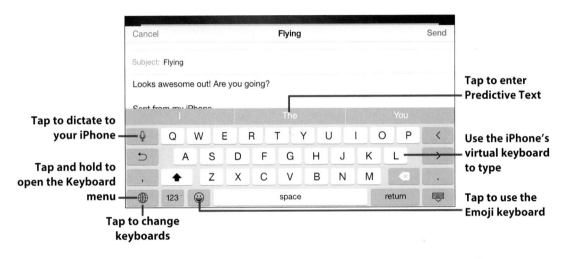

Tap to dictate to your iPhone

Tap and hold to open the Keyboard menu

Tap to change keyboards

Tap to enter Predictive Text

Use the iPhone's virtual keyboard to type

Tap to use the Emoji keyboard

You can also use Predictive Text, which is the feature that tries to predict text you want to enter based on the context of what you are currently typing and what you have typed before. Predictive Text appears in the bar between the text and the keyboard and presents you with three options. If one of those is what you want to enter, tap it and it is added to the text at the current location of the cursor. If you don't see an option you want to enter, keep typing and the options change as the text changes. You can tap an option at any time to enter it. The nice thing about Predictive Text is that it gets better at predicting your text needs over time. In other words, the more you use it, the better it gets at predicting what you want to type. You can also enable or disable Predictive Text as you see shortly.

Predictive Text Need Not Apply

When you are entering text where Predictive Text doesn't apply, such as when you are typing email addresses, the Predictive Text bar is hidden and can't be enabled. This makes sense because there's no way text in things such as email addresses can be predicted. When you move back into an area where it does apply, Predictive Text becomes active again.

The great thing about a soft (digital) keyboard like the iPhone has is that it can change to reflect the language or symbols you want to type. As you learn in Chapter 4, you can install multiple keyboards, such as one for your primary language and more for your secondary languages. You can also install third-party keyboards to take advantage of their features (this is also covered in Chapter 4).

By default, two keyboards are available for you to use. One is for the primary language configured for your iPhone (for example, mine is U.S. English). The other is the Emoji keyboard (more on this shortly). How you change the keyboard you are using depends on if you have installed additional keyboards and the orientation of the iPhone.

If you haven't installed additional keyboards, you can change keyboards by tapping the Emoji key, which has a smiley face on it.

If you have installed other keyboards, you change keyboards by tapping the Globe key.

Each time you tap this key (Globe if available, Emoji if there isn't a Globe), the keyboard changes to be the next keyboard installed; along with the available keys changing, you briefly see the name of the current keyboard in the Space bar. When you have cycled through all the keyboards, you return to the one where you started.

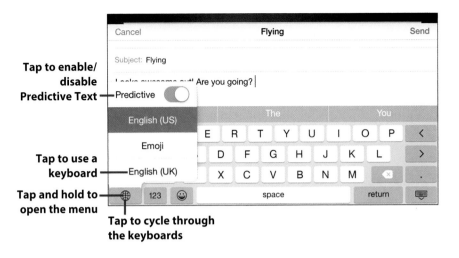

Tap to enable/ disable Predictive Text — Predictive

Tap to use a keyboard — English (UK)

Tap and hold to open the menu

Tap to cycle through the keyboards

You can also select the specific keyboard you want to use and enable/disable Predictive Text by tapping and holding on the Globe key (or the Emoji key if you don't see the Globe key). The Keyboard menu appears. Tap a keyboard to switch to it. Tap Predictive Text to enable or disable it; when the switch is green Predictive Text is enabled, when the switch is white, it is hidden.

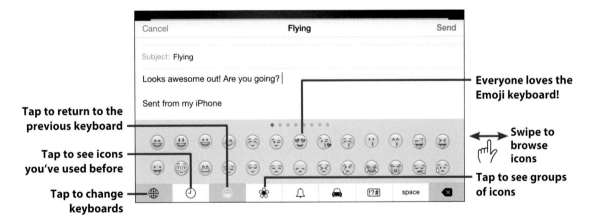

Tap to return to the previous keyboard

Tap to see icons you've used before

Tap to change keyboards

Everyone loves the Emoji keyboard!

Swipe to browse icons

Tap to see groups of icons

The Emoji keyboard enables you to insert a variety of icons into your text to liven things up, communicate your feelings, or just to have some fun (if you don't have this keyboard installed, see Chapter 4). You can open this keyboard by tapping its key (the smiley face). You see a palette containing many icons, organized into groups. You can change the groups of icons you are browsing by tapping the keys at the bottom of the screen. Swipe to the left or right on the icons to browse the icons in the current group. Tap an icon to enter it at the cursor's location in your message, email, or other type of document. To use an icon you've used before, tap the Clock key; you'll probably find that you use the recent set of icons regularly so this can save a lot of time. To return to the mundane world of letters and symbols, tap the Emoji or Globe key again.

The Keys, They Are A-Changin'

The keys on the keyboard can change depending on the orientation of the iPhone. For example, when you have more than one keyboard installed and hold the iPhone vertically, the Emoji key disappears and you see only the Globe key. Not to worry though, you can still get to the Emoji keyboard by tapping the Globe key until the Emoji keyboard appears, or by opening the Keyboard menu and tapping Emoji. When you have installed additional keyboards and hold the iPhone horizontally, you see both the Globe and Emoji keys. Tap the Emoji key to switch to that keyboard or the Globe key to cycle through all the keyboards.

Another Reason It's Called a Plus

When you rotate an iPhone 6 Plus to the horizontal position, the keyboard gains some extra keys. These include Cut (scissors), Copy (square with A in it), Paste (bottle of paste), bold (B), and undo (curved arrow).

What's Your Typing Orientation?

Similar to many other tasks, you can rotate the iPhone to change the screen's orientation while you type. When the iPhone is in the horizontal orientation, the keyboard is wider, making it easier to tap individual keys. When the iPhone is in the vertical orientation, the keyboard is narrower, but you can see more of the typing area. So, try both to see which mode is most effective for you.

If you type a word that the iPhone doesn't recognize, that word is flagged as a possible mistake and suggestions are made to help you correct it. How this happens depends on whether or not Predictive Text is enabled.

If Predictive Text is enabled, potential replacements for suspicious words appear in the Predictive Text bar. Tap a word to replace what you've typed with the suggested word.

If Predictive Text isn't enabled, a suspicious word is highlighted and a suggestion about what it thinks is the correct word appears in a pop-up box. To accept the suggestion, tap the Space key. To reject the suggestion, tap the pop-up box to close it and keep what you typed. You can also use this feature for shorthand typing. For example, to type "I've" you can simply type "Ive" and iPhone suggests "I've" which you can accept by tapping the Space key.

Typing Tricks

Many keys, especially symbols and punctuation, have additional characters. To see a character's options, tap it and hold down. If it has options, a menu pops up after a second or so.
To enter one of the optional characters, drag over the menu until the one you want to enter
is highlighted, and then lift your finger off the screen. The optional character you selected is
entered. For example, if you tap and hold on the period, you can select .com, .edu, or other
domain which is very helpful when you are typing a website or email addresses.

By default, the iPhone attempts to correct the capitalization of what you type.
It also automatically selects the Shift key when you start a new sentence, start a
new paragraph, or in other places where its best guess is that you need a capital letter. If you don't want to enter a capital character, simply tap the Shift key
before you type. You can enable the Caps Lock key by tapping the Shift key
twice. When the key is highlighted, everything you type is in uppercase letters.

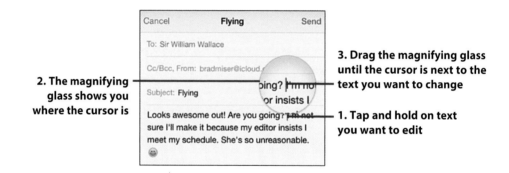

**2. The magnifying
glass shows you
where the cursor is**

**3. Drag the magnifying glass
until the cursor is next to the
text you want to change**

**1. Tap and hold on text
you want to edit**

To edit text you've typed, tap and hold on the text you want to edit. A magnifying glass icon appears on the screen, and within it you see a magnified view of
the location of the cursor. Drag the magnifying glass to where you want to make
changes (to position the cursor where you want to start making changes), and
then lift your finger from the screen. The cursor remains in that location, and you
can use the keyboard to make changes to the text or to add text at that location.

Your Own Shortcuts

You can create your own text shortcuts so you can type something like "eadd" and
it is automatically replaced with your email address. See Chapter 4 for the details.

Tap Select All to choose everything in the window

Tap Select to choose a portion of what's in the window

Tap to see more options

Tap where you want to start selecting

You can also select text or images to copy and paste the selected content into a new location. Tap and hold down briefly where you want to start the selection until the magnifying glass icon appears; then lift your finger off the screen. The Select menu appears. Tap Select to select part of the content on the screen, or tap Select All to select everything in the current window.

More Commands

Some menus that appear when you are making selections and performing actions have a right-facing arrow at the right end. Tap this to see a new menu that contains additional commands. These commands are contextual, meaning that you see different commands depending on what you are doing at that specific time. You can tap the left-facing arrow to move back to a previous menu.

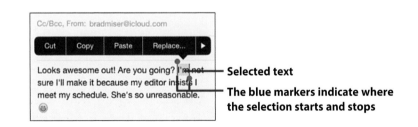

Selected text

The blue markers indicate where the selection starts and stops

You see markers indicating where the selection starts and stops. (The iPhone attempts to select something logical, such as the word or sentence.) New commands appear on the menu; these provide actions for the text currently selected.

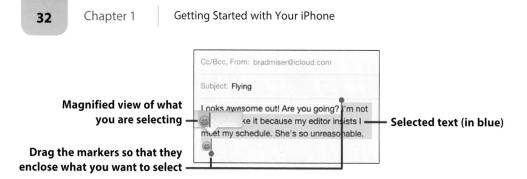

Magnified view of what you are selecting

Drag the markers so that they enclose what you want to select

Selected text (in blue)

Drag the two markers so that the content you want to select is between them; the selected portion is highlighted in blue. As you drag, you see a magnified view of where the selection marker is, which helps you place it more accurately. When the selection markers are located correctly, lift your finger from the screen. (If you tapped the Select All command, you don't need to do this because the content you want is already selected.)

Have I Got a Suggestion for You!

Tap the Suggestion option to see items that might be useful to you. These are also contextual. For example, when you have a word selected, one of the suggestions might be Define, which looks up the selected word in the Dictionary (tap Done to return to where you came from). As you use your iPhone, check out the Suggestions because you'll find some very useful options tucked away there.

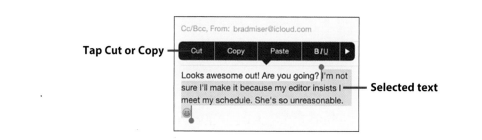

Tap Cut or Copy

Selected text

Tap Cut to remove the content from the current window, or tap Copy to just copy it.

Format It!

If you tap the **B/U** button, you can tap Bold, Italics, or Underline to apply those formatting options to the selected text. You also can tap multiple format options to apply them at the same time. You might need to tap the right-facing arrow at the end of the menu to see this command, depending on how many commands are on the menu.

Tap Paste

Tap where you
want to paste

Move to where you want to paste the content you selected; for example, use the App Switcher to change to a different app. Tap where you want the content to be pasted. For a more precise location, tap and hold and then use the magnifying glass icon to move to a specific location. Lift your finger off the screen and the menu appears. Then tap Paste.

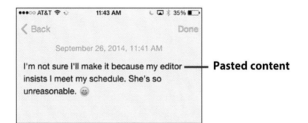

Pasted content

The content you copied or cut appears where you placed the cursor.

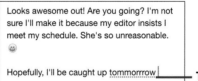

Text that may be misspelled

The iPhone also has a spell-checking feature that comes into play after you have entered text (as opposed to the autocorrect/suggest feature that changes text as you type it). When you've entered text the iPhone doesn't recognize, it is underlined in red.

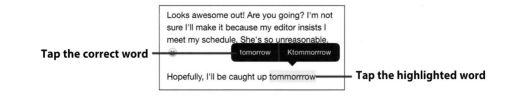

Tap the correct word

Tap the highlighted word

Tap the underlined word. It is shaded in red to show you what is being checked, and a menu appears with one or more replacements that might be the correct spelling. If one of the options is the one you want, tap it. The incorrect word is replaced with the one you tapped.

Contextual Menus and You

In some apps, tapping a word causes a menu with other kinds of actions to appear; you can tap an action to make it happen. For example, in the iBooks app, when you tap a word, the resulting menu enables you to look up the word in a dictionary. Other apps support different kinds of actions, so it's a good idea to try tapping words in apps that involve text to see which commands are available.

Dictating Text

You can also enter text by dictating it. This is a fast and easy way to type and you'll be amazed at how accurate the iPhone is at translating your speech into typed words. Dictation is available almost anywhere you need to enter text. (Exceptions are passcodes and passwords, such as for your Apple ID.)

To start dictating, tap the Microphone key. The iPhone goes into Dictation mode. A gray bar appears at the bottom of the window. As the iPhone "hears" you, the line oscillates.

Start speaking the text you want to enter. As you speak, the text is entered starting from the location of the cursor.

When you've finished dictating, tap Done. The keyboard reappears and you see the text you spoke. This feature is amazingly accurate and can be a much faster and more convenient way to enter text than typing it.

You can edit the text you dictated just like text you entered using the keyboard.

Tap to put the cursor where
you want dictated text to start

Tap the Microphone
key to start dictation

The iPhone is
taking dictation

Tap Done when
you're done speaking

The text you spoke

Meeting Siri

Siri is the iPhone's voice-recognition and control software. This feature enables you to accomplish many tasks by speaking. For example, you can create and send text messages, reply to emails, make phone calls, and much more. (Using Siri is explained in detail in Chapter 12, "Working with Siri.")

When you perform actions, Siri uses the related apps to accomplish what you've asked it to do. For example, when you create a meeting, Siri uses the Calendar app.

Siri is a great way to control your iPhone, especially when you are working in handsfree mode.

Your iPhone has to be connected to the Internet for Siri (and dictation for that matter) to work. That's because the words you speak are sent over the Internet, transcribed into text, and then sent back to your iPhone. If your iPhone isn't connected to the Internet, this can't happen and Siri reports that it can't connect to the network or simply that it can't do what you ask right now.

Using Siri is pretty simple because it follows a consistent pattern and prompts you for input and direction.

Activate Siri by pressing and holding down the Home button or pressing and holding down the center part of the buttons on the right EarPod wire until you hear the Siri chime. If so configured (see Chapter 12) and your iPhone is connected to power, you can say "Hey Siri" to activate it, too. This puts Siri in "listening" mode and the "What can I help you with?" text appears on the screen. This indicates Siri is ready for your command.

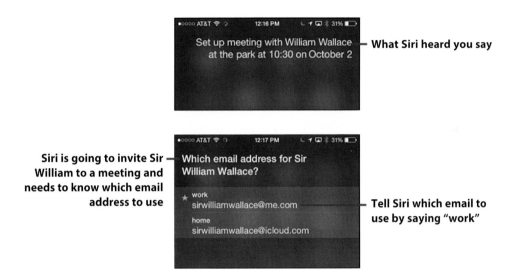

Speak your command or ask a question. When you stop speaking, Siri goes into processing mode. After Siri interprets what you've said, it provides two kinds of feedback to confirm what it heard: it displays what it heard on the screen and provides audible feedback to you. Siri then tries to do what it thinks you've asked and shows you what it is doing. If it needs more input from you, you're prompted to provide it and Siri moves into "listening" mode automatically.

If Siri requests that you confirm what it is doing or to make a selection, do so. Siri completes the action and displays what it has done; it also audibly confirms the result.

What Siri is doing for you

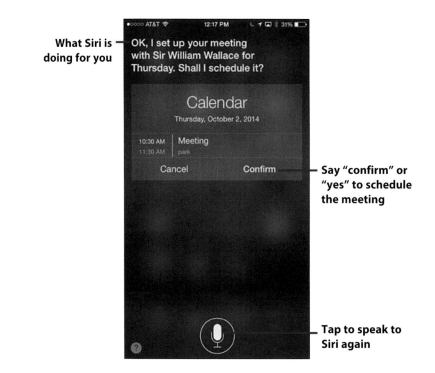

Say "confirm" or "yes" to schedule the meeting

Tap to speak to Siri again

Siri isn't quite like using the computer on the Starship Enterprise on *Star Trek*, but it's pretty darn close. Mostly, you can just speak to Siri as you would talk to someone else, and it is able to do what you want or asks you the information it needs to do what you want.

Understanding iPhone Status Icons

At the top of the screen is the Status bar with various icons that provide you with information, such as whether you are connected to a Wi-Fi or cellular data network, the time, sync in process, whether the iPhone's orientation is locked, and the state of the iPhone's battery. Keep an eye on this area as you use your iPhone. The following table provides a guide to the icons.

Table 1.1 iPhone Status Icons

Icon	Description	Where to Learn More
•••••	Signal Strength—Indicates how strong the cellular signal is.	Chapter 2
AT&T	Provider name—The provider of the current cellular network.	Chapter 2

Icon	Description	Where to Learn More
LTE	Cellular data network—Indicates which cellular network your iPhone is using to connect to the Internet.	Chapter 2
	Wi-Fi—Indicates your phone is connected to a Wi-Fi network.	Chapter 2
	Do Not Disturb—Your iPhone's notifications and ringer are silenced.	Chapters 1, 4
	Bluetooth—Indicates if Bluetooth is turned on or off and if your phone is connected to a device.	Chapter 2
97%	Battery percentage—Percentage of charge remaining in the battery.	Chapter 17
	Battery status—Relative level of charge of the battery.	Chapter 17
	Orientation Lock—Your iPhone's screen won't change when you rotate your iPhone.	Chapter 1
	Charging—The battery in the iPhone is being charged.	Chapter 17
	Location Services—An app is using the Location Services feature to track your iPhone's location.	Chapter 4
	Sync—Your iPhone is currently being synced with iTunes.	Chapter 5
	Airplane mode—The transmit and receive functions are disabled.	Chapter 1

Turning Your iPhone On or Off

If you want to turn off your iPhone, press and hold the Wake/Sleep button until the red slider appears at the top of the screen. Swipe the slider to the right to shut down the iPhone. The iPhone shuts down.

To restart your iPhone, press and hold the Wake/Sleep button until the Apple logo appears on the screen, and then let go of the button. After it starts up, you see the Lock screen if your iPhone has a passcode or Home screen if it doesn't, and it's ready for you to use.

Swipe to the right to turn your iPhone off

Sleeping/Locking and Waking/Unlocking Your iPhone

When an iPhone is asleep/locked, you need to wake it up and then unlock it to use it. How you do this depends on the type of iPhone you have.

If you have an iPhone 5s or later, and have configured it to recognize your fingerprint, press the Touch ID/Home button once to wake the iPhone up, and then touch the Touch ID button with your finger (you don't need to press it). When your fingerprint is recognized, your iPhone unlocks and you can start using it.

Be Recognized

To use the Touch ID, you need to train your iPhone to recognize your fingerprint. If you didn't do this when you first turned on your iPhone or you want to train your iPhone to recognize other people's fingerprints so they can also unlock your phone, see Chapter 4.

If you have an iPhone 5c or older, or you don't have any fingerprints configured, you first press the Wake/Sleep button or the Home button. The iPhone wakes up, the

Lock screen appears, and at the bottom of the screen, the Unlock slider appears. Swipe on the slider to the right to unlock the iPhone so you can work with it.

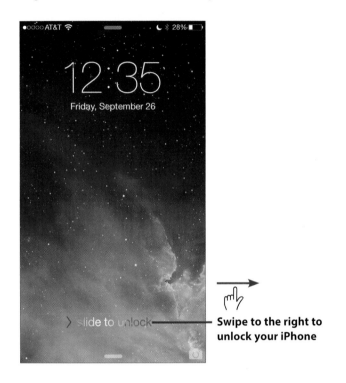

Swipe to the right to unlock your iPhone

If you require a passcode to unlock your iPhone—which you should for security— type your passcode at the prompt. (See Chapter 4 to learn how to configure a passcode.)

If you enter the correct passcode or you don't require a passcode, when you unlock the phone, you move to the last screen you were using.

The Time Is Always Handy

If you use your iPhone as a watch the way I do, just press the Wake/Sleep button. The current time and date appear; if you don't unlock it, the iPhone goes back to sleep after a few seconds.

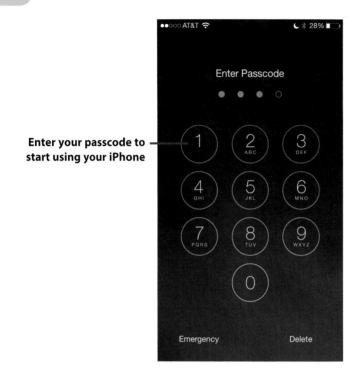

Enter your passcode to start using your iPhone

In most cases, you should just put the iPhone to sleep when you aren't using it instead of shutting it off. It doesn't use much power when it sleeps, and it wakes up immediately when you want to start using it again. Also, when you put your iPhone to sleep, it can't be used until it is unlocked. If you set it to require a passcode to unlock, this also protects your information. (You seldom need to turn off an iPhone.) Even when the iPhone is asleep, you can receive notifications, such as when you receive emails or text messages. (See Chapter 4 to configure which notifications you see on the Lock screen.)

To put your iPhone to sleep and lock it, press the Wake/Sleep button.

Signing In to Your Apple ID

As you learn throughout this book, an Apple ID is useful in many situations, such as to access iCloud services; purchase music, movies, and other content from the iTunes Store; download apps from the App Store; and more. If you have an iPhone 5s or later, you can quickly sign in to your Apple ID by using its Touch ID/Home button. (As referenced in the prior note, you need to configure your iPhone to recognize your fingerprint to use the Touch ID; see Chapter 4 for details.)

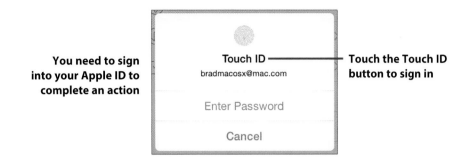

You need to sign into your Apple ID to complete an action

Touch ID

bradmacosx@mac.com

Enter Password

Cancel

Touch the Touch ID button to sign in

When you need to sign in to your Apple ID and have configured fingerprint recognition, you see a prompt. Simply touch your finger to the Touch ID/Home button. When your fingerprint is recognized, you sign in to your Apple ID and can complete whatever your were doing, such as downloading music from the iTunes Store.

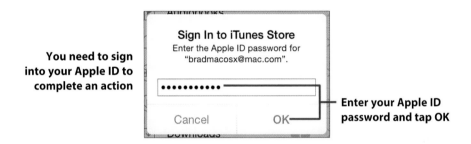

You need to sign into your Apple ID to complete an action

Sign In to iTunes Store
Enter the Apple ID password for "bradmacosx@mac.com".

Cancel   OK

Enter your Apple ID password and tap OK

If you have an older model or you don't have the settings configured to enable you to use Touch ID with your Apple ID, you need to type your Apple ID password, and then tap OK to sign in.

Setting the Volume

Setting the ringer volume

To change the iPhone's volume, press the up or down Volume button on the side of the iPhone. When you change the volume, your change affects the current activity. For example, if you are on a phone call, the call volume changes or if you are listening to music, the music's volume changes. If you aren't on a screen that shows the Volume slider, an icon pops up to show you the relative volume you are setting and the type, such as setting the ringer's volume. When the volume is right, release the Volume button.

Drag to the left or right to change the volume level

When you are using an app that produces sound, such as the Music app, you can also drag the volume slider to increase or decrease the volume.

When you use the iPhone's EarPods, you can change the volume by pressing the upper part of the switch on the right EarPod's wire to increase volume or the lower part to decrease it.

Using Airplane Mode

At times, such as when you are on an airplane, you may need to disable your iPhone's transmitting and receiving functions. When you place your iPhone in Airplane mode, its transmitting and receiving functions are disabled. While your device is in Airplane mode, you can't use the phone, the Web, Siri, or any other functions that require communication between your iPhone and other devices or networks.

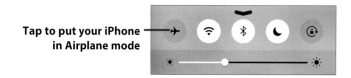

Tap to put your iPhone in Airplane mode

To put your iPhone in Airplane mode, swipe up from the bottom of the screen to open the Control Center and tap the Airplane mode button. All connections to the Internet and the cell network stop, and your iPhone goes into quiet mode in which it doesn't broadcast or receive any signals. The Airplane mode button becomes white and you see the Airplane mode icon at the top of the screen.

In Airplane mode, you can use your iPhone for all your apps that don't require an Internet connection, such as iBooks, Music, Videos, Photos, etc.

To turn off Airplane mode, open the Control Center and tap the Airplane mode button; it becomes black again and the Airplane mode icon disappears. The iPhone resumes transmitting and receiving signals, and all the functions that require a connection start working again.

Wi-Fi in Airplane Mode

Many airplanes support Wi-Fi onboard. To access a Wi-Fi network without violating the requirement not to use a cell network, put the iPhone in Airplane mode, which turns off Wi-Fi. On the Control Center, tap the Wi-Fi button to turn Wi-Fi back on. Wi-Fi starts up and you can select the network you want to join (see Chapter 2). You can use this configuration at other times, too, such as when you want to access the Internet but don't want to be bothered with phone calls. When your iPhone is in Airplane mode and Wi-Fi is on, all your calls go straight to voicemail but you can use your Internet-related apps. (I would never do this, you understand.)

Using the Settings App

—Tap to open the Settings app

The Settings app is where you do almost all of your iPhone's configuration, and you use it frequently throughout this book. To use the Settings app, tap Settings on the Home screen. The app opens. Swipe up and down the screen to browse the various settings tools. Tap an item to configure its settings. For example, to configure your notifications, you tap Notification Center. (You use the Settings app in a number of chapters in this book, especially Chapter 4.)

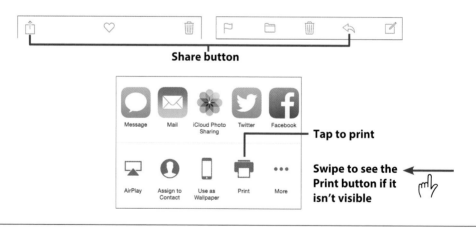

Printing from Your iPhone

You can also print from your iPhone to AirPrint-compatible printers.

First, set up and configure your AirPrint printer (see the instructions that came with the printer you use).

It Depends

When you tap the Share button, you might see a menu containing commands instead of the grid of icons shown in the figure. The way it appears is dependent upon the app you are using. Either way, tap Print to move to the Printer Options screen.

When you are in the app from which you want to print, tap the Share button. Tap Print on the resulting menu. You might need to swipe to the right to expose the

Print command. (If you don't see the Share button or the Print command, the app you are using doesn't support printing.) The Share button looks a bit different in some apps, but it works similarly.

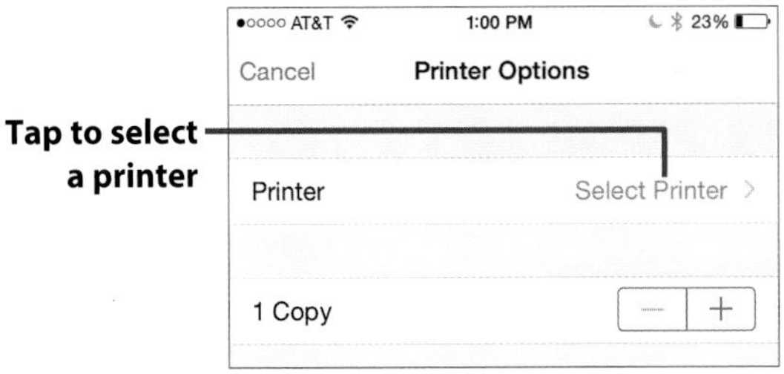

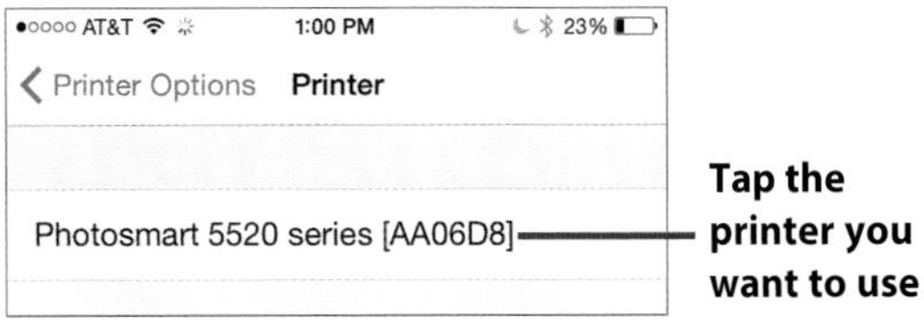

Tap to select a printer

Tap the printer you want to use

The first time you print, you need to select the printer you want to use. On the Printer Options screen, tap Select Printer. Then tap the printer you want to use. You move back to the Printer Options screen and see the printer you selected.

Don't Have an AirPrint Printer?

If you don't have an AirPrint printer, do a web search for a tool called "AirPrint for Windows" if you have a Windows PC or "handyPrint for Mac" if you have a Mac. Download and install the software on a computer that is capable of sharing its printers. Configure your computer to share the printer you want to use with your iPhone. Then launch the software on your computer and start it. The printers you configure in the AirPrint software are available for printing from your iPhone.

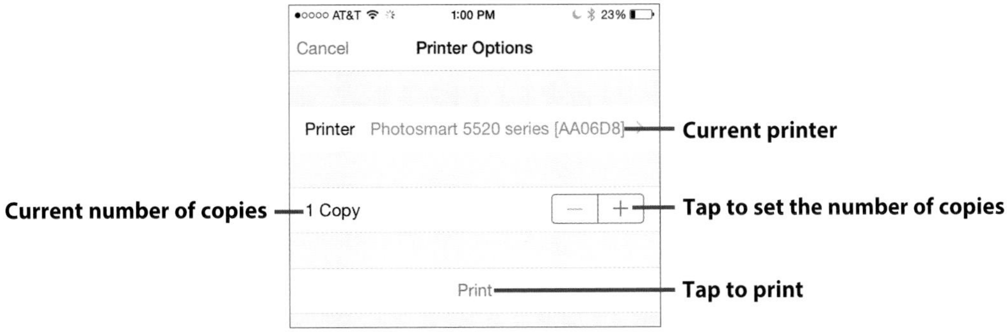

Current printer

Current number of copies

Tap to set the number of copies

Tap to print

Tap the – or + to set the number of copies; the current number of copies is shown to the left of the buttons. Tap Print to print the document.

The next time you print, if you want to use the same printer, you can skip the printer selection process because the iPhone remembers the last printer you used. To change the printer, tap Printer and tap the printer you want to use.

Connect to the Internet via
Wi-Fi or a cellular network

Use AirDrop to
share content
with other iOS
devices

Take advantage
of an Internet
connection in
many different
apps

Tap here to
join Wi-Fi
networks to
connect to
the Internet
and configure
Bluetooth to
connect to
other devices

In this chapter, you explore how to connect your iPhone to the Internet, Bluetooth devices, and other iPhones, iPod touches, and iPads. Topics include the following:

→ Getting started
→ Securing your iPhone
→ Using Wi-Fi networks to connect to the Internet
→ Using cellular data networks to connect to the Internet
→ Using Bluetooth to connect to other devices
→ Connecting your iPhone to other iPhones, iPod touches, or iPads
→ Using AirDrop to Share Content with Macs, Other iPhones, iPod Touches, or iPads

Connecting Your iPhone to the Internet, Bluetooth Devices, and iPhones/iPods/iPads

Your iPhone has many functions that rely on an Internet connection, with the most obvious being email, and web browsing. However, many default and third-party apps rely on an Internet connection to work as well. Fortunately, you can connect your iPhone to the Internet by connecting it to a Wi-Fi network that provides Internet access. You can also connect to the Internet through a cellular data network operated by your cell phone provider.

Using Bluetooth, you can wirelessly connect your iPhone to other devices, including keyboards, headsets, and headphones.

There are a number of ways to connect your iPhone to other iPhones, iPod touches, and iPads. This is useful to use collaborative apps, play games, and share information. For example, using AirDrop, you can quickly and easily share photos and other content with other people using iOS devices and Macintosh computers.

Before jumping into connecting your iPhone to the Internet or other devices, it's a good idea to understand some of the concepts and terms that you'll read about in this chapter.

Getting Started

The bad news is that there are lots of complex-sounding terms that you hear and see when you are connecting your iPhone to the Internet and other devices. The good news is that you don't need to understand these terms in-depth to be able to connect your iPhone to the Internet and other devices because the iPhone manages the complexity for you. You just need to make a few simple settings, and you'll be connected in no time. Here's a quick guide to the most important concepts you encounter in this chapter:

- **Wi-Fi**—This acronym stands for Wireless Fidelity and encompasses a whole slew of technical specifications around connecting devices together without using cables or wires. Wi-Fi networks have a relatively short range and are used to create a Local Area Network (LAN). The most important thing to know is that you can use Wi-Fi networks to connect your iPhone to the Internet. This is great because Wi-Fi networks are available just about everywhere you go. You probably have a Wi-Fi network available in your home, too. (If you connect your computers to the Internet without a cable from your computer to a modem or network hub, you are using a Wi-Fi network.) You can connect your iPhone to your home's Wi-Fi network, too.

- **Cellular data network**—In addition to your voice, your iPhone can transmit and receive data over the cellular network to which it is connected. This enables you to connect your iPhone to the Internet just about anywhere you are. You use the cellular network provided by your cell phone company. There are many different cell phone providers that support iPhones. In the United States, these include AT&T, Sprint, T-Mobile, and Verizon. You don't need to configure your iPhone to use the cellular data network as it is set up from the start to do so.

- **3G/4G/LTE**—The speed of the connection you have when using a cellular data network varies, which means the things you do on the Internet (such as browsing a web page) will be faster or slower depending on the current connection speed. These terms (this is not an exhaustive list; you may see these networks called by other names) refer to various types of cellular data networks you can use with your iPhone. Each type has a different speed. LTE networks are currently the fastest type. You usually don't choose which type of network you use because the iPhone connects to the fastest one available automatically.

- **Data Plan**—When you use your iPhone on the Internet (for web browsing, email, and apps), data is transmitted to your iPhone and the iPhone transmits data back to the Internet. Your cellular account includes a data plan that defines how much data you can send/receive during a specific time period (usually per month). It's important to know the size of your data plan so that you can be aware of how much of it you are using per month.

- **Overage charge**—If you use more data than is allowed under your data plan, you can be charged a fee. These fees can be quite expensive so you need to aware of how much data you are using so that you can avoid overage charges.

- **Roaming charge**—Your cellular provider's network covers a defined geographic area. When you leave your provider's network coverage area, your iPhone automatically connects to another provider's network when one is available. When your iPhone is connected to a different provider's network, this is called roaming. You need to aware when you are roaming because you can incur additional fees while using the roaming network.

- **Bluetooth**—This is the name of a technology that is used to wirelessly connect devices together. It is widely used for many different kinds of devices. Your iPhone can use Bluetooth to connect to speakers, the audio system in your car, keyboards, and headphones.

- **AirDrop**—This is Apple's technology for connecting iPhones, iPads, iPod touches, and Macintosh computers together to share information. AirDrop is a short-range technology—typically, the devices need to be in the same room or area for it to work. For example, you can use AirDrop to send photos from your iPhone to someone's iPad. The nice thing about AirDrop is that it requires very little setup and is quite easy to use, as you will see in this chapter.

Securing Your iPhone

Even though you won't often be connecting a cable to it, an iPhone is a connected device, meaning that it sends information to and receives information from other devices, either directly or via the Internet, during many different activities. Some are obvious, such as sending text messages or browsing the Web, while others might not be so easy to spot, such as when an app is determining your iPhone's location. Whenever data is exchanged between your iPhone and other devices, there is always a chance your information will get intercepted by someone you didn't intend or that someone will access your iPhone without you knowing about it.

The good news is that with some simple precautions, the chances of someone obtaining your information or infiltrating your iPhone are quite small (much less than the chance of someone obtaining your credit card number when you use it in public places, for example). Following are some good ways to protect the information you are using on your iPhone:

- Configure a passcode and fingerprint (if your iPhone supports fingerprint recognition) on your iPhone so that the passcode must be entered, or your fingerprint scanned, to be able to use it. Configuring a passcode is explained in Chapter 4, "Configuring an iPhone to Suit Your Preferences."

- Never let someone you don't know or trust use your iPhone, even if he needs it "just for a second to look something up." If you get a request like that, look up the information for the person and show him rather than letting him touch your iPhone.

- Learn how to use the Find My iPhone feature in case you lose or someone steals your iPhone. This is explained in Chapter 17, "Maintaining and Protecting Your iPhone and Solving Problems."

- Never respond to an email that you aren't expecting requesting that you click a link to verify your account. If you haven't requested some kind of change, such as signing up for a new service, virtually all such requests are scams, seeking to get your account information, such as username and password, or your identification, such as full name and Social Security number. And many of these scam attempts look like email from actual organizations; for example, I receive many of these emails that claim, and sometimes even look like, they are from Apple, but Apple doesn't request updates to account information using a link in an email unless you have made some kind of change, such as registering a new email address for iMessages. Legitimate organizations never include links in an email to update account information when you haven't requested or made any changes. Requests from legitimate organizations will provide instructions for you to visit a website to provide needed information.

To reinforce this concept, there are two types of requests for verification you might receive via email.

The legitimate type is sent to you after you sign up for a new service, such as creating a new account on a website, to confirm that the email address you provided is correct and that you are really you. If you make changes to an existing account, you might also receive confirmation request emails. You should respond to these requests to finish the configuration of your account.

If you receive a request for account verification, but you haven't done anything with the organization from which you received the request, don't respond to it. For example, if you receive a request that appears to be from Apple, PayPal, or other organizations, but you haven't made any changes to your account, the email request is bogus and is an attempt to scam you. Likewise, if you have never done anything with the organization apparently sending the email, it is also definitely an attempt to scam you.

If you have any doubt, contact the organization sending the request before responding to the email.

- If you need to change or update account information, always go directly to the related website using an address that you type in or have saved as a bookmark.

- Be aware that when you use a Wi-Fi network in a public place, such as a coffee shop, hotel, or airport, there is a chance that the information you send over that network might be intercepted by others. The risk of this is usually quite small, but you need to be aware that there is always some level of risk. To have the lowest risk, don't use apps that involve sensitive information, such as an online banking app, when you are using a Wi-Fi network in a public place.

- If you don't know how to do it, have someone who really knows what they are doing set up a wireless network in your home. Wireless networks need to be configured properly, so they are secure. Your home's Wi-Fi network should require a password to join. (Fortunately, as you learn shortly, your iPhone remembers your password, so you only have to enter it once.)

- For the least risk, only use your home's Wi-Fi network (that has been configured properly) or your cellular data connection (you can turn Wi-Fi off when you aren't home) for sensitive transactions, such as accessing bank accounts or other financial information.

- Never accept a request to share information from someone you don't know. Later in this chapter, you learn about AirDrop, which enables you to easily share photos and lots of other things with other people using iOS devices. If you receive an AirDrop request from someone you don't recognize, always decline it. In fact, if you have any doubt, decline such requests. It's much easier for someone legitimate to confirm with you and resend a request than it is for you to recover from damage that can be done if you inadvertently accept a request from someone you don't know.

- Only download apps through Apple's App Store, either through the App Store app on your iPhone or in iTunes on your computer. Fortunately, the way the iPhone is set up, you have to do something very unusual to install apps outside of the App Store. As long as you download apps only as described in this book, you are free of apps that can harm your information because Apple has strict controls over the apps that make it into the App Store. (Downloading apps is explained in Chapter 6, "Downloading Apps, Music, Movies, TV Shows, and More onto Your iPhone.")

Reality Check

Internet security is a complex topic, and it can be troublesome to think about. It's best to keep in mind the relative level of risk when you use your iPhone compared to other risks in the physical world that most of us don't think twice about. For example, every time you hand your credit card to someone, there is a chance that that person will record the number and use it without your knowledge or permission. Even when you swipe a credit card in a reader, such as at a gas station, that information is communicated across multiple networks and can be intercepted. (For example, there have been numerous compromises of credit card information at a number of well-known retailers.) If you take basic precautions like those described here, the risks to you when you are using your iPhone are similar to the other risks we all face in everyday life. My recommendation is to take the basic precautions, and then don't worry about it overly much. It might be a good idea to have identity theft insurance (try to find a company that assigns someone to do the work of recovering for you should your identity be stolen).

Using Wi-Fi Networks to Connect to the Internet

Much of the iPhone's amazing functionality relies on an Internet connection. Fortunately, you can easily connect your iPhone to just about any Wi-Fi network to get to the Internet, and Wi-Fi networks are available just about everywhere these days.

Almost all Wi-Fi networks broadcast their information so that you can easily see them with your iPhone; these are called *open networks* because anyone who is in range can attempt to join one since they appear on Wi-Fi devices automatically. The Wi-Fi networks you can access in public places (such as airports and hotels) are all open, and you can see them on your iPhone. Likewise, any Wi-Fi networks in your home or office are very likely to be open as well. Connecting to an open network typically requires selecting the network you want to join, based on its name, and then entering its password (if required).

By default, when you access one of your iPhone's Internet functions, such as Safari, your iPhone automatically searches for Wi-Fi networks to join if you aren't already connected to one. A box appears showing all the networks available. You can also select and join one of these networks, as you learn how to do in the following steps.

Connecting to Open Wi-Fi Networks

To connect to a Wi-Fi network, perform the following steps:

1. On the Home screen, tap Settings. Next to Wi-Fi, you see the status of your Wi-Fi connection. The options are: Off - if Wi-Fi is turned off; Not Connected - if Wi-Fi is turned on but your phone isn't currently connected to a Wi-Fi network; or you see the name of the Wi-Fi network to which your iPhone is connected (in which case, you can skip the rest of these steps or use them to change the network you are using).

(**2**) Tap Wi-Fi.

(**3**) If Wi-Fi isn't enabled already, slide the Wi-Fi switch to on (green) to allow your iPhone to start searching for available networks. When Wi-Fi is turned on, a list of available networks is displayed in the CHOOSE A NETWORK section (it can take a moment or two for your iPhone to list all the networks in the area). Along with each network's name are icons indicating whether it requires a password (the padlock icon) to join and the current signal strength (the radio signal icon).

●●●●● AT&T 4G	6:14 AM	⅄ 52% ▭
	Settings	
✈ Airplane Mode		◯
📶 Wi-Fi		Off ›
❋ Bluetooth		On ›
((ᴀ)) Cellular		›

2

Current Wi-Fi status

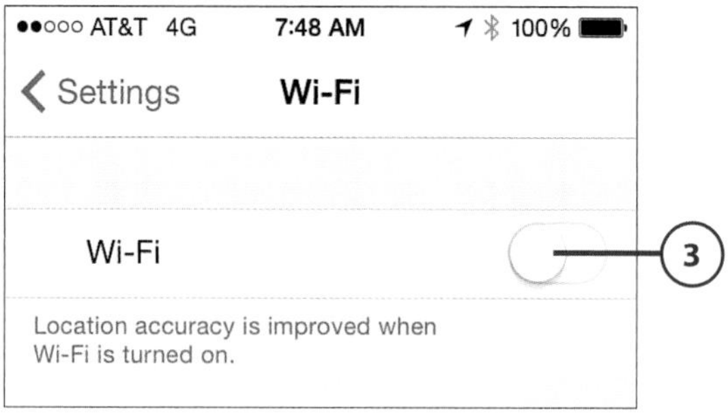

●●○○○ AT&T 4G	7:48 AM	⌁ ⅄ 100% ▰
‹ Settings	**Wi-Fi**	
Wi-Fi		◯ — **3**

Location accuracy is improved when Wi-Fi is turned on.

4 Tap the network you want to join. If multiple networks are available, you need to decide which one to join. If a network requires a password, of course, you must know what that password is to be able to join it. Another consideration should be signal strength; the more waves in the network's signal strength icon, the stronger the connection will be.

5 At the prompt, enter the password for the network. If you aren't prompted for a password, you selected a network that doesn't require one and can skip to step 7. You're likely to find networks that don't require a password in public places (hotels and airports); see the next section for information on using these types of networks.

6 Tap Join. If you provided the correct password, your iPhone connects to the network and gets the information it needs to connect to the Internet. If not, you're prompted to enter the password again. After you successfully connect to the network, you return to the Wi-Fi screen.

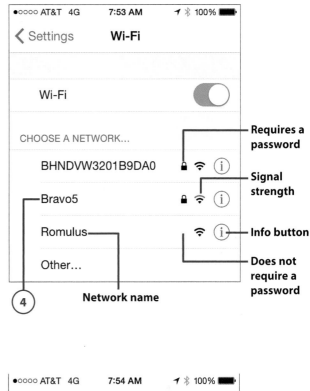

Requires a password

Signal strength

Info button

Does not require a password

Network name

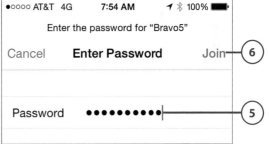

(7) Review the network informa-tion. The network to which you are connected appears just below the Wi-Fi switch and is marked with a check mark. You also see the signal strength for that network. (This indication is typically more accurate than the one you see before you are connected.) Assuming the Wi-Fi network is providing Internet access, you're able to use apps that require the Internet to work.

(7) **The network your iPhone is using**

Typing Passwords

As you type a password, each character is hidden by dots in the Password field except for the last character you entered, which is displayed on the screen for a few moments. This is helpful because you see each character as you type it, so you always see the most recent character you entered, which can prevent you from getting all the way to the end of a long password only to discover you've made a mistake along the way and have to start all over again.

Changing Networks

You can use these same steps to change the Wi-Fi network you are using at any time. For example, if you have to pay to use one network while a different one is free, simply choose the free network in step 4.

(8) Try to move to a web page, such as www.weather.com, to test your Wi-Fi connection. (See Chapter 13, "Surfing the Web," for details.) If the web page opens, you are ready to use the Internet on your phone. If you are taken to a login web page for a Wi-Fi provider rather than the page you were trying to access, see the following task. If you see a message saying the Internet is not available, there is a problem with the network you joined. Go back to step 4 to select a different network or contact the network's provider to see when the issue will be corrected.

Be Known

After your iPhone connects to a Wi-Fi network successfully, it becomes a known network. This means that your iPhone remembers its information so you don't have to enter it again. Your iPhone automatically connects to known networks when it needs to access the Internet. So unless you tell your iPhone to forget a network (explained later in this chapter), you need to log in to it only the first time you connect to it.

Connecting to Public Wi-Fi Networks

Many Wi-Fi networks in public places, such as hotels or airports, require that you pay a fee or provide other information to access the Internet through that network; even if access is free, you usually have to accept the terms and conditions for the network to be able to use it.

When you connect to one of these public networks, you're prompted to provide whatever information is required. This can involve different details for different networks, but the general steps are the same. You're prompted to provide whatever information is required so you just follow the instructions that appear.

Following are the general steps to connect to many types of public Wi-Fi networks:

1. Use the steps in the previous task to move to and tap the public network you want to join. The iPhone connects to the network, and you see the Log In screen for that network.

2. If prompted to do so, provide the information required to join the network, such as a name and room number. If a fee is required, you'll have to provide payment information. In almost all cases, you at least have to indicate that you accept the terms and conditions for using the network, which you typically do by checking a check box.

3. Tap the button to join the network. This button can have different labels depending on the type of access, such as Authenticate, Done, Free Access, and Login.

●●●●○ AT&T LTE	5:30 AM	46% ▭✦
‹ Settings	**Wi-Fi**	
Wi-Fi	⬤
CHOOSE A NETWORK...	
IHG-Guests	📶 ⓘ
Other...	

1

●●●●○ AT&T LTE	5:31 AM	47% ▭✦
🔒 p1512.superclick.com	
‹ › **Log In - IHG-Guests** Cancel	

number so that you may choose an internet access level

Last Name: | miser | 2

Room: | 1058 |

Authenticate 3

(4) Try to move to a web page, such as wikipedia.org, to test your Wi-Fi connection. (See Chapter 13 for details.) If the web page opens, you are ready to use the Internet on your phone. If you are taken to a login web page for the Wi-Fi network's provider, you need to provide the required information to be able to use the Internet.

No Prompt?

Not all public networks prompt you to log in as these steps explain. Sometimes, you use the network's website to log in instead. After you join the network (step 1), your iPhone is connected to the network without any prompts. When you try to move to a web page as explained in step 4, you're prompted to log in to or create an account with the network's provider on the web page that appears.

A Closed Network

Some Wi-Fi networks are closed, which means they don't broadcast their names. You don't see closed networks listed in the CHOOSE A NETWORK on the Wi-Fi screen. To be able to access a closed network, you need to know its name, its password, and the type of security it uses. With this information in hand, tap Other in the CHOOSE A NETWORK section. Then type the network's name. Tap Security, choose the appropriate type, and tap Back. Enter the required password and tap Join.

Cell Phone Provider Wi-Fi Networks

Many cell phone providers also provide other services, particularly public Wi-Fi networks. In some cases, you can access that provider's Internet service through a Wi-Fi network that it provides; ideally, you can do this at no additional charge. So, you can take advantage of the speed a Wi-Fi connection provides without paying more for it. You start connecting to these networks just like any other by selecting them on the available network list. What happens next depends on the specific network. In some cases, you need to enter your mobile phone number and then respond to a text message to that phone number. Check your provider's website to find out whether it offers this service and where you can access it.

Using Cellular Data Networks to Connect to the Internet

The cellular provider associated with your iPhone also provides a cellular Internet connection your iPhone uses automatically when a Wi-Fi connection isn't available. (Your iPhone tries to connect to an available Wi-Fi network before connecting to a cellular data connection because Wi-Fi is typically less expensive and faster to use.) These networks are great because the area they cover is large and the connection to them is automatic. Your iPhone chooses and connects to the fastest cellular network currently available because your phone is automatically configured to access your provider's cellular network as soon as you activate your iPhone. Access to these networks is usually part of your monthly account fee. Typically when you sign up for cellular service, you also choose from among various amounts of data per month at different monthly charges. One option might be where you have unlimited data, but not all providers offer this option. When there are options, usually the more data that is allowed per month, the more expensive the data plan is. It is a matter of choosing the plan that best balances how much data you will use and how much it will cost.

Most providers have multiple cellular data networks, such as a low-speed network that is available everywhere in that provider's coverage area and one or more higher-speed networks that have a somewhat smaller coverage area. For example, the higher-speed networks are usually available in populated areas, such as medium-to-large cities, but if you are in a remote area, you might be limited to a slower network. Your iPhone chooses the best connection available automatically.

The speed and name of the cellular data networks you can use are determined based on your provider, your data plan, the model of iPhone you are using, and your location within your provider's networks or the roaming networks available when you are outside of your provider's coverage area. The iPhone automatically uses the fastest connection available to it at any given time (assuming you haven't disabled that option, as explained later).

This iPhone is connected to a high-speed LTE cellular network

Whenever you are connected to a cellular data network, you can access the Internet for web browsing, email, etc.

One thing you do need to keep in mind when using a cellular network is that your account might include a set amount of data per month. When your data use exceeds this limit, you may be charged overage fees, which can be very expensive. Most providers send you warning texts or emails as your data use approaches your plan's limit, at which point you need to be careful about what you do while using the cellular data network to avoid an overage fee. Some tasks, such as watching YouTube videos or downloading large movie files, can chew up a lot of data. Other tasks, such as using email, typically don't use very much.

An App for That

Various apps that help monitor your data usage are available in the App Store. These apps are a good way to know where your data use is relative to your plan's monthly allowance so that you can avoid an overage situation. To get information on finding, downloading, and installing apps, see Chapter 6. (To find an app for this purpose, search for "data monitoring app.")

When you move outside of your primary network's geographic coverage area, you are in roaming territory, which means a different provider might provide both cellular phone or data access or both. The iPhone automatically selects a roaming provider if there is only one available or allows you to choose one if there is more than one available.

When you are outside of your primary provider's coverage area, roaming charges can be associated with phone calls or Internet access. These charges are often very expensive. The roaming charges associated with phone calls are easier to manage given that it's more obvious when you make or receive a phone call in a roaming area. However, data roaming charges are much more insidious because sometimes it is hard to tell when an app is connecting to the Internet. Because data roaming charges are harder to notice, the iPhone is configured by default to prevent data roaming. When data roaming is disabled, the iPhone is unable to access the Internet when you are outside of your provider's data network, unless you connect to a Wi-Fi network. (You can still use the cellular roaming network for telephone calls.)

You can configure some aspects of how your cellular network is used, as you see in this task. You can also allow individual apps to use, or prevent them from using, your cellular data network. This is important when your data plan has a monthly limit. You should be careful about enabling apps to use the cellular data network to help prevent overage charges (unless you have an account with unlimited data). In most cases, the first time you launch an app, you're prompted to allow or prevent it from using cellular data. At any time, you can use the Settings app to enable or disable an app's access to your cellular data network.

To configure how your iPhone uses its cellular network for data, perform the following steps:

1. Open the Settings app.
2. Tap Cellular.

3 To disable all cellular data connections, set the Cellular Data switch to off (white). The iPhone is no longer able to connect to any cellular data networks. To use the Internet when the Cellular Data switch is off, you have to connect to a Wi-Fi network that provides Internet access.

4 On an iPhone 6 or 6 Plus, tap Enable *high-speed network*, where *high-speed network* is the network name, such as LTE. On an iPhone 5s or earlier, this is a switch that enables or disables the high-speed network; set the switch to configure access to that network and then skip to step 7.

5 Tap Off to disable the high-speed network, tap Voice & Data to enable types of information to use the high-speed network, or Data Only to limit the high-speed connection to data only. The Data Only and Off settings don't affect your phone's ability to make phone calls; they only affect voice communication over the high-speed data network.

6 Tap Cellular.

7 If you want to allow data roaming, slide the Data Roaming switch to the on (green) position. When you move outside your primary network, data comes to the iPhone via an available roaming network. You should disable it again by sliding the Data Roaming switch to

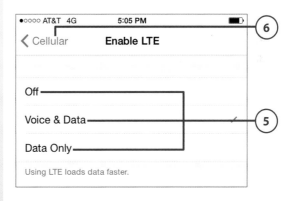

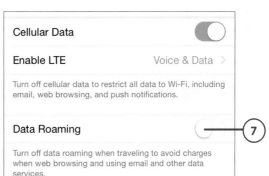

off (white) as soon as you're done with a specific task to limit the amount of roaming charges.

8. Swipe up the screen until you see the USE CELLULAR DATA FOR section. This section enables you to allow or prevent individual apps from accessing the cellular data network. Review this list and allow only those apps that you need to access frequently to use the cellular data network. Doing so helps to limit the amount of data you use. (Of course, if you are fortunate enough to have an unlimited data plan, you can leave all the apps enabled.)

9. Set an app's switch to on (green) if you want it to be able to use your cellular data network.

10. Set an app's switch to off (white) if you want it to be able to access the Internet only when you are connected to a Wi-Fi network.

11. Tap Settings when you're done configuring your cellular network use.

●○○○○ AT&T 4G	5:26 PM	✳ ▬▯
❮ Settings	**Cellular**	
CALL TIME		
Current Period		0 Minutes
Lifetime		0 Minutes
CELLULAR DATA USAGE		
Current Period		49.6 MB
Current Period Roaming		0 bytes
USE CELLULAR DATA FOR:		
📹 FaceTime		⬤▭
✉ Mail 1.4 MB		⬤▭
📑 Passbook		▭○
✿ Photos 3.1 MB		⬤▭
🎙 Podcasts 245 KB		⬤▭
System Services		44.9 MB ❯

Amount of data the app has used since last reset

Monitoring Data Use

In the CELLULAR DATA USAGE section of the Cellular screen, you see how much data you've used for the current period and how much you've used while roaming. This can help you see where your use is compared to your monthly plan allowance so you know whether you are getting close to exceeding that allowance (thus incurring overage charges). This isn't proactive at all, so you have to remember to move to this screen to see the information. If you are concerned about data use, you're better off getting an app with more active monitoring (refer to the earlier "An App for That" sidebar).

Erase the Past

You can reset all of the statistics on the Cellular screen by swiping up until you reach the bottom of the screen and tapping Reset Statistics. Tap Reset Statistics again at the prompt and all the statistics will be set to 0 and will count up from there. For example, you might want to do this at the end of each month of your data plan period, so the information you see reflects only the current month.

Using Bluetooth to Connect to Other Devices

Bluetooth is a short-range wireless communication technology that enables mobile and other devices to communicate with each other. Bluetooth is widely used on computers, mobile phones, tablets, and even home appliances, such as televisions. The iPhone includes built-in Bluetooth support so you can use this wireless technology to connect to other Bluetooth-capable devices. The most likely devices to connect to iPhone in this way are Bluetooth headphones or headsets or car audio/entertainment/information systems, but you can also use Bluetooth to connect to other kinds of devices, most notably keyboards, head-phones, computers, iPod touches, iPads, and other iPhones.

To connect Bluetooth devices together, you *pair* them. In Bluetooth, pairing enables two Bluetooth devices to communicate with each other. For devices to find and identify each other so they can communicate, one or both must be *discoverable*, which means they broadcast a Bluetooth signal other devices can detect and connect to.

There is a "sometimes" requirement, which is a pairing code, passkey, or PIN. All those terms refer to the same thing, which is a series of numbers, letters, or both that are entered on one or both devices being paired. Sometimes you enter this code on both devices, whereas for other devices you enter the first device's code on the second device. Some devices don't require a pairing code at all.

When you have to pair devices, you're prompted to do so, and you have to com-plete the actions required by the prompt to communicate via Bluetooth. This might be just tapping Connect, or you might have to enter a passcode on one or both devices.

Also, because Bluetooth works over a relatively short range, the devices have to be in the same proximity, such as in the same room.

Connecting to Bluetooth Devices

This task demonstrates pairing an iPhone with a Bluetooth keyboard; you can pair it with other devices similarly.

(1) Move to the Settings screen. The current status of Bluetooth on your iPhone is shown.

(2) Tap Bluetooth.

(3) If Bluetooth isn't on (green), tap the Bluetooth switch to turn it on. If it isn't running already, Bluetooth starts up. The iPhone immediately begins searching for Bluetooth devices. You also see the status Now Discoverable, which means other Bluetooth devices can discover the iPhone. In the MY DEVICES section, you see devices with which your iPhone is currently paired. You also see the current status of their connections, those being Connected (the iPhone is currently communicating with the device) or Not Connected (the iPhone is not currently communicating with the device). A device must show Connected for your iPhone to work with it. In the OTHER DEVICES section, you see the devices that are discoverable to your iPhone but that are not paired with it.

••○○○ AT&T 📶	7:04 AM	✳ 52% 🔋

Settings ──────── (1)

✈	Airplane Mode	⬭
📶	Wi-Fi	Bravo5 >
✳	Bluetooth	On → **Bluetooth is on**
ⒶⓌ	Cellular	>

(2)

••○○○ AT&T 📶	9:13 AM	➹ ✳ 71% 🔋

‹ Settings **Bluetooth**

Bluetooth ⬤ ─── (3)

Now discoverable as "Brad Miser's iPhone".

MY DEVICES

Brad Miser's iPad — Not Connected ⓘ ── **Paired device**

TOYOTA Highla… — Not Connected ⓘ

UE Mobile Boo… — Not Connected ⓘ ── **Current status of the device**

OTHER DEVICES ⚙

Bluetooth Keyboard ──────── (5)

Device that hasn't been paired

4 If the device you want to use isn't shown in the OTHER DEVICES section, put it into Discoverable mode. (See the instructions provided with the device.) When it is discoverable, it appears in the OTHER DEVICES section.

5 Tap the device to which you want to connect. If a passkey is required, you see a prompt to enter it on the device with which you are pairing. If you aren't prompted for a passkey, skip to step 7.

6 If it is required, input the pairing code, passkey, or PIN on the device, such as typing the passkey on a keyboard if you are pairing your iPhone with a Bluetooth keyboard.

7 If required, tap Connect—some devices connect as soon as you enter the passkey and you won't need to do this. You see the device to which the iPhone is connected in the MY DEVICES section of the Bluetooth screen and its status is Connected, indicating that your iPhone can communicate with and use the device. For example, if you paired your iPhone with a keyboard, you can type on the keyboard to enter text in an app on your iPhone.

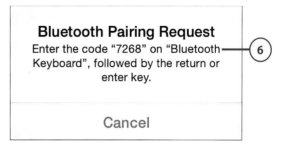

Bluetooth Pairing Request

Enter the code "7268" on "Bluetooth Keyboard", followed by the return or enter key. — **6**

Cancel

●○○○○ AT&T 🤶   9:18 AM   ✈ ❋ 71% ▰▹

❮ Settings   **Bluetooth**

Bluetooth ⬤

Now discoverable as "Brad Miser's iPhone".

MY DEVICES

Bluetooth Keyboard   Connected ⓘ

Brad Miser's iPad   Not Connected ⓘ

This keyboard is now connected and can be used

>>>Go Further
MANAGING BLUETOOTH

Following are a few pointers for using Bluetooth with other devices:

- Like other connections you make, the iPhone remembers Bluetooth devices to which you've connected before and reconnects to them automatically, which is convenient— most of the time anyway. If you don't want your iPhone to keep connecting to a device, move to the Bluetooth screen and tap the device's Info (i) button. Tap the Forget this Device button and then tap Forget Device. The pairing is removed. Of course, you can always pair the devices again at any time.

- If a device is already paired but has the Not Connected status, you need to connect it to use it. Move to the Bluetooth screen and tap the device to connect it to your iPhone. Once its status becomes Connected, your iPhone can communicate with the device again.

- You can use multiple Bluetooth devices with your iPhone at the same time.

Connecting Your iPhone to Other iPhones, iPod Touches, or iPads

The iPhone (and other devices that run the iOS software, including iPod touches and iPads) supports peer-to-peer connectivity, which is an overly complicated way of saying that these devices can communicate with one another directly via a Wi-Fi network or Bluetooth. This capability is used in a number of apps, especially multiplayer gaming, for information sharing, and for other collaborative purposes.

If the app you want to use communicates over a Wi-Fi network, such as a network you use to access the Internet, all the devices with which you want to communicate must be on that same network. If the application uses Bluetooth, you must enable Bluetooth on each device and pair them (as described in the previous section) so they can communicate with one another.

The specific steps you use to connect to other iOS devices using a collaborative app depend on the specific app you are using. The general steps are typically as follows:

1. Ensure the devices can communicate with each other. If the app uses Wi-Fi, each device must be on the same Wi-Fi network. If the app uses Bluetooth, the devices must be paired.

2. Each person opens the app on his device.

3. Use the app's controls to select the devices with which you'll be collaborating. Usually, this involves a confirmation process in which one person selects another person's device and that person confirms that the connection should be allowed.

4. Use the app's features to collaborate. For example, if the app is a game, each person can interact with the group members. Or, you can directly collaborate on a document with all parties providing input into the document.

Using AirDrop to Share Content with Macs, Other iPhones, iPod Touches, or iPads

You can use the iOS AirDrop feature to share content directly with people using a Mac running OS X Yosemite or later or using a device running iOS 7 or later. For example, if you capture a great photo on your iPhone, you can use AirDrop to instantly share that photo with iOS device users near you. AirDrop can use Wi-Fi or Bluetooth to share, but the nice thing about AirDrop is that it manages the details for you. You simply open the Share menu—which is available in most apps—tap AirDrop, and tap the people with whom you want to share.

When you activate AirDrop, you can select Everyone, which means you see anyone who has a Mac running OS X Yosemite or later or an iOS device running version iOS 7 or newer and is on the same Wi-Fi network as you are (or has a paired Bluetooth device); those people can see you, too. Or, you can select Contacts Only, which means only people who are in your Contacts app are able to use AirDrop to communicate with you. In most cases, you should choose the Contacts Only option so you have more control over who uses AirDrop with you.

When enabled, you can use AirDrop by opening the Share menu while using an app. Then you tap the people with whom you want to share content.

Is AirDrop Safe?

Anything you share with AirDrop is encrypted, so the chances of someone else being ables to intercept and use what you share are quite low. Likewise, you don't have to worry about someone using AirDrop to access your information or to add information to your device without your permission. However, like any networking technology, there's always some chance—quite small in this case—that someone will figure out how to use this technology for nefarious purposes. The best thing you can do is to be wary of any requests you receive to share information and ensure they are from people you know and trust before you accept them.

Enabling AirDrop

To use AirDrop, you must enable it on your iPhone.

1. Swipe up from the bottom of the screen to open the Control Center.

2. If AirDrop is not active—indicated by the text "AirDrop" being in black—tap AirDrop. If it is active, the "AirDrop" text is in white and you see its status (Everyone or Contacts Only); if this is the case, skip the next two steps.

Current AirDrop status (disabled)

3 Tap Contacts Only to allow only people in your Contacts app to communicate with you via AirDrop, or tap Everyone to allow anyone using a device running iOS 7 or later or Macs running OS X Yosemite in your area to do so.

4 Swipe down from the top of the Control Center to close it. You're ready to use AirDrop to share.

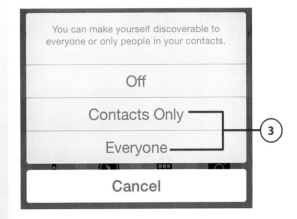

Share and Share Alike?

You should disable AirDrop when you aren't using it, especially if you use the Everyone option. By disabling it, you avoid having people in your area be able to try to communicate with you without you wanting them to do so. Generally, you should enable AirDrop only when you are actively using it and disable it when you aren't. To disable AirDrop, open the Control Center, tap AirDrop, and then tap Off.

People in your Contacts app can use AirDrop to communicate with you

Using AirDrop to Share Your Content

To use AirDrop to share your content, do the following:

(**1**) Open the app and move to the content you want to share. This example shows sharing a photo using the Photos app, but the steps to share in any app are quite similar.

(**2**) Tap the Share button.

(**3**) Tap AirDrop. The AirDrop button is replaced with icons for each person in your area who has AirDrop enabled that you have permission to access (such as being in her Contacts app if she is using the Contacts Only option).

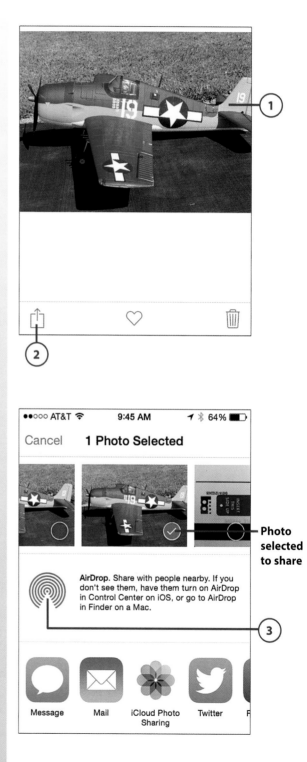

Photo selected to share

4 If necessary, swipe to the left or right to browse all the people with whom you can share.

5 Tap the person with whom you want to share the content. A sharing request is sent to those people's devices. Under their icons, the Waiting status is displayed. When a recipient accepts your content, the status changes to Sent. If a recipient rejects your content, the status changes to Declined.

Waiting for the recipient to accept or decline your sharing

(6) If the app supports it, browse and select more content to share.

(7) Tap the people with whom you want to share the content.

(8) When you're done sharing, tap Done.

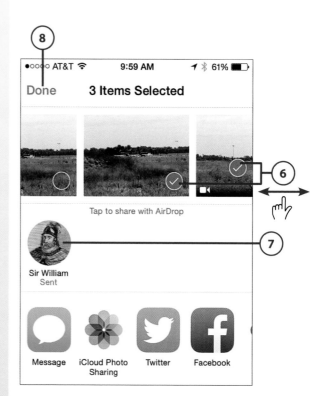

Recipient has accepted your content

Using AirDrop to Work with Content Shared with You

When someone wants to share content with you, you receive an AirDrop sharing request. Respond by doing the following:

(1) Make sure you know the person attempting to share with you.

(2) Make sure the content being shared with you is something you want. In this case, a photo is being shared.

(3) To accept the content on your iPhone, tap Accept. To reject it, tap Decline.

(4) If you accepted the content and the app enables you to review it in detail or edit it before saving it on your iPhone, swipe up and down the screen to see the detail of what you are accepting, or use the app's controls to edit it. For example, you can review the details of contact information being shared and you can edit photos shared with you.

(5) Use the app's controls to work with the shared content. For example, the Photos app provides tools to edit and share photos shared with you. In some cases, such as saving a contact shared with you, you need to tap Save to save the content on your iPhone or Cancel to not save it. (Other apps provide different controls depending on the type of content and the app it opens in.)

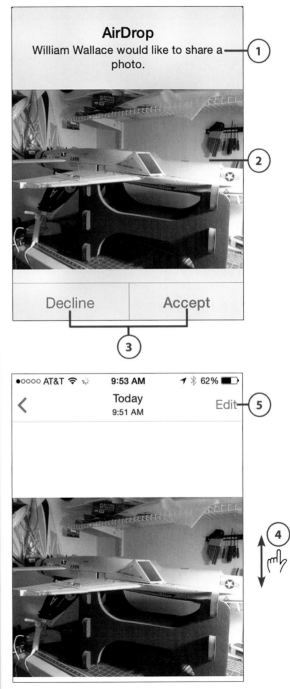

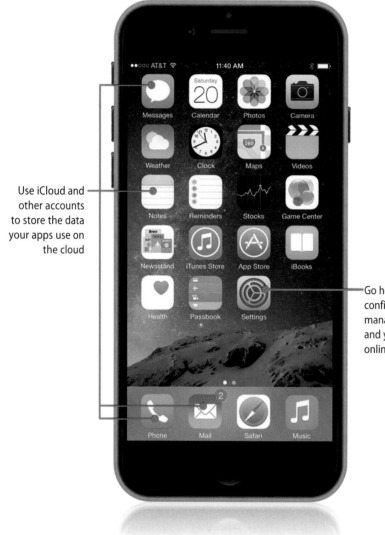

Use iCloud and other accounts to store the data your apps use on the cloud

Go here to configure and manage iCloud and your other online accounts

In this chapter, you learn how to connect your iPhone to various types of accounts, such as iCloud and Google, so that apps on your iPhone can access their data on the Internet cloud. The topics include the following:

→ Getting Started
→ Configuring and using iCloud
→ Setting up other types of online accounts on your iPhone
→ Configuring other types of online accounts
→ Setting how and when your accounts are updated

Setting Up and Using iCloud and Other Online Accounts

No iPhone is an island. Connecting your iPhone to the Internet enables you to share and sync a wide variety of content using online accounts such as iCloud and Google. Using iCloud, you can put your email, contacts, calendars, and more on the Internet so that multiple devices—most importantly your iPhone—can connect to and use that information. (There's a lot more you can do with iCloud, too, as you learn throughout this book.) There are lots of other accounts you might also want to use, such as Google for email, calendars, and contacts as well as Facebook for accessing social networks.

You need to configure each of these accounts on your iPhone to be able to use them; in this chapter, you'll see sections for several different accounts you might want to use. Of course, you only need to refer to the sections related to the accounts you actually use. You should also understand how you can determine how and when your information is updated along with tasks you might find valuable as you manage the various accounts on your iPhone.

Getting Started

One of the best things about using an iPhone is that you can configure it to use various types of online accounts that offer different types of services and information to you. Here are some of the key getting started terms for this chapter:

- **iCloud**—This is Apple's online service that offers lots of great features that you can use for free. It includes email, online photo storage and sharing, backup, calendars, Find My iPhone, and much more. You'll learn how to set up iCloud on your iPhone in this chapter and will see examples of how you can use it in many others.

- **Family Sharing**—This Apple service allows you to share content with a group of people. (They don't actually have to be related to you.) For example, you can share music you download from the iTunes Store with others automatically—when you set them up in your "family" group. It is also free.

- **Google account**—A Google account is similar to an iCloud account except it is provided by Google instead of Apple. It also offers lots of features, such as email, calendars, and contacts. You can use iCloud and a Google account on your iPhone at the same time.

- **Facebook**—Facebook is one of the largest social media sites that people and organizations use to share information, events, photos, and more. You can log into your Facebook account on your iPhone and use the Facebook app along with sharing information via that account in a number of apps (such as Photos).

- **Push, Fetch, or Manual**—Information has to get from your online account onto your iPhone. For example, when someone sends you an email, it actually goes to an email server, which then sends the message to devices that are configured with your email account. You can choose how and when new data is provided to your phone. Push means updates happen in real time; for example, as soon as a new email reaches the server, it is sent directly to your iPhone. Fetch means your phone connects to the servers periodically to retrieve new information. Manual means that new information is only retrieved when you cause it to be, such as by opening the Mail app.

Configuring and Using iCloud

iCloud is a service provided by Apple that gives you your own storage space on the Internet. In general, such Internet storage space is known as the cloud, so Apple's version of this space is called iCloud. You can store your information in your storage space on the cloud, and because it is on the Internet, all your devices are able to access that information at the same time. This means you can easily share your information on your iPhone, a computer, and an iPad so that the same information and content is available to you no matter which device you are using at any one time.

Although your iPhone can work with many types of online/Internet accounts, iCloud is integrated into the iPhone like no other type of account (not surprising because the iPhone and iCloud are both Apple technology). An iCloud account is really useful in a number of ways. For example, iCloud can be used for the following:

- **Family Sharing**—With Family Sharing, you can designate up to six people with whom you want to automatically share your iTunes and apps downloads, calendars, reminders, and more.

- **Photos**—iCloud can store your photos online to back them up, to make them easy to share, and to make them available on all your devices.

- **Email**—An iCloud account includes an @icloud.com email address. You can configure any device to use your iCloud email account, including an iPhone, an iPad, an iPod, and a computer.

- **Contacts**—You can store contact information in iCloud so that you can access it from lots of different devices.

- **Calendars**—Putting your calendars in iCloud makes it much easier to manage your time.

- **Reminders**—Through iCloud, you can be reminded of things you need to do or anything else you want to make sure you don't forget. Like the other features, you can have the same reminders on any device you've connected to your iCloud account.

- **Safari**—iCloud can store your bookmarks, letting you easily access the same websites from all your devices. And you can easily access websites open on other devices, such as a Mac, on your iPhone.

- **Notes**—With the Notes app, you can create text notes for many purposes; iCloud enables you to access these notes on any iCloud-enabled device.

- **Passbook**—The Passbook app stores coupons, tickets, boarding passes, and other documents so you can access them quickly and easily. With iCloud, you can ensure that these documents are available on any iCloud-enabled device.

- **Documents**—The iCloud Drive enables you to store your documents on the cloud so that you can seamlessly work with them using different devices.

- **Backup**—You can back up your iPhone to the cloud so that you can recover your data and your phone's configuration should something ever happen to it.

- **Keychain**—The Keychain securely stores sensitive data, such as passwords, so that you can easily use that data without having to remember it.

- **Find My iPhone**—This service enables you to locate and secure your iPhone and other devices.

You'll learn about iCloud's many useful features throughout this book (such as using iCloud with your photos, which is covered in Chapter 15, "Working with Photos and Video You Take with Your iPhone"). The tasks in this chapter show you how to set up and configure the iCloud features you want to use.

Obtaining an iCloud Account

To use iCloud on your iPhone, you need to have an iCloud account. The good news is that you probably already have one. The other good news is that even if you don't, obtaining one is simple and free.

If you have any of the following accounts, you already have an iCloud account and are ready to start using iCloud and can skip ahead to the next section:

- **iTunes Store**—If you've ever shopped at the iTunes Store, you created an account with an Apple ID and password. You can use that Apple ID and password to access iCloud.

- **Apple Online Store**—As with the iTunes Store, if you made purchases from Apple's online store, you created an account with an Apple ID and password that also enables you to use iCloud.

- **Find My iPhone**—If you obtained a free Find My iPhone account, you can log in to iCloud using that Apple ID.

During the initial iPhone startup process, you were prompted to sign into or create an iCloud account. If you created one at that time, you are also good to go and can move to the next task.

If you don't have an iCloud account, you can use your iPhone to create one by performing the following steps:

(1) On the Home screen, tap Settings.

(2) Swipe up the screen and tap iCloud.

(3) Tap Create a new Apple ID.

●○○○○ AT&T 📶	10:26 AM	🔀 ∗ 72% 🔋
	Settings	
☁ iCloud		›
Ⓐ iTunes & App Store		›

Create a new Apple ID

An Apple ID is the login you use for just about everything you do with Apple.

(4) Provide the information required on the following screens; tap Next to move to the next screen after you've entered the required information. You start by entering your birthday.

During the process, you'll be prompted to use an existing email address or to create a free iCloud email account. You can choose either option. The email address you use will become your Apple ID that you use to sign into iCloud. If you create a new iCloud email account, you can use that account from any email app on any device, just like other email accounts you have.

You'll also create a password, enter a rescue email address (optional), set up security questions, and agree to license terms. When your account has been created, you're prompted to enter your password.

After you successfully create your password, you are logged into your iCloud account and may be prompted to merge information already stored on your iPhone, such as Safari bookmarks, onto iCloud. Tap Merge to move your existing data to the cloud or Don't Merge to keep it out of the cloud.

When you've worked through merging your information, you're prompted to allow iCloud to track the location of your iPhone.

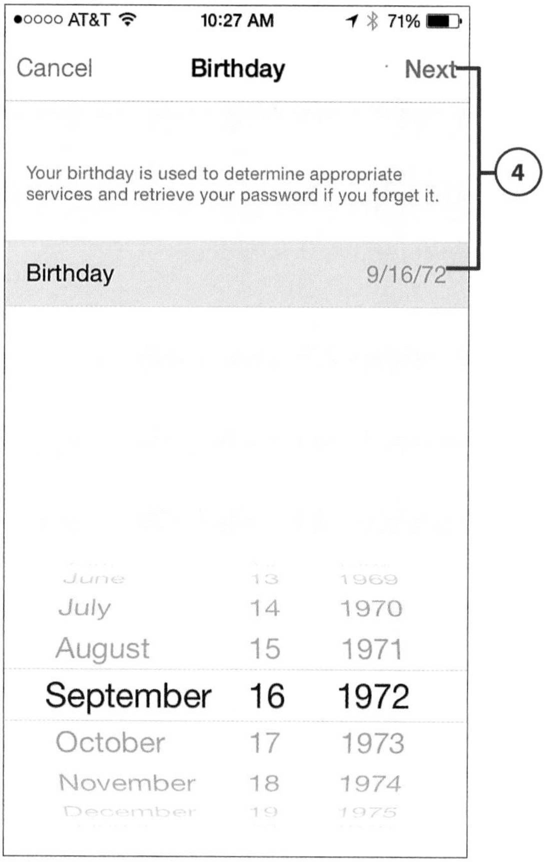

●oooo AT&T 🤝   10:27 AM   ✈ ⅜ 71% ▪️◻️

Cancel   **Birthday**   · Next

Your birthday is used to determine appropriate
services and retrieve your password if you forget it.

Birthday   9/16/72

June   13   1969
July   14   1970
August   15   1971
September   16   1972
October   17   1973
November   18   1974
December   19   1975

(4)

(5) Tap OK to activate Find My iPhone. You are ready to complete the configuration of your iCloud account, which is covered in the next section.

Allow iCloud to Use the Location of Your iPhone?

This enables Find My iPhone features, including the ability to show the location of this iPhone on a map.

Don't Allow   OK ——(5)

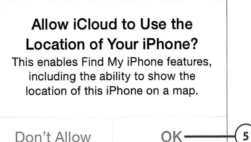

Multiple iCloud Accounts

You can have more than one iCloud account. However, you can have only one iCloud account active on your iPhone at a time.

Signing Into Your iCloud Account

To be able to use an iCloud account on your iPhone, you need to first sign into your account and then enable the services you want to use and disable those that you don't want to use. After iCloud is set up on your iPhone, you rarely need to change your account settings. If you restore your iPhone at some point, you might need to revisit these steps to ensure iCloud remains set up as you want it.

To get started, sign into your iCloud account—if you created your iCloud account on your iPhone using the prior task, you can skip to the next task, because when you created the account, you also signed into it.

(1) On the Home screen, tap Settings.

(2) Swipe up the screen and tap iCloud.

(3) Enter your Apple ID. If you see account information instead of the Apple ID field, an iCloud account is already signed into on the iPhone. If it is your account, skip to the next task. If it isn't your account, swipe up the screen and tap Sign Out; tap Delete to delete various data from your iPhone at the prompts and continue with these steps.

(4) Enter your Apple ID password.

(5) Tap Sign In. You are logged in to your iCloud account.

(6) If prompted to do so, tap Merge (not shown) to merge existing data, such as Safari bookmarks, already stored on the iPhone onto the cloud.

(7) At the prompt, tap either OK to allow iCloud to access your iPhone's location or Don't Allow if you don't want this to happen. You need to allow this for Find My iPhone, which enables you to locate your phone, to work. You're ready to configure the rest of iCloud's services.

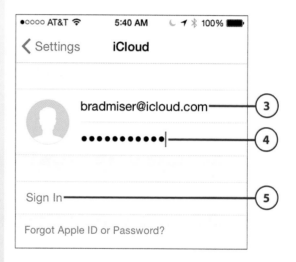

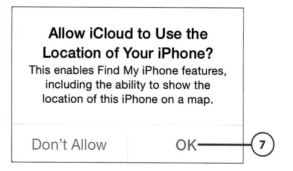

Enabling iCloud to Store Your Information on the Cloud

One of the best things about iCloud is that it stores data on the cloud so that all your iCloud-enabled devices can access the same information. You can choose the types of data stored on the cloud by performing the following steps:

(1) Move to the iCloud screen by tapping Settings, iCloud. Just below the Storage information are the iCloud data options. Some of these have a right-facing arrow that you tap to configure while others have a two-position switch. When a switch is green, it means that the related data is stored to your iCloud account and kept in sync with the information on the iPhone.

(2) If you don't want a specific type of data to be stored on the cloud and synced to your iPhone, tap its switch to turn that data off (the switch becomes white instead of green). The types of data that have switches are: Mail, Contacts, Calendars, Reminders, Safari, Notes, and Passbook.

Account currently signed in (tap to make changes)

Family Sharing (tap to configure)

Space available to you on the cloud (tap for more detail)

Green indicates the data is being stored on the cloud and synced with your iPhone

White indicates the data isn't being synced between the cloud and your iPhone

When you turn a switch off, you might be prompted to either keep the associated information on your iPhone or delete it.

If you choose Keep on My iPhone, the information remains on your iPhone but is no longer connected to the cloud; this means any changes you make will exist only on the iPhone. If you choose Delete from My iPhone, the information is erased from your iPhone. Whether you choose to keep or delete the information, any information of that type that was previously stored on the cloud remains available there.

After you've configured each data switch on the iCloud screen, you're ready to configure the rest of the data options, which are explained in the following tasks.

Share and Share Alike

Family Sharing enables you to share iTunes and App Store downloads, reminders, photos, and other information with a group of people. Configuring Family Sharing is explained in "Using Family Share to Share your iTunes Store Content" in Chapter 6, "Downloading Apps, Music, Movies, TV Shows, and More onto Your iPhone."

iCloud Drive

An iCloud account comes with storage space on which you can store documents that you work on using more than one device. For example, you can create a Pages document on an iPad and work on the same document using Pages on your iPhone. If you don't work with documents on your iPhone, you can ignore the iCloud Drive settings.

Configuring iCloud to Store Photos

Storing your photos on the cloud provides many benefits, not the least of which is that the photos you take with your iPhone are automatically saved on the cloud so that you can access them from computers and other iOS devices (such as iPads) and your photos remain available even if something happens to your iPhone, such as you lose it. Using iCloud also makes it easy for you to share your photos with others. To configure your photos to be stored in iCloud, do the following:

(1) On the iCloud screen, tap Photos.

(2) To keep all of the photos and video you take with your iPhone stored on the cloud, set the iCloud Photo Library switch to on (green). This stores all of your photos and video in iCloud, which both protects them by backing them up and makes them accessible on other iOS devices (iPads, iPod touches, and iPhones) and via the Web.

(3) If you enable the iCloud Photo Library feature, tap Optimize iPhone Storage to keep lower resolution versions of photos and videos on your iPhone (this means the file sizes are smaller so that you can store more of them on your phone) or Download and Keep Originals if you want to keep the full-resolution photos on your iPhone. In most cases, you should choose the Optimize option so that you don't use as much of your iPhone's storage space for photos.

Photos Revealed

Using the iCloud-enabled photo features is explained in detail in Chapter 15.

●○○○○ AT&T 🤶   7:43 AM   ⁎ ▰

‹ Settings   **iCloud**

Brad Miser
bradmacosx@mac.com   ›

☁️ Set Up Family Sharing…

Storage   12.7 GB Available ›

☁️ iCloud Drive   On ›

💮 Photos   On → (1)

●○○○○ AT&T 🤶   7:43 AM   ⁎ ▰

‹ iCloud   **Photos**

iCloud Photo Library (Beta)   ⬤— (2)

Automatically upload and store your entire library in iCloud to access photos and videos from all your devices.

Optimize iPhone Storage ———
    (3)
Download and Keep Originals ——

This iPhone is storing device-optimized versions. Turn on Download and Keep Originals to store full resolution photos and videos on your iPhone.

(4) Ensure the My Photo Stream switch is on (green). Any photos you take with the iPhone's camera are copied onto iCloud, and from there they are copied to your other devices on which the Photo Stream is enabled. If you use a Windows computer or a Mac, Photo Stream is useful because your photos are automatically downloaded to your computers. If you only use iOS devices, you don't really need to use Photo Stream if you enable the iCloud Photo Library on all the devices. Note that Photo Stream only affects photos that you take with the iPhone from the time you enable it, while the iCloud Photo Library feature uploads all of your photos, those you took in the past and will take in the future.

(5) If you want all of your burst photos (see Chapter 15) to be uploaded to iCloud, set the Upload Burst Photos switch to on (green). In most cases, you should leave this off (white) because you typically don't want to keep all the photos in a burst. When you review and select photos to keep, the ones you keep are uploaded through Photo Stream.

(6) To be able to share your photos and to share other people's photos, set the iCloud Photo Sharing switch to on (green).

(7) Tap iCloud.

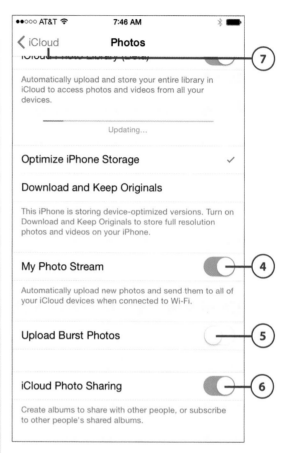

Configuring Your iCloud Backup

Like other digital devices, it is important to back up your iPhone's data so that you can recover should something bad happen to your iPhone. You can back up your iPhone's data and settings to iCloud, which is really useful because that means you can recover the backed-up data using a different device, such as a replacement iPhone. Configure your iCloud backup with the following steps:

(1) On the iCloud screen, tap Backup.

(2) Set the iCloud Backup switch to on (green). Your iPhone's data and settings are backed up to the cloud automatically.

(3) Tap iCloud.

Back Me Up on This

You can manually back up your iPhone's data and settings at any time by tapping Back Up Now on the Backup screen. This can be useful to ensure recent data or settings changes are captured in your backup. For example, if you know you are going to be without a Wi-Fi connection to the Internet for a while, back up your phone to ensure that your current data is saved in the backup.

Configuring Your iCloud Keychain

A keychain can be used to store usernames, passwords, and credit cards so you can access this information without retyping it every time you need it. Enabling keychain syncing through iCloud makes this information available on multiple devices. For example, if you've configured a credit card on your keychain on a Mac, that credit card is available though the keychain being synced via iCloud. Follow these steps to enable keychain syncing through iCloud:

Assumptions

These steps assume you have a keychain already configured for iCloud syncing on another device, such as a Mac or iPad, and that you know your security code. If not, your steps may be slightly different than those shown here. For example, you create a security code if this is the first time you set up keychain syncing.

(1) On the iCloud screen, tap Keychain.

(2) Set the iCloud Keychain switch to on (green).

(3) Enter your Apple ID password and tap OK. Next, you need to approve with your security code or via another device that uses your keychain.

(4) Tap Approve with Security Code.

(5) Enter your security code. You're prompted to enter a verification code, which is texted to your phone.

(6) Enter the verification code you receive via text. Your keychain syncing starts and your keychain information is stored on the cloud and synced onto your iPhone.

(7) Tap iCloud.

Advanced Keychain Syncing

When keychain syncing has been enabled, Advanced appears on the Keychain screen. Tap this to access additional Keychain commands. Use the Approve with Security Code switch to determine if your code can be used to set up keychain syncing on other devices. Tap Change Security Code to change your security code. Use the controls in the VERIFICATION NUMBER section to see or change the phone number to which the verification code is texted.

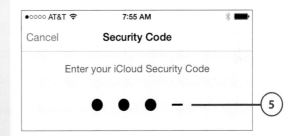

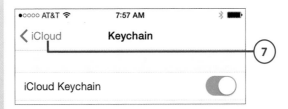

It's Not All Good

If you store a lot of sensitive information in your keychain on a Mac, such as usernames and passwords to websites, and credit cards, be careful about enabling keychain syncing. When you enable that, all this data becomes available on your iPhone and can be used by anyone who can use your phone. Assuming you have a passcode to the phone, you are protected from someone using your phone without you knowing it, but anyone using your phone can also access your sensitive information. You may choose to leave keychain syncing off and just keep a minimum sensitive of information on your phone.

Configuring Find My iPhone

Find My iPhone enables you to locate and secure your iPhone if needed. If you didn't enable Find My iPhone when you signed into your iCloud account, do so with the following steps:

1. On the iCloud screen, tap Find My iPhone.

2. Set the Find My iPhone switch to on (green).

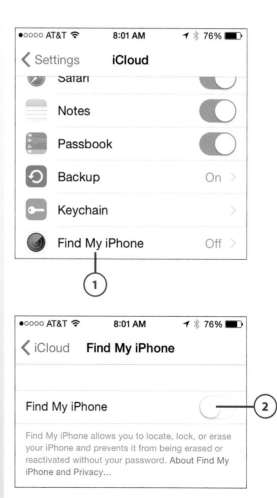

3 Tap Allow.

4 To have the location of the phone sent to Apple when the battery is low, set the Send Last Location switch to on (green). This can be useful if you lose your phone and it runs out of power. At least you will know where it was when the power ran out.

5 Tap iCloud.

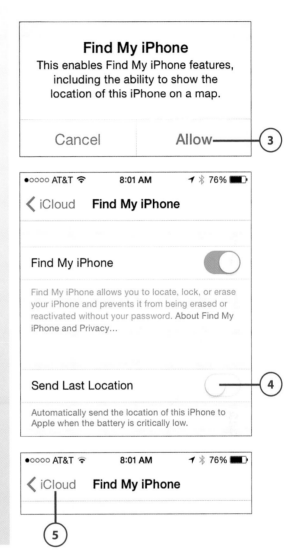

Setting Up Other Types of Online Accounts on Your iPhone

Many types of online accounts provide different services, including email, calendars, contacts, and social networking. To use these accounts, you need to configure them on your iPhone. The process you use for most types of accounts is similar to the steps you used to set up your iCloud account. In this section, you'll learn how to configure Google and Facebook accounts.

Configuring a Google Account

A Google account provides email, contacts, calendar, and note syncing that is similar to iCloud. To set up a Google account on your iPhone, do the following:

1. On the Home screen, tap Settings.

2. Tap Mail, Contacts, Calendars.

3. Tap Add Account.

4. Tap Google.

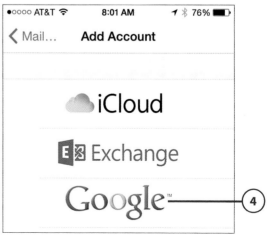

5 Enter your name.

6 Enter your Google email address.

7 Enter your Google account password.

8 Change the default description, if you want to. This description appears on various lists of accounts, so you should use something easily recognizable.

9 Tap Next. If your account information is verified, you briefly see check marks next to each item and move to the account options screen. If there is a problem with the information you entered, you need to correct it before your account can be verified.

10 Enable the features of the account you want to access on the iPhone, which are Mail, Contacts, Calendars, and Notes. Do this by setting the switch for the feature to on (green) to add it to your iPhone or to off (white) if you do not want to include it on your iPhone.

11 Tap Save. The account is saved, and the data you enabled becomes available on your iPhone.

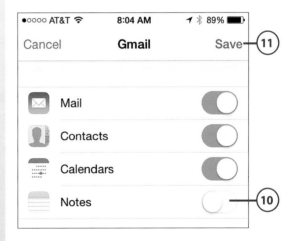

Configuring Other Types of Online Accounts

There are a number of other online accounts you can use on your iPhone. Some, such as Exchange, Yahoo!, AOL, and Outlook.com, are "built in," and you configure them similarly to how you configure a Google account. Just select the account type you want to use and provide the information for which you are prompted.

There are lots of other accounts you might want to use that aren't "built in." An email account included with an Internet access account, such as one from a cable Internet provider, is one example. Although support for these accounts isn't built in to the iOS, you can usually set up such accounts on your iPhone fairly easily.

There are two basic ways to set up other types of accounts.

- Using iTunes Sync
- Manually

If you already have an account set up on your computer, you can use iTunes syncing to configure the account on your iPhone. This is the easiest and best method because you don't have to enter that account's information manually. Just include the account in the sync settings and sync the iPhone. The account becomes available for you to use on your iPhone. See Chapter 5, "Working with iTunes on Your Computer," for information on syncing your iPhone with iTunes.

If you don't already have the account configured on a computer or you don't want to use iTunes to sync it onto your iPhone, you can manually configure it with just a bit more work.

When you obtain an account, such as email accounts that are part of your Internet service, you should receive all the information you need to configure those accounts in an application on a computer, which is the same information you need to configure those accounts on your iPhone. If you don't have this information, visit the provider's website and look for information on configuring the account in an email application. You need to have this information to configure the account on the iPhone.

Setting Up an Account Manually

With the configuration information for the account in hand, you're ready to set it up:

(1) In the Settings app, move to the Mail, Contacts, Calendars screen and tap Add Account.

(2) Tap Other.

(3) Tap the type of account you want to add. For example, to set up an email account, tap Add Mail Account.

(4) Enter the information by filling in the fields you see; various types of information are required for different kinds of accounts. You just need to enter the information you received from the account's provider.

(5) Tap Next. If the iPhone can set up the account automatically, its information is verified and it is ready for you to use (if the account supports multiple types of information, you can enable or disable the types with which you want to work on your iPhone). If the iPhone can't set up the account automatically, you're prompted to enter additional information to complete the account configuration. When you're done, the account appears on the list of accounts and is ready for you to use.

Multiple Accounts

There is no limit (that I have found so far) on the number of online accounts (even of the same type, such as Gmail) that you can access on your iPhone.

●●●○○ AT&T 🤍   8:41 AM   ⏎ ❋ 84% 🔋

❮ Add Account **Other**

MAIL

Add Mail Account ———————————— (3)

CONTACTS

Add LDAP Account   ❯

Add CardDAV Account   ❯

CALENDARS

Add CalDAV Account   ❯

Add Subscribed Calendar   ❯

●○○○○ AT&T 🤍   8:41 AM   ⏎ ❋ 84% 🔋

Cancel   **New Account**   Next—(5)

Name   Brad Miser

Email   bradmiser@indy.rr.com—(4)

Password   ●●●●●●●●

Description   Brighthouse

Configuring a Facebook Account

Facebook is one of the most popular social media channels you can use to keep informed about other people and inform them about you. Facebook is integrated into the iOS so you can share photos, messages, and such via your Facebook page, along with using the Facebook app.

To configure Facebook, perform the following steps:

(1) Move to the Home screen and tap Settings.

(2) Swipe up the screen and tap Facebook. If you see INSTALLED at the top of the screen, the Facebook app is installed on your iPhone and you can get right into your account. If not, tap INSTALL to install the app (downloading and installing apps is covered in Chapter 6); when the app is done installing, continue with these steps.

(3) Type your Facebook username.

(4) Type your Facebook password.

(5) Tap Sign In. Your account information is verified and you are signed into your account.

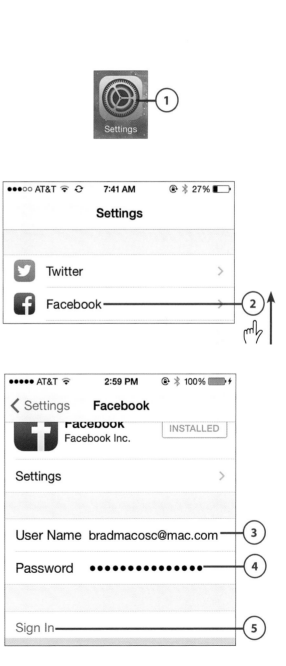

(6) Tap Sign In.

(7) To prevent apps from accessing your Facebook information, slide their switches to the off position (white).

(8) Tap Update All Contacts. Facebook attempts to match as much of your contact information with your friends as it can. When the process is complete, you are ready to access your Facebook account within the Facebook app or in any number of other apps.

No Facebook Account?

If don't have a Facebook account and want one, tap Create New Account and follow the onscreen instructions to create one. When you are done creating the new account, you're signed into it automatically.

More Facebook Settings

If you tap Settings on the Facebook Settings screen, you can do some additional configuration such as enabling or disabling sound and vibration for Facebook notifications. If you tap your name on that screen, you can change your password (which you might need to do from time to time).

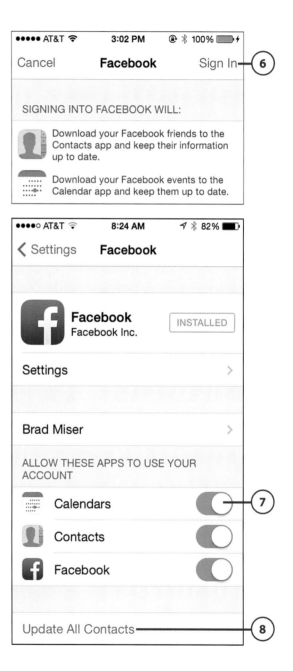

Setting How and When Your Accounts Are Updated

The great thing about online accounts is that their information can be updated any time your iPhone can connect to the Internet. This means you have access to the latest information, such as new emails and changes to your calendars.

As you learned in the "Getting Started" section, there are three ways that information on your iPhone is updated: Push, Fetch, and Manual. You can choose the methods that are used to update the information on your iPhone.

Push automatically provides the most current information, but also uses the most power, which shortens how long you can use your iPhone between charges. Fetch updates information automatically though less frequently, but uses less power than Push, so your battery lasts longer. Manual requires that you take action to update information.

You can configure the update method that is used globally, and you can set the method for specific accounts. Some account types, such as iCloud, support all three options while others might support only Fetch and Manual. The global option for updating is used unless you override it for individual accounts. For example, you might want your personal account to be updated via Push so your information there is always current, while configuring Fetch on a club email account may be frequently enough.

Configuring How New Data is Retrieved for Your Accounts

To configure how your information is updated, perform the following steps:

(1) Move to the Mail, Contacts, Calendars screen of the Settings app.

(2) Tap Fetch New Data.

(3) To enable data to be pushed to your iPhone, slide the Push switch to on (green). To disable push to extend battery life, set it to off (white). This setting is global, meaning that if you disable Push here, it is disabled for all accounts even though you can still configure Push to be used for individual accounts. For example, if your iCloud account is set to use Push but Push is globally disabled, the iCloud account's setting is ignored and data is fetched instead.

(4) To change how an account's information is updated, tap it. The account's screen displays. The options on this screen depend on the kind of account it is. You always have Fetch and Manual; Push is displayed only for accounts that support it.

●○○○○ AT&T 📶 8:56 AM ⬈ ❄ 80% 🔋

‹ Settings **Mail, Contacts, Calendars** ──(1)

Brighthouse
Mail ›

Add Account ›

──(2)

Fetch New Data 15 min ›

●●○○○ AT&T 📶 10:33 AM ⬈ ❄ 74% 🔋

‹ Mail... **Fetch New Data**

Push ⬤──(3)

New data will be pushed to your iPhone from the server when possible.

●○○○○ AT&T 📶 10:38 AM ⬈ ❄ 72% 🔋

‹ Mail... **Fetch New Data**

Push ⬤

New data will be pushed to your iPhone from the server when possible.

Brad Miser
Contacts, Calendars Fetch ›

Brighthouse
Mail Fetch ›

iCloud ──────────────────(4)
Mail, Contacts, Calendars and 8 more... Push ›

5 Tap the option you want to use for the account: Push, Fetch, or Manual.

If you choose Manual, information is retrieved only when you manually start the process by opening the related app (such as Mail to fetch your email) or by using the refresh gesture, regardless of the global setting.

If you choose Fetch, information is updated according to the schedule you set in step 9.

6 If you choose the Push option, choose the mailboxes whose information you want to be pushed by tapping them so they have a check mark; to prevent a mailbox's information from being pushed, tap it so that it doesn't have a check mark. (The Inbox is selected by default and can't be unselected.)

7 Tap Back.

●○○○○ AT&T 🤶   10:39 AM   🢁 ⁑ 72% ▮▮▯

❮ Back   **iCloud**

SELECT SCHEDULE

Push

Fetch   ✓   **5**

Manual

7

●○○○○ AT&T 🤶   10:43 AM   🢁 ⁑ 71% ▮▮▯

❮ Back   **iCloud**

SELECT SCHEDULE

Push   ✓

Fetch

Manual

If Push is not available, the Fetch schedule will be used.

PUSHED MAILBOXES

📭 Inbox   ✓

📄 Drafts

📨 Sent   ✓   **6**

🗑 Trash

8 Repeat steps 5-7 until you have set the update option for each account. (The current option is shown to the right of the account's name.)

9 Tap the amount of time when you want the iPhone to fetch data when Push is turned off globally or for those accounts for which you have selected Fetch or that don't support Push; tap Manually if you want to manually check for information for fetch accounts or when Push is off. Information for your accounts is updated according to your settings.

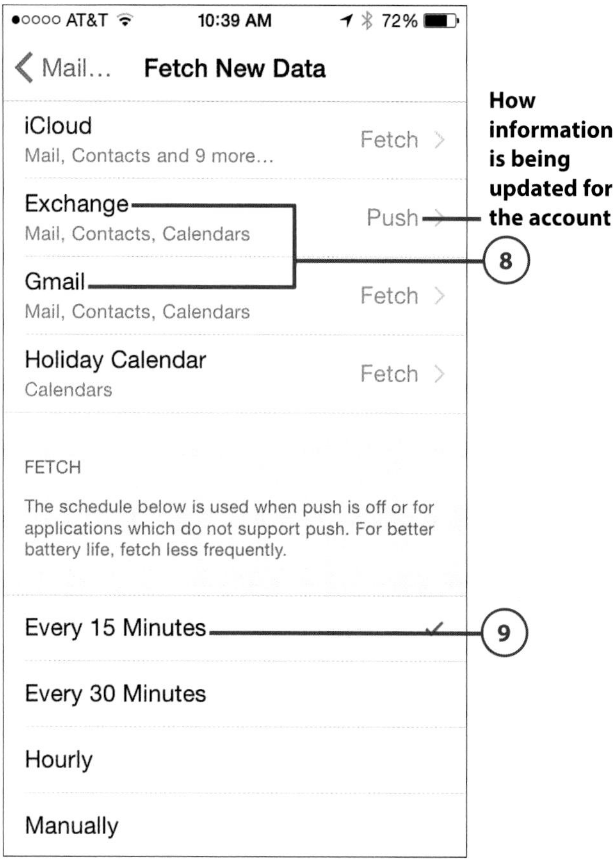

●○○○○ AT&T 📶   10:39 AM   ✈ ❄ 72% ▭

❮ Mail...   **Fetch New Data**

iCloud   Fetch ❯
Mail, Contacts and 9 more...

Exchange   Push ❯
Mail, Contacts, Calendars

Gmail   Fetch ❯
Mail, Contacts, Calendars

Holiday Calendar   Fetch ❯
Calendars

FETCH

The schedule below is used when push is off or for applications which do not support push. For better battery life, fetch less frequently.

Every 15 Minutes   ✓

Every 30 Minutes

Hourly

Manually

How information is being updated for the account

>>>*Go Further*

TIPS FOR MANAGING YOUR ACCOUNTS

As you add and use accounts on your iPhone, keep the following points in mind:

- You can temporarily disable any data for any account by moving to the Mail, Contacts, Calendars screen and tapping that account. Set the switch for the data you don't want to use to off (white). You might be prompted to keep or delete that information; if you choose to keep it, the data remains on your iPhone but is disconnected from the account and is no longer updated. If you delete it, you can always recover it again by simply turning that data back on. For example, suppose you are going on vacation and don't want to deal with club email. Move to your club account and disable all its data. That data disappears from the related apps; for example, the account's mailboxes no longer appear in the Mail app. When you want to start using the account again, simply re-enable its data.

- If you want to completely remove an account from your iPhone, move to its configuration screen, swipe up the screen, and tap Delete Account. Tap Delete in the confirmation dialog box and the account is removed from your iPhone. (You can always sign into the account to start using it again.)

- You can have different notifications for certain aspects of an account, such as email. See Chapter 4, "Configuring an iPhone to Suit Your Preferences," for the details of configuring and using notifications.

- You can change how information is updated at any time, too. If your iPhone is running low on battery, disable Push and set Fetch to Manually so you can control when the updates happen. When your battery is charged again, you can re-enable Push or set a Fetch schedule.

Place icons in folders to keep your Home screens organized

Tap to personalize your iPhone to make it your own

Choose the image you want as wallpaper

Customize the layout of the icons on your Home screens by placing icons where you want them

In this chapter, you learn how to make *an* iPhone into *your* iPhone. Topics include the following:

→ Getting started
→ Setting the screen's brightness, view, text size, and wallpaper
→ Setting Passcode, Touch ID, and Auto-Lock preferences
→ Choosing the sounds your iPhone makes
→ Configuring notifications
→ Configuring the Control Center
→ Setting Do Not Disturb preferences
→ Setting keyboard, language, and format options
→ Setting restrictions for content and apps
→ Setting accessibility options
→ Customizing your Home screens

Configuring an iPhone to Suit Your Preferences

There are lots of ways that you can turn *an* iPhone into *your* iPhone so that it works, looks, and sounds the way you want it to. Some examples include changing how text appears on the screen, creating and using text shortcuts, choosing the sounds your iPhone uses, configuring the notifications your iPhone displays and plays to keep you informed about what's happening, and more. One important customization that goes beyond just looks or sounds is to make your phone more secure by configuring and using a passcode (all models) and fingerprint (iPhone 5s and later) and restricting access to content and apps.

Getting Started

To do most of this personalization of your iPhone, you use the Settings app, which you've seen several times in the previous chapters. This app is the starting place for almost all of the customization of your iPhone's settings, such as the email accounts you use and the sounds your iPhone makes, and of the iPhone's default apps, such as Mail, Messages, and Photos along with any apps you download and install.

If you've read previous chapters, you've already used the Settings app a couple of times. Aptly named, the Settings app is where you configure the many settings that change how your iPhone looks, sounds, and works. Most of the tasks in this chapter involve the Settings app.

Using the Settings App on Any iPhone

You can work with the Settings app on any iPhone as follows:

(1) On the Home screen, tap Settings. The Settings app opens. The app is organized in sections starting at the top with controls you use to enable, disable, or configure key functions of your iPhone including Airplane mode, Wi-Fi, and so on. The next set of tools configures notifications, the Control Center, and the Do No Disturb function. The third group includes General, Display & Brightness, Wallpaper, Sounds, Touch ID & Passcode, and Privacy. Beneath those is a section with iCloud and iTunes & App Store settings. The remainder of the sections are the settings you use to configure how specific apps work, such as Notes, Reminders, and so on.

2 Swipe up or down the screen to get to the settings area you want to use.

3 Tap the area you want to configure, such as Sounds.

4 Use the resulting controls to configure that area. The changes you make take effect immediately.

5 When you're done, you can leave the Settings app where it is or tap the Back button, which is always located in the upper-left corner of the screen, until you get back to the main Settings screen to go into other Settings areas.

••ooo AT&T 🗢	6:24 AM	@ ✈ ✳ 59% ■⊃
	Settings	

✈	Airplane Mode	◯
🗢	Wi-Fi	MISER >
✳	Bluetooth	On >
(·)	Cellular	>

| 📷 | Notifications | > |
| 🎛 | Control Center | > |

2

••ooo AT&T 🗢	6:28 AM	@ ✈ ✳ 57% ■⊃
	Settings	

| 🎛 | Control Center | > |
| 🌙 | Do Not Disturb | > |

⚙	General	>
AA	Display & Brightness	>
🌸	Wallpaper	>
🔊	Sounds	**3**
☝	Touch ID & Passcode	>

••ooo AT&T 🗢	6:28 AM	@ ✈ ✳ 57% ■⊃
‹ Settings	**Sounds**	**5**

VIBRATE

Vibrate on Ring ◯

Vibrate on Silent ◯

RINGER AND ALERTS

◂ ——————◯—————— ◀ൈ **4**

Change with Buttons ◯

The volume of the ringer and alerts can be adjusted using the volume buttons.

Using the Settings App on an iPhone 6 Plus

When you hold an iPhone 6 Plus in the horizontal orientation and use the Settings app, you can take advantages of the iPhone 6 Plus' split-screen feature as follows:

(1) Hold the iPhone 6 Plus so it is horizontal.

(2) Tap the Settings app to open it. In the left pane, you see the areas of the Settings app that you can configure. In the right pane, you see tools you can use to configure the selected function. The two panes are independent, making navigation easier than with other iPhones.

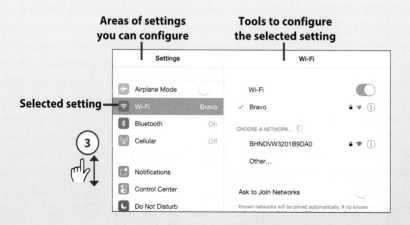

(3) Swipe up or down on the left pane until you see the function, feature, or app you want to configure.

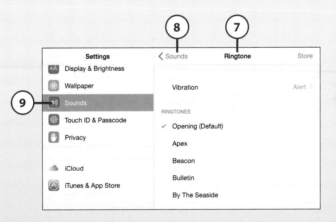

(4) Tap the function, feature, or app you want to configure, such as Sounds. Its controls appear in the right pane.

(5) Swipe up or down on the right pane until you see the specific setting you want to change.

(6) Tap the setting you want to configure, such as Ringtone. It's controls appear in the right pane.

(7) Use the tools in the right pane to configure the setting you selected in step 6. These work just as described in the previous task and throughout this chapter except that you move within the right pane instead of changing the entire screen.

(8) To move back through the screens in the right pane, use the Back button, which is labeled with the name from the screen you came from.

(9) Tap another area in the left pane to configure it. The split screen makes it very easy to quickly switch between Settings.

Chapter Shorthand

For almost all the tasks you read about in this chapter, you use the Settings app. The first step in these tasks is always to open the related settings area; you use the steps in the previous tasks to do this. These steps are not repeated in the following tasks. Instead, the tasks start with you selecting the settings area you need. So, when you see something like "Tap Display & Brightness," it means you should move into the Settings app, swipe up or down until you see the area you need (Display & Brightness for example), and then tap it. If you were previously using a different area in the Settings app, you need to tap the Back button to return to the main Settings screen and then find and tap the area you want to use.

Setting the Screen's Brightness, View, Text Size, and Wallpaper

Because you continually look at your iPhone's screen, it should be the right brightness level for your eyes. However, the screen is also a large user of battery power, so the dimmer an iPhone's screen is, the longer its battery lasts. You have to find a good balance between viewing comfort and battery life. Fortunately, your iPhone has an Auto-Brightness feature that automatically adjusts for current lighting conditions.

The iPhone 6 and iPhone 6 Plus offer two views. The Standard view maximizes screen space and the Zoomed view makes things on the screen larger, making them easier to see but less content fits on the screen.

As you use your iPhone, you'll be constantly working with text so it's also important to configure your text to meet your preferences.

Although it doesn't affect productivity or usability of the iPhone, choosing your own wallpaper to see in the background of the Home and Lock screens makes your iPhone more personal to you and is just plain fun.

Setting the Screen Brightness, View, and Text Size

To set the screen brightness, view, and text size, perform the following steps:

1. In the Settings app, tap Display & Brightness.

2. Drag the slider to the right to raise the base brightness or to the left to lower it. A brighter screen uses more power but is easier to see.

3. If you don't want to use the Auto-Brightness feature, slide the switch to off (white) to disable this feature. The Auto-Brightness feature adjusts the screen brightness based on the lighting conditions in which you are using the iPhone. You'll get more battery life with Auto-Brightness on, but you might not be comfortable with the screen when you use the iPhone where there isn't a lot of ambient light. Try using your iPhone with this feature enabled to see whether the automatic adjustment bothers you. You can always set the brightness level manually, as described in step 2, if it does.

(4) Tap View; if you don't see this option, your model doesn't support it and you can skip to step 17. The View settings enables you to set the zoom level you want to use.

(5) Tap Standard.

(6) Look at the sample screen.

(7) Swipe to the right to see examples of what other screens look like in the Standard view.

(8) Look at the sample screen.

(9) Swipe to the right to see examples of what other screens look like in the Standard view.

(10) Tap Zoomed. The sample screens change to reflect the Zoomed view.

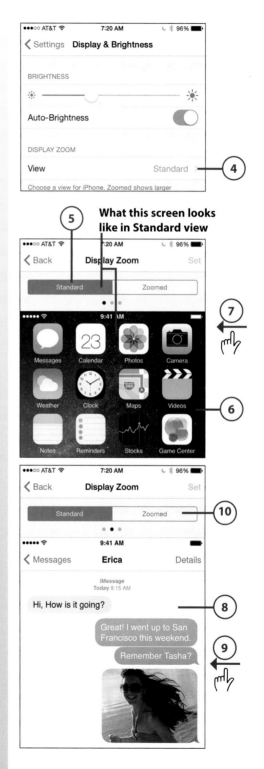

11 Swipe to the left and right to preview the other sample screens in the Zoomed view.

12 If you want to keep the current view, tap Cancel and skip to step 16.

13 To change the view, tap the view you want.

14 Tap Set (if Set is grayed out, the view you selected is already set and you can skip to step 16).

15 Tap Use Zoomed (this is Use Standard if you are already using the Zoomed view). Your iPhone restarts and uses the new view.

16 Move back into the Settings app and tap Display & Brightness.

17 Tap Text Size. This control changes the size of text in all the apps that support the iPhone's Dynamic Type feature.

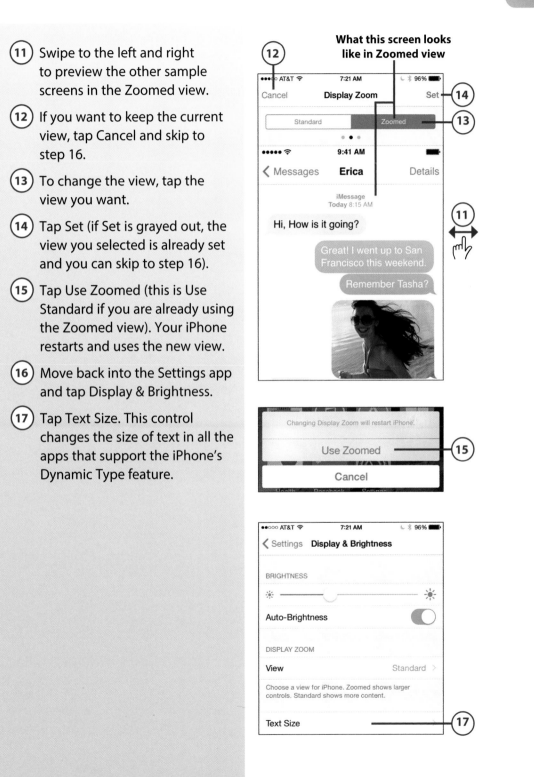

(18) Drag the slider to the right to increase the size of text or to the left to decrease it. As you move the slider, the text at the top of the screen resizes so you can see the impact of the change you are making.

(19) When you are happy with the size of the text, tap Back.

(20) If you want to make all of the text on your iPhone bold, set the Bold Text switch to on (green) and move to step 21. If you don't want to bold the text, skip the next step.

(21) Tap Continue. Your iPhone restarts. All the text is in bold, making it easier to read.

Setting the Wallpaper on the Home and Lock Screens

Wallpaper is the image you see "behind" the icons on your Home screens. Because you see this image so often, you might as well have an image that you want to see or that you believe makes using the Home screens easier and faster. You can use the iPhone's default wallpaper images, or you can use any photo available on your iPhone. You can also set the wallpaper you see on the iPhone's Lock screen (you can use the same image as on the Home screens or a different one). To configure your wallpaper, perform the following steps:

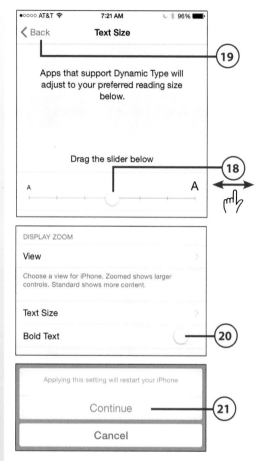

(1) In the Settings app, tap Wallpaper. You see the current wallpaper set for the Lock and Home screens.

(2) Tap Choose a New Wallpaper. The Choose screen has two sections. The APPLE WALLPAPER section enables you to choose one of the default wallpaper images while the PHOTOS section shows you the photos available on your iPhone. If you don't have any photos stored on your iPhone, you can only choose from the default images. To choose a default image, continue with step 3; to use one of your photos as wallpaper, skip to step 8.

(3) Tap Dynamic if you want to use dynamic wallpaper or Stills if you want to use a static image. Dynamic wallpaper has motion (kind of like a screen saver on a computer). Stills are static images. These steps show selecting a still image, but using a dynamic one is similar.

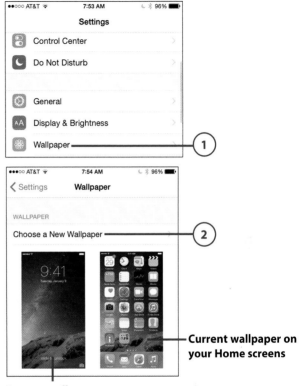

Current wallpaper on your Home screens

Current wallpaper on your Lock screen

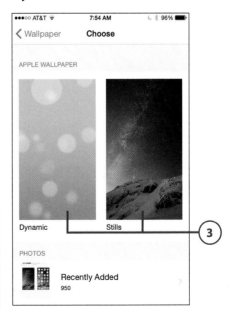

(**4**) Swipe up and down the screen to browse the images available to you.

(**5**) Tap the image you want to use as wallpaper.

(**6**) Tap Perspective Zoom to turn it off or on; the current setting is indicated by On or Off. When you tap Perspective Zoom, it toggles between these states. (See the sidebar "Perspective Zoom" at the end of this task for an explanation of this feature.)

(**7**) Tap Set and skip to step 15.

(**8**) To use a photo as wallpaper, swipe up the screen to browse the sources of photos available to you; these include All Photos, albums, and so on.

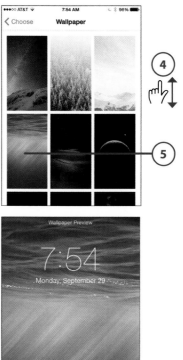

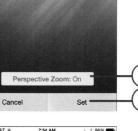

Working with Photos

To learn how to work with the photos on your iPhone, see Chapter 15, "Working with Photos and Video You Take with Your iPhone."

9. Tap the source containing the photo you want to use.

10. Swipe up and down the selected source to browse its photos.

11. Tap the photo you want to use. The photo appears on the Move and Scale screen, which you can use to resize and move the image around.

12. Use your fingers to unpinch to zoom in or pinch to zoom out, and hold down and drag the photo around the screen until it appears how you want the wallpaper to look.

13. Tap Perspective Zoom to turn it off or on; the current setting is indicated by On or Off. When you tap Perspective Zoom, it toggles between these states. (See the sidebar "Perspective Zoom" at the end of this task for an explanation of this feature.)

14. Tap Set.

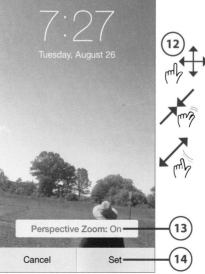

(15) Tap Set Lock Screen or Set
Home Screen to apply the
wallpaper to only one of those
screens; tap Set Both to apply
the same wallpaper in both
locations. The next time you
move to the screen you selected, you see the wallpaper you
chose.

(16) If you set the wallpaper in
only one location, tap Choose
to move back to the Choose
screen and repeat steps 3–15 to
set the wallpaper for the other
screen.

New wallpaper on the Lock screen

New wallpaper on the Home screens

Perspective Zoom

The Perspective Zoom feature can be a bit difficult to describe because it is subtle. This feature magnifies the wallpaper image when you tilt your iPhone. It is sometimes noticeable and sometimes not, depending on the image you are using for wallpaper. The best thing to do is to enable it to see if you notice any difference or disable it if you prefer not to use it for the specific images you use as wallpaper. You can enable or disable it anytime for your wallpaper on the Lock and Home screens. To change this setting without changing the wallpaper, move to the Wallpaper screen and tap the wallpaper (tap Lock or Home screen) setting you want to change. Tap Perspective Zoom at the bottom of the screen; it toggles the setting between off and on. When on, Perspective Zoom is highlighted and displays as On; when you turn it off, it dims and displays Off. To save the new setting, tap Set or to leave it as it is, tap Cancel.

Setting Passcode, Touch ID, and Auto-Lock Preferences

Your iPhone contains data you probably don't want others to access. You can require a passcode so your iPhone can't be unlocked without the proper passcode being entered. This gives you a measure of protection should you lose control of your phone. If you have an iPhone 5s or later, you can record your fingerprints so that you can unlock your phone (by automatically entering the passcode) and enter your Apple ID password by touching the Touch ID/Home button. The capability can also be used in other apps and services that require confirmation, such as Apple Pay.

The Auto-Lock feature automatically locks your phone after a specific period of time. This is useful because your iPhone automatically locks and, assuming you require a passcode, the passcode must be provided to be able to unlock your phone.

Securing Your iPhone with Auto-Lock

To configure your phone so it locks automatically, perform the following steps.

(1) On the Settings screen, tap General.

(2) Swipe up the screen until you see Auto-Lock.

(3) Tap Auto-Lock.

(4) Tap the amount of idle time you want to pass before the iPhone automatically locks and goes to sleep. You can choose from 1 to 5 minutes; choose Never if you only want to manually lock your iPhone. I recommend that you keep Auto-Lock set to a relatively small value to conserve your iPhone's battery and to make it more secure. Of course, the shorter you set this time to be, the more frequently you have to unlock it.

(5) Tap General. You're ready to configure your passcode and fingerprints (iPhone 5S and later).

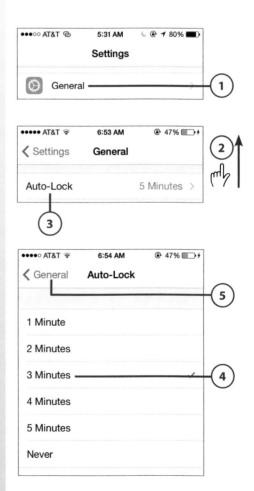

Configuring Your Passcode and Fingerprints (iPhone 5s and later)

To configure the passcode you have to enter to unlock your iPhone, perform the following steps (note these steps show an iPhone that has Touch ID; if your model doesn't have this, the steps will be slightly different as you will only be configuring a passcode):

(1) On the Settings screen, tap Touch ID & Passcode.

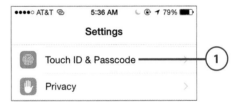

Already Have a Passcode?

If your iPhone already has a passcode set, when you perform step 1, you're prompted to enter your current passcode. When you enter it correctly, you move to the Touch ID & Passcode (iPhone 5s and later) or Passcode (other models) screen and you can make changes to the current passcode, add new fingerprints, and delete fingerprints. In this case, you can skip directly to step 5. If you want to change your current passcode, tap Change Passcode and follow steps 3 and 4 to change it. Then continue with step 5.

(2) Tap Turn Passcode On.

(3) Enter a four-digit passcode.

(4) Reenter the passcode. If the two passcodes match, the passcode is set.

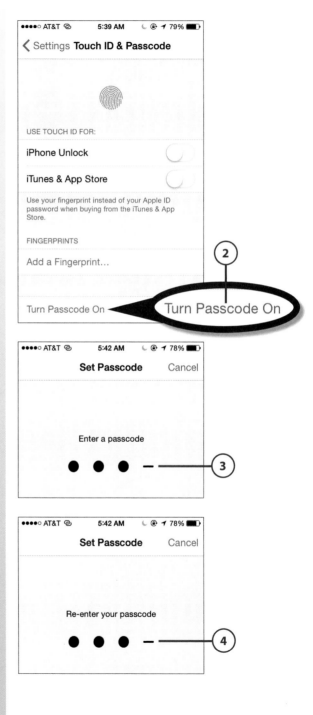

5 Tap Require Passcode.

6 Tap the amount of time the iPhone is locked before the passcode takes effect. The shorter this time is, the more secure your iPhone is, but also the more times you'll have to enter the passcode if your iPhone locks frequently.

7 Tap Back.

8 If you have an iPhone 5s or later, tap Add a Fingerprint and continue to step 9; if you have a model that doesn't support Touch ID, skip to step 20.

9 Touch the finger you want to be able to use to unlock your phone and enter your Apple ID password to the Touch ID/Home button, but don't press it. An image of a fingerprint appears.

Are You Complex?

By default, your passcode is a simple four-digit number. If you want to have a more complex (and more secure) passcode, set the Simple Passcode switch to off (white). You are prompted to create a new, complex passcode. The passcode field becomes more flexible, and you can enter text and numbers. This is more secure, especially if you use a code that is eight characters or longer that includes both letters and numbers. The steps to set a complex password are similar; the difference is that you use the keyboard to configure the passcode instead of just the numeric keypad.

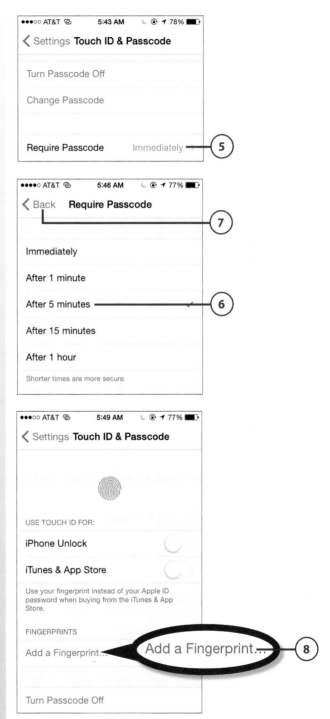

10. Leave your finger on the Touch ID/Home button until you feel the phone vibrate, which indicates part of your fingerprint has been recorded and you see some segments turn red. The parts of your fingerprints that are recorded are indicated by the red segments, gray segments are not recorded yet.

11. Take your finger off the Touch ID/Home button and touch the button again, adjusting your finger on the button to record other parts that currently show gray lines instead of red ones. Other segments of your fingerprint are recorded.

12. Repeat step 11 until all the segments are red. You are prompted to change your grip so you can record more of your fingerprint.

13. Tap Continue.

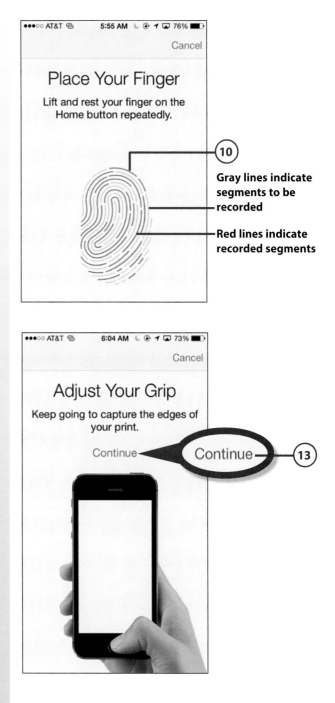

Gray lines indicate segments to be recorded

Red lines indicate recorded segments

14 Repeat step 11, again placing other areas of your finger to fill in more gray lines with red ones. When the entire fingerprint is covered in red lines, you see the Complete screen.

15 Tap Continue. The fingerprint is recorded and you move back to the Touch ID & Passcode screen. You see the fingerprint that has been recorded.

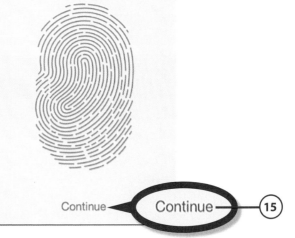

(16) Repeat steps 8 through 15 to record up to five fingerprints. These can be yours or someone else's if you want to allow another person to access your iPhone.

(17) If you don't want to use Touch ID to unlock your iPhone, set the iPhone Unlock switch to off (white). (This is enabled by default when you record a fingerprint.)

(18) If you want to be able to send payments via Apple Pay, set the Apple Pay switch to on (green). This enables you to register an Apple Pay payment by opening your Passbook app to the Apple Pay screen and touching your finger to the Home/Touch ID button

(19) If you want to also be able to enter your Apple ID password by touching your finger to the Touch ID/Home button, set the iTunes & App Store switch to on (green). (If you don't want to be able to sign into the stores using your fingerprint, skip to step 20.)

(20) Enter your Apple ID password and tap OK.

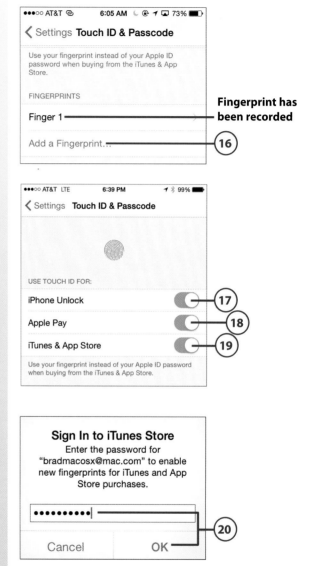

Fingerprint has been recorded

Name that Fingerprint!

To give a fingerprint a more descriptive name, tap it. On the resulting screen, tap the Clear button (x) to delete the current name. Then type the fingerprint's new name, maybe something like Right Thumb. Then tap Back. You see the fingerprint listed by its new name in the FINGERPRINTS section. This can make the fingerprints easier to recognize than the default names (such as Finger 1).

(21) Swipe up the screen until you see the Voice Dial switch.

(22) To prevent Voice Dial from working when your phone is locked, set the Voice Dial switch to off (white). (Voice Dial enables you to make calls by speaking even if you don't use Siri.)

(23) Use the switches in the ALLOW ACCESS WHEN LOCKED section to enable or disable the related functions when your iPhone is locked. The options are Today (the Today tab on the Notifications Center), Notifications View (the Notifications tab of the Notifications Center), Siri, Passbook, and Reply with Message. If you set a switch to off (white), you won't be able to access the corresponding function when your iPhone is locked.

(24) If you don't want the iPhone to automatically erase all your data after an incorrect passcode has been entered 10 times, set the Erase Data switch to off (white).

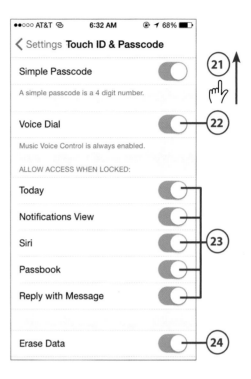

Automatic Erase

When you have enabled the Erase Data function and you enter an incorrect passcode when unlocking your iPhone, you see a counter showing the number of unsuccessful attempts. When this reaches 10, all the data on your iPhone will be erased on the next unsuccessful attempt.

Making Changes

Any time you want to make changes to your passcode and fingerprint (iPhone 5s or later) settings, move back to the Touch ID & Passcode (iPhone 5s or later) or Passcode (other models) screen. Before you can move back to this screen, you must enter your current passcode at the prompt. After you enter your current passcode, you move to the Touch ID & Passcode (iPhone 5s or later) or Passcode (other models) screen. To disable the passcode, tap Turn Passcode Off, tap Turn Off, and enter the passcode. To change your passcode, tap Change Passcode. You then enter your current passcode and enter your new passcode twice. You return to the Passcode Lock screen, and the new passcode takes effect. You can change the other settings similar to how you set them initially as described in these steps. For example, you can add new fingerprints. To remove a fingerprint, move to the Fingerprints screen, swipe to the left on the fingerprint you want to remove, and tap Delete. As you learned in the earlier note, you can rename a fingerprint by tapping it, editing its name on the resulting screen, and tapping Back (you might want to name the fingerprints so you recognize them, such as Right Thumb).

Choosing the Sounds Your iPhone Makes

Sound is one important way your iPhone uses to communicate with you. You can configure the sounds the phone uses in two ways. One is by choosing the general sounds your iPhone makes, which is covered in this section. You can also configure sounds specific apps use to notify you about certain events; this is covered in the next section.

To configure your iPhone's general sounds, do the following:

(1) On the Settings screen, tap Sounds.

(2) If you want your iPhone to also vibrate when it rings, set the Vibrate on Ring switch to on (green).

(3) If you want your iPhone to vibrate when you have it muted, set the Vibrate on Silent switch to on (green).

(4) Set the volume of the ringer and alert tones by dragging the slider to the left or right.

(5) If you want to also be able to change this volume using the volume buttons on the side of the phone, set the Change with Buttons switch to on (green).

(6) Tap Ringtone. On the resulting screen, you can set the sound and vibration your iPhone uses when a call comes in.

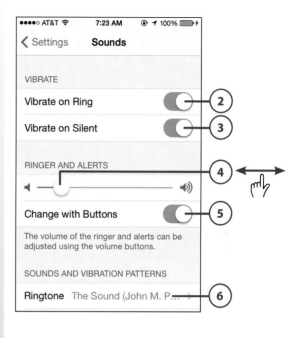

Individual Ringtones and Vibrations

The ringtone and vibration you set in steps 6–14 are the default or general settings. These are used for all callers except for people in your Contacts app for whom you've set specific ringtones or vibrations. In that case, the contact's specific ringtone and vibration are used instead of the defaults. See Chapter 7, "Managing Contacts," to learn how to configure ringtones and vibrations for contacts.

7 Swipe up and down the screen to see all the ringtones available to you. There are two sections of sounds on this screen: RINGTONES and ALERT TONES. These work in the same way; alert tones tend to be shorter sounds. At the top of the RINGTONES section, you see any custom ringtones you have configured on your phone; a dark line separates those from the default ringtones that are below the custom ones.

8 Tap a sound, and it plays.

9 Repeat steps 7 and 8 until you have selected the sound you want to have as your general ringtone.

10 If necessary, swipe down the screen so you see the Vibration section at the top.

11 Tap Vibration. A list of Standard and Custom vibrations available is displayed.

12 Swipe up and down the screen to see all the vibrations available. The STANDARD section contains the default vibrations while the CUSTOM section shows vibrations you have created.

13 Tap a vibration. It "plays" so you can feel it.

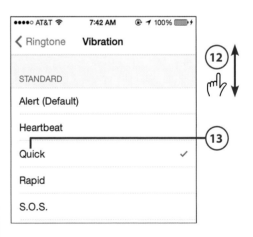

14 Repeat steps 12 and 13 until you've selected the general vibration you want to use; you can tap None at the bottom of the Vibration screen below the CUSTOM section if you don't want to have a general vibration.

15 Tap Ringtone.

16 Tap Sounds. The ringtone you selected is shown on the Sounds screen next to the Ringtone label.

17 Tap Text Tone.

18 Use steps 7–16 to set the sound and vibration used when you receive a new text. The process works the same as for ringtones, though the screens look a bit different. For example, the ALERT TONES section is at the top of the screen because you are more likely to want a short sound for new texts.

19 When you're done setting the text tone, tap Sounds.

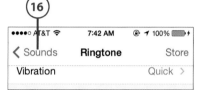

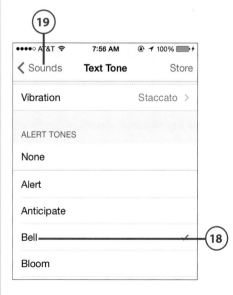

(20) Using the same pattern as you did for ringtones and text tones, set the sound and vibrations for the rest of the events you see.

(21) If you don't want your iPhone to make a sound when you lock it, slide the Lock Sounds switch to off (white). Your iPhone no longer makes this sound when you press the Sleep/Wake button to put it to sleep and lock it.

(22) If you don't like the audible feedback when you tap keys on the iPhone's virtual keyboard, slide the Keyboard Clicks switch to off (white) to disable that sound. The keyboard is silent as you type on it.

(23) Tap Settings. Your iPhone uses the sounds and vibrations you selected to notify you of events of which you want to be aware.

Text Tone	Bell >
New Voicemail	Tri-tone >
New Mail	Ding >
Sent Mail	Swoosh >
Tweet	Tweet >
Facebook Post	Swish >
Calendar Alerts	Alert >
Reminder Alerts	Update >
AirDrop	Typewriters >
Lock Sounds	
Keyboard Clicks	

>>>Go Further

SOUNDING OFF

Following are some other sound- and vibration-related pointers:

- You can tap the Store button on the Ringtone, Text Tone, and other screens to move to the iTunes Store, where you can download ringtones to your iPhone. See Chapter 6, "Downloading Apps, Music, Movies, TV Shows, and More onto Your iPhone," for more information about downloading content from the iTunes Store.

- You can also create your own ringtones using an audio app on a computer, such as GarageBand. GarageBand enables you to move ringtones you create directly into iTunes. If you use a different app, you need to export the sound from that app and then add it to your iTunes Library. In either case, you can then sync the tones onto your iPhone. See Chapter 5 for information about syncing.

- You can create custom vibration patterns, too. On the Vibration screen, tap Create New Vibration. Tap the vibration pattern you want to create; when you're done tapping, tap Stop. Tap Record to start over if you don't like the one you created. When you're done, tap Save. Name the pattern and tap Save. The patterns you create are available in the CUSTOM section on the Vibration screen, so you can use them just like the iPhone's default vibration patterns. To remove a custom pattern, swipe to the left on it and tap Delete.

Configuring Notifications

Many apps use notifications to communicate information to you, such as to inform you about new information, provide status updates, new email messages, and new text messages. You can use the Notifications settings to enable or disable notifications and to configure them for specific apps. Configuring notifications is one of the most important ways to customize your iPhone so that it keeps you informed as much as you want it to without overwhelming you with too many notifications.

Understanding Notifications and the Notification Center

There are several types of notifications, which include badges, banners, alerts, vibrations, and sounds.

 —Number of new items in the app

Badges are the counters that appear on an app's or folder's icon to let you know how many new of something you have, such as email messages, texts, event invitations, etc. You can enable or disable the badge for an app's icon. (Remember that when a badge appears on a folder's icon, it counts all the events for all the apps it contains.)

Banner notification for a new email message —

Swipe down to reply (some apps)

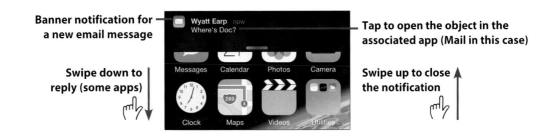

Tap to open the object in the associated app (Mail in this case)

Swipe up to close the notification

Type your reply ———— | That's great! ———— Send —— **Tap Send to send it**

Banners are small messages that appear at the top of the screen when something happens, such as when you receive an email message. Banners contain the icon of the app from which they come, and they can show a preview (if you enable the preview setting). Banners are nice because they don't interfere with what you are doing. If you ignore a banner, after a few seconds, it disappears. If you tap a banner, you move into the app producing the banner and can work with whatever the banner is for, such as a new email message. You can swipe up on a banner to close it. You can swipe down on a banner to reply (for some apps, such as Messages). When you receive a new banner when one is visible on the screen, the first one rotates out of the way so the newest one is displayed. If you receive a lot of notifications at the same time, you see a summary of how many you have received.

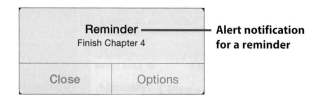

Reminder ———— **Alert notification**
Finish Chapter 4 **for a reminder**

Alerts are another means that apps can use to communicate with you. There are alerts for many types of objects, such as texts, emails, reminders, missed call notifications, and more. The differences between a banner and an alert are that alerts appear in the center of the screen and you must do something to make the alert go away, such as listen to or ignore a voice message. Some alerts have an Options button; tap this button to see and do actions related to the notification. Tap Close to close it without taking any action.

You should use alerts when you want to be sure to take action on the occurrence about which a reminder is being sent. For example, you might want to use alerts for calendar events so you have to respond to the notice that the event is coming up, such as the start of a meeting. Banners are better for those notifications that you want to be aware of but that you don't want to interrupt what you are doing, such as email messages. (If an alert appeared each time you received an email message, they could be very disruptive.)

Cellular Emergency Notifications

Depending on where you live and which provider you use, you might receive emergency notifications from government agencies for such things as weather emergencies or Amber Alerts (in the United States, these are issued when a child is abducted). These alerts appear on your iPhone when they are issued to keep you informed of such events. You can enable or disable certain of these notifications.

Sounds are audible indicators that something has happened. For example, when something happens in the Game Center, you can be notified via a sound. Earlier in this chapter, you learned how to configure your iPhone's general sounds. You also can configure the sounds used for a specific app's notifications.

Vibrations are a physical indicator that something has happened. Like sounds, you can configure general vibrations, and you can also configure an app's vibration pattern for its notifications.

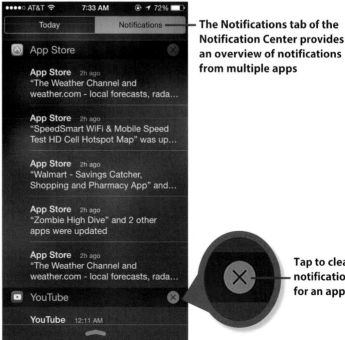

The Notifications tab of the Notification Center provides an overview of notifications from multiple apps

Tap to clear notifications for an app

The Notification Center enables you to access all your notifications on one screen. As you learned in Chapter 1, "Getting Started with Your iPhone," swipe down from the top of the screen to reveal the Notification Center. Tap the Notifications tab, and you see your current notifications grouped by the associated app. Swipe up and down the screen to review them. Tap the delete (x) button and tap Clear to clear all of the notifications for an app. You can configure which apps provide notifications here and how many are allowed.

Setting Global Notification Preferences

Use the following steps to configure general notification settings:

(1) On the Settings screen, tap Notifications.

(2) In the NOTIFICATIONS VIEW section, tap Sort By Time if you want the notifications shown in the Notification Center to be organized based on the most recent information being toward the top of the screen and skip to step 6; tap Sort Manually if you want to set the order (from top to bottom) of how apps appear in the Notification Center.

(3) Tap Edit to continue with the manual sorting.

Maintaining Order

You can set the order of the apps when either Manually or By Time is selected. The order you set persists when you switch between the two options, so you can change back and forth whenever you want without having to manually reset the order in which the apps are listed.

(4) Drag items by their order button up and down to change the order in which they appear in the Notification Center. If many apps are listed in the INCLUDE section, you need to swipe up the screen to see all of them.

(5) When you are done manually sorting the order, tap Done.

(6) Configure each app's notification settings; the details of this are explained in the next task.

(7) Swipe up the screen until you see the GOVERNMENT ALERTS section.

(8) If you don't want to receive AMBER alert notifications, set the AMBER Alerts switch to off (white).

(9) If you don't want to receive other types of emergency alerts, set the Emergency Alerts switch to off (white).

More Alerts

Depending on where you live, you might see a different set of alert options in the GOVERNMENT ALERTS section. You can enable or disable any of the alerts you see in this section as explained in steps 8 and 9.

Configuring Notifications for Specific Apps

You can configure which apps can provide notifications and, if you allow notifications, which type. You can also configure other aspects of notifications, such as whether an app displays in the Notification Center, whether its notifications appear on the Lock screen, and if they include an alert sound. Apps support different notification options, and not all apps support all options. Some apps, such as Mail, support notification configuration by account (for example, you can set a different alert sound for new mail in each account). However, you can follow the same general steps to configure notifications for each app; you should explore all the options for the apps you use most often to ensure they work the best for you.

The following steps show how to configure Mail's notifications, which is a good example because it supports a lot of notification features; other apps might have fewer features or might be organized slightly differently. But, configuring the notifications for any app follows a similar pattern.

1. Continuing on the Notifications screen from the previous task, swipe up to see the INCLUDE section. Here, you see each app on your iPhone that supports notifications. The INCLUDE sections shows apps for which notifications are enabled, while those for which notifications are disabled are shown in the DO NOT INCLUDE section.

2. Tap the app whose notifications you want to configure.

3 If you want the app to provide notifications, set the Allow Notifications switch to on (green) and move to step 4. If you don't want notifications from the app, set the Allow Notifications switch to off (white) and skip the rest of these steps.

4 Tap Show in Notification Center.

5 Tap the number of individual notifications you want to be shown in the Notification Center.

6 Tap the Back button, which is labeled with the name of the app you are configuring (Mail, in this example). If an app supports multiple accounts, you can configure the notifications for each account. If not, you see the Notifications screen showing all the options for that app and you can skip to step 8.

7 Tap the account for which you want to configure notifications.

8 If you want notifications from the account you selected in step 7 to appear in the Notification Center, set the Show in Notification Center switch to on (green); set the switch to off (white) if you don't want notifications for the account to appear in the Notification Center.

9 Tap Notification Sound.

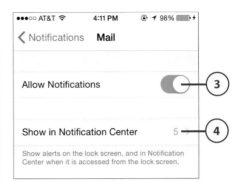

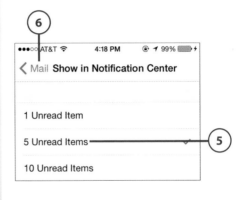

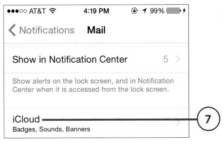

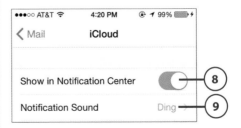

10 Use the resulting Notification Sound screen to choose the alert sound and vibration for new email messages to the account (refer to the section on setting general sound preferences earlier in this chapter for details).

11 Tap the Back button located in the upper-left corner of the screen (it is labeled with the account's name).

12 To display the app's badge, set the Badge App Icon switch to on (green); if you set it to off (white), the badge is not displayed when new email arrives.

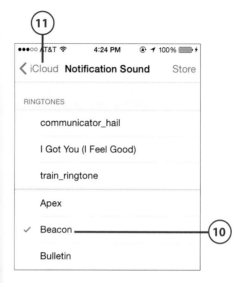

Installed App Not Shown?

You must have opened an app at least once for it to appear on the Notifications screen.

13 If you want the app's notifications for the account to appear on the Lock screen, slide the Show on Lock Screen switch to on (green); if you set it to off (white), you won't see notifications from the app for the account when your iPhone is locked.

14 Choose the type of notification you want the app for the account to provide by tapping None, Banners, or Alerts. The selected alert type is the one whose name is enclosed in an oblong.

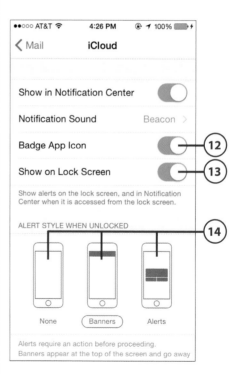

15 If you don't want a preview to appear in the app's notifications, slide the Show Previews switch to off (white). For example, you might want to keep some types of messages private; to do so, disable the preview option for that account.

16 Tap the Back button, which is located in the upper-left corner of the window and is labeled with the app you are configuring (Mail, in this example).

17 Configure notifications for the other accounts used in the app.

18 Configure notifications for VIP email and threads.

19 Tap Notifications.

VIPs Are Special

Mail supports VIPs, which are people from whom email messages are treated specially, such as having a dedicated mailbox in the Mail app. You can apply specific notification settings to VIP messages using the VIP option. These override the notification settings for the email account to which messages from VIPs are sent.

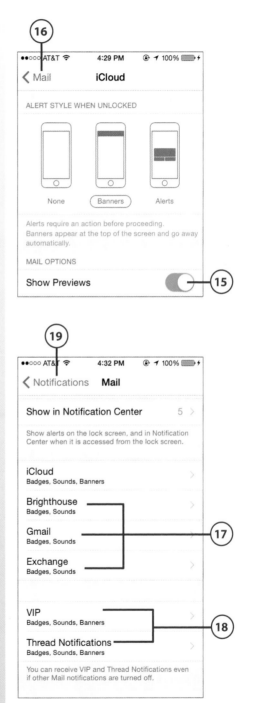

20. Repeat these steps for each app shown on the Notification Center screen. Certain apps might not have all the options shown in these steps, but the process to configure their notifications is similar.

Configuring the Control Center

As you learned in Chapter 1, the Control Center provides quick access to various settings, app controls, and even apps.

There are a couple of Control Center preferences you can set:

1. On the Settings screen, tap Control Center.

2. To be able to access the Control Center from the Lock screen, set the Access on Lock Screen switch to on (green).

3. To be able to access it when you are using an app, set the Access Within Apps switch to on (green).

Setting Do Not Disturb Preferences

As you learned in Chapter 1, the Do Not Disturb feature enables you to temporarily silence notifications; you can also configure quiet times during which notifications are automatically silenced.

You can set an automatic Do Not Disturb schedule by performing the following steps:

(1) On the Settings screen, tap Do Not Disturb.

(2) To activate Do Not Disturb manually, set the Manual switch to on (green). (This is the same as activating it from the Control Center.)

(3) To configure Do Not Disturb to activate automatically on a schedule, slide the Scheduled switch to on (green).

(4) Tap the From and To box.

(5) Tap From.

(6) Swipe on the time selection wheels to select the hour and minute (AM or PM) when you want the Do Not Disturb period to start.

(7) Tap To.

(8) Swipe on the time selection wheels to set the hour and minute (AM or PM) when you want the Do Not Disturb period to end.

(9) Tap Do Not Disturb.

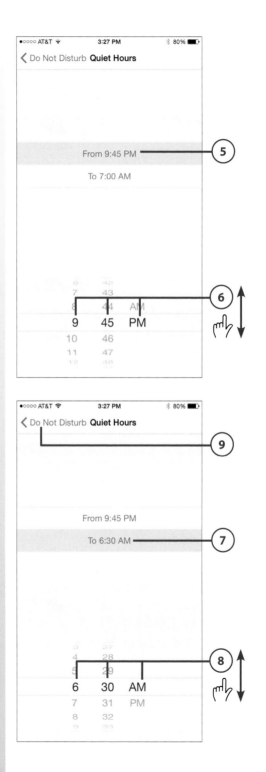

10 Tap Allow Calls From.

11 Tap the option for whose calls should be allowed during the Do Not Disturb period. The options are Everyone, which doesn't prevent any calls; No One, which sends all calls to voicemail; Favorites, which allows calls from people on your Favorites lists to come through but all others go to voicemail; or one of your contact groups, which allows calls from anyone in the selected group to come through while all others go to voicemail.

12 Tap Do Not Disturb.

Scheduled	⬤
From	9:45 PM
To	6:30 AM ›
Allow Calls From — All Contacts ›	**10**

Incoming calls from your contacts will not be silenced.

12

●●○○○ AT&T 🛜   3:31 PM   🔋 79% 🔋

‹ Do Not Disturb **Allow Calls From**

Everyone

No One

Favorites ——————————— **11**

GROUPS

All Contacts

Book Group

My Favorite People

Presidents I Wish I Knew

App Settings

Many apps (default and those you install) include settings you can use to configure how the apps work or look. On the Settings screen, tap the app whose settings you want to configure and use the resulting screen to configure its options. You'll be learning how to use many of the app settings in detail throughout this book.

(13) Set the Repeated Calls switch to on (green) if you want a second call from the same person within three minutes to be allowed through. This feature is based on the assumption that if a call is really important, someone will try again immediately.

(14) If you want notifications to be silenced only when your phone is locked during the Do Not Disturb period, tap Only while iPhone is locked. Tap Always if you want notifications to be silenced regardless of the Lock status.

(15) Tap Settings. During the Do Not Disturb period, your iPhone is silent, except for any exceptions you configured. When the period ends, your iPhone resumes its normal notification activity.

(15)

●●○○○ AT&T 📶	4:48 PM	@ ⌁ 100% ▭⫶⚡

‹ Settings Do Not Disturb

Scheduled ⬤

From   9:45 PM ›
To   6:30 AM

Allow Calls From   Favorites ›

Incoming calls from your favorites will not be silenced.

Repeated Calls ⬤――(13)

When enabled, a second call from the same person within three minutes will not be silenced.

SILENCE:

Always ――――――――――――――――

Only while iPhone is locked ―――― ✓   ――(14)

Incoming calls and notifications will be silenced while iPhone is locked.

Setting Keyboard, Language, and Format Options

You'll be working with text in many apps on your iPhone. You can customize a number of keyboard- and format-related options so text appears and behaves the way you want it to. You can also choose the language your iPhone uses to communicate to you.

Setting Keyboard Preferences

You use the iPhone's keyboard to input text in many apps, including Mail, and Messages. A number of settings determine how the keyboard works.

1. On the Settings screen, tap General.

2. Swipe up the screen.

3. Tap Keyboard.

4. Tap Keyboards. This enables you to add more keyboards so that you can choose a specific language's keyboard when you are entering text. At the top of the screen, you see the keyboards that are available to you.

5. Tap Add New Keyboard.

Fun in Text

If you want to be able to include a huge variety of smiley faces, symbols, and other icons whenever you type, add the Emoji keyboard (it might be installed by default). Using this keyboard is explained in Chapter 1.

6. Swipe up and down the screen to browse the available keyboards.

7. Tap the keyboard you want to add.

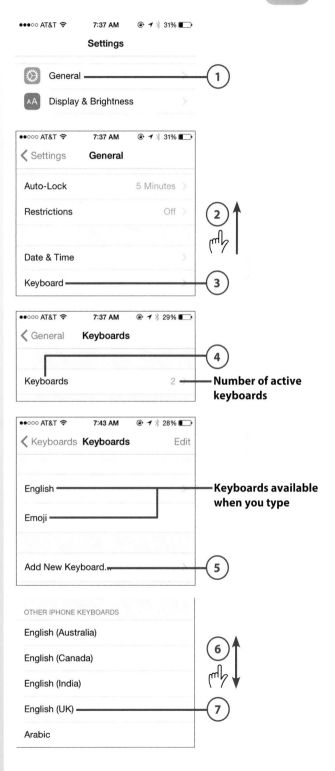

8. Tap the keyboard you added in step 7.

9. Tap the keyboard layout you want to use.

10. Tap Keyboards.

11. Repeat steps 5–10 to add and configure additional keyboards.

12. Tap Keyboards. (Note that the Shortcuts option is explained in the next task.)

More Options

Depending on the language and keyboards you have configured, you might see additional options. For example, when English is selected, you can use the Check Spelling switch to enable and disable the spell checker.

>>>Go Further

THIRD-PARTY KEYBOARDS

You can install and use keyboards on your phone that are sold in the App Store by third-party developers (third-party means someone other than Apple). To do this, open the App Store app and search for "keyboards for iPhone" or you can search for a specific keyboard by name if you know of one you want to try. (See Chapter 6, "Downloading Apps, Music, Movies, TV Shows, and More onto Your iPhone," for help using the App Store app.) After you have downloaded the keyboard you want to use, use steps 1 through 5 to move back to the Keyboards Settings screen. When you open the Add New Keyboard screen, you see a section called THIRD-PARTY KEYBOARDS in which you see the additional keyboards you have installed. Tap a keyboard in this section to activate it. When you move back to the Keyboards screen, you see the keyboard you just activated. Tap it to configure its additional options. Then, you can use the new keyboard just like the default keyboard or others you have activated. Check out the documentation for any keyboards you download to ensure you take advantage of all of their features.

13 To prevent your iPhone from automatically capitalizing as you type, set Auto-Capitalization to off (white). The iPhone no longer changes the case of letters as you type them.

14 To disable the automatic spell checking/correction, set Auto-Correction to off (white). Your iPhone no longer automatically suggests corrections to what you type.

15 To disable the iPhone's Spell Checker, set the Check Spelling switch to off (white). You'll be on your own spelling-wise.

16 To disable the Caps Lock function, set the Enable Caps Lock to off (white). The Cap Locks function won't be available to you when you tap the Shift key twice.

17 To disable the iPhone's Predictive Text feature (see Chapter 1), set the Predictive switch to off (white). You won't be able to use the predictive text bar to enter text.

18 To disable the shortcut that types a period followed by a space when you tap the space-bar twice, set the "." Shortcut switch to off (white). You must tap a period and the spacebar to type these characters when you end a sentence.

Auto-Capitalization	13
Auto-Correction	14
Check Spelling	15
Enable Caps Lock	16
Predictive	17
"." Shortcut	18

Double tapping the space bar will insert a period followed by a space.

Changing Keyboards

To delete a keyboard, move to the Keyboards Settings screen and swipe to the left on the keyboard you want to remove. Tap Delete. The keyboard is removed from the list of activated keyboards and is no longer available to you when you type. (You can always activate it again later.) To change the order in which keyboards appear, move to the Keyboards screen, tap Edit, and drag the keyboards up and down the screen. When you've finished, tap Done.

Creating and Working with Text Shortcuts

Text shortcuts are useful because you can use just a few letters to type a series of words. You type the shortcut, and it is replaced by the phrase with which it is associated. To configure your text shortcuts, do the following:

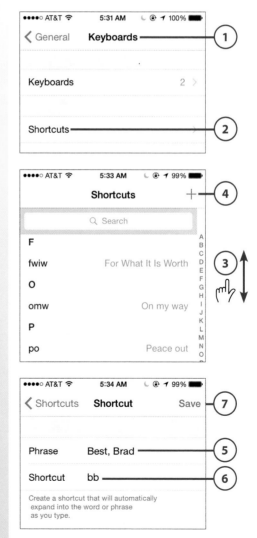

1. Move to the Keyboards screen as described in steps 1–3 in the previous task.

2. Tap Shortcuts.

3. Review the current shortcuts.

4. To add a shortcut, tap Add (+).

5. Type the phrase for which you want to create a shortcut.

6. Type the shortcut you want to be replaced by the phrase you created in step 5.

7. Tap Save. If the shortcut doesn't contain any disallowed characters, it is created and you move back to the Shortcuts section where you see your new shortcut. If there is an error, you see an explanation of the error; you must correct it before you can create the shortcut.

8 Repeat steps 4–7 to create other text shortcuts.

9 When you've created all the shortcuts you want, tap Keyboards.

Shortcuts to Shortcuts

To change a shortcut, tap it. Use the resulting screen to change the phrase or shortcut, and tap Save to update the shortcut. To remove a shortcut, swipe to the left on it and tap Delete. To search for a shortcut, tap in the Search bar at the top of the screen and type the shortcut you want to see; you can also use the index along the right side of the screen to find shortcuts. You can also tap Edit on the Shortcuts screen to change your shortcuts. And, yes, you can create a phrase without a shortcut, but I don't really see much use for that!

Setting Language and Region Preferences

There are a number of formatting preferences you can set that determine how information is formatted in various apps. For example, you can choose how addresses are formatted by default by choosing the region whose format you want to follow.

1 On the Settings screen, tap General.

2 Swipe up the screen.

3 Tap Language & Region.

New shortcut

4 Tap iPhone Language.

5 Swipe up and down the screen to view the languages with which your iPhone can work; or tap in the Search bar and type a language you want to use to find it. The current language is marked with a check mark.

6 Tap the language you want to use.

7 Tap Done. Your iPhone starts using the language you selected.

8 Tap Other Languages.

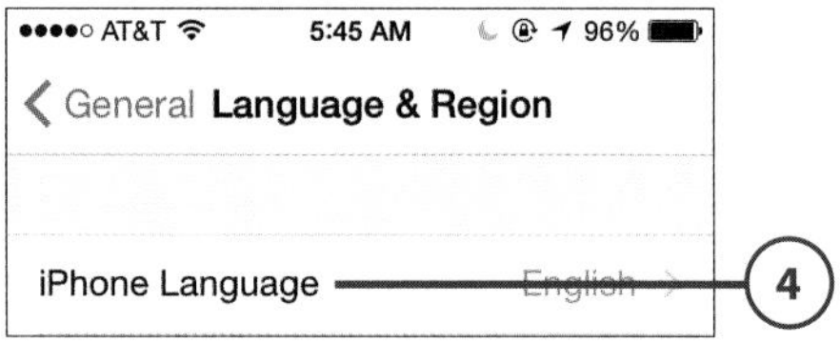

●●●●○ AT&T 🖵   5:45 AM   ◔ @ ➹ 96% 🔋

〈 General **Language & Region**

iPhone Language   English 〉   **4**

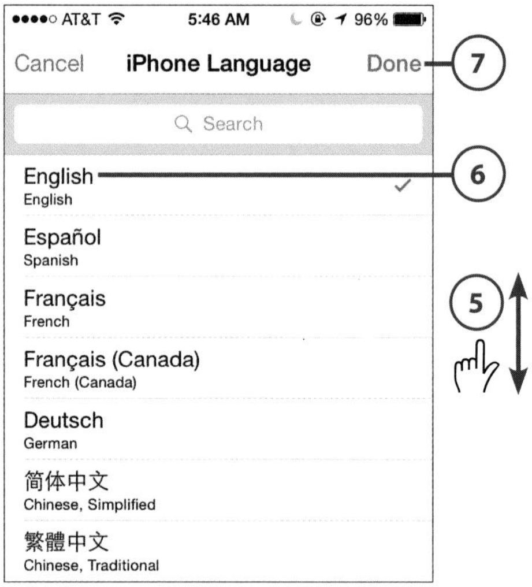

●●●●○ AT&T 🖵   5:46 AM   ◔ @ ➹ 96% 🔋

Cancel   **iPhone Language**   Done   **7**

🔍 Search

English
English   ✓   **6**

Español
Spanish

Français
French

Français (Canada)
French (Canada)   **5**

Deutsch
German

简体中文
Chinese, Simplified

繁體中文
Chinese, Traditional

●●●●○ AT&T 🖵   5:51 AM   ◔ @ ➹ 94% 🔋

〈 General **Language & Region**

iPhone Language   English 〉

Other Languages...   **8**

9 Using steps 5 through 7, find and tap a secondary language. This language is used when your primary language can't be, such as on websites that don't support your primary language.

10 Tap Done.

11 Tap the language you want to be primary to confirm it. The language you selected is configured and you move back to the Home screens.

12 Use steps 1 through 3 to return to the Language & Region screen. You see the languages and order of preference below the iPhone Language section.

13 To add more languages, tap Add Language and follow steps 9 through 12.

14 Tap Region.

Order, Order!

To change the order of preference for the languages you have configured, tap Edit, drag the languages up or down the screen to set their order, and tap Done to save your changes.

●●●○○ AT&T 🤛   5:52 AM   🌙 ⓐ ⏶ 94% ▊▊▊

Cancel   **Language**   Done — **10**

Corsican

ཇོང་ཁ
Dzongkha

English (Canada)   ✓ — **9**
English (Canada)

English (U.S.)
English (U.S.)

Esperanto
Esperanto

Eesti
Estonian

Eʋegbe
Ewe

Føroyskt
Faroese

If you prefer English (Canada), English will be used as the iPhone language and by apps and websites where English (Canada) is not supported.

Prefer English (Canada)

Prefer English — **11**

Cancel

Fulah

●●●●○ AT&T 🤛   6:02 AM   ⓐ ⏶ 92% ▊▊▊

‹ General **Language & Region**   Edit — **12**

iPhone Language   English ›

PREFERRED LANGUAGE ORDER

English

English (Canada)

Add Language... — **13**

Apps and websites will use the first language in this list that they support.

REGION FORMATS

Region — United States › — **14**

15 Swipe up and down the regions available to you. The current region is marked with a check mark.

16 Tap the region whose formatting you want to use; if there are options within a region, you move to an additional screen and can tap the specific option you want to use.

17 Tap Back. Your iPhone starts using the formatting associated with the region you selected.

18 Tap Calendar.

19 Tap the calendar you want your iPhone to use.

20 Tap Back. You move back to the Language & Region screen. At the bottom of the screen are examples of the format options you have selected, such as the time and date format.

Setting Restrictions for Content and Apps

You can restrict the access to specific content and apps on your phone. Suppose you let other people borrow your iPhone but don't want them to use certain apps or to see data you'd rather keep to yourself. For example, you might want to let children use your iPhone, but prevent them from installing apps on it or making purchases. You can enable a restriction to prevent someone from accessing these areas without entering the restriction code. You can also restrict the use of apps, movies, music, and other content based on the age rating that the app or other content has.

To restrict access to content or apps, perform the following steps:

(1) On the Settings screen, tap General.

(2) Swipe up the screen until you see Restrictions.

(3) Tap Restrictions.

(4) Tap Enable Restrictions.

(5) Create a restrictions passcode. You have to enter this passcode to change the content restrictions or to be able to access restricted content.

(6) Reenter your restrictions passcode. You return to the Restrictions screen, and the ALLOW switches are enabled.

Dueling Passcodes

There are two passcodes: the Lock passcode and the Restrictions passcode. Each controls access to its respective functions. If you will be letting someone else use your phone, the person needs to have the Lock passcode. You should use different Lock and Restrictions passcodes. If they are the same, anyone who can use your iPhone has the Lock passcode and can also access the restrictions, which defeats the purpose of having a Restrictions passcode.

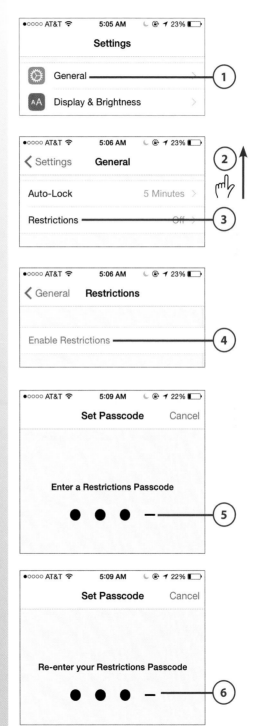

7 In the ALLOW section, set the switch next to each function you want to disable to off (white). For example, to prevent web browsing, set the Safari switch to off (white); the Safari icon is removed from the Home screen and can't be used. With the other controls, you can prevent access to the Camera, FaceTime, iTunes Store, etc.

8 Swipe up to see the ALLOWED CONTENT section.

9 Tap Ratings For.

10 Tap the country whose rating system you want to use for content on your iPhone.

11 Tap Restrictions.

Preventing In-App Purchases and App Installs

Some apps, especially games, allow you to make purchases while you are using the app (called in-app purchases). For example, you can buy additional levels for a game. To prevent in-app purchases, set the In-App Purchases switch on the Restrictions screen to off (white). This is especially important if you let your phone be used by children or others who might inadvertently make purchases. You might also want to set the Installing Apps switch to off (white) to prevent others from installing apps on your iPhone without entering the Restrictions passcode.

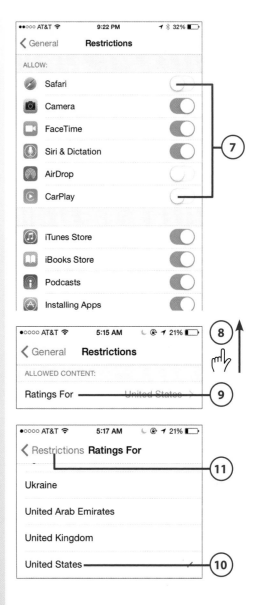

Whose Ratings?

The country you select in step 10 determines the options you see in the remaining steps because the restrictions available depend on the location you select. The steps show the United States rating systems; if you select a different country, you see rating options for that country instead.

(12) Tap Music & Podcasts.

(13) To prevent content tagged as explicit in the iTunes Store from being played, set the EXPLICIT switch to off (white). Explicit content will not be available in the Music or Podcasts app.

(14) Tap Restrictions.

(15) Tap Movies.

●●○○○ AT&T 🔋 5:18 AM 🌙 ⊛ ⏺ 21% 🔋

❮ General **Restrictions**

ALLOWED CONTENT:

Ratings For   United States ❯

Music & Podcasts   Explicit ❯ —(12)

●○○○○ AT&T 🔋 5:18 AM 🌙 ⊛ ⏺ 20% 🔋

❮ Restrictions **Music & Podcasts** —(14)

ALLOW MUSIC & PODCASTS RATED

EXPLICIT ⬤ —(13)

Allow Playback of Music, Music Videos and Podcasts containing Explicit Content.

●○○○○ AT&T 🔋 5:18 AM 🌙 ⊛ ⏺ 20% 🔋

❮ General **Restrictions**

ALLOWED CONTENT:

Ratings For   United States ❯

Music & Podcasts   Explicit ❯

Movies   All ❯ —(15)

16 Tap the highest rating of movies that you want to be playable (for example, tap PG-13 to prevent R and NC-17 movies from playing); tap Allow All Movies to allow any movie to be played; or tap Don't Allow Movies to prevent any movie content from playing. Prevented movie ratings are highlighted in red.

17 Tap Restrictions.

18 Tap TV Shows and use the resulting screen to set the highest rating of TV shows that you want to be playable (for example, tap TV-14 to prevent TV-MA shows from playing); tap Allow All TV Shows to allow any show to be played; or tap Don't Allow TV Shows to prevent any TV content from playing. Prevented ratings are highlighted in red. Tap Restrictions to return to the Restrictions screen.

19 Use the Books option to enable or disable access to sexually explicit books.

20 Tap Apps and set the highest rating of app that you want to be available (for example, tap 12+ to prevent 17+ applications from working); tap Allow All Apps to allow any application to be used; or tap Don't Allow Apps to prevent all applications. Tap Restrictions to return to the Restrictions screen.

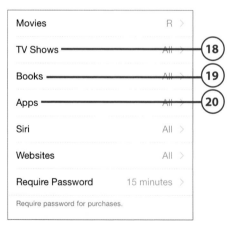

21 Use the Siri option to restrict explicit language for searching the Web.

22 Use the Websites option to control the websites that can be accessed. The options are to limit sites with adult content or to allow only specific websites to be visited. When you select Websites, you can create a list of sites and only those sites can be visited unless the restrictions passcode is entered.

23 Tap Require Password.

24 Tap Immediately if you want a password to be required for every purchase, or 15 minutes if you don't want a password to be required for each purchase within a 15-minute window.

25 Tap Restrictions.

26 Swipe up the screen until you see the PRIVACY section.

27 Use the settings in the PRIVACY section to determine whether apps can access information stored in each area and whether they should be locked in their current states. For example, you can prevent apps from accessing your calendars or photos. Configuring these is similar to the Privacy settings you read about earlier.

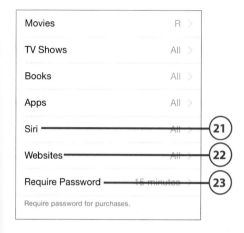

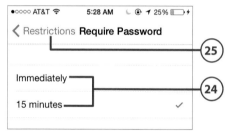

(28) Swipe up the screen until you see the ALLOW CHANGES section.

(29) Tap areas that you want to restrict, such as Cellular Data Use and then tap Don't Allow Changes to prevent changes to that area.

(30) To prevent multiplayer games in the Game Center, set the Multiplayer Games switch to off (white). Users will no longer be able to play games against other people.

(31) To prevent new friends from being added in the Game Center, set the Adding Friends switch to off (white). Players will be restricted to the friends already allowed.

ALLOW CHANGES:

Accounts >

Cellular Data Use ———————— (29)

Background App Refresh >

Volume Limit >

GAME CENTER:

Multiplayer Games ⬤———(30)

Adding Friends ⬤———(31)

(28)

Removing Restrictions

To remove all restrictions, move to the Restrictions screen (your passcode is required) and tap Disable Restrictions. Enter your passcode, and the restrictions are removed.

Setting Accessibility Options

The iPhone has a lot of features designed to help people who are hearing-impaired, visually-impaired, or who have a number of other physical challenges, to be able to use it effectively. These features can be enabled and configured under the Accessibility Settings screen.

1. On the Settings screen, tap General.

2. Swipe up the screen until you see Accessibility.

3. Tap Accessibility. The Accessibility screen is organized into different sections for different kinds of limitations. The first section is VISION, which includes options to assist people who are visually impaired.

4. Use the controls in the VISION section to change how the iPhone's screens appear. Some of the options include:

- **VoiceOver**—The iPhone guides you through screens by speaking their contents.

- **Zoom**—This magnifies the entire screen.

- **Invert Colors**—This changes the screen from dark characters on a light background to light characters on a dark background.

- **Grayscale**—This option causes the screen to use grayscale instead of color.

- **Speech**—Under the Speech option, Speak Selection has the iPhone speak text you have selected, Speak Screen provides the option to have the screen's content spoken, and Speak Auto-text has the iPhone speak corrections it suggests to you, such as auto-capitalizations.

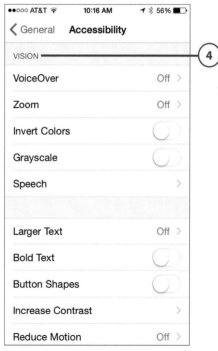

- **Larger and Bold Text**—These increase the text size and add bold; these are in addition to the Text Size and Bold settings described earlier. You can make the text even larger.

- **Other options**—You can also change button shapes, change contrast, reduce motion, and turn labels on or off.

⑤ Swipe up to see the HEARING section.

⑥ Use the controls in this section to configure sounds and to configure the iPhone to work with hearing-impaired people. The controls in this section include:

- **Hearing Aids**—You can pair an iPhone to work with a Bluetooth-capable hearing aid and put it in hearing aid mode.

- **LED Flash for Alerts**—When you set this switch to on (green), the flash flashes whenever an alert plays on the phone.

- **Mono Audio**—This causes the sound output to be in mono instead of stereo.

- **Phone Noise Cancellation**—This switch turns noise cancellation on and off. Noise cancellation reduces ambient noise when you are using the Phone app.

- **Balance**—Use this slider to change the balance of stereo sound between left and right.

7) Swipe up to see the MEDIA section.

8) Use the controls in this section to add features to video playback, including:

- **Subtitles & Captioning**—Use these controls to enable subtitles and captions for video and choose the style of those elements on the screen.

- **Video Descriptions**—This causes a description of a video to be played when available.

9) Use the Guided Access setting if you want to limit the iPhone to using a single app and to further configure the features, such as Passcode Settings and Time Limits.

10) Swipe up to see the INTERACTION section.

11) Use the controls in this section to adjust how someone can interact with the iPhone. The controls here include:

- **Switch Control**—The controls on this screen enable you to configure an iPhone to work with an adaptive device.

- **Assistive-Touch.**—These controls make an iPhone easier to manipulate; if you enable this, a white button appears on the screen at all times. You can tap this to access the Home screen, Notification Center, and other

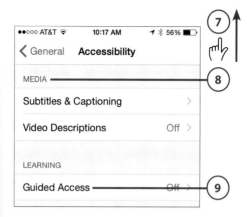

areas. You can also create new gestures to control other functions on the iPhone.

- **Call Audio Routing**—Use this to configure where audio is heard during a phone call or FaceTime session, such as headset or speaker.

- **Home-click Speed**—Use this to adjust the speed at which you need to press the Touch ID/Home button to register a double- or triple-press.

(12) Use the Accessibility Shortcut control to determine what happens when you press the Touch ID/Home button three times.

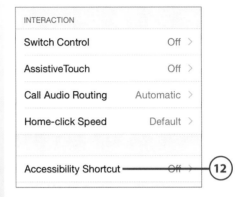

Lots More to the Settings App

There's a lot more you can do with the Settings app than is explained in this chapter; here you've learned about most of the "general" iPhone customization/configuration for which you can use the Settings app. You also learn how to use it to configure app- or function-specific settings throughout this book. For example, you learn how to use Settings to configure Internet access in Chapter 2, "Connecting Your iPhone to the Internet, Bluetooth Devices, and iPhones/iPods/iPads," and to configure email preferences in Chapter 9, "Sending, Receiving, and Managing Email."

Customizing Your Home Screens

The iPhone's Home screens are the starting point for anything you do because these screens contain the icons that you tap to access the apps and web page icons that you want to use; you can also place icons within folders which also have icons on your Home screens. You see and use the Home screens constantly, so it's a good idea to make them look the way you want them to.

In the background of the Lock screen and every Home screen is the wallpaper image. In the section called "Customizing the Wallpaper on the Home and Lock Screens," you learned how to configure your iPhone's wallpaper.

As you know, you can access apps and web page icons on your Home screens by tapping them. The Home screens come configured with icons in default locations. You can change the location of these icons to be more convenient for you. As you install more apps and create your own web page icons, it's a good idea to organize your Home screens so that you can quickly get to the items you use most frequently. You can move icons around the same screen, move icons between the pages of the Home screen, and organize icons within folders. You can even change the icons that appear on the Home screens' toolbar. You can also delete icons you no longer want.

Moving Icons Around Your Home Screens

You can move icons around on a Home screen, and you can move icons among screens to change the screen on which they are located.

(1) Press the Touch ID/Home button to move to a Home screen.

(2) Swipe to the left or right across the Home screen until the page containing an icon you want to move appears.

(3) Tap and hold any icon. After a moment, the icons begin jiggling and you can then move icons on the Home screens. You might also see Delete buttons (an x) in the upper-left corner of some icons, which indicate that you can delete both the icon and app or the web page link (more on this later in this section).

4 Tap and hold an icon you want to move; it becomes larger to show that you have selected it.

5 Drag the icon to a new location on the current screen; as you move the icon around the page, other icons separate and are reorganized to enable you to place the icon in its new location.

6 When the icon is in the location you want, lift your finger up. The icon is set in that place.

7 Tap and hold on an icon you want to move to a different page.

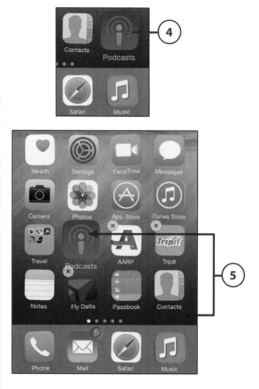

8 Drag the icon to the left edge of the screen to move it to a previous page or to the right edge of the screen to move it to a later page. As you reach the edge of the screen, you move to the previous or next page.

9 Drag the icon around on the new screen until it is in the location where you want to place it.

10 Lift your finger up. The icon is set in its new place.

11 Continue moving icons until you've placed them in the locations you want; then press the Touch ID/Home button. The icons are locked in their current positions, they stop jiggling, and the Delete buttons disappear.

Creating Folders to Organize Apps on Your Home Screens

You can place icons into folders to keep them organized and to make more icons available on the same page. To create a folder, do the following:

1 Move to the Home screen containing two icons you want to place in a folder.

2 Tap and hold an icon until they start jiggling; the Delete buttons appear.

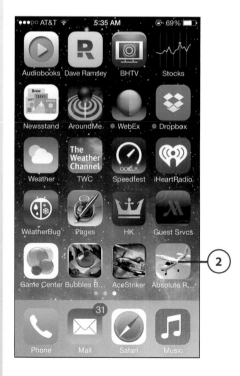

(3) Drag one icon on top of another one that you want to be in the new folder together.

(4) When the first icon is on top of the second and a border appears around the second icon, lift your finger off the screen. The two icons are placed into a new folder, which is named based on the type of icons you place within it. The folder opens and you see its default name.

(5) To edit the name, tap in the name field.

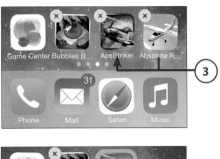

(6) Edit the folder's name.

(7) Tap Done.

(8) Tap outside the folder to close it.

(9) If you're done organizing the Home screen, press the Touch ID/Home button. The icons stop jiggling.

Locating Folders

You can move a folder to a new location in the same way you can move any icon. Tap and hold an icon until the icons start jiggling. Drag the folder icon to where you want it to be.

Placing Icons in Existing Folders

You can add icons to an existing folder like so:

(1) Move to the Home screen containing an icon you want to place in a folder.

(2) Tap and hold an icon until the icons start jiggling and the Delete buttons appear.

3 Drag the icon you want to place into a folder on top of the folder's icon so that the folder's icon enlarges. (The icon doesn't have to be on the same Home screen page; you can drag an icon from one page and drop it on a folder on a different page.)

4 When the folder opens, lift up your finger. The icon is placed within the folder and you see its current location within the folder. (If you don't want to change the icon's location when you place it in the folder, lift up your finger as soon as the folder's icon enlarges; this places the icon in the folder but doesn't cause the folder to open. This is more efficient when you want to place multiple icons within a folder during the same time period.)

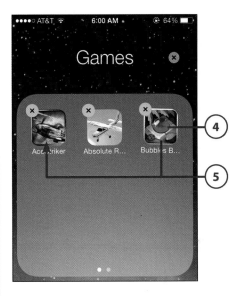

5 Drag the new icon to its location within the folder.

Removing Icons from Folders

To remove an icon from a folder, tap the folder from which you want to remove the icon to open it. Tap and hold the icon you want to remove until it starts jiggling. Drag the icon you want to remove from inside the folder to outside the folder. When you cross the border of the folder, the folder closes and you can place the icon on a Home screen.

(6) Tap outside the folder. The folder closes.

(7) When you're done adding icons to folders, press the Touch ID/ Home button.

Folders and Badges

When you place an icon that has a badge (the red circle with a number in it that indicates the number of new items in an app) in a folder, the badge transfers to the folder so that you see it on the folder's icon. You still see the number of new items, but you can't really tell which of the apps in the folder is generating the badge. When you place more than one app with a badge in the same folder, the badge on the folder becomes the total number of new items for all the apps in the folder. You need to open a folder to see the badges for individual apps it contains.

Configuring the Home Screen Toolbar

The toolbar on the bottom of the Home screen appears on every page. You can place any four icons on the toolbar that you want, including folder icons.

(1) Move to the Home screen containing an icon you want to place on the toolbar.

(2) Tap and hold an icon until the icons start jiggling and the Delete buttons appear.

3. Drag an icon that is currently on the toolbar from the toolbar onto the Home screen. This creates an empty space on the toolbar.

4. Drag an icon or folder containing icons from the Home screen onto the toolbar.

5. Drag the icons on the toolbar around so they are in the order you want them to be.

6. Press the Touch ID/ Home button to set the icons in their current places.

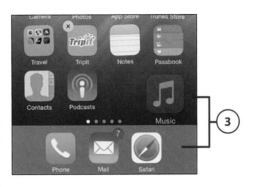

Deleting Icons

You can delete icons from a Home screen to remove them from your iPhone. When you delete an app's icon, its data is also deleted and you won't be able to use the app anymore (of course, you can download it again if you change your mind). When you delete a web page's icon (see Chapter 13, "Surfing the Web," for information on creating web page icons), the bookmark to that web page is deleted.

(1) Move to the Home screen containing an icon you want to delete.

(2) Tap and hold an icon until the icons start jiggling and the Delete buttons appear.

(3) Tap the icon's Delete button.

(4) Tap Delete. If the icon was for an app, it and any associated data on your iPhone are deleted. If the icon was for a bookmark, the bookmark is deleted.

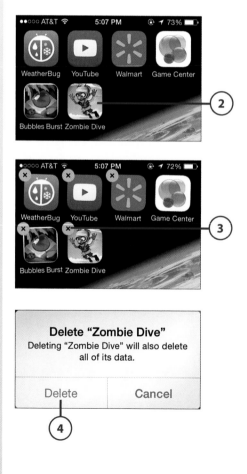

>>>Go Further

MORE ON ORGANIZING HOME SCREENS

Organizing your Home screens can make the use of your iPhone more efficient and make it more what you want it to be. Here are a few more things to keep in mind:

- You can place many icons in the same folder. When you add more than nine, any additional icons are placed on new pages within the folder. As you keep adding icons, pages keep being added to the folder. You can swipe to the left or right within a folder to move among its pages, just as you can to move among your Home screen.

- To change a folder's name, move to a screen showing the folder. Tap and hold an icon until the icons jiggle. Tap the folder so it opens, and then tap the current name. Type the new name, tap Done, and tap outside the folder to close it. Press the Touch ID/Home button to complete the process.

- To delete a folder, remove all the icons from it. The folder is deleted as soon as you remove the last icon from within it.

- You can delete only icons for things you've added to your iPhone, which are either apps you've installed or bookmarks to web pages you've added. You can't delete any of the default apps, which is why their icons don't have Delete buttons when you press and hold the Touch ID/Home button to move into Edit mode. If you don't use some of these default icons, move them to pages of your Home screen that you don't use very often so they don't get in your way, or create a folder for unused icons and store them there, out of your way.

- To return your Home screens to how they were when you first started using your iPhone, open the Settings app, tap General, Reset, Reset Home Screen Layout, and Reset Home Screen. The Home screens return to their default configurations. Icons you've added are moved onto the later pages.

- You can also organize your iPhone's Home screens using iTunes on a computer. Move to the Sync screen in iTunes and click Apps. You see thumbnails for each of your Home page screens. Using techniques similar to those you've learned in this chapter, you can move icons around, create folders, place icons in folders, and name folders. When you sync the iPhone, the Home screens change accordingly. Refer to Chapter 5, "Working with iTunes on Your Computer," for information about using iTunes on a computer.

Sync the content of your
iTunes Library, such as
your music, to enjoy it
on your iPhone

iTunes is a good
partner for your
iPhone

In this chapter, you learn how iTunes on a computer is useful for your iPhone. Topics include the following:

→ Getting started
→ Converting music on audio CDs for your iPhone
→ Using iTunes to download movies, music, books, and more from the iTunes Store
→ Synchronizing content on your computer with your iPhone
→ Keeping your iPhone in sync

5

Working with iTunes on Your Computer

iTunes is a great application you can use to store, organize, and enjoy all sorts of music, movies, TV shows, podcasts, and other types of digital content. You can also access the iTunes Store from within iTunes so you can seamlessly shop for and download new content from the Store's vast selection. iTunes enables you to create, organize, and manage your digital media, enabling you to quickly access and enjoy anything in your digital library.

Getting Started

The reason this chapter exists is that iTunes is also useful as a partner to your iPhone. You can use iTunes on your computer to manage your iPhone's operating system software (iOS). You can also use the sync process to move any content in your iTunes Library onto your iPhone so you can listen to, watch, or read it there.

You'll definitely want to be able to use iTunes to restore your iPhone's software should that become necessary to solve a problem (doing this is explained later in this chapter).

If you download all your music, movies, books, and other content from the iTunes Store, then you don't have to use iTunes on a computer to move that content onto your iPhone because you can do that directly on the iPhone using the iTunes app (this is covered in Chapter 6, "Downloading Apps, Music, Movies, TV Shows, and More onto Your iPhone"). However, you might find it easier to shop in the iTunes and App Stores using iTunes on a computer because of the computer's larger screen. If you set up your iPhone as described in Chapter 6, any music you download in iTunes on a computer gets added to your iPhone automatically.

If you have music on audio CDs, you can use iTunes to convert that music into a format compatible with your iPhone so you can listen to it with the Music app on your phone. (You can move music from iTunes onto your iPhone through the sync process which is explained in this chapter.) If you have content on DVD, such as movies or TV shows, that you want to watch on your iPhone, you'll need to first store that content in iTunes and then use the sync process to move it onto the iPhone.

If you have a Windows PC, iTunes might not be installed on your computer (iTunes is automatically installed on Macs). To download and install iTunes on a Windows PC, go to http://www.apple.com/itunes/download/ and click the Download Now button. Follow the onscreen instructions to complete the installation.

Converting Music on Audio CDs for Your iPhone

iTunes enables you to convert music on an audio CD into an iPhone-compatible format and store the converted music in your iTunes Library on your computer. After that's done, you can move the music onto your iPhone by syncing your iPhone with iTunes on a computer.

To get started, configure iTunes to convert the music on audio CDs into files stored on your computer; you only need to do this when you first get started or if you want to change how the conversion process works at a later time. After iTunes is configured, importing CDs into your iTunes Library is a snap.

Free is Good

The best thing about converting CDs and adding them to iTunes is that you can then use their music on your iPhone at no additional charge. Because you've already paid for CDs you own, there's no need to pay for their music again just to be able to listen to it on your iPhone (as you would if you downloaded that music from the iTunes Store).

Setting Up iTunes to Import Audio CDs

There are a few import preferences you should set for iTunes:

(1) Launch iTunes by double-clicking its application icon, selecting it on the Windows Start menu, or clicking it on the Mac's Dock.

(2) On a Windows PC, hold down the Alt key (so the iTunes menu bar appears) and select Edit, Preferences; on a Mac, select iTunes, Preferences. The Preferences dialog box appears.

(3) Click the General tab.

(4) On the When a CD is inserted menu, select Import CD and Eject.

(5) Click Import Settings.

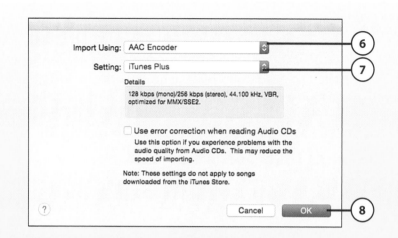

6. On the Import Using drop-down menu, select AAC Encoder.
7. On the Setting drop-down menu, select iTunes Plus.
8. Click OK.

9. Check Automatically retrieve CD track names from Internet.
10. Click OK. You're ready to start importing your CDs.

Importing Audio CDs to the iTunes Library

When you've configured iTunes as described in the previous task, importing music from your audio CDs is a snap:

(1) Launch iTunes by double-clicking its application icon, selecting it on the Windows Start menu, or clicking it on the Mac's Dock.

CD being imported →

Imported song →

Information about the import process

Song being imported

(2) Insert the CD you want to import into the computer. iTunes connects to the Internet and identifies the CD. When that's done, the import process starts. As songs are imported, they are marked with a check mark. The process is done at several times faster than playback speed, so importing a typical CD requires only a few minutes. When the process finishes, iTunes plays an alert sound and ejects the disc. The songs on the disc are in your iTunes Library, and you can use iTunes to listen to them, put them in playlists, and move them onto your iPhone.

(3) Insert the next CD you want to import. After it has been ejected, insert the next CD and continue this process until you've added all the CDs you want to have in your iTunes Library (and so you can have them on your iPhone).

No Duplicates, Please

After you import a CD into your iTunes Library, you won't likely ever need to use it again on your computer. So after you import all your CDs, change the "When a CD is inserted" setting on the General tab of the iTunes Preferences dialog to Ask to Import CD setting so that you don't accidentally import multiple copies of the same CD (in the rare case you do insert a CD into your computer again). (Don't worry, though—if you leave the setting as is, iTunes prompts you the next time you insert the CD to see if you want to replace the previous version.)

>>>*Go Further*

ADDING DVD CONTENT TO iTUNES

Adding movies and TV shows that you have on DVD to your iTunes Library is a bit more complicated because iTunes can't import that content directly. You need another application to convert the DVD content into a digital format. Many of these are available for Mac and Windows PCs—just do a web search to find and download the application you want to use. Most offer multiple format options; if you are going to move the content onto your iPhone, you need to choose a compatible format when you convert the content. After you've set up the import application, you convert (also called *encode* or *rip*) the DVD content into the iPhone-compatible format. When that is done, you can add the converted content to your iTunes Library on a Windows PC by pressing the Alt key (so the iTunes menu appears), selecting File, selecting Add File to Library, moving to and selecting the converted content, and clicking Open. You can do the same on a Mac by selecting File, selecting Add to Library, moving to and selecting the converted file, and clicking OK. After the converted content has been added to your iTunes Library, you can watch it in iTunes or move it onto your iPhone through the sync process (which is explained later in this chapter).

Using iTunes to Download Movies, Music, Books, and More from the iTunes Store

The iTunes Store has a large selection of music, movies, TV shows, books, and other content that you can preview, purchase or rent, and download to your iTunes Library. You can listen to or watch that content in iTunes on a computer, and you can do the same on an iPhone.

To download content from the iTunes Store, you must have an iTunes Store account, also known as an Apple ID. (You can preview content without an Apple ID.) You can sign into your account within iTunes and begin shopping for and downloading content.

No Sync Required—Most of the Time

For almost all the content you download from the iTunes Store, you don't need to sync your iPhone with iTunes because you can always download that content directly onto your iPhone. As you learn in Chapter 6, you can configure your iPhone so that all the content you download from the Store on any device is automatically downloaded to your iPhone, too. The exception to this is rented movies; rented movies can exist on only one device at a time. So, if you rent a movie in iTunes on a computer, you must use the sync process to move that rented movie onto your iPhone if you want to watch it there.

Obtaining an iTunes Store Account (Apple ID)

An account with the iTunes Store enables you to purchase music, movies (or rent movies), TV shows, apps, ringtones, books, and other content that is then downloaded to your iTunes Library. From there, you can move it onto your iPhone (you can set up your phone so this happens without syncing your iPhone with iTunes on your computer, as explained in Chapter 6). Even if you don't intend to purchase movies, books, or other content from the iTunes Store, you still need an account to download and install free apps for your iPhone.

If you already have an Apple ID, you don't need to create another one to use the iTunes Store—if some form of payment isn't associated with your current account, you need to add that to be able to download any content that isn't free (you're prompted to provide the required information when it is needed). If you have a current Apple ID, you can just sign into that account by skipping to the next section.

To create a new Apple ID, perform the following steps:

1. Open iTunes.
2. Click Sign In. The Sign In dialog box appears.

That's My Name

If you see your name instead of the Sign In menu, you are already signed in using your Apple ID. If the name is yours, you can skip the rest of these steps and the next task as well. If the current name isn't yours and you are using a Mac, select the name shown and on the resulting menu, select Sign Out. If you are using a Windows PC, open the iTunes menu (located in the upper-left corner of the window), select iTunes Store, and then select Sign Out. Then return to step 2 and click Sign In.

3) Click Create Apple ID. You move to the first screen in the account creation process.

4) Read the information and follow the onscreen instructions to create an Apple ID. After you complete the steps, you receive your Apple ID and password and are ready to sign into your new account in iTunes.

iTunes Store Security

You might be concerned about including personal and payment (credit card) information in your iTunes Store account. You don't need to worry because the iTunes Store is very secure. Apple has been serving many, many customers in the iTunes Store for a long time, and has protected its customers' data quite well. If you don't want to include a credit card in your iTunes Store account, you can purchase a gift card at a local retailer and redeem it in the Store when you want to buy something. To redeem a gift card, move into the iTunes Store, click the Redeem link in the QUICK LINKS section on the Home page, sign into your iTunes Store account, and enter the code from the gift card. Your account is credited with the amount of the card, and you can use that to buy and download content from the iTunes Store.

Signing Into the iTunes Store

The first step to use the iTunes Store is to sign into your account. iTunes remembers your account, so unless you sign out (as described in the "No Sign In Seen?" sidebar) you need to sign in only once.

1. Open iTunes.
2. Click Sign In. You connect to the Internet and move into the iTunes Store. (If you see your name instead of Sign In, you are already signed in and can skip to the next task.)

(**3**) Enter your Apple ID and password.

(**4**) Click Sign In. You are logged into your iTunes Store account.

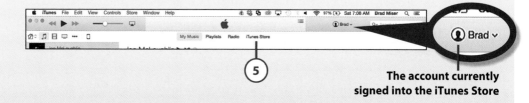

The account currently signed into the iTunes Store

(**5**) Click iTunes Store. You move into the iTunes Store and are ready to shop.

One Login to Rule Them All

You can use the same Apple ID in the iTunes Store, for an iCloud account, and in the Apple online store. When you get an Apple ID via the iTunes Store, you can just use your iCloud account email address as the login. Although iCloud is free, you need to provide payment information to use your Apple ID in the iTunes Store. You don't have to use just one account, though. For example, if you want to share iTunes content with your family, you can get one Apple ID for shopping in the iTunes Store but get a different Apple ID for your personal iCloud account.

Shopping in the iTunes Store

When you are signed into your iTunes account, using the iTunes Store is simple because it is integrated into iTunes and it uses an interface that is intuitive and easy to use.

Here are three general steps to download iTunes Store content to your iTunes Library:

- **Find the content of interest to you**—There are a couple of ways to do this:

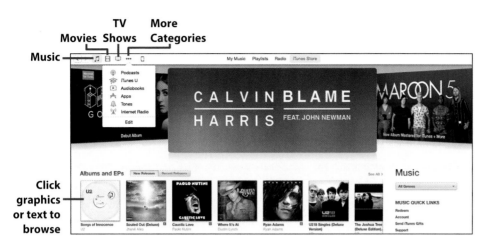

One way to find content is by browsing. Just about every graphic and almost all the text you see are linked to either categories of content or to specific content. You can browse the store just by clicking around. For example, you can click the Music button to browse music and click any of the other links you see on the Music Home page to browse music in the Store. The current type of content you are browsing is indicated by the button highlighted in light blue. If you want to browse movies, click the Movies button or to browse TV shows, click the TV Shows button. To browse other types of content, click the ellipsis (…), and then make a selection on the menu that appears (such as Tones to browse ringtones). There are numerous ways to browse, but all of them involve just clicking around. If you don't have something specific in mind, browsing is a great way to discover, preview, and purchase content.

Another way is to search for specific content. This is useful when you know something about the content you want, such as the artist, because it gets you to that content very quickly. Steps to search are provided shortly.

- **Preview the content**—You can listen to portions of songs, watch trailers for movies, and read information to get a good idea of whether the content is something you want to have in your Library. If it is, you can move to the next step. If not, keep looking until you find something you want to download.

- **Download the content**—This involves clicking the appropriate download button. If the content has a cost, you see that cost in the download button. If there are options, such as High Definition (HD) and Standard Definition (SD) versions of a movie, you see a button for each option. Some content is free, in which case it has a Free button. Whichever path you take, the content is downloaded to your computer and becomes available in your iTunes Library (and music becomes available on your iPhone automatically if you've configured the automatic download Music setting).

Shop on your iPhone, too

You can shop for music, movies, and other content using the iTunes app on your iPhone, too (which is explained in Chapter 6), but shopping in iTunes on a computer is easier because you have a lot more screen space to work with. Also, you have to use different apps on your iPhone, such as iTunes to buy music or movies and the App Store app to download other apps, while you can get everything available in one place when you access the iTunes Store using iTunes on a computer. If you configure your iPhone to automatically download new music (see Chapter 6), any music you buy on your computer is downloaded to your iPhone, too.

A quick example of searching for content to download from the iTunes Store will show you how easy shopping in the Store is:

(1) Click iTunes Store. iTunes connects to the iTunes Store, and the Store's Home page displays.

(2) Click in the Search Store bar.

(3) Type the information for which you want to search. You can perform a general search by typing a small amount of text, such as "rat pack," which finds all the content associated with that term. Make the search more specific by combining text phrases, such as "the beatles abbey road" (which would find a specific album by that group). As you type, iTunes tries to complete your search; if you want to use one of the terms it recommends, click it. If not, keep typing until you've entered all of the search term.

(4) Press the Enter key on your computer's keyboard (if you clicked a search term in step 3, you don't need to do this). Items that meet your search criteria appear. The results are

organized into logical collections based on the type of content for which you searched. For example, when you search for music, you see albums, songs, and music videos. You see different kinds of information for each type of content available in the Store.

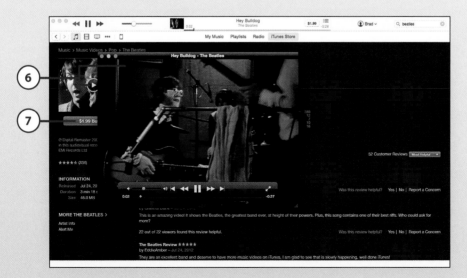

5 To preview content, move the pointer over it and click the Play button that appears; where it appears depends on what you hover over. When you hover over a song, the Play button replaces the track number; when you hover over a video, the Play button appears in the center of the thumbnail. After you click the button, a preview plays. The length of the preview depends on the specific content you are previewing. For example, when you preview most songs, the preview lasts 90 seconds.

6 If you select a video, watch the video in the preview window that appears.

7 When you want to purchase and download content, click its *buy* button. This button can include different information depending on the content you are viewing. It always shows the price of the content. It can also describe what you are buying. For example, when you browse a TV show, one *buy* button enables you to purchase the entire season, whereas you can use the *buy* buttons next to each episode to purchase one episode at a time.

Sign In to the iTunes Store.
If you have an Apple ID, sign in with it here.

Apple ID
bradmacosx@mac.com

Password   Forgot?
••••••••••••

Cancel   Buy —— **8**

8 If prompted, enter your account's information and click Buy—or just click the Buy button depending on the prompt that displays. The content you purchase is downloaded to your computer and added to your iTunes Library.

Playlists —— **9**

9 To see content you've downloaded, click Playlists.

10 Click the Purchased playlist to see content you've downloaded from the iTunes Store. You can listen to or watch this content, put it in other playlists, and move it onto your iPhone.

More Than Buy

If you click the downward-facing arrow to the right of the *buy* buttons in the iTunes Store, a menu with various commands appears; commands on this menu include Gift, which enables you to give the content to someone and share via Facebook. One useful option enables you to add content to your wish list, which is much like a shopping cart where you can store content you might be interested in purchasing at a later time; after you add content to your wish list, you can move back to it by clicking the My Wish List item on the Quick Links section of the various home pages (Music, Movies, etc.). From your wish list, you can preview or purchase content.

>>>*Go Further*

ORGANIZING YOUR iTUNES CONTENT

As you build up your iTunes Library, you'll end up with a lot of content of all types. It's a good idea to organize your content to make it easier to find, and much easier to move onto your iPhone through the sync process. You can use playlists to manually place content into your own collections, sorted in just the way you want. With a smart playlist, you can define a set of criteria (such as a specific artist) and iTunes collects the associated content into a group automatically. You can also use folders to group your playlists to keep those organized, too. Playlists and folders make configuring and syncing content using iTunes easier and also make finding and using that content on your phone easier.

Synchronizing Content on Your Computer with Your iPhone

iTunes communicates with your iPhone for a number of purposes. Configuring some aspects of how your iPhone works and copying or moving content from your iTunes Library onto your iPhone so you can use that content in your iPhone's apps are just a few of the ways iTunes interacts with your iPhone. This is called *syncing* because you are synchronizing the content of your iPhone with your iTunes Library. You can determine the kind of data that is copied or moved to your iPhone by configuring the various sync settings available in iTunes. Each of these has its own screen with controls that are appropriate for what you are doing. The sync areas available are:

- **Summary**—Use this to configure some aspects of how your iPhone works, such as if you can sync wirelessly and how your iPhone is backed up.

- **Info**—This enables you to sync contacts, calendars, email accounts, and other information on your iPhone. If you keep this information in an online account, such as iCloud, you don't need to include these in the sync process and can ignore this. However, it can be useful to sync content that is only stored on your computer; for example, if you have calendar information that is only stored on the computer, rather than on iCloud, Google, or other such account.

- **Apps**—Use this to add apps to or remove them from your iPhone. You can also organize your Home screens on this along with moving files, such as documents, from the computer onto the iPhone.

- **Tones**—With this, you can choose the custom ring and alert tones to copy onto your iPhone.

- **Music**—Use this to copy music onto your iPhone. There are many ways to choose the music you want to copy onto the iPhone, such as playlists or specific artists.

- **Movies**—You can copy movies onto your iPhone so you can watch them in the Videos app. You can also move rented movies from the computer onto your iPhone (unlike other content, rented movies can exist on only one device at a time).

- **TV Shows**—Here, you can choose which series, and which episodes of those series, that you want to copy onto your phone.

- **Podcasts**—This enables you to select the podcasts you want to copy from the computer onto the iPhone. If you use the Podcasts app on the iPhone, you probably won't need to use this (see Chapter 16, "Using Other Cool iPhone Apps and Features," for information about the Podcasts app).

- **Books**—Use this to copy ebooks and PDF documents onto your iPhone.

- **Audiobooks**—Use this to copy audiobooks onto your iPhone.

- **Photos**—This enables you to copy photos from your desktop or a photo app (such as iPhoto or Photoshop Elements) onto your phone.

- **On My Device**—Using this, you can browse the current contents on your iPhone and manually copy content from the computer onto the iPhone.

Understanding the Sync Process

The general steps to sync your iPhone follow:

(1) Connect your iPhone to your computer using its USB cable (after it's configured, you can sync wirelessly, too).

(2) Open iTunes, if it doesn't open automatically.

(3) Click the iPhone button. If your computer can communicate with more than one iOS device and you click this button, you see a menu showing each device with which iTunes can communicate. Click your iPhone in this menu. You see the sync controls for your iPhone along the left side of the window.

(4) Click the area you want to configure.

(5) Use the controls to configure that aspect of the sync process, such as what content you want to move or sync.

(6) Repeat steps 4 and 5 for each tab.

(7) Click Apply (if you haven't changed any settings, you see the Sync button instead). The iPhone is synced according to your settings.

Although each area has different controls, the process you follow to configure most of them is similar. Because it is a bit different from the others, the detailed steps to configure the Summary settings are listed next.

Show Some Trust

The first time you connect your iPhone to a computer to try to sync it, you're prompted in iTunes on the computer and on the iPhone to trust the computer. On your iPhone, you must indicate that you trust the computer by tapping Trust. If you don't, you won't be able to sync it and you will see the prompt again the next time you connect it to your computer.

Configuring Summary Sync Settings

The Summary tab is where you configure how certain aspects of your iPhone work, and you can also use it to maintain your iPhone's software. To configure the Summary sync settings, do the following:

(1) With your iPhone connected to your computer (or within range once wireless syncing is enabled), click Summary.

(2) If you have an iCloud account configured and want to back up your iPhone on the cloud, click the iCloud radio button.

(3) If you want to back up to your computer instead of iCloud or if you don't use iCloud at all, click This computer.

(**4**) If you back up to your computer and want to protect the backup of your iPhone's data (used to restore your iPhone) with encryption, check Encrypt iPhone backup, create and verify a password, and click Set Password; this password is required to restore the backed-up information onto the iPhone.

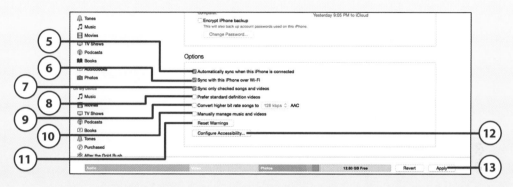

(**5**) Check the Automatically sync when this iPhone is connected check box if you want the sync process to start automatically when you connect the iPhone to your computer.

(**6**) Check Sync with this iPhone over Wi-Fi if you want to be able to sync your iPhone via a Wi-Fi network. This is useful because you don't have to physically connect your iPhone to your computer to sync it. If you enable this option, you can still connect your iPhone to your computer using the USB cable to sync it and charge its battery.

(**7**) If you don't want content that you have configured iTunes to ignore to be copied onto the iPhone, check the Sync only checked songs and videos check box. (You configure iTunes to ignore content by unchecking the check boxes next to songs or other content you want to be skipped; enabling this sync setting mirrors those selections and unchecked items won't be copied onto your iPhone.)

(**8**) If you want to copy only the standard definition of HD video, check the Prefer standard definition videos check box; this saves space because the HD versions are larger files.

(**9**) To cause iTunes to convert songs that have been encoded so they are high quality (larger file sizes) to files that have smaller sizes (so more content fits onto the iPhone), check the Convert higher bit rate songs to check box and select the conversion you want to use, such as 128 kbps, on the menu. (You aren't likely to hear the difference when playing this content with your iPhone.) This is useful to save some storage space on your iPhone if you've included audio encoded to a higher quality setting in your iTunes Library. If you've imported audio from CD using the settings earlier in the chapter, or downloaded it from the iTunes Store, you don't need to set this because your content is already using an efficient format.

(10) If you check the Manually manage music and videos check box, you can place content on the iPhone by dragging music, movies, and other video content onto the iPhone in addition to moving it via the sync process.

(11) To reset various warnings on your iPhone to their defaults, click the Reset Warnings button.

(12) Click Configure Accessibility to configure various accessibly options on your iPhone.

(13) To save and apply the settings to your iPhone and sync it now, click Apply. If you are also going to configure other settings, you can skip this step and wait until you have configured the other tabs to apply and save the changes and sync your iPhone.

Backing Up Isn't Hard to Do

Like other data, you should back up the contents of your iPhone so you don't lose data if something happens to your iPhone. The backup process occurs automatically when you back up to iCloud. If you back up to your computer only, the phone needs to be connected to the computer via the USB cable or within range of the computer if you use Wi-Fi; this means that when you are away from your computer, your iPhone won't be backed up. If you have an iCloud account, you should use the iCloud backup option. When you do, you can also manually back up your iPhone on your computer by clicking the Back Up Now button on the Summary tab, which backs up your content on your computer regardless of the backup option you have selected. So, you can choose to automatically back up your iPhone to iCloud and periodically also back it up on your computer manually to be extra safe.

Syncing Content onto Your iPhone

As mentioned previously, the process to configure each of the Sync screens is similar. Walking through the details for one (the following steps show Music) will help you understand what you need to do to configure the other areas (the controls you have change for each area, but using them is similar to using the options for Music). To configure the music you want to copy from your computer onto your iPhone, perform the following steps:

1 Click Music.

2 Check the Sync Music check box.

3 If you have enough room on the iPhone to store all the music content you have in your Library, check the Entire music library radio button and skip to step 5. Unless you have a small amount of music and other content in your Library, you'll probably need to choose specific music you want to be copied on your iPhone by performing step 4.

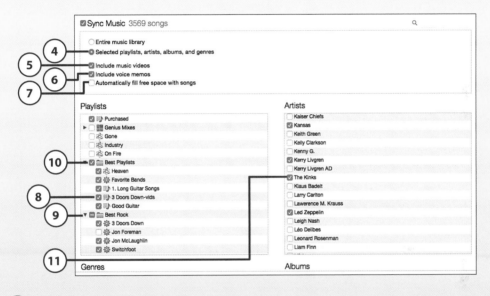

4 Check the Selected playlists, artists, albums, and genres radio button; this enables you to select specific music to move onto the iPhone. When you select it, the Playlists, Artists, Albums, and Genres selection tools appear.

5 Check Include music videos if you want music videos in your collection to be copied onto the iPhone.

6 Check Include voice memos if you use the Voice Memos or another app to record audio notes and want those memos to be included in the sync.

7 If you selected Entire music library in step 3, skip to step 14; if you performed step 4 and you want any free space on the iPhone to be filled with music that iTunes selects, check the Automatically fill free space with songs check box.

8 To include a playlist in the sync so that all the items that playlist contains are moved onto the iPhone, check the check box next to it on the Playlists list.

9 To expand or collapse a folder to see or hide the playlists it contains, click its triangle.

10 To copy all the items within a folder of playlists onto the iPhone, check the folder's check box.

11 To copy all the songs by specific artists onto the iPhone, check the artist's name on the Artists list.

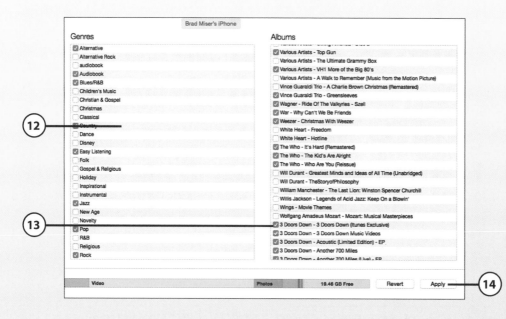

12 Click the check box next to each genre whose contents you want to copy onto the iPhone. For example, to move all the music in the Classical genre, check its check box.

13 Check the check boxes for albums you want to copy onto the iPhone.

14 To apply the settings to your iPhone and sync it now, click Apply. The music you selected is copied onto your iPhone and is available in the Music app. If you are also going to sync other content, you can skip this step and wait until you have configured the other sync areas so that you sync everything at one time.

Scrolling, Scrolling, Scrolling

Each box on the Music tab has its own scroll bar that you can use to browse the content in that section. For example, you can scroll up and down within the Genres box. You can also use the iTunes scroll bar to move up and down the tab, which you might need to do to see all of the sections on it.

Keeping Your iPhone in Sync

Following are some additional points to ponder when it comes to keeping your iPhone in sync:

Use this gauge to see if your iPhone has enough room for the content you've selected to sync

- As you select content to sync onto your iPhone, the Capacity gauge at the bottom of the screen is updated to show you how much of your iPhone's storage the current sync settings will use. The gauge is segmented by type of content, including audio, video, and photos. If you have more content selected than will fit, the gauge is full and a warning icon is displayed. You'll need to remove content from the sync to be sure of the content that will be moved onto the iPhone (if you sync anyway, some of the content won't be moved onto the iPhone or the sync process won't finish).

  If there's enough space on the iPhone for the content you've selected, the sync process continues until all the content has been copied or moved onto the phone. If you've selected more content than there is room for on the iPhone, a warning dialog box explaining how much content you selected versus how much space is available displays. (You can tell this is a problem before the sync process begins if a warning icon appears to the right of the Capacity gauge.)

  If you have selected too much content, you need to decrease the amount of content you are syncing and perform the sync again by clicking Apply.

- Not having enough space on the iPhone to complete the sync is just one type of warning you might see during the sync process. If you've included content that can't be synced for some reason, such as a movie that isn't in the correct format, you also see a warning. Or if you want to sync content from more than five iTunes Store accounts, that content won't be synced onto the iPhone. In most cases, the sync process continues but the content with problems is not copied onto the iPhone. Just click OK to clear any warnings so the sync process continues. You can also get more detail about issues in the warning dialog boxes, usually by clicking the right-facing arrow to expand their contents.

- The sync process can work in the background so you can use iTunes for other things while your iPhone is being synced. Progress information appears in the information area at the top of the iTunes window.

- When the sync is complete, the iPhone sync is complete message appears in the Information area at the top of the iTunes window.

- When you've made changes to the sync settings, the Apply button appears at the bottom of the screen. Clicking this saves your current settings and starts the sync process. When the process completes, the button becomes the Sync button. When you click this button, the sync process starts using the current settings; even though the settings are the same, different content can be involved, such as new songs being added to a smart playlist.

- If you decide you don't want to use changes you've made to the sync settings, click Revert. Any changes you have made are discarded and the prior sync settings are restored.

- To exit the sync screens, click one of the other buttons on the toolbar at the top of the window, such as Music. If you've made changes to the settings but haven't synced, you are prompted to Apply the settings and sync—or you can choose Don't Apply, which discards the changes you have made.

- If you've configured automatic syncing, the sync process starts as soon as you connect your iPhone to your computer.

- Don't disconnect your iPhone during the sync process because it might not complete correctly.

- You can sync your iPhone with more than one iTunes Library, but you can sync the same type of content, such as Music, with only one computer at a time.

- If you configured Wi-Fi syncing, you can use the sync screen whenever your iPhone and computer are on the same Wi-Fi network. This works just like when your phone is connected to the computer with a USB cable, except the phone isn't charged as it is when connected with the cable.

Tap to sync your iPhone wirelessly

- With Wi-Fi syncing enabled, you can start the sync process on the iPhone. Move to the Settings app, tap General, tap iTunes Wi-Fi Sync, and tap Sync Now. If you have synced the phone with more than one computer, tap the computer with which you want to sync and then tap Sync Now; if you have synced with only one computer, you skip this step. The sync process occurs using the current settings. You can change the sync settings when you are syncing over Wi-Fi, too; just select the iPhone as you do when it is connected with a cable and configure the sync in the same way as when it is connected to the computer. If you don't see your iPhone in iTunes, make sure your iPhone is on the same Wi-Fi network as the computer, or connect it to your computer using the USB cable and ensure that the Sync with this iPhone over Wi-Fi is enabled in the Summary tab.

>>>Go Further
KEEPING iTUNES CURRENT

Apple updates iTunes regularly to correct issues and add features. You can configure iTunes so that it notifies you when updates are available. On a Windows PC, open the iTunes Preferences dialog box, click the Advanced tab, check the Check for new software updates automatically check box, and click OK; when updates are available, you're prompted to download and install them.

On a Mac, open the System Preferences app and click App Store. Then check all the check boxes in the App Store window. When an iTunes update is available, it downloads and is installed automatically.

Use the iTunes Store app to load your phone with great music, movies, TV shows, and more

Use the App Store app to download and install cool and useful apps on your iPhone

Use the Settings app to configure your store preferences

In this chapter, you learn how to add apps, music, TV shows, and other content onto your iPhone, and how to share your goodies with others. Topics include the following:

→ Getting started
→ Configuring store settings
→ Using the App Store app to find and install iPhone apps
→ Using the iTunes Store app to download music, ringtones, movies, and TV shows
→ Downloading apps or iTunes Store content you've purchased previously
→ Using Family Sharing to share your store downloads with others

Downloading Apps, Music, Movies, TV Shows, and More onto Your iPhone

One of Apple's past marketing campaigns for the iPhone stated that if you want to do something with an iPhone, there was an app for it. That was quite a claim, but it also was, and continues to be, pretty accurate. Your iPhone is a powerful device and supports a full suite of programming tools. That's a good thing because this capability has unleashed the creativity of developers around the world, and many thousands of apps are available now. You can use the App Store app to download and install any of these apps on your iPhone.

Along with all these great apps, there is also lots of music, movies, TV shows, ebooks, audiobooks, and much more content available to enjoy on your iPhone. Using the iTunes Store app, you can easily browse and search for content and then download it to your iPhone with just a couple of taps.

A benefit of using the App Store and iTunes Store apps is that anything you download once can be downloaded again at no cost. If you happen to lose some of your content, you can simply download it again. Or, when you upgrade your iPhone, you can re-download content you've previously purchased onto it at no cost (you can also download the content onto other iOS devices, such as an iPad, or a Mac too). And, you can use the Family Sharing to share content you purchase with other people.

Another nice thing about using the iTunes and Apps Stores is that you only have to download something once and it can automatically appear on all your devices. See the "Configuring Store Settings" task in this chapter to learn how to automatically download your purchases to all your iOS devices.

Getting Started

Because adding the apps you want to use along with the music and other content you want to enjoy is part of making an iPhone into your iPhone, you'll know how to download items to your iPhone. Here are the major concepts related to this topic:

- **App Store**—This is both a location where all the apps are available for your iPhone and an app on your iPhone that you use to download apps. You can also download apps from the App Store using iTunes on a computer.

- **iTunes Store**—Like the App Store, this is both a store and an app on your iPhone. You use the iTunes Store app to download content, such as music, ringtones, and books, onto your iPhone. You can also download this content from the iTunes Store using the iTunes app on a computer.

- **iTunes**—This app is on a computer and you can use it to store, organize, and play all sorts of content, such as music, movies, and books. You can also download apps and content from the App Store and iTunes Store onto your computer, which is automatically downloaded to your iPhone with the settings discussed in the following task. You can learn about iTunes on a computer in Chapter 5, "Working with iTunes on Your Computer."

- **Family Sharing**—You can define a group of up to six people (they don't have to be actual family members) with whom you want to share content you download. The people in your Family Sharing group can download and use your content without having to pay for it again. When people put you in their Family Sharing group, you can use the content they purchase.

Configuring Store Settings

You'll likely be accessing the iTunes Store using more than one device, such as a computer, an iPad, and of course, your iPhone. You can configure your iPhone so that music, apps, and books that you download on any of your devices are automatically downloaded to your phone as well. For example, if you purchase an album on your iPad, that same album can be immediately downloaded to your iPhone, too. You can also have any updates to apps installed on your iPhone downloaded and installed automatically.

Configuring Automatic Store Downloads

To have content you purchase from the iTunes Store be automatically downloaded to your iPhone, perform the following steps:

1. Tap Settings.

2. Tap iTunes & App Store.

3. To show all the music you've purchased from the iTunes Store on your iPhone, even if it is not currently stored on your phone, set the Music switch to on (green). This enables you to access the music from the Store at any time.

4. To show all videos you've downloaded from the Store on your phone even if they aren't currently stored there, set the Videos switch to on (green).

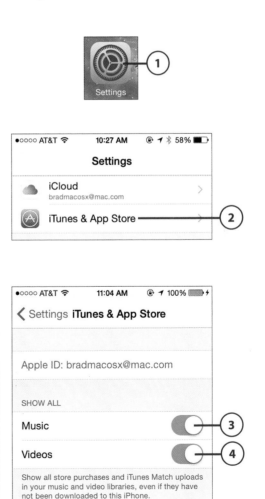

(5) Slide the switches to on (green) for the types of content you want to be downloaded to your iPhone automatically; the options are Music, Apps, Books, and Updates (which causes any updates to the apps installed on your iPhone to be downloaded and installed automatically).

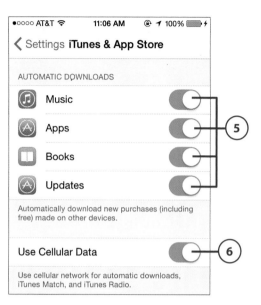

(6) If you don't have an unlimited data plan, you might want to set the Use Cellular Data to off (white) so content is downloaded only when you are on a Wi-Fi network. If this is enabled (green), content is downloaded to your iPhone when you are using a cellular network, which can consume significant amounts of your data plan. If you exceed your data plan allowance, the overage can be quite expensive, so you need to be careful about allowing cellular downloads.

After you've completed these steps, any content you enabled in step 6 is downloaded to your iPhone automatically when it is purchased on any of your devices (content you've purchased before you configured the Store settings is not downloaded automatically, but as you learn at the end of this chapter, you can manually download that content at any time).

(7) If you want apps that are currently installed to be suggested to
you based on your current location, set the My Apps switch to on
(green). With this enabled, as you
change locations, apps that are
relevant to that location are suggested on the Lock screen and
when you open the App Switcher.

(8) If you want to see suggestions
for apps based on your current
location when you use the App
Store app, set the App Store
switch to on (green). When you
search or browse for apps in
the App Store (which you learn
about in the next section), you
see recommendations based on
your current location.

Use Cellular Data	
Use cellular network for automatic downloads, iTunes Match, and iTunes Radio.	
SUGGESTED APPS	
My Apps	———(7)
App Store	———(8)
Show installed apps or App Store suggestions for apps relevant to your current location, on the lock screen and in the app switcher.	

Apple ID

To work with the Apple ID you use in the App and iTunes Stores, tap the account
shown at the top of the iTunes & App Store screen. On the resulting prompt, you
can view your Apple ID, sign out of your account, or reset your password (the iFor-
got option). If you sign out of your account, the Store screen only has the Sign In
button. Tap this and sign into the Apple ID you want to configure.

Using the App Store App to Find and Install iPhone Apps

You might think that with so many thousands of apps available, it might be difficult
to find and download apps on your iPhone. The good news is that the App Store app
enables you to quickly and easily browse and search for apps, view information about
them, and then download and install them on your iPhone with just a few taps.

When you use the App Store app, you can find apps to download using any of the following options:

- **Categories**—This link shows you various categories of apps that you can browse.
- **Featured**—This tab takes you to apps featured in the iTunes Store. This screen organizes apps in several categories. These categories change from time to time, but they typically include "best new" types of apps (such as games) and apps for specific purposes (for example, back-to-school shopping). Swipe up and down the screen to see all the categories available.
- **Top Charts**—This takes you to lists of the top iPhone apps. This screen has three sections: Paid shows you the top apps for which you have to pay a license fee; Free shows you a similar list containing only free apps; and Top Grossing shows the apps that have been downloaded the most (rather than those that have made the most money).
- **Explore**—This option shows apps that are popular or relevant based on your current location. The first time you choose it, you're prompted to allow the App Store app to use your iPhone's Location Services feature to identify your location.
- **Search**—This button enables you to search for apps. You can search by name, developer, and other keywords.
- **Updates**—Through this, you can get to the Purchased screen, which enables you to find and download apps you have previously downloaded to your iPhone or other device and shows you the update status of your apps on your iPhone (this topic is covered in the last section of this chapter). If you have automatic updates enabled, you see the list of updates made to the apps on your iPhone; if you don't have automatic updates enabled, you can use this screen to download and install updates for your apps.

Finding and downloading any kind of app follows this same pattern:

1. **Find the app you are interested in.** You can use the options described previously, find apps by browsing for them, or use the search option to find a specific app quickly and easily.

2. **Evaluate the app.** The information screen for apps provides lots of information that you can use to decide whether you want to download an app (or not). The information available includes a text description, screenshots, and ratings and reviews of other users.

3. **Download and install the app.**

The following sections provide detailed examples for each of these steps.

Suggestions, Suggestions

If you enabled the App Store setting described in the previous section, when you move around the App Store app, you may see various suggestion screens that present apps that may be of interest to you based on your location, or sometimes Apple apps are suggested to you regardless of location. You can download and install apps from the suggestion screen, very similarly to the steps you'll find in this chapter for downloading them from other locations. If you don't want to download any of the suggested apps, tap Not Now. None of the tasks in this chapter show the suggestion screens for clarity's sake so to follow the steps as written, just tap Not Now when a suggestion screen opens to close it. You also might see app icons for suggested apps appear in the lower-left corner of the Lock screen when you are in a location related to the app. You can swipe on these icons to move into the App Store app to download the suggested app.

Searching for Apps

If you know something about an app, such as its name, its developer, or just about anything else, you can quickly search the App Store to find the app. Here's how to search for an app:

1. Move to the Home screen and tap App Store.

2. Tap Search.

3. Tap in the Search box.

(4) Type a search term. This can be the type of app you are looking for based on its purpose (such as travel) or the name of someone associated with the app, its title, its developer, or even a topic. As you type, the app suggests searches that are related to what you are typing.

(5) Tap the search you want to perform (to see the full list of search results, tap Search). The apps that meet your search term appear.

(6) Swipe up and down on the screen to review the apps that were found by your search.

(7) If none of the apps are what you are looking for, tap the x in the Search box and repeat steps 4–6 (or use the Related Searches as described in the Related Apps note).

(8) When you find an app of interest to you, tap it. You move to the app's information screen.

●oooo AT&T 📶 11:01 AM 📶 ✈ ✳ 52% 🔋

Q data ————————————————— ⊗ **(4)**

data supply ——————————————— **(5)**

data monitor - manage data usage in...

data monitor - manage your usage

data usage

data usage - onavo count - data man...

data counter - universal data usage...

aviation data systems inc

Q W E R T Y U I O P

A S D F G H J K L

⬆ Z X C V B N M ⊗

123 😊 🎤 space Search

●oooo AT&T 📶 11:03 AM 📶 ✈ ✳ 51% 🔋

Q data monitor - manage y... 79 Results ⊗ **(7)**

Related: bandwidth ›

Related searches

Data Monitor - Manage Your Usa...
Amos Epstein GET
★★★★☆ (217) In-App Purchases

Data usage from previous
2 days 14 days 30 days 60 days

(8)

(6)

My Data Manager –
Track your mobile... GET
Mobidia Technology

☆ 📋 ◎ Q ⬇️
Featured Top Charts Explore Search Updates

9 Use the information on the app's information screen to evaluate the app and decide if it's what you are looking for; this is explained in the task called "Evaluating Apps."

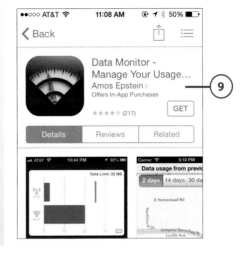

Related Apps

When the search results are on the screen, at the top (just under the Search bar), you see app searches that are related to the one you performed in some way in the Related Searches bar. Tap a related search on this bar to use it to find other apps. As you use related searches, back (<) and forward (>) buttons appear in the Related Searches bar so that you can move back and forth among the searches you have done. For example, tap the Back button to get back to a previous search.

Follow the Trends?

Before you enter a search term on the Search screen, you see the Trending Searches, which are the searches that are being performed most frequently. You can tap one of these to use it to search for apps.

Searching for Apps

You can also search for apps using the Web. Using your favorite search page, such as google.com, search for something like "best iPhone apps for *subject*," where *subject* is the topic of interest to you. Examples of subjects you might use include travel, retirement, and health. The results are likely to include at least one app (usually more than one) that is related to the subject. Use the links provided by the search to explore the apps it found. Then, you can go back into the App Store app to search for (by their title) and download the apps that look the most promising to you.

Browsing for Apps

If you don't know of a specific app you want, you can browse the App Store. To browse, you can tap any graphics or links you see in the App Store app. There are a number of ways to start the browsing process: Categories, Featured, Top Charts, or Explore. When you select one of these options, you can then browse apps associated with or organized by the option you selected. The following steps show you how to browse for apps by category; the other options are similar:

1. Move to the Home screen and tap App Store. The App Store app opens and at the bottom of the screen, you see the tabs you can use to choose a method to find apps.

2. Tap Featured.

3. Tap Categories.

4. Swipe up and down the screen to browse the list until you see a category of interest.

5. Tap a category in which you are interested.

This arrow indicates a category has subcategories

6. If the category has subcategories, swipe up and down the screen to browse the subcategories; if you moved directly to apps, skip to step 7.

7. Tap a subcategory in which you are interested.

8. Swipe up and down to browse the groupings of apps, such as New and What's Hot.

9. Swipe left and right on a grouping to browse the apps it contains.

10. Tap an app in which you are interested. You move to that app's information screen.

See All, Know All

To browse all the apps in a category, tap See All at the top of the category's screen. You see all the apps in that category; swipe up and down the screen to browse the list. Tap an app to see its information.

Universal Apps

When you see a "+" inside an app's price or free button, it means the app is a universal app, which means it runs equally as well on iPhones, iPads, and iPod touches.

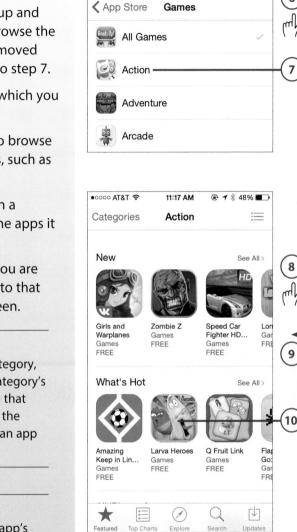

(11) Use the information on the information screen to evaluate the app; this is explained in the next task, "Evaluating Apps."

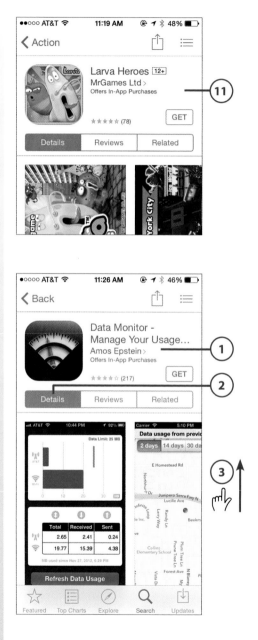

Evaluating Apps

The App Store provides lots of information about apps that you can use to evaluate an app to decide whether it is worth downloading. When you move to an app's information screen, you can evaluate it using the following steps:

(1) Review the name, average user rating, and cost (displayed in the app's download button).

(2) Tap the Details tab.

(3) To read a description, swipe up on the screen.

But Wait, There's More

If you continue to swipe up the screen, you see the Information section, which shows the seller, category, update date, and version number. Below that are various sections you can tap on to get even more information. For example, if you tap In-App Purchases, you see a list of the purchases you can make from inside the app, such as add-ons, or ad-free versions. Other such sections include Version History, Developer Website, Privacy Policy, and Developer Apps. If you really want to get into the details, you can tap each of these to get even more information.

(4) If not all of the description is currently displayed, tap More; the Description area expands so you can read the entire description.

(5) Read the What's New section to see the changes made for the current version.

(6) Swipe down on the screen to view screenshots of the app shown above the description.

(7) Tap the screenshots.

Video Previews

Some apps include video previews. When you see the Play button on an image, it is a video preview. Tap the Play button to watch it. Tap the Done button in the upper-left corner of the screen to move back to the screenshots.

Make Your Voice Known

After you have used an app, you can add your own review by moving back to its Reviews tab and tapping Write A Review. You move to the Write a Review screen where you have to enter your iTunes Store account information before you can write and submit a review.

(8) Look at the app's screenshots. If the app is horizontally-oriented, rotate the iPhone so the screenshots make sense. (Note that the screen you view doesn't reorient like most screens do, but at least the screenshots themselves look better.)

(9) Swipe on the screenshots to see them all.

(10) Tap Done. The screenshot screen closes and you move back to the app's screen.

(11) Tap Reviews. (If you've rotated the iPhone, you'll need to move it back to the vertical orientation.)

(12) Read the user reviews for the app; you'll have to swipe up to see them all. You should have all the information you need about the app to be able to decide if it is worth your time and cost, if any, to download it.

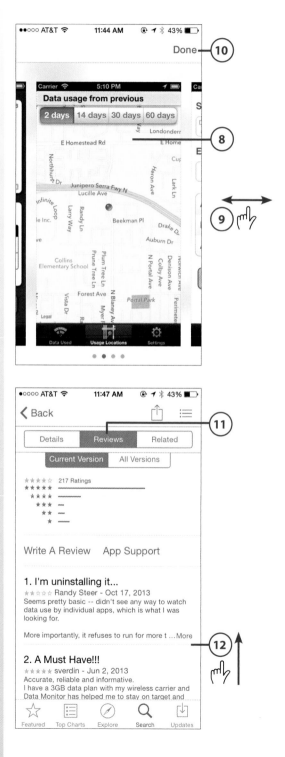

Downloading Apps

Downloading and installing apps is about as easy as things get, as you can see:

1. Move to the information screen for the app you want to download.

2. To download the app, tap GET if it is a free app or tap the price to download the app if there is a cost to download it. The button then becomes INSTALL if it is a free app or BUY if it has a cost.

3. Tap INSTALL or BUY. Depending on how long it's been since you signed into your Apple ID, you might be prompted to sign in to start the download. If you have recently downloaded an app under your account, you can skip the next step because the app starts downloading immediately.

4. If you are using an iPhone 5s or later, touch the Touch ID /Home button at the prompt; if you are using another model, or you don't use Touch ID, type your Apple ID password and tap OK.

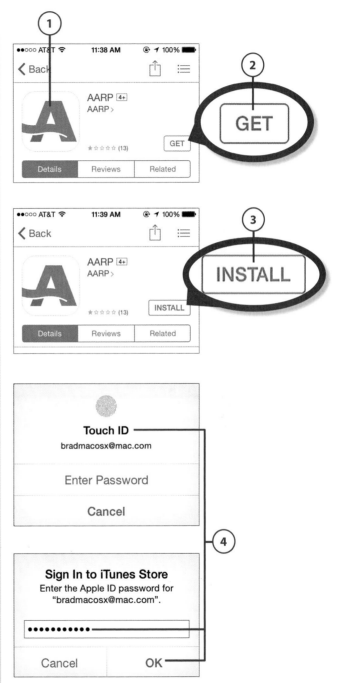

You see the progress of the process.

When the process is complete, the status information is replaced by the Open button. This indicates the app has been downloaded and installed. (Its icon appears on the next available spot on your Home screens and you see it the next time you press the Touch ID/Home button to move there.) Tap Open to launch the app.

You don't have to wait for apps to download. You can start the process and then use your iPhone normally as the download occurs in the background.

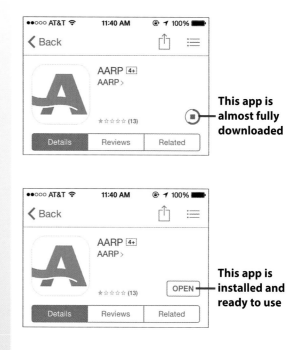

This app is almost fully downloaded

This app is installed and ready to use

Adding Apps to the Wish List

The Wish List is a nice tool you can use to collect apps in which you might be interested; this works similarly to a shopping cart on a retail website. You can collect apps on your Wish List and then go back and easily locate them again. The Wish List can be used only for apps that have a license fee, which makes sense because you can just download any free apps you are interested in.

To add an app to your Wish List, do
the following:

1 Move to the information screen
for the app that you want to add
to your Wish List.

2 Tap the Share button.

3 Tap Add to Wish List. The app is
added to your Wish List.

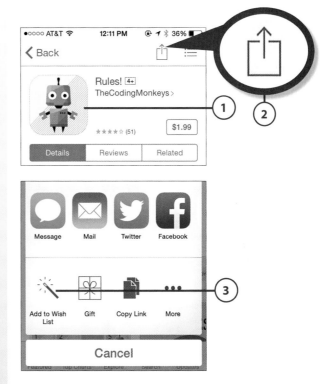

Using Your Wish List

To work with your Wish List, do the
following:

1 Tap the Wish List button.

2 To move to an app's Information
screen, tap it.

3 To download an app, tap its
price button.

4 To remove apps from the list,
tap Edit.

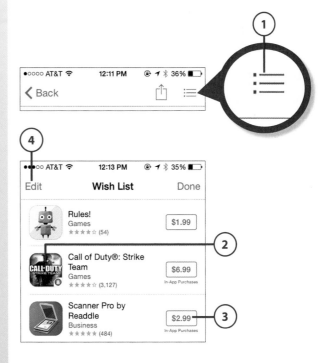

⑤ Tap the apps you want to remove to select them.

⑥ Tap Delete.

⑦ Tap Done to close the Wish List.

Deleting Wish List Apps

You can also remove an app from the list by swiping to the left on it and tapping Delete.

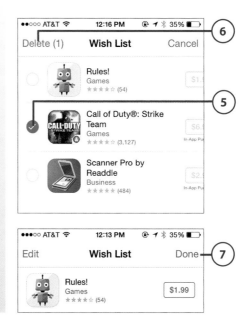

>>>Go Further

MORE ON APPS

As you use the App Store app to install apps on your iPhone, keep the following hints handy:

- If you have to pay to download an app, the fee is a one-time payment for the app, at least in its current version (most apps provide unlimited updates, too). Some apps, such as TripIt, have an associated service (such as TripIt Pro) that might have an annual fee, but in most cases, you only have to spend money on an app the first time you download it and from there, you can use it and download it again (even on other devices) for free.

- Like other software, apps are updated regularly to fix problems, add features, or make other changes. If you set the iTunes & App Store AUTOMATIC DOWNLOADS Updates setting to on (green) as described earlier in this chapter, updates to your apps happen automatically in the background. Your apps are always current and so you don't have to update them manually. (More information on updating apps is in Chapter 17, "Maintaining and Protecting Your iPhone and Solving Problems.")

- If you see the Download button (which is a cloud with a downward-pointing arrow) on an app's page, that means you have already downloaded the app but it is not currently installed on your iPhone. Tap the button to download and install it.

- To let someone else know about an app, tap the Share button and then tap how you want to let him know; the options are AirDrop, Message, Mail, Twitter, and Facebook.
- Apps can work in the background to keep their information current, such as Weather and Stocks. To configure this, open the Settings app, tap General, and tap Background App Refresh. Set Background App Refresh to on (green). To enable an app to work in the background, set its switch to on (green). To disable background activity for an app, set its switch to off (white).
- To give the app to someone, tap the Share button and tap Gift.
- To send the link to the app to someone, tap Copy Link and then past the link into an email message or other location where you want to use it.
- To see apps that are related to the one you are evaluating, tap the Related tab and browse the resulting screen.
- If you want to report a problem you're having with an app, move to the app's Details tab, swipe up the screen, and tap Developer Website. You move to the developer's website and can get information and help with the app.
- Anytime you download an app, it is automatically download to all devices that you have connected to your App Store account and for which you have enabled the AUTOMATIC DOWNLOADS setting.
- Using the Family Sharing feature, you can share apps you download with others. You learn about this in "Using Family Sharing to Share Your Store Downloads with Others, "at the end of this chapter.
- The next time you sync your iPhone (by connecting it to your computer or via a Wi-Fi network), the apps you've added using the App Store app will be copied into your iTunes Library. If you have configured the iTunes Store Preferences to allow automatic downloads, this happens automatically.
- Tap an app's icon on the Home screen to launch it.
- After you install an app, move to the Settings screen and look for the app's icon. If it is there, the app has additional settings you can use to configure the way it works. Tap the app's icon and use its Settings screen to configure it.
- To remove an app you have installed, tap and hold on its icon on the Home screen. When the icons starting jiggling, raise your finger. Tap the Delete button (x). Confirm the deletion at the prompt that appears, and the app is deleted. (Any data stored only with the app on the iPhone is also deleted, so be careful. If the app stores its data on the cloud, you don't have to worry about this; if you re-install the app at a later time, you get your data back, too.) As you see in a later section of this chapter, you can download the app again at any time—but your data might not be restored when you do.

Using the iTunes Store App to Download Music, Ringtones, Movies, and TV Shows

You can use the iPhone's iTunes Store app to download audio and video content from the iTunes Store directly onto your iPhone. You can listen to music you download in the Music app, watch movies and TV shows in the Videos app, and use tones for ringtones and alert tones.

Using the iTunes Store app involves the following general steps:

1. **Find the content you are interested in**—Like the App Store app, there are a number of ways to do this. You can search for specific content, or you can browse for content by type, which includes the following (to get to some of these, such as Audiobooks and Tones, tap the More button and then tap the category of interest to you):

    • Music enables you to download music.

    • Movies takes you to the movies in the iTunes Store so you can browse, preview, and download them.

    • TV Shows does the same for TV programming.

    • Audiobooks enables you to download audiobooks to listen to.

    • Tones enables you to purchase ringtones and alert tones that you can use as various sounds on your iPhone.

    • Genius shows you recommendations based on content you have previously downloaded that you might also be interested in.

2. **Preview the content**—You can sample content before you download it. For example, you can listen to a preview of songs (typically 90 seconds' worth), watch movie trailers, and listen to tones.

3. **Download the content**—You can download content with just a couple of taps. After you download content to your iPhone, it immediately becomes available in the related app.

In the following tasks, you see examples of each of these steps.

Searching for iTunes Store Content

When you know something about the content you want, searching is a good way to find it because it is easy and fast. Also, when you search, your results can include multiple types of content. For example, searching on a title can yield an album, a movie, a song, or an audiobook. Here's how to search in the Store:

1. On the iPhone's Home screen, tap iTunes Store. You move to the iTunes Store app. At the bottom of the screen, you choose how you want to look for content by tapping one of the buttons on the iTunes Store toolbar.

2. Tap Search.

3. Tap in the Search box.

4. Type a search criterion, such as an artist's name, a movie title, or even a general topic (for example, a franchise, such as *Star Trek*). As you type, content that matches your search appears under the Search bar.

5. When you see something of interest on the results list, tap it, or to see the entire list of search results, tap the Search key on the keyboard (not shown) and then tap the result you want to explore. For example, tap an artist's name or a more general

topic. A list of content related to your search appears. If there are multiple types of content associated with the search, you see tabs at the top of the screen showing you the available types.

(6) Swipe up, down, right, and left to browse the search results, which are organized into categories, such as Movies, Albums, Songs, Ringtones, and Music Videos.

(7) To limit the results to a specific type of content, tap the related tab. For example, to see the movies related to what you searched for, tap Movies.

(8) Swipe on the screen to browse the list of results for the type of content you selected.

(9) When you see something of interest, tap it. You see the Information screen for that content.

More Trends

Similar to the App Store app, when you haven't entered a search term on the Search screen, you see the searches that are trending. You can tap a trending search to see its results.

Stop the Search!

To clear a search, tap the Clear button (x) in the Search bar. Swipe down on the keyboard to close it so that you can see the iTunes toolbar at the bottom of the screen again.

Tap to clear search

10 Use the Information screen to preview and explore the content. Details are provided later in this chapter in the task titled, "Previewing iTunes Store Content."

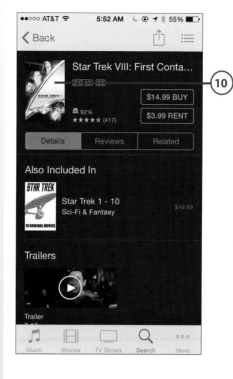

Browsing for iTunes Store Content

Even though browsing isn't as efficient as searching, it is a good way to discover content you might not know about. Sometimes you can get to specific content by browsing almost as quickly as searching. The details of browsing depend on the type of content for which you are looking. The following example shows browsing music to demonstrate the general process:

1 On the iPhone's Home screen, tap iTunes Store. You move to the iTunes Store app. At the bottom of the screen, you can choose how you want to look for content by tapping one of the buttons on the iTunes Store toolbar.

2 Tap Music. You move to the Music Home page. At the top of the screen, you see options you can use to browse: Genres, Featured (the default), and Charts.

(3) Swipe the screen to browse the current contents. The rest of these steps show browsing by genre. The steps for using the other browse options are similar.

(4) Tap Genres. You see the list of genres.

(5) Swipe up and down the screen to browse the list of genres.

(6) Tap the genre you want to explore.

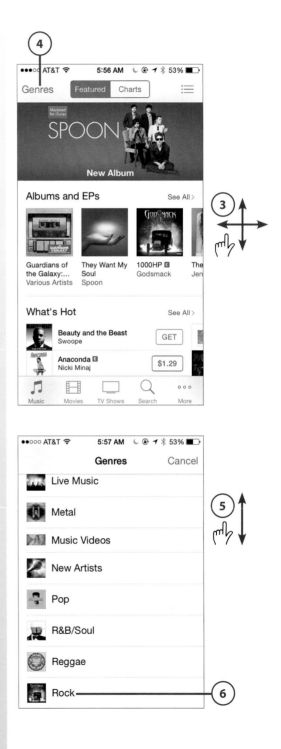

7 Swipe the screen to browse the contents being displayed.

8 Tap something of interest to see more detail. Tap the See All link for a category to see all the items in that category.

9 Swipe the results to browse them.

10 Tap an item for which you'd like to see more detail.

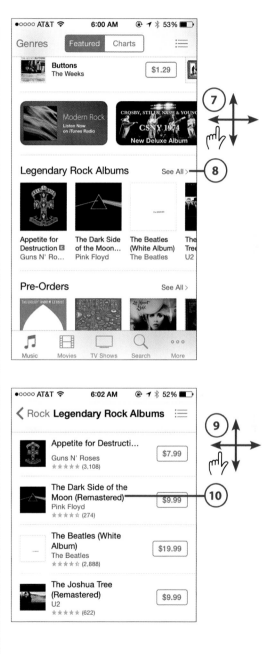

11 Use the Information screen to preview and explore the content. Details are provided in the task "Previewing iTunes Store Content."

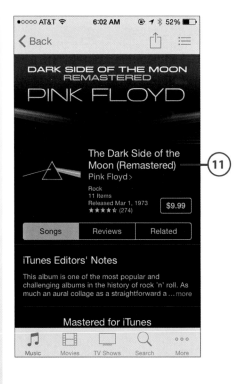

Previewing iTunes Store Content

You can use the Information screen to explore content in which you are interested. This screen looks a bit different for various kinds of content, such as a movie versus an album. However, the general features of this screen are similar, so the following steps showing an album's Information screen will get you started:

1 Move to the Information screen for content you might want to download.

2 Review the summary information at the top of the screen.

3 On the Songs tab (this is called Details for some other types of content), tap More.

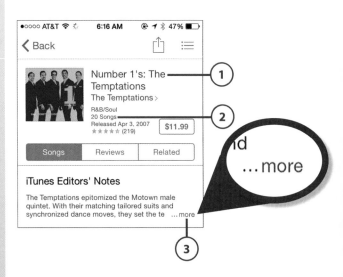

4 Read the detailed description/notes. (Be aware that not all content has notes or other information about it.)

5 Tap the Reviews tab.

6 Swipe up and down the screen to read all the review information. At the top, you see an overview of the reviews, indicated by the star ratings. Toward the bottom of the screen, you can read the individual reviews.

7 Tap Songs.

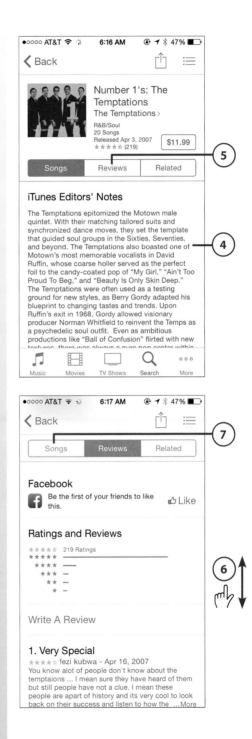

8 Swipe up the screen to see the list of songs the album or collection contains.

9 To preview a track, tap it. A short preview plays. While it's playing, the track's number is replaced by the Stop button, which you can tap to stop the preview.

10 Continue previewing the content until you are ready to make a decision to download it—or not.

Previewing Video

When you preview video content, such as watching a trailer for a movie, it plays in a video player. Tap the Play button to play the video preview. Tap Done when you're finished watching it. You return to the screen you came from.

But Wait, There's More

You can access additional categories of content by tapping the More button. On the More screen, you see Audiobooks, Tones, and Genius. Tap Audiobooks to browse audiobooks you can download and listen to. Tap Tones to download sound snippets from songs or special effects to use as ringtones or alert tones. Tap Genius to see recommended content based on content you have downloaded or content related to content you have downloaded.

A preview is playing

Downloading iTunes Store Content

Like downloading apps, downloading movies, tones, songs, and albums is just a tap away:

1. Move to the Information screen for content you want to download.

2. Tap the appropriate buy button, which shows the price of the item. For example, to buy an album, tap its buy button. To buy a song, tap its price button instead. Likewise, you can buy a movie by tapping its price button (some movies are offered in different formats, and each one has its own price button). The button changes to show what you are buying.

3. Tap the Buy button again, such as BUY ALBUM. If it's been a while since you signed into your Apple ID, you're prompted to sign into your account. If you recently signed in, the download starts without you signing in and you can skip step 4.

4. If you are using an iPhone 5s or later, at the prompt, touch the Touch ID/Home button. If you are using a different model or don't use Touch ID, enter the password for your Apple ID and tap OK.

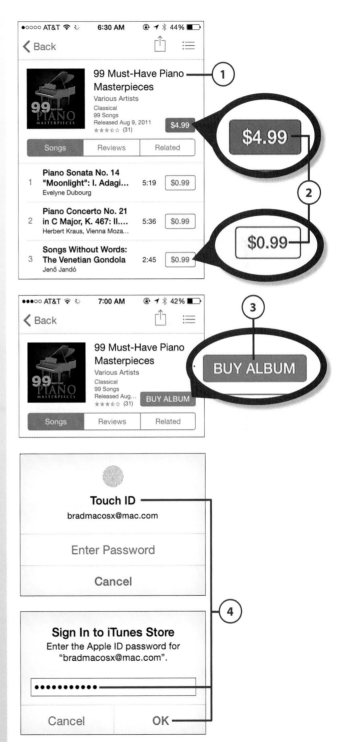

The download process starts and you can continue to shop in the Store or move into a different app; the download process occurs in the background. If you want to, you can monitor the download process by continuing with these steps.

(5) Tap More.

(6) Tap Downloads. You move to the Downloads screen, which displays the progress of the tracks you are purchasing.

When the process is complete, the Downloads screen becomes empty. This indicates that all of the content you purchased has been added to the iPhone and is ready for you to listen to or watch in the related app.

Procrastinate If You Wish

When you download some content that is large, such as a movie, you have the option to download it later. For example, you might decide you want the movie while you are using your cellular data network but don't want to use a lot of your data plan's monthly allocation to download it. Tap the Later button to defer the download to a later time. You can do the same thing with the Pause button for any content that is downloaded. Tap the Pause button and the download stops where it is. Tap the Resume button to complete the download (for example, when you return to a Wi-Fi network).

Freebies

Some content (not a lot) in the iTunes Store is free to download. Similar to apps that are free, instead of a button showing the content's price, you see the FREE button. Tap FREE to start the download process, which works just like that for content you have to pay for, except that you aren't charged for it of course.

Using Your iTunes Store History List

As you are looking at content in the iTunes Store, you'll likely encounter music, movies, etc. that you are interested in but are not sure you want to download. It would be a pain to get back to content via searching or browsing. Fortunately, you can use the History List to go back to content you have previewed.

The History List contains content that you've interacted with in the following ways:

- **Wish List** —To add something to your Wish List, open an item's information screen, tap the Share button, and then tap Add to Wish List.

- **Siri Tag**—When music is playing around you, press and hold the Touch ID/ Home button and say, "What song is this?" Siri identifies the music playing and adds it to your History List. This is a great way to add music that you hear when you are out and about so you can easily find it again later.

- **Radio**—Songs you listen to via iTunes Radio are added to your History List automatically so that you can purchase them easily. So, if you remember that you heard a great song on iTunes Radio, but don't remember who performed it, you can use this option to easily find it.

- **Preview**—Any content you preview is added to your History List automatically.

When you preview content, such as watching a TV show's preview, it is added to your History List

You can use your History List to find, preview, and download content similarly to how you do these things from other areas. The following example shows content captured by previewing it, but the other options work in the same way:

① Tap the History List button.

② Tap the source of content you want to see. For example, tap Previews to see the content you have previewed. (Tap Wish List to see your Wish List items, Siri to see items Siri has identified, or Radio to see iTunes Radio content to which you've listened.)

3. Swipe the screen to browse the list of items.

4. To move to an item's Information screen, tap its title.

5. To preview an item, taps its icon.

6. To buy an item, tap its price button and then tap its BUY button.

7. If you've purchased something on this list, tap PLAY to play it.

8. To clear your list, tap Clear and then tap Clear History.

9. To close the list, tap Done.

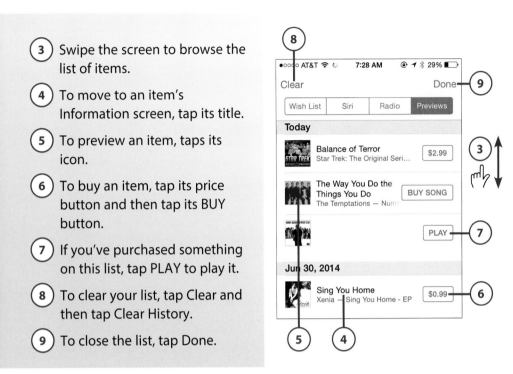

>>>Go Further
SHOPPING LIKE A PRO

Here are a few more pointers to make your iTunes Store experience even better:

- **Preorder** —You can order content that isn't released yet, such as movies, or a full season of a TV show that is in a current season. When the content you have preordered becomes available, it is downloaded to your iPhone automatically.

- **Renting**—You can rent movies, too. This is less expensive than buying them, but it comes with limitations. You can keep a rented movie for only 30 days. And, after you start watching it, you will have 24 (or, less often, 48) hours to watch it. When the time period for rented content expires, the rented movie is deleted from your iPhone automatically.

- **Customizing the iTunes Store app toolbar**—You can place any four buttons on the iTunes Store app toolbar by customizing it (the More button is always visible on the toolbar). To change the buttons displayed, tap More and then tap Edit. Drag the buttons you want to place on the bar from the upper part of the screen, and drop them on the toolbar at the location you want them to appear. You can also drag icons around the toolbar to change their locations. When the toolbar is what you want it to be, tap Done.

• **Add Your Own Review**—To add your own review of an item, move to its Reviews tab and tap Write a Review. Complete the resulting form to record your feedback.

• **Related**—Tap the Related tab to see content that is "related to" the content you are exploring. This shows you other content that was purchased by the same people who downloaded the content you are considering.

• **Move from Song to Album**—When you browse a list of songs, tap a song's title twice to move to the Information screen for the album from which the song comes.

• **Pausing Downloads**—You can tap the Pause button for items being downloaded to temporarily stop the download process. For example, if you are leaving the area covered by the Wi-Fi network you are using, you might want to delay completion of a download until you return so it isn't completed over the cellular data network.

• **Share and Share Alike**—Tap the Share button at the top of iTunes screens to share the content you are exploring. You can share by email, message, Twitter, and Facebook. The messages you send contain a link to the item. You can also share via AirDrop or tap Copy Link to copy the item's link to the Clipboard, from where you can paste into other areas such as a document. Tap Gift to give the content to someone else.

• **The Next Time You Sync**—The next time you sync after purchasing audio and video from the iTunes Store on the iPhone, that audio and video is moved into your iTunes Library. If you've created any smart playlists with live updating enabled and the new audio and video matches that playlist's criteria, the new audio and video become part of those playlists automatically.

• **Clear History**—The Clear button on the History List only deletes the items from the tab you are currently viewing. For example, if you use it on the Previews tab, all the items you have previewed are erased. To clear the other lists, tap the tab for the content you want to clear, tap Clear, and then tap Clear History at the prompt.

• **Automatic Downloads**—If you have other iOS devices or iTunes on your computers configured to automatically download iTunes Store purchases, the content is downloaded to those locations, too.

Downloading Apps or iTunes Store Content You've Purchased Previously

You can download any content you've purchased from the App or iTunes Stores again without paying a fee (rented movies are an exception because you can download those only once and have to pay for them again to download them again). For example, you might download an app, decide that you don't want it any more, delete it, and then change your mind and want it again. (Of course, this doesn't really apply to free apps since you can always download those at no cost.) Similarly, you might delete music from your iPhone to free up some memory, and then download it again later when you want to listen to it.

Downloading Previously Purchased App Store Apps

To download apps you previously purchased, perform the following steps:

1. Tap the App Store icon to open the app.
2. Tap Updates.
3. Tap Purchased.

Family Sharing?

If you have enabled Family Sharing for your account and if others have added you to their Family Sharing, after step 3, you see the All Purchases screen. On this screen, you see My Purchases; tap this to download content you've purchased and move to step 4. You also see the people who have shared their content with you in the FAMILY PURCHASES section. In this section, tap the person whose content you want to download in this section and then move to step 4.

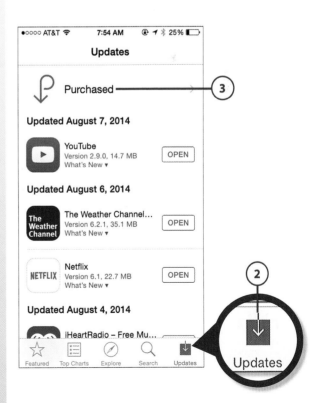

(4) Tap Not on This Phone.

(5) Swipe up and down the list to browse the apps you've downloaded, but that are not currently installed on your iPhone.

(6) Tap the Download button for the app that you want to re-install; if prompted to do so, confirm your Apple ID by tapping the Touch ID button or entering your Apple ID and tapping OK. The app is downloaded and installed on your iPhone. When the process is complete, the OPEN button appears. This indicates that the app has been re-installed on your iPhone and is ready for you to use.

Downloading Previously Purchased iTunes Content

To download music, movies, or other content you previously downloaded, perform the following steps:

(1) Open the iTunes Store app.

(2) Tap More.

(3) Tap Purchased.

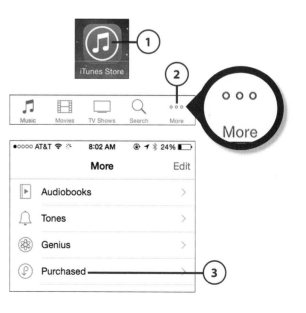

Family Sharing?

If you have enabled Family Sharing for your account and if others have added you to their Family Sharing, after step 3, you see the Purchased screen. On this screen, you see the MY PURCHASES section; here, you see Music, Movies, and TV Shows as shown in step 4. You also see the people who have shared their content with you in the FAMILY PURCHASES section. In this section, tap the person whose content you want to download in this section and then move to step 4.

4 Tap Music, Movies, or TV Shows. The rest of these steps show downloading music, but the steps to download other content are similar.

5 Tap Not on This iPhone. The list shows all the music you've purchased from the iTunes Store but that is not currently stored on your iPhone. At the top of the screen is the number of songs you've purchased recently that aren't on the iPhone (you can tap to browse the list of recent purchases). Below this are all the artists associated with content you haven't downloaded to the iPhone as well as the number of tracks for each artist.

6 Swipe up and down to browse the list.

7 Tap the artist whose music you want to download. A list of content for that artist, organized into categories such as albums or songs, is displayed.

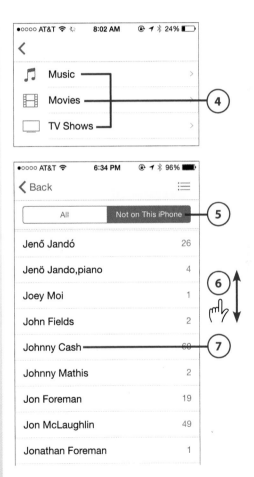

(8) Swipe up and down the screen to browse the content you have from the artist (if you have content from only one album, skip to step 12).

(9) To download an entire album, tap its Download button and skip to step 15.

(10) To download all of the content from that artist, tap Download All and skip to step 15.

(11) To download individual songs, tap the album containing the songs you want to download.

(12) Browse the contents of the album.

(13) Tap a song's Download button to download it and skip to step 15.

(14) To download all of the album's songs, tap its Download button.

(15) If prompted and you are using an iPhone 5s or later, touch the Touch ID/Home button; if you are using a different model, enter your Apple ID password and tap OK. The content is downloaded to your iPhone. When that process is complete, you can watch or listen to it in the related app, such as the Music app for songs you download.

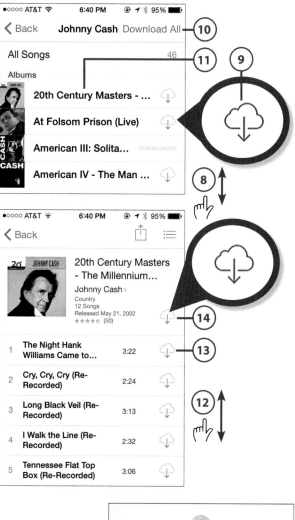

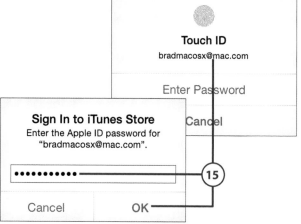

Using Family Sharing to Share Your Store Downloads with Others

New! With Family Sharing, you can share your iTunes content with up to six other people. The people with whom you share content don't have to be related to you in any way despite the name of this feature. People with whom you share content can then download content you have purchased to their devices without needing to use your Apple ID or password.

To start using Family Sharing, you need to set it up and then designate the people with whom you will share content.

Setting Up Family Sharing

To set up Family Sharing on your iPhone, do the following:

(**1**) Open the Settings app.

(**2**) Tap iCloud.

(**3**) Tap Set Up Family Sharing.

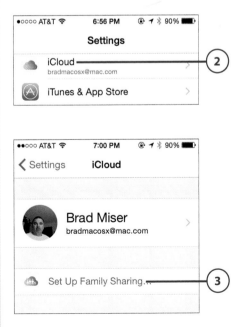

4 Tap Get Started.

5 If you want to share content under your current iCloud account, tap Continue; if you want to change accounts, tap the link at the bottom of the screen and follow the onscreen instructions to change the account you are configuring.

6 If you want to share purchases that were made using your current Apple ID, tap Continue; if not tap Share purchases from a different account and follow the prompts to change the account whose content you are sharing.

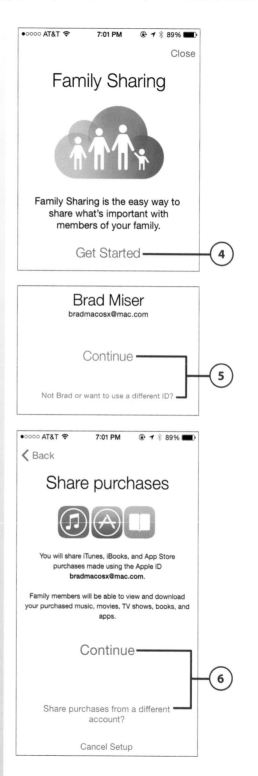

7. To accept changes on the credit card currently associated with your Apple ID, tap Continue; to change the payment method, tap Managing Family Purchases and follow the prompts to make changes.

8. To share your location with the people in your Family Sharing group, tap Share Your Location; if you prefer to not share your location, tap Not Now. You move to the Family screen and are ready to share content with others as described in the next task.

Adding People to Family Sharing

To be able to share content with someone, she must be using a device running iOS 8 or later or a Mac running OS X Yosemite or later. To share your content with someone else, add them to your Family Sharing as follows:

1. If you just completed the previous task and are still on the Family screen, skip to step 4; if this isn't the case, open the Settings app.

2. Tap iCloud.

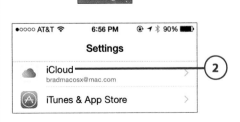

3 Tap Family.

4 Tap Add Family Member.

5 Enter the email address of the person with whom you are sharing content and then select the person when he appears on the list. If the email address you enter isn't associated with an Apple ID, an invitation is sent to the person and you return to the Family screen where you see the person with whom you are sharing content. You can skip the rest of these steps. If the email address is already associated with an Apple ID, you see two options for sharing with the person.

6 Enter the three-digit security code located on the back of the credit card associated with your account.

7 Tap Next.

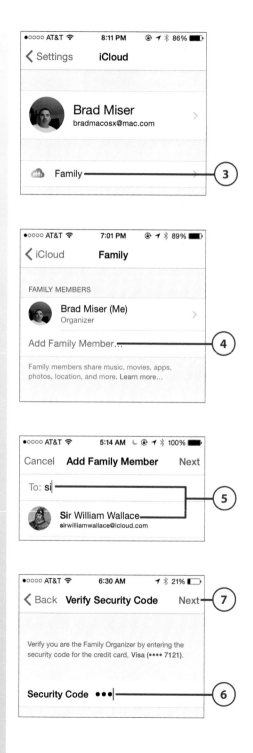

8 Tap Ask *name* to Enter Password, where *name* is the name of the person with whom you are sharing content, if the person with whom you are sharing can enter their Apple ID password on your iPhone; then move to step 7. Tap Send an Invitation to send an invitation to him instead.

If you choose the invitation option, an invitation is sent to the person and you return to the Family screen where you see the person with whom you are sharing content. You can skip the rest of these steps.

9 Have the person with whom you are sharing content enter his Apple ID password on your phone.

10 Tap Done.

11 To have the person share his location with the people in your Family Sharing group, tap Share Your Location; if he prefers to not share his location, tap Not Now. The person is added to your FAMILY MEMBERS list and can share your content immediately.

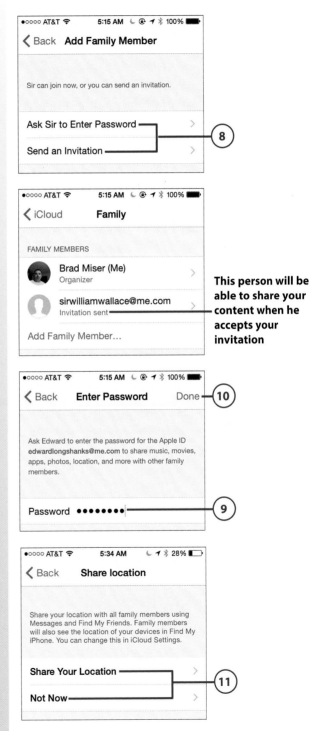

This person will be able to share your content when he accepts your invitation

Your Options Might Be Limited

In some cases, you might not have the option to ask the person you are sharing with to enter the password and only have the invitation option.

> **New Family Member** now
> Edward the Longshanks has been added to Family Sharing.
>
> FAMILY MEMBERS
>
> **Brad Miser (Me)** ›
> Organizer
>
> **Edward the Longshanks** ›
> Adult
>
> **sirwilliamwallace@me.com** ›
> Invitation sent
>
> Add Family Member…

This person can share your content immediately

Create an Apple ID for a Child

If the person with whom you want to share content doesn't have an account, you can create an Apple ID for that person. Tap Create an Apple ID for a child at the bottom of the Family screen. Tap Next. You then have to indicate you had parental consent, confirm your payment information, enter the child's birthday, enter the child's name, create the Apple ID and password, and configure security questions. You then turn Ask to Buy on or off. If you leave it on, you will have to approve a purchase the child tries to make; if you turn it off, you won't have to approve purchases. Note that any purchases the child makes use the payment information associated with your account. Finally, you accept the terms and conditions. Once the account is created, provide the Apple ID and password to the child, and he will be able to purchase apps and iTunes Store content under your account.

Birthdays

If the person who you are trying to add to Family Sharing doesn't have a birthday configured in her iCloud settings, you might not be able to complete the process. Ask that person to update their birthday in her iCloud settings either on her iOS device or via the iCloud website.

Managing Family Sharing

You can use the Family screen to manage the people with whom you are sharing content. When you access the Family screen, you see the people with whom you are sharing content and their status.

Tap your name (the organizer) to move to the screen labeled with your name where you can perform the following tasks:

- If you tap the email address, you can change the Apple ID being used to share. People who are currently sharing your content will lose access to your content if you change the account being used to share.

- Set the Share My Purchases switch to off (white) if you don't want those with whom you are sharing to be able to share your content.

- Tap Stop Family Sharing and then tap Stop Sharing at the prompt to turn Family Sharing off (see the following It's Not All Good sidebar before doing this).

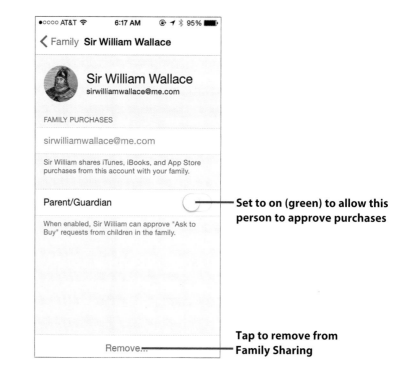

Set to on (green) to allow this person to approve purchases

Tap to remove from Family Sharing

It's Not All Good

You can stop and restart Family Sharing once during a year. If you stop it a second time, you're unable to restart it again until a year passes. If you want to prevent others from sharing your content, set the Share My Purchases switch to off (white) because this doesn't limit your ability to access Family Sharing.

Tap the name of people with whom you are sharing to perform the following tasks:

- Set the Parent/Guardian switch to on (green) to allow the person to approve purchases others make.
- Tap Remove and then tap Remove at the prompt to remove the person from Family Sharing. He is no longer able to access shared content and disappears from the list of people shown on the Family screen.

Accessing Shared Content

Accessing content being shared via Family Sharing is very similar to downloading apps and iTunes Store content previously purchased (see "Downloading Previously Purchased App Store Apps" and "Downloading Previously Purchased iTunes Content"). Following is an example of downloading iTunes content being shared with you:

1. Using steps 1 through 3 in "Downloading Previously Purchased iTunes Content," move to the Purchased screen of the iTunes app.

2. Tap the person sharing content with you.

3. Tap the type of content you want to download.

4. Tap Not on This iPhone. You see the content being shared with you.

5. Tap the content you want to download.

6. Tap Download All to download all the content you see. Tap the download button next to individual items to download specific content, or tap an item (such as album) to explore its content. These options work just like downloading content you purchased from the iTunes Store. When the content is downloaded to your iPhone, you can use the related app to listen to or watch it.

Share and Share Alike

When a person is added to the group shown on the Family tab, any content purchased by any member is immediately available to be shared with all the other members of the group. You should periodically check the Not on This iPhone tab for the people sharing with you to see what new content is available.

Use Settings to configure how contacts are displayed

Tap here to work with your contact information

Use your contact information in many apps

In this chapter, you learn how to ensure that your iPhone has the contact information you need when you need it. Topics include the following:

→ Getting started
→ Setting your contacts preferences
→ Creating contacts on your iPhone
→ Working with contacts on your iPhone
→ Managing contacts on your iPhone

7

Managing Contacts

Contact information, including names, phone numbers, email addresses, and physical addresses, is useful to have on your iPhone. For example, when you send email, it's much easier to select the appropriate email addresses by tapping the recipients' names rather than having to remember the email addresses and type them in. When you want to call someone, you don't need to remember a phone number; instead, just tap the name of the person you want to call. Likewise, you might want to see a contact's address on a map in the Maps app.

Getting Started

The Contacts app enables you to do all these things plus much more. This app makes using your contact information seamless. You can access contact information directly in the Contacts app and take action on it (such as placing a call), or you can use your contact information within other apps, such as Mail, Phone, and Messages.

To use contact information, it first must be stored in the Contacts app. You can add this information to your iPhone via syncing with a computer or via iCloud, Google, and other similar accounts; by capturing it when you perform tasks (such as reading email); or by entering information manually. And, you'll need to manage your contact information over time, such as adding to it and updating it.

Setting Your Contacts Preferences

Before you start using the Contacts app, you should set your preferences for contact information. You can determine how contacts are sorted and displayed, if or how names are shortened on various screens, your contact information, and which account should be the default for contact information.

To configure your contacts settings, perform the following steps:

1. On the Home screen, tap Settings.

2. Swipe up the screen until you see Mail, Contacts, Calendars.

3. Tap Mail, Contacts, Calendars.

4. Swipe up the screen until you see the Contacts section.

5. Tap Sort Order.

6. To have contacts sorted by first name and then last name, tap First, Last.

7. To have contacts sorted by last name and then first name, tap Last, First.

8. Tap Mail.

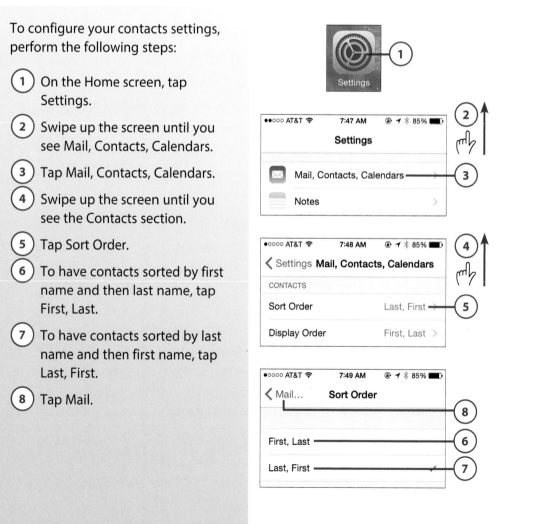

9 Tap Display Order.

10 To show contacts in the format *first name, last name,* tap First, Last.

11 To show contacts in the format *last name, first name,* tap Last, First.

12 Tap Mail.

13 Tap Show In App Switcher.

14 Set the Phone Favorites switch to on (green) if you want icons for people who are set as Favorites to be shown at the top of the screen when you open the App Switcher by pressing the Home button twice. If you set this to off, icons for your Favorites won't be shown.

15 Set the Recents switch to on (green) if you want icons for people whom you have communicated with (via the Phone, FaceTime, or Message apps) to be shown at the top of the screen when you open the App Switcher. If you set this to off, icons for your Recents won't be shown.

16 Tap Mail.

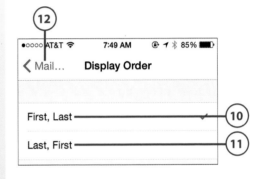

17 Tap Short Name. If enabled, short names are displayed for your contacts in various locations instead of full names (for example, showing only a person's first name on an email message). You can choose whether short names are used and if they are, what form they take. Short names are useful because more contact information can be displayed in a smaller area, and they look "friendlier."

18 To use short names, tap the Short Name switch to move it to the on position (green); if the switch is already green, skip this step.

19 Tap the format of short name you want to use. You can choose from a combination of initial and name or just first or last name. The selected format is marked with a check mark.

20 If you want nicknames for contacts used for the short name when available, set the Prefer Nicknames switch to on, which is indicated by it being green.

21 Tap Mail.

22 Tap My Info.

23 Browse or search the All Contacts screen (to learn different ways to browse this screen, jump ahead to the section called "Using the Contacts App" and then come back here).

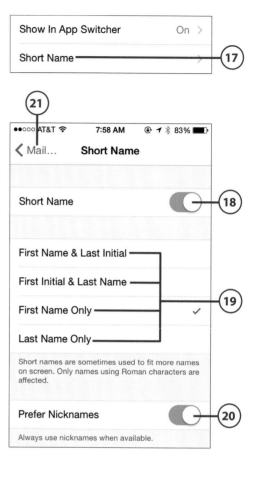

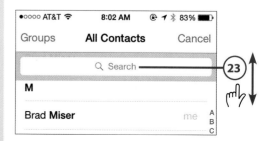

24 Tap your name. This tells the Contacts app your contact information, which it can insert for you in various places; your contact information is indicated by the label "me" next to the alphabetical index. You return to the Mail, Contacts, Calendars screen where your name appears next to My Info.

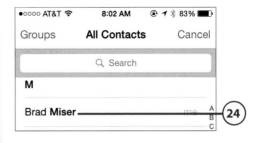

25 To determine the default account for your contacts, tap Default Account. (You see this option only if you have configured at least two accounts that can store contact information on your phone. If you don't have any accounts that can store contact information set up, your only option is to store them on your phone.)

26 Tap the account in which you want new contacts to be created by default (which is then marked with a check mark); if you want new contacts to be created on your iPhone instead of under an account, tap On My iPhone.

27 Tap Mail. Your contacts are configured according to your preferences.

Creating Contacts on Your iPhone

You can create new contacts on an iPhone in a number of ways. You can start with some information, such as the email address on a message you receive, and create a contact from it, or you can create a contact manually "from scratch." In this section, you learn how to use both of these options.

Creating New Contacts from Email

When you receive an email, you can easily create a contact to capture the email address. (To learn how to work with the Mail app, see Chapter 9, "Sending, Receiving, and Managing Email.")

(1) On the Home screen, tap Mail.

(2) Use the Mail app to read an email message (see Chapter 9 for details).

(3) Tap the email address from which you want to create a new contact. The Info screen appears—the label of the screen depends on the type of email address you tapped. For example, if you tapped the address from which the email was sent, the screen is labeled Sender. You see as much information as could be gleaned from the email address, which is typically the sender's name and email address.

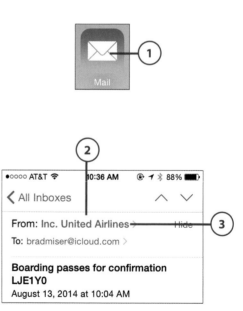

4 Tap Create New Contact. The New Contact screen appears. The name and email address are added to the new contact. The email address is labeled with iPhone's best guess, such as other or home.

5 Use the New Contact screen to enter more contact information and save the new contact. This works just like when you create a new contact manually, except that you already have some information—in this case, a name and an email address. For details on adding and changing more information for the contact, see the next task, which is "Creating Contacts Manually."

More Information for New Contacts

In some cases, such as when an email comes from an email server that includes full contact information, you will see a bar at the top of the email message above the From and To section. This bar shows the sender's name and phone number. Under this, you see Ignore and Add to Contacts. Tap Ignore to ignore this additional contact information. Tap Add to Contacts to create a new contact with all of the information available; this does the same thing as steps 3 through 5 except the resulting new contact contains more information than just name and email address.

>>>Go Further

MORE ON CREATING CONTACTS FROM APPS

It's useful to be able to create contact information by starting with some information in an app. Keep these points in mind:

- Mail is only one of the apps from which you can create contacts. You can start a contact in just about any app you use to communicate with people, such as Messages and Phone. The steps to start a contact in these apps are similar to those for Mail. Tap the person for whom you want to create a contact, and then tap Create New Contact. The Contacts app fills in as much of the information as it can, and you can complete the rest yourself.

- You can also add more contact information from an app you are currently using to an existing contact. You can do this by tapping Add to Existing Contact instead of Create New Contact. You then search for and select the contact to which you want to add the additional information. After it's saved, the additional information is associated with the contact you selected. For example, suppose you have created a contact for a company, but all you have is its phone number. You can quickly add the address to the contact by using the Maps app to look it up and then add the address to the company's existing contact information by tapping Add to Existing Contact and selecting the company in your contacts.

Creating Contacts Manually

Most of the time, you'll want to get the information for a new contact from an app, as the previous example demonstrated, or through an online account, such as contacts stored in your iCloud account. If these aren't available, you can also start a contact from scratch and add all the information you need to it. Also, you use the same steps to add information to an existing contact that you do to create a new one, so even if you don't start from scratch often, you do need to know how to do so.

The following steps show creating a new contact containing just some of the common information you will want to have; there are a lot more fields you can add if needed. Often, you'll create a new contact with only a few bits of information and add to it over time.

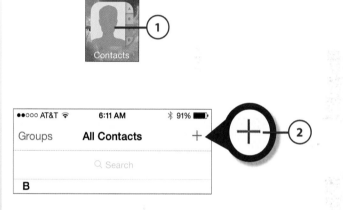

1. On the Home screen, tap Contacts. (If you don't see the Contacts app on the Home screen, tap the Extras folder to open it and you should see the app's icon. You may want to move the Contacts icon from this folder to a more convenient location on your Home screens; see Chapter 4, "Configuring an iPhone to Suit Your Preferences," for the steps to do this.) The All Contacts screen displays.

   If you see the Groups screen instead, tap Done to move to the All Contacts screen.

   If you have only one account that provides contact information, you see its contact list rather than the All Contacts screen, and you are ready to create a new contact.

2. Tap the Add button (+). The New Contact screen appears with empty fields for lots of the information you can include. (You can add more data fields as needed using the add field command.)

One of the most interesting things to store for your contacts is a photo. To associate a photo with a contact, that photo has to be stored on the iPhone. You can use a photo previously stored there or you can use the iPhone's camera to take a photo. (See Chapter 15, "Working with Photos and Video You Take with Your iPhone," for the info you need to use the iPhone's Camera app to take photos and the Photos app to work with your photos.)

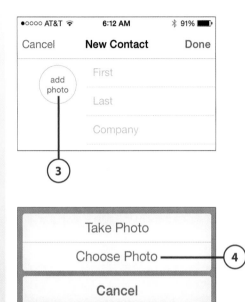

(3) To associate a photo with the contact, tap add photo. You can choose a photo already on your phone or take a new photo. These steps show using an existing photo. See the "Taking Photos" note for the steps to take a new photo.

(4) Tap Choose Photo.

(5) Use the Photos app to move to, select, and configure the photo you want to associate with the contact (see Chapter 15 for help with the Photos app).

(6) Tap Choose. You return to the New Contact screen where the photo you selected is displayed.

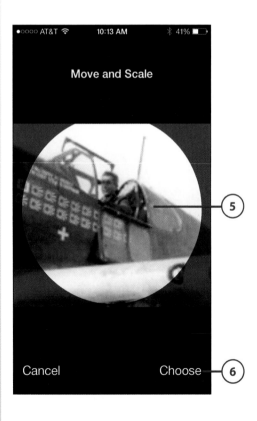

⑦ Tap in the First field and enter the contact's first name; if you are creating a contact for an organization only, leave this field empty. (The Display Order preference you set earlier determines whether the First or Last field appears at the top of the screen. It doesn't really matter because the fields are so close that you always see them at the same time.)

⑧ Tap in the Last field and enter the contact's last name (except if you are creating a contact for an organization, in which case, leave this field empty).

⑨ Enter the organization, such as a company, with which you want to associate the contact, if any.

⑩ To add a phone number, tap add phone. A new phone field appears along with the keypad.

⑪ Use the keypad to enter the contact's phone number, including any prefixes you need to dial it, such as area code and country code. The app formats the number for you as you enter it. Note that the information for a contact is labeled because you can have more than one of the same type. For example, you might have a work and a mobile phone number.

⑫ Tap the label for the phone number, such as home, to change it to another label. The Label screen appears.

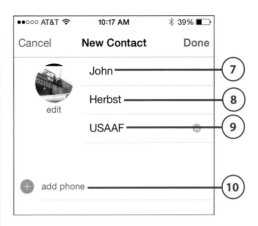

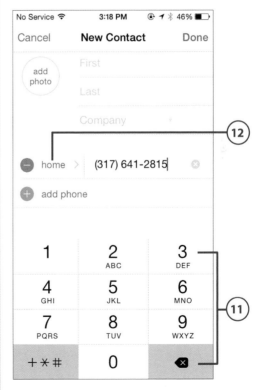

Taking Photos

To take a new photo for a contact, tap Take Photo in step 4 instead of Choose Photo. The Camera app's screen appears. Use the iPhone's camera to capture the photo you want to associate with the new contact (taking photos is covered in Chapter 15). Use the Move and Scale screen to adjust the photo so it is what you want to use. Then, tap Use Photo. The photo is pasted into the image well on the New Contact screen.

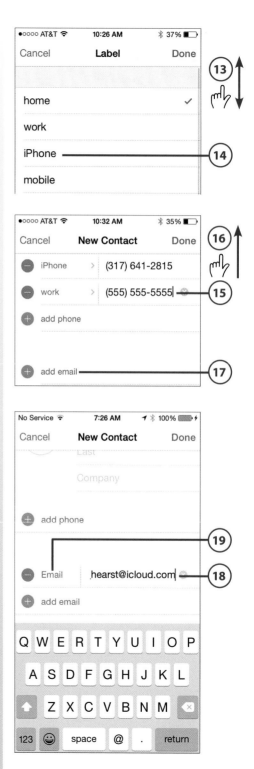

13) Swipe up and down the Label screen to see all the options available.

14) Tap the label you want to apply to the number, such as iPhone. That label is applied and you move back to the New Contact screen.

15) Repeat steps 10–14 to add more phone numbers to the contact.

16) Swipe up the screen until you see add email.

17) Tap add email. The keyboard appears.

18) Type the contact's email address.

19) Tap the label for the email address to change it.

20 Tap the label you want to apply to the email address. You move back to the New Contact screen.

21 Repeat steps 17–20 to add more email addresses.

22 Swipe up the screen until you see Ringtone.

23 Tap Ringtone. The list of ringtones and alert tones available on your iPhone appears.

24 Swipe up and down the list to see all of the tones available.

25 Tap the ringtone you want to play when the contact calls you. When you tap a ringtone, it plays so you can experiment to find the one that best relates to the contact. You can choose any ringtone stored on your iPhone or an alert tone. Setting a specific ringtone helps you identify a caller without looking at the phone.

26 Tap Done. You return to the New Contact screen, where the tone you selected appears.

You've probably noticed that the Contacts app leads you through creating each type of information you want to capture. You can choose to enter any or all of the default information on the New Contact screen.

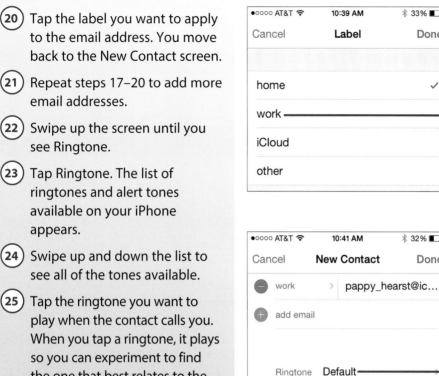

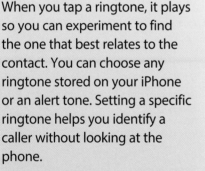

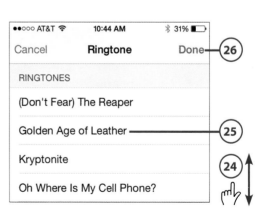

(27) Using the pattern you have learned in the previous steps, move to the next item you want to set and tap it.

(28) Use the resulting screens to enter the information you want to store and apply a label. After you've done a couple of the fields, it is easy to do the rest because the same pattern is used throughout. To move from field to field, tap in the field you want to move to and then either configure that field or tap Done. You can set a vibration when the contact calls and a tone and vibration for text messages, URLs, addresses, birthday, dates, related names, and notes.

(29) When you've added all the information you want to capture, tap Done. The New Contact screen closes and the new contact is created and ready for you to use in the Contacts and other apps. It is also moved onto other devices with which your contact information is synced.

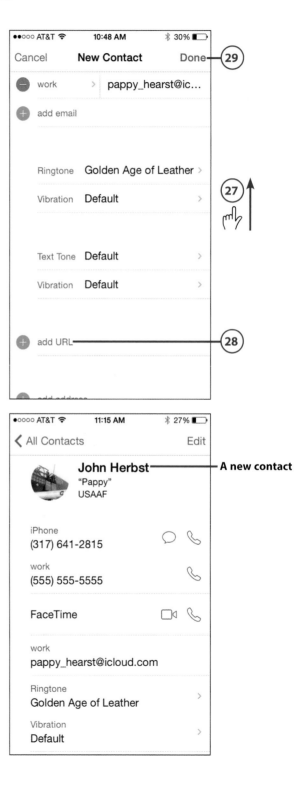

>>>Go Further

CREATING CONTACTS EXPANDED

Contacts are useful in many ways so you should make sure you have all the contact information you need. Here are a few points to ponder:

- You can (and should) sync contacts on multiple devices (computers and other iOS devices) by using iCloud, Gmail, or other similar accounts to store your contact information on the cloud from where all these devices can access it. Refer to Chapter 3, "Setting Up and Using iCloud and Other Online Accounts," for the details of setting up an account through which you can sync your contacts. You can also sync contacts with a computer (Mac or Windows PC) via iTunes; refer to Chapter 5, "Working with iTunes on Your Computer," to learn how to configure iTunes contact syncing.

- By the way, syncing your contacts works in both directions. Any new contacts you create or any changes you make to existing contact information on your iPhone move back to your other devices through the sync process. The bottom line is that you always have the same contact information available no matter which device you are using, which is a very good thing indeed.

- To remove a field in which you've entered information, tap the red circle with a dash in it next to the field and then tap Delete. If you haven't entered information into a field, just ignore it because empty fields don't appear on a contact's screen.

- The address format on the screens in the Contacts app is determined by the country you associate with the address. If the current country isn't the one you want, tap it and select the country in which the address is located before you enter any information; the fields appropriate for that country's address format appear on the screen.

- If you want to add a type of information that doesn't appear on the New Contact screen, swipe up the screen and tap add field. A list of additional fields you can add displays. Tap a field to add it; for example, tap Nickname to add a nickname for the contact. Then enter the information for that new field.

- When you add more fields to contact information, those fields appear in the appropriate context on the Info screen. For example, if you add a nickname, it is placed at the top of the screen with the other "name" information. If you add an address, it appears with the other address information.

Working with Contacts on Your iPhone

There are many ways to use contact information. The first step is always finding the contact information you need, typically by using the Contacts app. Whether you access it directly or through another app (such as Mail), it works the same way. Then, you select the information you want to use or the action you want to perform.

Using the Contacts App

You can access your contact information directly in the Contacts app. For example, you can search or browse for a contact and then view the detailed information for the contact in which you are interested.

(1) On the Home screen, tap Contacts. The contacts screen displays with the contacts listed in the view and sort format you selected when you set your Contacts preferences (refer to the task, "Setting Your Contacts Preferences," at the beginning of this chapter).

The title of the screen depends on what you have selected to view; if All Contacts appears, you are browsing all your contact information. If Contacts appears, you are browsing only some of your contact information based on the contact groups you have elected to view; you learn how to change the groups of contacts you are viewing shortly. (If the Groups screen appears, tap Done. You move back to the All Contacts or Contacts screen.)

You can find a contact to view by browsing (step 2), using the index (step 3), or searching (step 4). You can use combinations of these, too, such as first using the index to get to the right area and then browsing to find the contact in which you are interested.

2 Swipe up or down to scroll the screen to browse for contact information; swipe on the index to browse rapidly.

3 Tap the index to jump to contact information organized by the first letter of the selected format (last name or first name).

4 Use the Search tool to search for a specific contact; tap in the tool, type the name (last, first, company, nickname, etc.), and then tap the contact you want to view on the results list.

5 To view a contact's information, tap the contact you want to see.

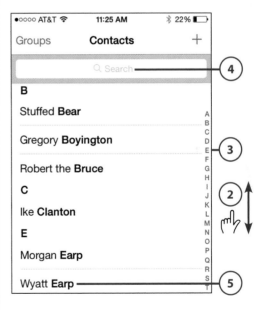

6 Swipe up and down the screen to view all the contact's information.

7 Tap the data or icons on the screen to perform actions, including the following:

- **Phone numbers**—Tap a phone number or the receiver icon to dial it.

- **Email addresses**—Tap an email address to create a new message.

- **URLs**—Tap a URL to move to the associated website.

- **FaceTime**—Tap the video camera icon to start a FaceTime call.

- **Text**—Tap the quote bubble icon and choose the phone number or email address to which you want to send a text message.

- **Share Contact**—Tap Share Contact. The Share menu appears. Tap how you want to share it, such as Mail or Messages. Then use the associated app to complete the task. For example, when you choose Mail, a new email message is created with the contact added as a vCard (virtual address card). Recipients of the email can add the contact information to their own contact applications by importing the vCard.

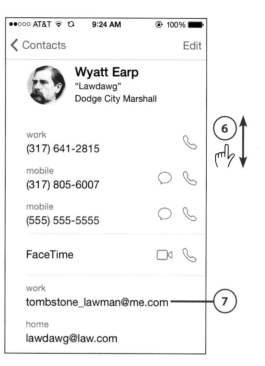

- **Favorites**—Tap Add to Favorites and choose the phone number or email address you want to designate as a favorite. You can use this in the associated app to do something faster. For example, if it's the Phone app, you can tap the Favorites tab to see your favorite contacts and quickly dial one by tapping it. You also can see your favorites on the App Switcher screen to use them even faster and easier. You can add multiple items (such as phone numbers) as favorites for one contact.

(8) To return to the Contacts list without performing an action, tap Contacts.

```
●●○○○ AT&T ⌁ ↻      9:24 AM        ⊕ 100% ▬

< Contacts                              Edit

              Wyatt Earp
              "Lawdawg"
              Dodge City Marshall

   work                                    ☏
   (317) 641-2815

   mobile                            ◯     ☏
   (317) 805-6007

   mobile                            ◯     ☏
   (555) 555-5555


   FaceTime                          ☐◁    ☏


   work
   tombstone_lawman@me.com

   home
   lawdawg@law.com
```

>>>Go Further

MAKE CONTACT

When working with your contacts, keep the following points in mind:

- **Last known contact**—The Contacts app remembers where you last were and takes you back there whenever you move into the app. For example, if you view a contact's details and then switch to a different app and then back to Contacts, you return to the screen you were last viewing. To move to the Contacts screen, tap Contacts in the upper-left corner of the screen.

- **Groups**—In a contact app on a computer, such as Contacts on a Mac, contacts can be organized into groups, which in turn can be stored in an online account, such as iCloud. When you sync, the groups of contacts move onto the iPhone along with the contacts. You can limit the contacts you browse or search; tap Groups on the Contacts screen.

  The Groups screen displays the accounts (such as iCloud) with which you are syncing contact information; under each account are the groups of contacts stored in that account. If a group has a check mark next to it, its contacts are displayed on the Contacts screen. To hide a group's contacts, tap it so that the check mark disappears. To hide or show all of a group's contacts, tap the All *account*, where *account* is the name of the account in which those contacts are stored. Tap Show All Contacts or Hide All Contacts to show or hide all the groups and contacts; then tap each group whose contacts you want to show on the Contacts screen.

  Tap Done to move back to the Contacts screen.

- **Speaking of contacts**—You can use Siri to speak commands to work with contacts, too. You can get information about contacts by asking for it, such as "What is William Wallace's work phone number?" If you want to see all of a contact's information, you can say "Show me William Wallace." When Siri displays contact information, you can tap it to take action, such as tapping a phone number to call it. (See Chapter 12, "Working with Siri," for more on using Siri.)

- **Managing Groups**—You can't create groups in the Contacts app, nor can you change the group with which contacts are associated. You have to use a contacts app on a computer to manage groups and then sync your iPhone (which happens automatically when you use an online account, such as iCloud) to see the changes you make to your contact groups.

Accessing Contacts from Other Apps

You can also access contact information while you are using a different app. For example, you can use a contact's email address when you create an email message. When you perform such actions, you use the Contacts app to find and select the information you want to use. The following example shows using contact information to send an email message, and using your contact information in other apps (such as Phone or Messages) is similar.

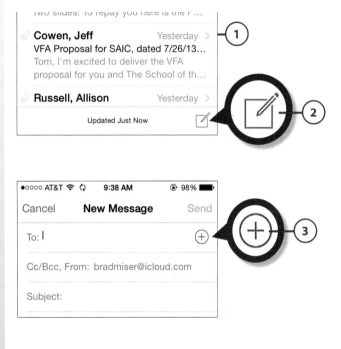

1. Open the app from which you want to access contact information (this example uses Mail).

2. Tap the New Message button.

3. In the To: field, tap the Add button (+).

4. Search, browse, or use the index to find the contact whose information you want to use.

5. Tap the contact whose information you want to use.

   If the contact has only one type of the relevant information (such as a single email address, if you started in the Mail app), you immediately move back to the app and the appropriate information is entered, and you can skip to step 7.

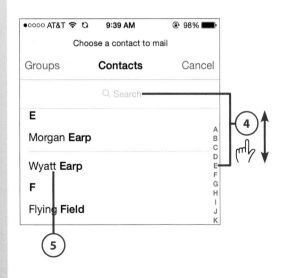

(6) If the contact has multiple entries of the type you are trying to use, tap the information you want to use—in this case, the email address. The information is copied to the app.

(7) Complete the task you are doing, such as sending an email message.

```
•oooo AT&T 🤔 🔃    9:39 AM        98% ▪▪▪
            Choose a contact to mail
< Contacts
┄┄┄┄┄┄┄┄┄┄┄┄┄┄┄┄┄┄┄┄┄┄┄┄┄┄┄┄┄┄┄
              Wyatt Earp
              "Lawdawg"
              Dodge City Marshall

work
tombstone_lawman@me.com ──────(6)

home
lawdawg@law.com

other
sorebruiser@gmail.com
```

```
••ooo AT&T 🤔 🔃    9:39 AM        98% ▪▪▪
Cancel      New Message      Send

To: Wyatt Earp, ⊕ ───────  The email
                           address from the
Cc/Bcc, From: bradmiser@icloud.com   Contacts app

Subject: ──────────────(7)

Sent from my iPhone
```

Managing Your Contacts on Your iPhone

When you sync contacts with an iCloud, Google, or other account (or with a contact application via iTunes on a computer), the changes go both ways. For example, when you change a contact on the iPhone, the synced contact manager application, such as Outlook, makes the changes for those contacts on your computer. Likewise, when you change contact information in a contact manager on your computer, those changes move to the iPhone. If you add a new contact in a contact manager, it moves to the iPhone, and vice versa. You can also change contacts manually.

Updating Contact Information

You can change any information for an existing contact, such as adding new email addresses or deleting out-dated information.

(1) View the contact's Info screen.

(2) Tap Edit. The Info screen moves into Edit mode, and you see Unlock buttons.

(3) Tap current information to change it; you can change a field's label by tapping the current label, or you can change the data for the field by tapping the information you want to change. Use the resulting tools, such as the phone number entry keypad, to make changes to the information. These tools work just like when you create a new contact (refer to "Creating Contacts Manually," earlier in this chapter).

(4) To add more fields, tap add in the related section, such as add phone in the phone number section; then, select a label for the new field and complete its information. This also works just like when you add a field to a contact you create manually.

(5) To remove a field from the contact, tap its Unlock button.

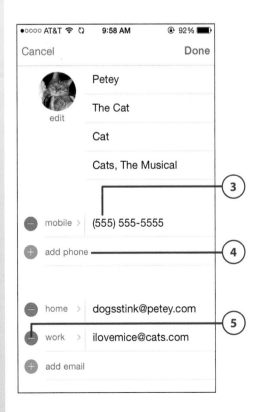

(6) Tap Delete. The information is removed from the contact.

(7) To change the contact's photo, tap the current photo, or the word *edit* under the current photo, and use the resulting menu and tools to select a new photo, take a new photo, delete the existing photo, or edit the existing one.

(8) When you finish making changes, tap Done. Your changes are saved, and you move out of Edit mode.

No Tones or Vibes?

If you leave the default tones or vibration patterns set for a contact, you won't see those fields when you view the contact. However, when you edit a contact, all the fields you need to add these to a contact become available.

●○○○○ AT&T 🛜 🔄   10:04 AM   @ 91% ▭▷

Cancel   Done ─(8)

Petey

The Cat

edit ──────────────────────────(7)

Cat

Cats, The Musical

⊖ mobile ›   (555) 555-5555

⊕ add phone

⊖ home ›   dogsstink@petey.com

›   ilovemice@cats.com   Delete ─(6)

Adding Information to an Existing Contact While Using Your iPhone

As you use your iPhone, you'll encounter information related to a contact but that isn't part of that contact's information. For example, a contact might send you an email from a different email address than the one you have stored for her. When this happens, you can easily add the new information to an existing contact. Just tap the information to select it (such as in an email address), and then tap Add to Contacts (or Add to Existing Contact, if you already have some contact info for that person) on the screen that holds the info you want to add. For example, to add an email address, tap the name or email address in the email message and then tap Add to Existing Contact. Then select the contact to which you want to add the new information.

Deleting Contacts

To get rid of contacts, you can delete them from the Contacts app.

1. Find and view the contact you want to delete.

2. Tap Edit.

3. Swipe to the bottom of the Info screen.

4. Tap Delete Contact.

5. Tap Delete Contact again to confirm the deletion. The app deletes the contact, and you return to the Contacts screen.

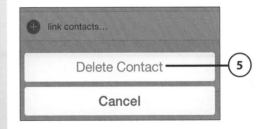

Tap to
configure
Phone and
FaceTime
settings

Tap to hear *and see* the
person with whom
you want to talk

Tap to make calls,
listen to voicemail,
and more

Communicating with the Phone and FaceTime Apps

Although it's also a lot of other great things, such as a music player, web browser, and email tool, there's a reason the word *phone* is in *iPhone*. It's a feature-rich cell phone that includes some amazing features, two of which are visual voicemail and FaceTime. Other useful features include a speakerphone, conference calling, and easy-to-use onscreen controls. The iPhone's phone functions are integrated with its other features. For example, when using the Maps application, you might find a location, such as a business, that you're interested in contacting. You can call that location just by tapping the phone number directly on the Maps screen. No need to fumble around switching to phone mode and dialing the number manually. The iPhone makes your mobile phone use quicker, easier, and smarter in so many ways, as you'll see in the pages that follow.

Getting Started

Using an iPhone as a phone is easy, and you'll get to take advantage of the wonderful features it offers. Some of the key concepts you'll learn about in this chapter include:

- **Phone App**—The iPhone can run many different kinds of apps that do all sorts of useful things. The iPhone's phone functionality is provided by the Phone app. You use this app whenever you want to make calls or answer calls.

- **Visual Voicemail**—The Phone app allows you to see information about your voicemails, such as the person who left each message, a time and date stamp, and the length of the message. In addition to more information, the Phone app provides a lot more control over your messages; for example, you can easily fast forward to specific parts of a message that you want to hear. (This is particularly helpful for capturing information, such as phone numbers.)

- **FaceTime**—This app enables you to have videoconferences with other people so that you can both see and hear them. Using FaceTime is intuitive so you won't find it any more difficult than making a phone call.

- **FaceTime Audio Only**—You can also make FaceTime calls using only audio; this is similar to making a phone call. One difference is that when you are using a Wi-Fi network to place a FaceTime call, there are no extra costs for the call, no matter if you are calling someone next-door or halfway around the world.

Setting Phone Preferences

Before jumping into making voice calls, take a few minutes to configure your iPhone's phone functions to work the way you want them to. You can set your phone's sounds, such as ringtones, and notifications so that you always know what is happening with phone activity. You can also configure some other less visible settings to further tweak how the phone works.

Setting Phone Sounds and Notifications

Of course, we all know that your ringtone is the most important phone setting, and you'll want to make sure your iPhone's ringtones are just right. Use the iPhone's Sounds settings to configure custom or standard ringtones and other phone-related sounds, including the new voicemail sound. These are explained in

Chapter 4, "Configuring an iPhone to Suit Your Preferences."

You can also set ringtones for specific contacts; you can have different ringtones for different people so you can know who is calling just by the ringtone (configuring contacts is explained in Chapter 7, "Managing Contacts").

You'll also want to configure notifications for the Phone app. These include alerts and the app's badge. Configuring notifications is also explained in Chapter 4.

Configuring Phone Settings

There are a number of settings you can use to configure the way the phone functions work.

1. On the Home screen, tap Settings.

2. Swipe up the screen.

3. Tap Phone. You move to the Phone screen. (Your number is shown at the top of the screen in case you ever forget it. And, yes, I have forgotten my own number.)

4. To see the images associated with contacts on the Favorites list, set the Contact Photos in Favorites switch to on (green). (You learn about your Favorites list a little later in this chapter.) When this is enabled, a small image showing the contact's photo appears next to each favorite on the list. If you set this to off (white), you see only names on the Favorites list.

●●○○○ AT&T 4G   6:29 AM   100%

Settings

▤ Reminders

☏ Phone

●●●●● AT&T   10:28 AM   64%

‹ Settings   **Phone**

My Number   +1 ( )

Contact Photos in Favorites

CALLS

Respond with Text

(5) To create a custom text reply that a caller sees if you choose to send the text rather than answer a call, tap Respond with Text. (More on this later in this chapter.) On the Respond with Text screen, you see the three default text responses that are available. If you just want to use the default messages such as, "I'll call you later," skip to step 8.

(6) To replace one of the default responses, tap it and type a custom reply. Custom replies are shown in a darker text, while the defaults are shown in the lighter text.

(7) To remove a custom reply, tap its delete button. It is replaced with a default reply.

(8) When you're done customizing replies, tap Phone.

(9) To forward your calls to another number, tap Call Forwarding; if you don't want to forward calls, skip to step 14.

(10) Turn Call Forwarding on (green). The Forwarding To screen appears.

Contact Photos in Favorites	

CALLS

Respond with Text ————— **(5)**

●●●●○ AT&T 📶 11:09 AM 🔋 63% 🔋

❮ Phone **Respond with Text** ————— **(8)**

CAN'T TALK RIGHT NOW...

I'll call you later.

I'm on my way. ————— **(6)**

On another call, will call you back ASAP ⊗ ————— **(7)**

These quick responses will be available when you respond to an incoming call with a text. Change them to say anything you like.

CALLS

Respond with Text ❯

Call Forwarding ————— **(9)**

●●●●○ AT&T 📶 11:10 AM 🔋 62% 🔋

❮ Phone **Call Forwarding**

Call Forwarding ⚪ ————— **(10)**

Provider Differences

The settings available to you in the CALLS section depend on the cellular provider you are using. These steps show the options for AT&T in the United States; other providers (such as Verizon or Sprint in the United States or Rogers in Canada) might offer more, fewer, or different options (for example, no Call Waiting). You can configure the specific options available to you using steps similar to these.

11. Enter the number to which you want to forward calls. Include the number's area code, and country code, if applicable (enter it just as if you are dialing it though in some cases, the country code is added automatically). You can use the special symbols located in the lower-left corner of the keypad to enter pauses and such.

12. Tap Back. The number is saved, and you return to the Call Forwarding screen. The number to which your iPhone forwards calls shows next to the Forward to text. The forward icon appears at the top of the screen.

13. Tap Phone.

14. To disable call waiting, tap Call Waiting; the Call Waiting screen appears. To leave Call Waiting active, skip to step 17.

15. To disable call waiting, turn Call Waiting off (white). When call waiting is turned off and you receive a second call while you're already on another call, the second call immediately goes to voicemail.

16. Tap Phone.

17. To hide your information when you make calls, tap Show My Caller ID; to leave it showing, skip to step 20.

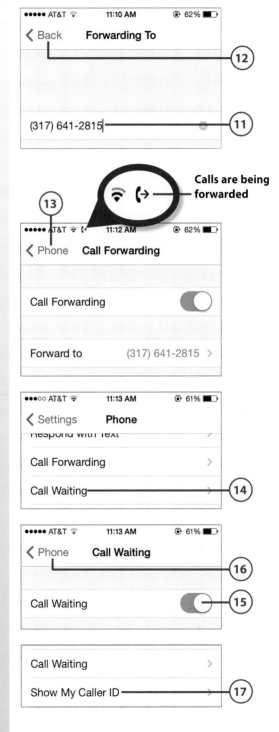

Calls are being forwarded

(18) Turn Show My Caller ID off (white) and your information won't be transmitted when you make a call.

(19) Tap Phone.

(20) Enable the Dial Assist feature if you want the correct country code to be added to numbers in your country when dialing those numbers from outside your country or if you want the correct area codes to be added when you dial a local number. For example, if you live in the United States and don't want the correct prefixes added to U.S. phone numbers when you dial them from outside the United States, turn Dial Assist off (white). You now have to add any prefixes manually when dialing a U.S. number from outside the United States. (This step is specific to the iPhone in the United States with service provided by AT&T. If you have a different provider, this function might perform a different action.)

(21) Tap Settings.

(19)

•••○○ AT&T 🔋	11:41 AM	⊕ 60% 🔋

‹ Phone **Show My Caller ID**

Show My Caller ID ⬤ **(18)**

(21)

‹ Settings **Phone**

Call Waiting ›

Show My Caller ID ›

Blocked ›

TTY ◯

Change Voicemail Password

Dial Assist ⬤ **(20)**

Dial assist automatically determines the correct international or local prefix when dialing.

Blocking Calls

To block calls, tap Blocked. Tap Add New and choose the contact whose calls (messages and FaceTime requests, too) you want to block. Tap Add New again to block more contacts; when you've blocked all that you want to block, tap Phone. The step-by-step instructions to block calls are in Chapter 17, "Maintaining and Protecting Your iPhone and Solving Problems."

>>>*Go Further*

OTHER PHONE SETTINGS

Here are some other phone settings you should be aware of:

- TTY devices enable hearing-impaired people to use a telephone. To use TTY with your iPhone, you need an adapter to connect your iPhone to a TTY device. You also need to turn on TTY support by turning TTY on (green).

- The Change Voicemail Password command enables you to reset your voicemail password; this is covered at the end of this chapter.

- Your iPhone uses a Subscriber Identity Module (SIM) card to store certain data about your phone; the SIM PIN setting (near the bottom of the Phone screen) enables you to associate a personal ID number (PIN) with the SIM card in an iPhone. You can remove the SIM card from your iPhone and install it in other phones that support these cards to use your account with a different phone. If you set a PIN, that PIN is required to use the card in a different phone.

- The Provider Services option (where *Provider* is the name of your cell phone provider, such as AT&T and Sprint) located at the bottom of the Phone screen enables you to get information about your account. When you send a request for information, you receive the answer via a text message. The options available to you here depend on the provider you use.

Making Voice Calls

There are a number of ways to make calls with your iPhone; after a call is in progress, you can manage it in the same way no matter how you started it.

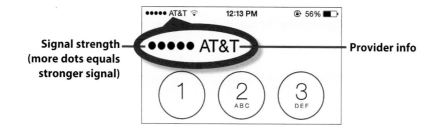

Signal strength (more dots equals stronger signal) — Provider info

You can tell you are able to make a call or receive calls when you see your provider's information at the top of the screen along with strength of the signal your phone is receiving. As long as you see at least one dot, you should be good to go. More dots are better because they mean you have a stronger signal, meaning the call quality will be better.

With a reasonably strong signal, you are ready to make calls.

Which Network?

When you leave the coverage area for your provider and move into an area that is covered by another provider that supports roaming, your iPhone automatically connects to the other provider's network. When you are roaming, you see a different provider near the signal strength indicator at the top of the screen. For example, if AT&T is your provider and you travel to Toronto, Canada, the provider might become Rogers instead of AT&T, which indicates you are roaming. (In some cases, your provider might send you a text message explaining the change in networks, including information about roaming charges.) Although the connection is automatic, you need to be very aware of roaming charges, which can be significant depending on where you use your iPhone and what your default network is. Before you travel outside of your default network's coverage, check with your provider to determine the roaming rates that apply to where you are going. Also, see if there is a discounted roaming plan for that location. If you don't do this before you leave, you might get a nasty surprise when the bill arrives showing substantial roaming charges.

When you are roaming, use Wi-Fi instead of the cellular network whenever possible. For example, instead of making a cellular voice call, use an audio-only FaceTime call instead, because you can do that for no additional charge.

Dialing with the Keypad

The most obvious way to make a call is to dial the number.

1. On the Home screen, tap Phone. The Phone app opens.

2. If you don't see the keypad, tap Keypad.

3. Tap numbers on the keypad to dial the number you want to call. If you dial a number associated with one or more contacts, you see the contact's name and the type of number you've dialed just under the number. (If you make a mistake in the number you are dialing, tap the Delete button located to the right of the number you are dialing at the top of the screen to delete the most recent digit you entered.)

4. Tap the receiver button. The app dials the number, and the Call screen appears.

5. Use the Call screen to manage the call; see "Managing In-Process Voice Calls" later in this chapter for the details.

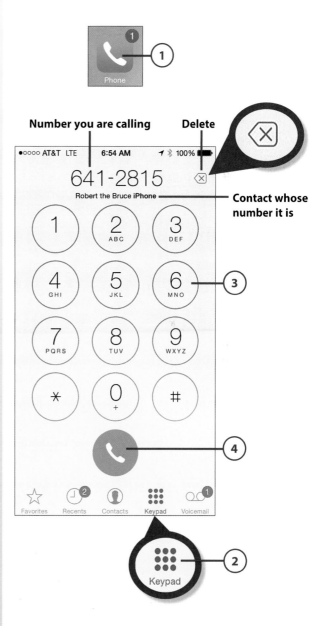

Number you are calling   **Delete**

Contact whose number it is

Dialing with Contacts

As you saw in Chapter 7, the Contacts app is a complete contact manager so you can store various kinds of phone numbers for people and organizations. To make a call using a contact, follow these steps.

(1) On the Home screen, tap Phone.

(2) Tap Contacts.

(3) Browse the list, search it, or use the index to find the contact you want to call. (Refer to Chapter 7 for information about using the Contacts app.)

(4) Tap the contact you want to call.

(5) Tap the number you want to dial. The app dials the number, and the Call screen appears.

(6) Use the Call screen to manage the call; see "Managing In-Process Voice Calls" later in this chapter for the details.

One and Only

If the contact has only one method of contact, such as one phone number and no email address, the app dials the contact immediately when you select him in step 4. In other words, if the app has only one option, it uses that option automatically.

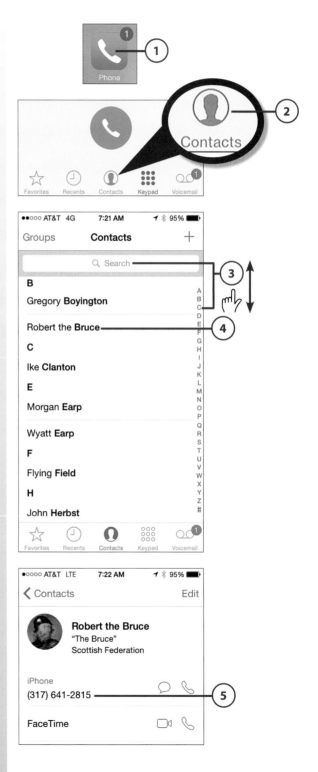

Dialing with Favorites

You can save contacts and phone numbers as favorites to make dialing them even simpler. (You learn how to save favorites in various locations later in this chapter. You learn how to make a contact into a favorite in Chapter 7.)

(1) On the Home screen, tap Phone.

(2) Tap Favorites.

(3) Browse the list until you see the favorite you want to call. Along the right side of the screen, you see the type of favorite, such as a phone number (identified by the label in the Contacts app, for example, iPhone or mobile) or FaceTime.

(4) Tap the favorite you want to call; to place a voice call, tap a phone number (if you tap a FaceTime contact, a FaceTime call is placed instead). The app dials the number, and the Call screen appears.

(5) Use the Call screen to manage the call; see "Managing In-Process Voice Calls" later in this chapter for the details.

Type of favorite

Nobody's Perfect

If your iPhone can't complete the call for some reason, such as not having a strong enough signal, the Call Failed screen appears. Tap Call Back to try again or tap Done to give up. When you tap Done, you return to the screen from which you came.

Dialing with Recents

As you make, receive, or miss calls, your iPhone keeps tracks of all the numbers for you on the Recents list. You can use the Recents list to make calls.

1. On the Home screen, tap Phone.

2. Tap Recents.

3. Tap All to see all calls.

4. Tap Missed to see only calls you missed.

5. If necessary, browse the list of calls.

6. To call the number associated with a recent call, tap the title of the call, such as a person's name, or the number if no contact is associated with it. The app dials the number, and the Call screen appears. Skip to step 10.

7. To get more information about a recent call, tap its Info button. The Info screen appears.

Info on the Recents Screen

If you have a contact on your iPhone associated with a phone number, you see the person's name and the label for the number (such as mobile). If you don't have a contact for a number, you see the number itself. If a contact or number has more than one call associated with it, you see the number of recent calls in parentheses next to the name or number. If you initiated a call, you see the phone icon next to the contact's name and label.

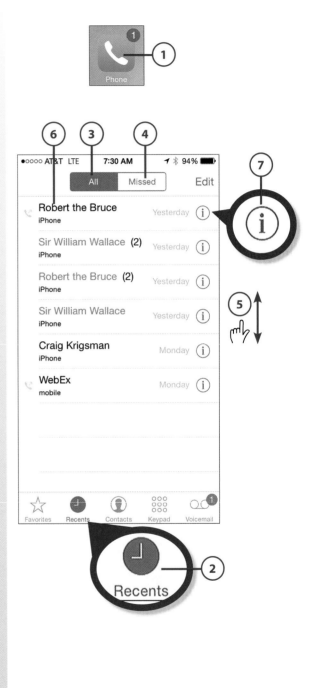

(8) Read the information about the call. For example, if the call is related to someone in your Contacts list, you see detailed information for that contact. The numbers associated with the call are highlighted in red if they were missed or in blue if the call went through. If there are multiple recent calls, you see information for each call, such as its status (Canceled Call or Outgoing Call, for example) and time.

(9) Tap a number on the Info screen. The app dials the number, and the Call screen appears.

(10) Use the Call screen to manage the call; see "Managing In-Process Voice Calls" later in this chapter for the details.

Going Back

To return to the Recents screen without making a call, tap Recents in the upper-left corner of the screen.

Seeing Red

When you see a contact's name or number in red, it means the call was missed or was not answered. If you don't answer a call to you, it is counted as a missed call, even if a message is left.

●○○○○ AT&T LTE   7:33 AM   ✈ ✳ 93% ▮▮▯

‹ Recents   **Info**   Edit

Robert the Bruce
"The Bruce"
Scottish Federation

(8)

Yesterday
12:22 PM   **Canceled Call**

iPhone ★
(317) 641-2815   💬 📞

(9)

FaceTime   📹 📞

work
robert_the_bruce_1@me.com

home ★
rob_bruce@me.com   💬 ✉

work
http://www.robertbruce_1.com

☆ Favorites   Recents   Contacts   Keypad   Voicemail ①

Dialing from the App Switcher

New! Using the App Switcher, you can quickly call someone you have recently communicated with, or who is on your Favorites list. The steps are as follows:

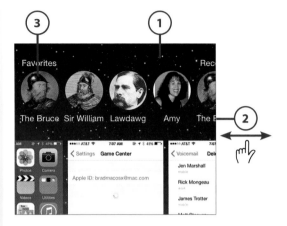

(1) Press the Touch ID/Home button twice to open the App Switcher. At the top of the screen, you see lists of your Favorites and Recents.

(2) Swipe to the left or right on the icons until you see the person you want to call.

(3) Tap the person you want to call. The ways you are able to contact the person appear next to the person's icon at the top of the screen. Phone numbers are represented by the receiver icon and either have the number's label, such as iPhone, or the actual number under each receiver icon.

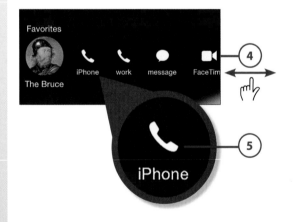

(4) Swipe to the left or right to see all of the ways you can contact the person, including phone numbers, message, and FaceTime.

(5) Tap the number you want to call. The app dials the number you tapped.

(6) Use the Call screen to manage the call; see "Managing In-Process Voice Calls" later in this chapter for the details.

Managing In-Process Voice Calls

When you place a call, there are several ways to manage it. The most obvious is to place your iPhone next to your ear and use your iPhone like any other phone you've ever used. As you place your iPhone next to your ear, the controls on its screen become disabled so you don't accidentally tap onscreen buttons with the side of your face or your ear. When you take your iPhone away from your ear, the Call screen appears again and the Phone app's controls become active again.

When you are on a call, press the Volume buttons on the left side of the iPhone to increase or decrease its volume. Some of the other things you can do while on a call might not be so obvious, as you'll learn in the next few tasks.

Following are some of the buttons on the Call screen that you can use to manage an active call:

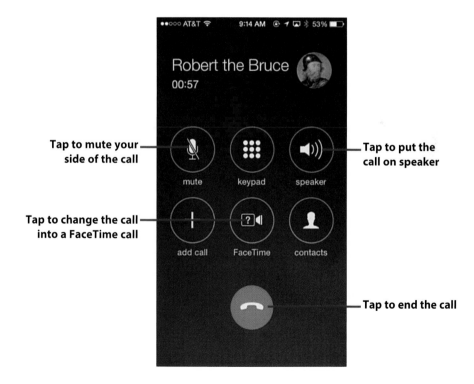

Tap to mute your side of the call

Tap to change the call into a FaceTime call

Tap to put the call on speaker

Tap to end the call

- To mute your side of the call, tap mute. You can hear the person on the other side of the call, but he can't hear anything on your side.

- Tap speaker to use the iPhone's speakers to hear the call. You can speak with the phone held away from your face, too.

- Tap FaceTime to convert the voice call into a FaceTime call (more on FaceTime later in this chapter).

- When you're done with the call, tap the receiver button.

Contact Photos on the Call Screen

If someone in your contacts calls you, or you call her, the photo associated with the contact appears on the screen. Depending on how the image was captured, it either appears as a small icon at the top of the screen next to the contact's name or fills the entire screen as the background wallpaper.

Entering Numbers During a Call

You often need to enter numbers during a call, such as to log in to a voicemail system, access an account, or enter a meeting code for an online meeting.

(1) Place a call using any of the methods you've learned so far.

(2) Tap keypad.

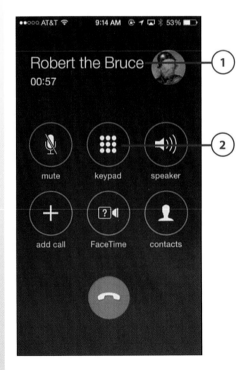

3 Tap the numbers you want to enter.

4 When you're done, tap Hide. You return to the Call screen.

Making Conference Calls

Your iPhone makes it easy to talk to multiple people at the same time. You can have two separate calls going on at any point in time. You can even create conference calls by merging them together. For example, you might want to have a conversation with multiple family members at the same time, or you might receive a call from one family member while you are already talking to another one; you can quickly join those calls together. Not all cell providers support two on-going calls or conference calling, though. If yours doesn't, you won't be able to perform the steps in this section.

1 Place a call using any of the methods you've learned so far.

2 Tap add call.

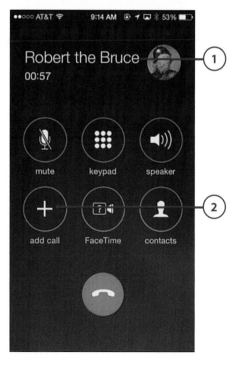

3 Tap the button you want to use to place the next call. Tap Favorites to call a favorite, tap Recents to use the Recents list, tap Contacts to place the call via contacts, or tap Keypad to dial the number. These work just as they do when you start a new call.

4 Place the call using the option you selected in step 3. Doing so places the first call on hold and moves you back to the Call screen while the Phone app makes the second call. The first call's information appears at the top of the screen, including the word hold so you know the call is on hold. The app displays the second call just below that, and it is currently the active call.

5 Talk to the second person you called; the first remains on hold.

6 To switch to the first call, tap it on the list or tap swap. This places the second call on hold and moves it to the top of the call list, while the first call becomes active again.

Similar but Different

If you tap contacts instead of add call, you move directly into the Contacts screen. This might save you one screen tap if the person you want to add to the call is on your contacts list.

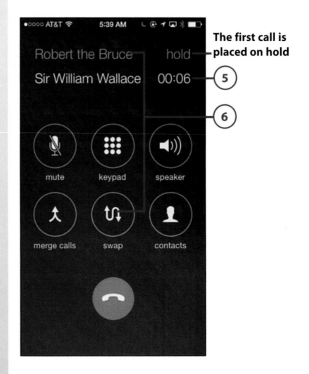

The first call is placed on hold

(7) To join the calls so all parties can hear you and each other, tap merge calls. The Phone app combines the two calls, and you see a single entry at the top of the screen to reflect this.

(8) To add another call, repeat steps 2–7. Each time you merge calls, the second line becomes free so you can add more calls.

(9) To manage a conference call, tap the Info button at the top of the screen.

Merging Calls

As you merge calls, your iPhone attempts to display the names of the callers at the top of the Call screen. As the text increases, your iPhone scrolls it so you can read it. Eventually, the iPhone replaces the names with the word Conference.

Number of Callers

Your provider and the specific technology of the network you use can limit the number of callers you place in a conference call. When you reach the limit, the add call button is disabled.

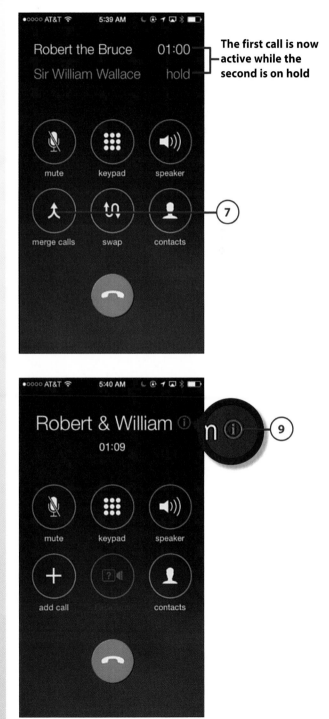

The first call is now active while the second is on hold

10 To speak with one of the callers privately, tap Private. Doing so places the conference call on hold and returns you to the Call screen showing information about the active call. You can merge the calls again by tapping merge calls.

11 To remove a caller from the call, tap End. The app disconnects that caller from the conference call. You return to the Call screen and see information about the active call.

12 To move back to the Call screen, tap Back. You move to the Call screen and can continue working with the call, such as adding more people to it.

13 To end the call for all callers, tap the receiver button.

It's Not All Good

When you have multiple calls combined into one, depending on your provider, the minutes for each call can continue to count individually. If you've joined three people into one call, each minute of the call may count as three minutes against your calling plan. Before you use this feature, check with your provider to determine what policies govern conference calling for your account.

Using Another App During a Voice Call

If your provider's technology supports it, you can use your iPhone for other tasks while you are on a call. When you are on a call, press the Touch ID/Home button once to move to the Home screen and then tap a different app (placing the call in speaker mode is the most convenient for this). Or, you can press the Touch ID/ Home button twice and use the App Switcher to move into a different app. The call remains active and you see the active call information in a green bar at the top of the screen. You can perform other tasks, such as looking up information and sending emails. You can continue to talk to the other person just like when the Call screen is showing. To return to the call, tap the green bar.

Tap to return to the call ⎯⎯⎯

A call is active, and you can use other apps while still talking

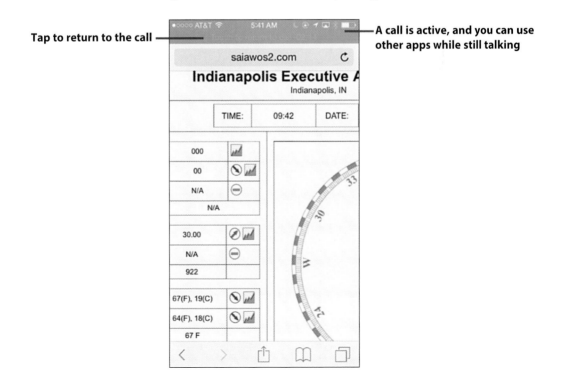

Receiving Voice Calls

Receiving calls on your iPhone enables you to access the same great tools you can use when you make calls, plus a few more for good measure.

Answering Calls

When your iPhone rings, it's time to answer the call—or not. If you configured the ringer to ring, you hear your default ringtone or the one associated with the caller's contact information when a call comes in. If vibrate is turned on, your iPhone vibrates whether the ringer is on or not. And if those two ways aren't enough, a message appears on iPhone's screen to show you information about the incoming call. If the number is in your Contacts app, you see the contact with which the number is associated, the label for the number, and the contact's image if there is one. If the number isn't in your contacts, you see the number only.

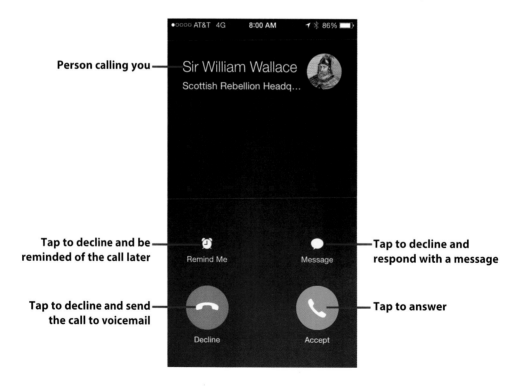

Person calling you

Tap to decline and be reminded of the call later

Tap to decline and send the call to voicemail

Tap to decline and respond with a message

Tap to answer

Wallpaper

If the photo associated with a contact was taken with your iPhone or came from a high-resolution figure, you see the contact's image at full screen when the call comes in, otherwise, you see a small icon at the top of the screen.

Calls on Other Devices

By default, when you receive a call on your iPhone, it also comes to any iOS 8 devices or Macs running Yosemite that are on the same Wi-Fi network, and you can take the call on those devices. To disable this, see "Configuring FaceTime Settings."

If your iPhone is locked when a call comes in, swipe the slider to the right to answer it. You can also use the Remind Me and Message icons, which work just like they do when a call comes in when the iPhone isn't locked.

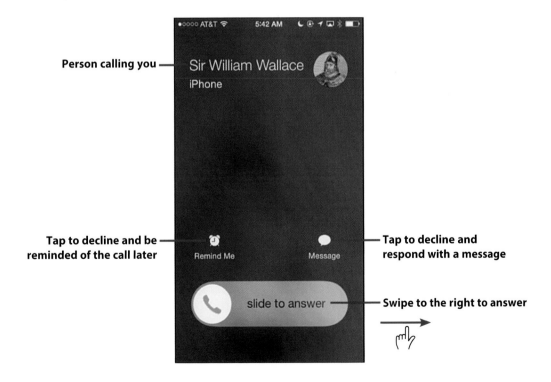

When you receive a call, you have the following options:

- **Answer**—Tap Accept (if the iPhone is unlocked) or swipe the slider to the right (if the iPhone is locked) to take the call (you don't have to unlock the phone to answer a call). You move to the Call screen and can work with the call just like calls you place. For example, you can add a call, merge calls, place the call on hold or end the call.

- **Decline**—If you tap Decline (when the iPhone is unlocked), the Phone app immediately routes the call to voicemail. You can also decline a call by quickly pressing the Sleep/Wake button twice.

- **Silence the ringer**—To silence the ringer without sending the call directly to voicemail, press the Sleep/Wake button once or press either volume button. The call continues to come in, and you can answer it even though you shut off the ringer.

- **Respond with a message**—Tap Message to send the call to voicemail and send a message back in response. You can tap one of the default messages, or you can tap Custom to create a unique message (earlier in the chapter, you learned how to configure these messages). Of course, the device the caller is using to make the call must be capable of receiving messages for this to be useful.

- **Decline the call but be reminded later**—Tap Remind Me and the call is sent to voicemail. Tap In 1 hour, When I leave, or When I get home to set the timeframe in which you want to be reminded. A reminder is created in the Reminders app to call back the person who called you, and it is set to alert you at the time you select.

Silencio!

To mute your iPhone's ringer, slide the Mute switch located above the Volume switch toward the back so the orange line appears. The Mute icon (a bell with a slash through it) appears on the screen to let you know you turned off the ringer. To turn it back on again, slide the switch forward. The bell icon appears on the screen to show you the ringer is active again. To set the ringer's volume, use the Volume controls (assuming that setting is enabled) when you aren't on a call and aren't listening to an app, such as the Music app.

Answering Calls During a Call

As you saw earlier, your iPhone can manage multiple calls at the same time. If you are on a call and another call comes in, you have a number of ways to respond.

- **Decline incoming call**—Tap Send to Voicemail to send the incoming call directly to voicemail.

- **Place the first call on hold and answer the incoming call**—Tap Hold & Accept to place the current call on hold and answer the incoming one. After you do this, you can manage the two calls just as when you call two numbers from your iPhone. For example, you can place the second call on hold and move back to the first one, merge the calls, and add more calls.

- **End the first call and answer the incoming call**—Tap End & Accept to terminate the active call and answer the incoming call.

Auto-Mute

If you are listening to music or video when a call comes in, the app providing the audio, such as the Music app, automatically pauses. When the call ends, that app picks up right where it left off.

Managing Voice Calls

You've already learned most of what you need to know to use your iPhone's cell phone functions. In the following sections, you learn the rest.

Clearing Recent Calls

Previously in this chapter, you learned about the Recents list that tracks call activity on your iPhone. As you read, this list shows both completed and missed calls; you can view all calls by tapping the All tab or only missed calls by tapping Missed. On either tab, missed calls are always in red, and you see the number of missed calls in the badge on the Recents tab since you last looked at the list. You also see how you can get more detail about a call, whether it was missed or made.

Over time, you'll build a large Recents list, which you can easily clear.

1. Tap Phone.
2. Tap Recents.
3. Tap Edit.
4. To clear the entire list, tap Clear; to delete a specific recent call, skip to step 6.
5. Tap Clear All Recents. The Recents list is reset.

Delete Faster

On the Recents screen, you can delete an individual recent item by swiping to the left on it (starting to the left of the i button) and tapping Delete.

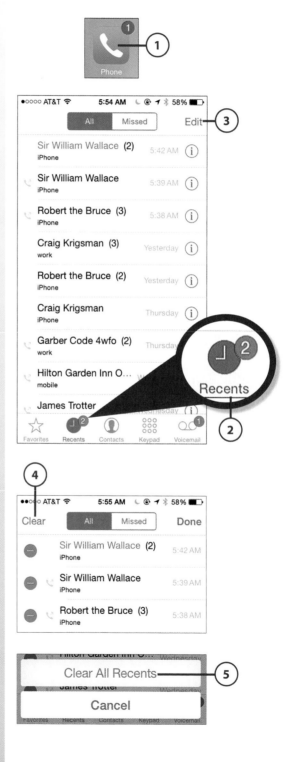

6 Tap a recent item's unlock button.

7 Tap Delete. The recent item is deleted.

8 When you are done managing your recent calls, tap Done.

Adding Calling Information to Favorites

Earlier you learned how simple it is to place calls to someone on your Favorites list. There are a number of ways to add people to this list, including adding someone on your Recents list.

1 Move to the Recents list.

2 Tap the Info button for the person you want to add to your Favorites list. The Info screen appears. If the number is associated with a contact, you see that contact's information.

3 Swipe up to move to the bottom of the screen.

4 Tap Add to Favorites. If the person has multiple numbers associated with his contact information, you see each available number. Numbers that are already set as favorites are marked with a blue star. If the contact has email addresses, you can set them as favorites for FaceTime conversations (video or audio only).

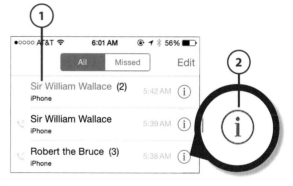

(5) Tap the number or email address you want to add as a favorite.

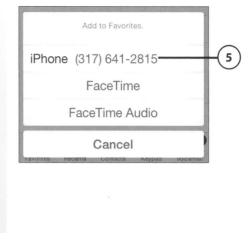

(6) Repeat steps 4 and 5 if you want to add the contact's other numbers to the Favorites list. Any numbers or email addresses that are set as favorites are highlighted in blue and marked with a blue star. If all the numbers and email addresses are assigned as favorites, the Add to Favorites button doesn't appear on the contact's screen.

Make Contact First

To make someone a favorite, he needs to be a contact in the Contacts app. Refer to Chapter 7 to learn how to make someone who has called you into a contact.

Using the iPhones Headset for Calls

Your iPhone includes an EarPods headset with a microphone on one of its cords. The mic includes a button in the center of the switch on the right side of the EarPod's cable that you can use to do the following:

- **Answer**—Press the mic button once to answer a call.

- **End a call**—Press the mic button while you are on a call to end it.

- **Decline a call**—Press and hold the mic button for about two seconds. Two beeps sound when you release the button to let you know that your iPhone sent the call to voicemail.

- **Put a current call on hold and switch to an incoming call**—Press the mic button once and then press again.

- **End a current call on hold and switch to an incoming call**—Press the mic button once and hold for about two seconds. Release the button and you hear two beeps to let you know you ended the first call. The incoming call is ready for you.

- **Activate Siri**—Press and hold the mic button until you hear the Siri chime. This is useful when you want to make a call to someone without looking at or touching your phone.

Oh, That Ringing in My Ears

When you have EarPods plugged into your iPhone and you receive a call, the ring-tone plays on both the iPhone's speaker (unless the ringer is muted, of course) and through the EarPods.

Using Visual Voicemail

Visual voicemail just might be the best of your iPhone's many great features. No more wading through long, uninteresting voicemails to get to one in which you are interested. You simply jump to the message you want to hear. And because voicemails are stored on your iPhone, you don't need to log in to hear them. If that isn't enough for you, you can also jump to any point within a voicemail to hear just that part, such as to repeat a phone number that you want to write down.

Recording a Greeting

The first time you access voicemail, you are prompted to record a voicemail greeting. Follow the onscreen instructions to do so.

You can also record a new greeting at any time.

(1) Move to the Phone screen and tap Voicemail.

(2) Tap Greeting.

(3) To use a default greeting that provides only the iPhone's phone number, tap Default and skip to step 10.

(4) To record a custom greeting, tap Custom. If you have previously used a custom greeting, it is loaded into the editor. You can replace it by continuing with these steps.

(5) Tap Record. Recording begins.

For the First Time

Some providers require that you dial into your voicemail number the first time you use it. If you tap the Voicemail button and the phone starts to dial instead of you seeing the Visual Voicemail controls as shown in these figures, this is your situation. You call the provider's voicemail system, and you're prompted to set up your voicemail. When you've completed that process, you can use these steps to record your greeting.

6 Speak your greeting. As you record your message, the red area of the timeline indicates (relatively) how long your message is. It's good practice to keep your greeting relatively short as a courtesy to people who call you. Something like, "Hi, you've reached Brad, but I can't take your call right now. Please leave a message." works well. Make sure you include your name in the greeting so the caller knows they've reached the right phone.

7 When you're done recording, tap Stop.

8 Tap Play to hear your greeting.

9 If you aren't satisfied, drag the Playhead to the beginning and repeat steps 5–8 to record a new message.

10 When you are happy with your greeting, tap Save. The Phone app saves the greeting as the active greeting and returns you to the Voicemail screen.

Adding to a Custom Message

To add onto an existing greeting, drag the playhead to where you want to start recording and tap Record. Tap Stop when you're done.

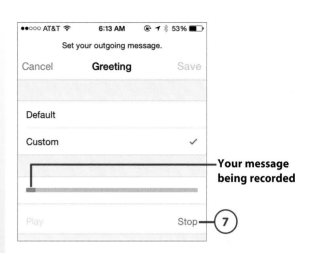

Your message being recorded

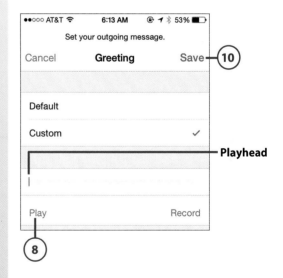

Playhead

No Visual Voicemail?

If your voicemail password isn't stored on your iPhone when you tap Voicemail, your phone dials into your voicemail instead of moving to the Voicemail screen. If that happens, something has happened to your voicemail password and you need to reset it. Follow your provider's instructions to reset the password. When you have the new password, open the Phone Settings screen, tap Change Voicemail Password, enter the reset password, create a new password, and re-enter your new password. (You need to tap Done after each time you enter a password.)

Change Greeting

To switch between the default and the current custom greeting, move to the Greeting screen, tap the greeting you want to use (which is marked with a check mark), and tap Save. When you choose Custom, you use the custom greeting you most recently saved.

Listening to and Managing Voicemails

Unless you turned off the voicemail sound, you hear the sound you selected each time a caller leaves a voicemail for you. The number in the badge on the Phone icon and on the Voicemail button on the Phone screen increases by 1 (unless you've disabled the badge). (Note that the badge number on the Phone icon includes both voicemails left for you and missed calls while the badge number on the Voicemail button indicates only the number of voicemails left for you.) A new voicemail is one to which you haven't listened.

If you receive a voicemail while your iPhone is locked, you see a message on the screen alerting you that your iPhone received a voicemail (unless you have dis-abled these notifications from appearing on the Lock screen). (It also indicates a missed call, which is always the case when a call ends up in voicemail.) Swipe to the right on the notification to jump to the Voicemail screen so that you can work with your messages.

Missing Password

If something happens to the password stored on your iPhone for your voicemail, such as if you restore the iPhone, you are prompted to enter your password before you can access your voicemail. Do so at the prompt and tap OK. The iPhone signs you in to voicemail, and you won't have to enter your password again (unless something happens to it again of course).

And in yet another scenario, if you are using your iPhone when a message is left, you see a notification (either a banner or an alert unless you have turned off notifications for the Phone app) that enables you to ignore the new message or to listen to it.

Contacts or Numbers?

Like phone calls, if a contact is associated with a number from which you've received a voicemail, you see the contact's name associated with the voicemail message. If no contact exists for the number, you see the number only.

Finding and Listening to Voicemails

Working with voicemails is simple and quick.

1. Move into the Phone app and tap Voicemail (if you tapped a new voicemail banner or the Listen button on an alert, you jump directly to the Voicemail screen).

2. Swipe up and down the screen to browse the list of voicemails. Voicemails you haven't listened to are marked with a blue circle.

3. To listen to a voicemail, tap it. You see the timeline bar and controls and the message plays.

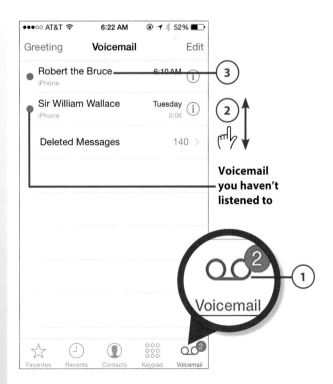

Voicemail you haven't listened to

④ To pause a message, tap its Pause button.

⑤ To hear the message on your iPhone's speaker, tap Speaker.

⑥ To move to a specific point in a message, drag the Playhead to the point at which you want to listen.

⑦ Tap the Play button.

⑧ To call back the person who left the message, tap Call Back.

⑨ To delete the message, tap Delete.

⑩ To get more information about a message, tap its Info button. The Info screen appears. If the person who left the message is on your contacts list, you see her contact information. The number associated with the message is highlighted in blue.

⑪ Swipe up or down the screen to review the caller's information.

⑫ Tap Voicemail.

Moving Ahead or Behind

You can also drag the Playhead while a message is playing to rewind or fast-forward it. This is also helpful when you want to listen to specific information without hearing the whole message again.

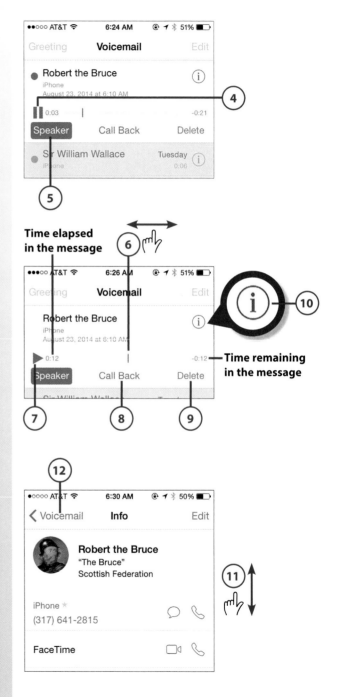

Time elapsed in the message

Time remaining in the message

13 To listen to a message you have listened to before (one that doesn't have a blue dot), tap the message and it expands so you see the playback controls; tap the Play button. It plays.

Deleting Messages

To delete a voicemail message that isn't the active message, tap it so it becomes the active message and then tap Delete. Or swipe to the left on the message you want to delete and tap Delete.

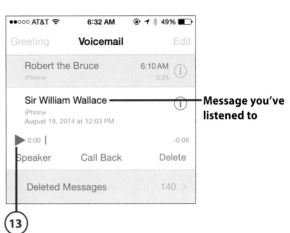

Message you've listened to

Listening to and Managing Deleted Voicemails

When you delete messages, they are moved to the Deleted Message folder. You can work with deleted messages as follows.

1 Move to the Voicemail screen.

2 If necessary, swipe up the screen until you see the Deleted Messages option.

3 Tap Deleted Messages.

4 Swipe up or down the screen to browse all the deleted messages.

5 Tap a message to listen to it.

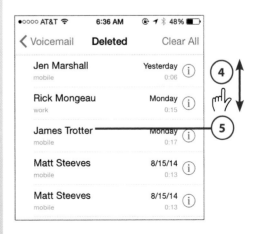

What's Missed?

In case you're wondering, your iPhone considers any call you didn't answer as a missed call. So if someone calls and leaves a message, that call is included in the counts of both missed calls and new voicemails. If the caller leaves a message, you see an alert informing you that you have a new voicemail and showing whom it is from (if available). If you don't answer and the caller doesn't leave a message, it's counted only as a missed call and you see an alert showing a missed call along with the caller's identification (if available).

(6) Tap the Play button. You can use the other playback tools just like you can with undeleted messages.

(7) Tap Undelete to restore the deleted message. The iPhone restores the message to the Voicemail screen.

(8) To remove all deleted messages permanently, tap Clear All. (If this is disabled, close the open message by tapping it.)

(9) Tap Clear All at the prompt. The deleted messages are erased and you return to the Deleted screen.

(10) To return to the Voicemail screen, tap Voicemail.

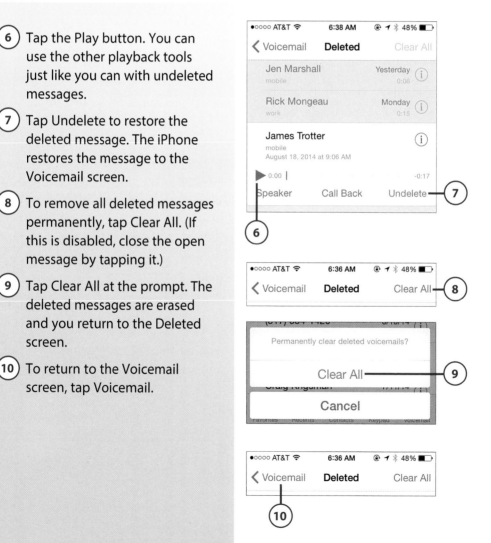

Lost/Forgot Your Password?

If you have to restore your iPhone or it loses your voicemail password for some other reason and you can't remember it, you need to have the password reset to access your voicemail on the iPhone. For most cell phone providers, this involves calling the customer support number and accessing an automated system that sends a new password to you via a text message. For AT&T, which is one of the iPhone provider's in the United States, call 611 on your iPhone and follow the prompts to reset your password (which you receive via a text). No matter which provider you use, it's a good idea to know how to reset your voicemail password because it is likely you will need to do so at some point.

Communicating with FaceTime

FaceTime enables you to see, as well as hear, people with whom you want to communicate. This feature exemplifies what's great about the iPhone; it takes complex technology and makes it simple. FaceTime works great, but there are two conditions that have to be true for you and the people you want some FaceTime with. To be able to see each other, both sides have to use a device that has the required cameras (this includes iPhone 4s and newer, iPod touches third generation and newer, iPad 2s and newer, and Macs running Snow Leopard and newer), and have FaceTime enabled (via the settings on an iOS device as you saw earlier or via the FaceTime application on a Mac). Also, each device has to be able to communicate over a network; an iPhone or iPad can use a cellular data network (if that setting is enabled) or a Wi-Fi network. When these conditions are true, making and receiving FaceTime calls are simple tasks.

In addition to making video FaceTime calls, you can also make audio-only FaceTime calls. These work similarly to making a voice call except the minutes don't count against your voice plan when you use a Wi-Fi network (if you are making the call over the cellular network, the data does count against your data plan so be careful about this).

Assuming you are in a place where you don't have to pay for the data you use, such as when you use a Wi-Fi network, you don't have to pay for a FaceTime call (video or audio-only) either.

FaceTime Equals Free (When You Use the Internet)

FaceTime calls—whether video or only audio—cost you nothing extra as long as you are using a Wi-Fi network. This means you can literally call anywhere in the world for no cost, as long as the person you are communicating with has FaceTime and an Internet connection. Using an audio-only FaceTime call is a good alternative to using your iPhone's Phone app when you are calling somewhere that involves fees for the call (such as international calling).

Configuring FaceTime Settings

FaceTime is a great way to use your iPhone to hear and see someone else. Like the phone function, there are a few FaceTime settings you should configure. You can connect with other FaceTime users via your phone number, an email address, or your Apple ID.

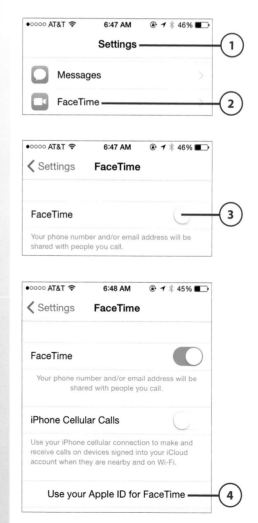

(**1**) Move to the Settings screen.

(**2**) Tap FaceTime.

(**3**) If the FaceTime status is off (white), tap the FaceTime switch to turn it on (green).

(**4**) To use your Apple ID for FaceTime calls, tap Use your Apple ID for FaceTime. If you see your Apple ID, it means you are signed in already and can skip to step 7. (If you don't sign in to an Apple ID, you can still use FaceTime but it is always via your cellular connection, which isn't ideal because then FaceTime counts under your voice minutes on your calling plan.)

5 Enter your Apple ID password. (If you haven't recorded your Apple ID in another app on your iPhone, such as by registering your iCloud account, you need to enter your Apple ID along with the password.)

6 Tap Sign In.

7 Configure the email addresses you want people to use to contact you for FaceTime sessions by tapping them to enable each address (enabled addresses are marked with a check mark) or to disable addresses (these don't have a check mark). (If you don't have any email addresses configured on your iPhone, you are prompted to enter email addresses.)

8 Tap Next. The information you entered is verified. If a problem is detected, you must correct it.

9 To prevent your cellular connection from being used for FaceTime from other devices (such as an iPad) near you and on the same Wi-Fi network, set the iPhone Cellular Calls switch to off (white). When this is enabled (the switch is green), your iPhone acts as a relay for other devices so they can be used to place FaceTime calls via your iPhone's cellular connection. This is useful when the person you want to FaceTime with only has a cellular connection available for FaceTime.

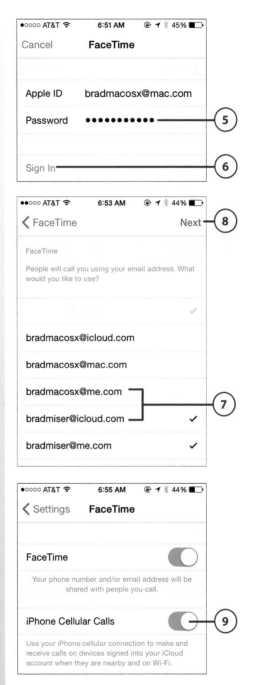

(10) Swipe up the screen until you see the CALLER ID section.

(11) Tap the phone number or email address by which you will be identified to the other caller during a FaceTime call.

(12) Tap Settings.

More on iPhone Cellular Calls

If the iPhone Cellular Calls switch is on (green) when a calls comes into your iPhone, it also comes to iOS 8 and Macs running Yosemite that are on the same Wi-Fi network. If you set this switch to off (white), calls don't go to these other devices.

---

(12)

●●●○○ AT&T 📶   6:59 AM   🅐 ✈ ❋ 43% 🔋

‹ Settings   **FaceTime**

bradmacosx@mac.com   ⓘ

bradmacosx@me.com   ⓘ

✓ bradmiser@icloud.com   ⓘ

bradmiser@me.com   ⓘ   (10)

Add Another Email…

CALLER ID

✓ bradmiser@icloud.com   (11)

bradmiser@me.com

Blocked   ›

Managing Addresses

You can add more email addresses at any time by tapping Add Another Email and following the onscreen prompts to add and confirm the new addresses. To remove an address from FaceTime, tap its Info button (i) and then tap Remove This Email.

Blocking FaceTime

If you tap Blocked at the bottom of the FaceTime Settings screen, you can block people from making calls, sending messages, or making FaceTime requests to your iPhone. Tap Add New and then tap the contact you want to block. See Chapter 17 for detailed steps to do this.

Making FaceTime Calls

FaceTime is a great way to communicate with someone because you can hear and see him (or just hear him if you choose an audio-only FaceTime call). Because iPhones have cameras facing each way, it's also easy to show something to the person you are talking. You make FaceTime calls starting from the FaceTime, Contacts, or Phone apps and from the App Switcher. No matter which way you start a FaceTime session, you manage it in the same way.

To start a FaceTime call from the Contacts app, do the following:

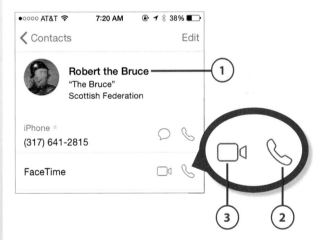

(1) Use the Contacts app to open the contact with whom you want to chat (refer to Chapter 7 for information about using the Contacts app).

(2) To place an audio-only FaceTime call, tap the FaceTime audio button. (The rest of these steps show a FaceTime video call, but a FaceTime audio-only call is very similar to voice calls described earlier in this chapter.)

(3) Tap the contact's FaceTime video button. The iPhone attempts to make a FaceTime connection. You hear the FaceTime "chirping" and see status information on the screen while the call is attempted.

When the connection is complete, you hear a different tone and see the other person in the large window and a preview of what she is seeing (whatever your iPhone's front-side camera is pointing at—mostly likely your face) in the small window. If the person you are trying to FaceTime with isn't available for FaceTime for some reason (perhaps he doesn't have a FaceTime-capable device or is not connected to the Internet), you see a message saying that the person you are calling is unavailable for FaceTime and the call terminates.

Preview window

4 After the call is accepted, manage the call as described in the "Managing FaceTime Calls" task.

Careful

If your iPhone is connected to a Wi-Fi network, you can make all the FaceTime calls you want because you have unlimited data. However, if you are using the cellular data network, be aware that FaceTime calls may use data under your data plan. If you have a limited plan, it's a good idea to use FaceTime primarily when you are connected to a Wi-Fi network. (Refer to Chapter 2, "Connecting Your iPhone to the Internet, Bluetooth Devices, and iPhones/iPods/iPads," for information on connecting to Wi-Fi networks.)

Playing Favorites

If you've set a FaceTime contact as a favorite, you can open the Phone app, tap Favorites, and tap the FaceTime favorite to start the FaceTime session.

Failing FaceTime

If a FaceTime request fails, you can't really tell the reason why. It can be a technical issue, such as none of the contact information you have is FaceTime-enabled, the person is not signed into a device, or the person might have declined the request. If you repeatedly have trouble connecting with someone, contact him to make sure he has a FaceTime-capable device and that you are using the correct FaceTime contact information.

On the FaceTime Unavailable screen, you can tap Leave a Message to send a text or iMessage to the person with whom you are trying to FaceTime.

Transforming a Call

You can transform a voice call into a FaceTime session by tapping the FaceTime button on the Call screen. When you transform a call into a FaceTime session and you are using a Wi-Fi network, the minutes no longer count against the minutes in your calling plan because all communication happens over the Wi-Fi network or your cellular data plan if you enabled that option and aren't connected to a Wi-Fi network. (The voice call you started from automatically terminates when the switch is made.)

Other Ways to FaceTime

To use the FaceTime app to start a call, tap the FaceTime icon on the Home screen. Tap the Video tab to make a video call or the Audio tab to make an audio-only call. Tap the Add button to use your contacts to start the call. You can also enter a name, email address, or phone number in the bar at the top of the screen. Tap a person on the Recents list to place a FaceTime call to that person. Once you've connected, you manage the FaceTime session as described in the rest of this chapter.

You can also place a FaceTime call using Siri by activating Siri and saying "FaceTime *name*" where *name* is the name of the person with whom you want to FaceTime. If there are multiple options for that contact, you must tell Siri which you want to use. After you've made a selection, Siri starts the FaceTime call.

And for yet another option, you can open the App Switcher, swipe on the Favorites and Recents icons at the top of the screen until you see the person with whom you want to FaceTime, tap that person's icon, and then tap the FaceTime icon shaped like a video camera to make a FaceTime video call, or tap the FaceTime icon that is shaped like a phone receiver to make an audio-only FaceTime call.

Receiving FaceTime Calls

When someone tries to FaceTime with you, you see the incoming FaceTime request screen message showing who is trying to connect with you and the image you are currently broadcasting. Tap Accept to accept the request and start the FaceTime session. Manage the FaceTime call as described in the "Managing FaceTime Calls" task.

Tap Remind Me to decline the FaceTime request and create a reminder or Message to decline the request and send a message. These options work just as they do for a voice call (you have the same custom message options). You can also press the Sleep/Wake button to decline the request.

However you decline the FaceTime request, the person trying to call you receives a message that you're not available (and a message if you choose that option). She can't tell whether there is a technical issue or if you simply declined to take the call.

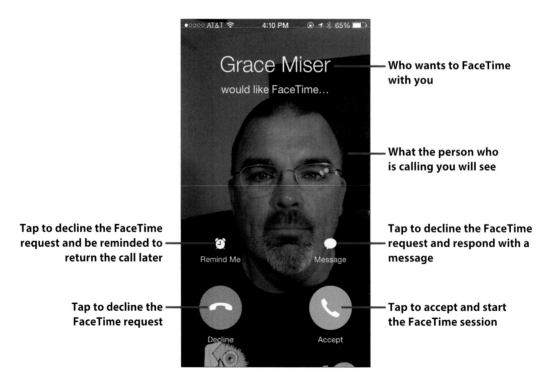

Who wants to FaceTime with you

What the person who is calling you will see

Tap to decline the FaceTime request and be reminded to return the call later

Tap to decline the FaceTime request and respond with a message

Tap to decline the FaceTime request

Tap to accept and start the FaceTime session

Tracking FaceTime Calls

FaceTime calls are tracked just as voice calls are. Open the FaceTime app and tap Recents. On the Recents list, FaceTime calls are marked with the video camera icon. FaceTime audio-only calls are marked with a telephone receiver icon. FaceTime calls that didn't go through are in red and are treated as missed calls. You can do the same tasks with recent FaceTime calls that you can with recent voice calls.

Managing FaceTime Calls

During a FaceTime call (regardless of who placed the call initially), you can do the following:

Drag to change the location of the preview window

- Drag the preview window, which shows the image that the other person is seeing, around the screen to change its location. It "snaps" into place in the closest corner when you lift your finger up.

- Move your iPhone and change the angle you are holding it to change the images you are broadcasting to the other person. Use the preview window to see what the other person is seeing.

- Tap Mute to mute your side of the conversation. Your audio is muted and you see the Mute icon in the preview window. Video continues to be broadcast so the other person can still see you.

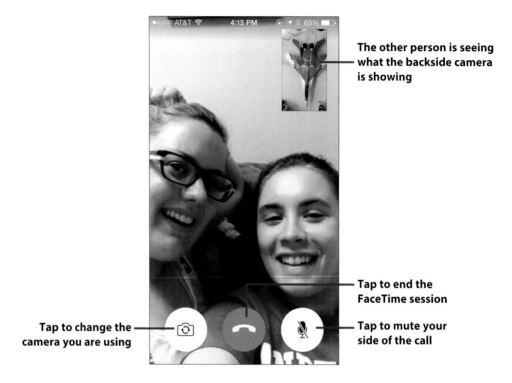

The other person is seeing what the backside camera is showing

Tap to end the FaceTime session

Tap to change the camera you are using

Tap to mute your side of the call

- To use the camera on the backside of the iPhone, tap the Change Camera button. The other person now sees whatever you have the camera on the back of the iPhone pointed at. If the other person changes her camera, you see what her backside camera is pointing at.

- After a few moments, the controls disappear. Tap the screen to make them reappear.

- Rotate your iPhone to change the orientation to horizontal. This affects what the other person sees (as reflected in your preview), but you continue to see the other person in her iPhone's current orientation.

- Tap the receiver button to end the FaceTime call.

Tap the screen to make the controls reappear

FaceTime works in landscape orientation, too

Preview shows the landscape orientation

FaceTime Break

Just like when you are on a voice call, you can move into and use other apps (if your provider's technology supports this functionality). You see the green FaceTime in progress bar at the top of the screen. The audio part of the session continues, but the other person sees a still image with a camera icon and the word "Paused." As soon as you move back into the FaceTime session, the video resumes. Likewise, if the other person moves out of the FaceTime app, you'll see the Paused icon.

Tap to configure email settings

Tap to use email

In this chapter, you explore all the email functionality that your iPhone has to offer. Topics include the following:

→ Getting started
→ Configuring email accounts
→ Setting Mail app preferences
→ Working with email
→ Managing email

Sending, Receiving, and Managing Email

For most of us, email is an important way we communicate with others. Fortunately, your iPhone has great email tools so you can work with email no matter where you are. Of course, you need to be connected to the Internet through a Wi-Fi or cellular data connection to send or receive email—although you can still read downloaded messages, reply to messages, and compose messages when you aren't connected.

To use email on your iPhone, you use the Mail app. This app has lots of great features that help you really take advantage of email from all your accounts. Before jumping into the app, you need to have email accounts configured on your iPhone; there are also a number of email-related settings that you should configure to tailor how the Mail app works.

Getting Started

You send and receive email through an email account. There are many sources for email accounts, such as your Internet service provider, iCloud, and Google (Gmail). One thing to keep in mind is that email isn't sent between devices, such as a computer to an iPhone. Rather all email flows through an email server. It moves from the server into each device, such as an iPhone and a computer. This means you can have the same email messages on more than one device at a time. You can also determine how often email is moved from the server onto your iPhone.

Before you can start using an iPhone for email, you have to configure the email accounts you want to access with it. The iPhone supports many kinds of email accounts, including iCloud, Exchange, and Gmail. In fact, you can configure any kind of email account on your iPhone. Setting up the most common types of email accounts is covered in Chapter 3, "Setting Up and Using iCloud and Other Online Accounts," so if you haven't done that already, go back to that chapter and get your accounts set up. Then, come back here to start using those accounts for email.

You can have multiple email accounts configured on your iPhone at the same time, such as an iCloud account and a Google account. This chapter assumes you use only one email account on your iPhone. If you configure more than one email account on your iPhone, some of the screens you see might look a bit different than those in this chapter. The information contained in this chapter still applies to you; some of the screens you see are slightly different than those shown here.

Setting Mail App Preferences

Your iPhone includes a number of settings that determine certain aspects of how the Mail app works. For example, you can determine how many lines of emails appear as a preview when you are viewing a list of emails. Or, you can determine whether you want Mail to organize your email in threads.

Configure Mail's settings by performing the following steps:

1. Tap Settings on the Home screen.

2. Swipe up the screen.

3. Tap Mail, Contacts, Calendars.

4. Swipe up the screen until you see the MAIL section.

5. Tap Preview.

6. Tap the number of lines you want to display for each email when you view the Inbox and in other locations, such as alerts. This preview enables you to get the gist of an email without opening it. More lines give you more of the message, but take up more space on the screen so you see fewer messages without swiping up or down (when you are in the Inbox).

7. Tap Mail.

8. Slide the Show To/Cc Label switch to on (green) to always see the To and Cc labels in email headers. (With this disabled, you can still view this information for an email by tapping Details on the Message screen.)

9. Tap Swipe Options. This screen enables you to configure what happens when you swipe on emails in the Inbox.

Change Text Size

To change the size of text used in the Mail app (and all apps that support Dynamic Type), open the Settings app, tap Display & Brightness, and tap Text Size. Drag the slider to the right to make text larger or to the left to make it smaller.

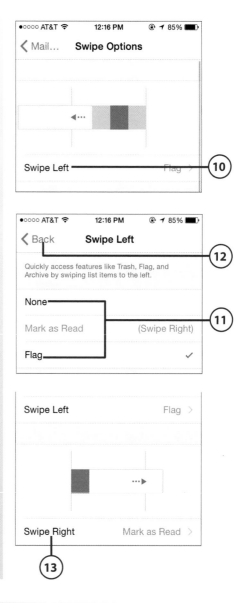

(10) Tap Swipe Left.

(11) Tap the action you want to happen when you swipe left on a message; the options are None, which means nothing will happen, or Flag, which causes the message to be marked with the flag (more on this later).

(12) Tap Back.

(13) Tap Swipe Right.

(14) Tap the action you want to happen when you swipe right on a message; the options are None, which means nothing will happen; Mark as Read, which causes the message to not be marked as a new message; or Archive, which causes the message to be moved into the Archive folder.

Where Has My Email Gone?

When you send an email to the Archive folder, it isn't deleted. To access messages you've archived, tap the Back button in the upper left corner of the screen until you get to the Mailboxes screen. Tap the account to which email you've archived was sent. Then tap the Archive folder.

15 Tap Back.

16 Tap Mail.

17 Tap Flag Style.

18 Tap Color to use a colored circle to flag messages, or tap Shape to use the flag shape to flag them. Flagging messages marks messages that you want to know are important or that need your attention.

19 Tap Mail.

20 If you don't want to confirm your action when you delete messages, slide the Ask Before Deleting switch to off (white). When you delete a message, it immediately goes into the Trash or Archive folder depending on the account to which it was sent. If this switch is on (green), you have to tap Delete or Archive in a prompt before a message you are deleting is moved into the Trash or Archive folder.

21 If you want images in HTML email messages to be displayed automatically when you read messages, slide the Load Remote Images switch to on (green). If you disable this, you can manually load images in a message. If you receive a lot of spam, you should disable this so that you won't see images in which you might not be interested.

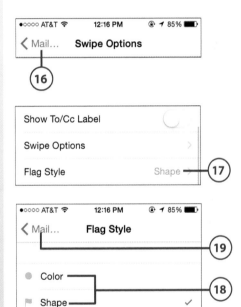

22 If you don't want Mail to organize your messages by thread (which means grouping them based on their subject so you see all the messages on a single topic on the same screen), disable this feature by sliding the Organize By Thread switch to off (white). With this set to off, messages appear individually in the Inbox. If Organize By Thread is on (green), messages in a conversation are grouped together as a "thread" on one screen. This makes it easier to read all the messages in a thread. You learn more about working with threads in "Working with Email," later in this chapter.

23 If you want to receive a blind copy of each email you send, slide the Always Bcc Myself switch to on (green). Each time you send a message, you'll also receive a copy of it but your address isn't shown to the message's other recipients.

24 Tap Mark Addresses. This feature highlights (marks) messages in red that aren't from domains that you specify; if you don't want to use this feature, skip to step 27.

25 Enter the domains (everything after the @ in email addresses) from which you don't want messages to be marked (highlighted in red) in your Inbox; for example, enter icloud.com to prevent messages from icloud.com accounts from being highlighted in red. Add multiple domains by separating them with commas. Email from any domains except those listed on the Mark Addresses screen are in red text on the New Message screen. This is useful to prevent accidental email going to places where you don't want it to go. For example, you might want to leave domains associated with organizations of which you are a member off this list so that whenever you deal with email for that organization, the addresses appear in red to remind you to pay careful attention.

26 Tap Mail.

27 Tap Increase Quote Level.

28 If you don't want the Mail app to automatically indent current content (quoted content) when you reply or forward email, slide the switch to off (white). Generally, you should leave this enabled so it is easier for the recipients to tell when you have added text to an email thread versus what is the previous part of the conversation (quoted content).

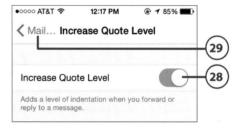

29 Tap Mail.

30 Tap Signature to configure a default signature that is automatically added to new email messages you create. A signature is just any text that you want to automatically appear at the end of every email that you send.

31 Type the signature you want to use.

32 Tap Mail. The configuration is complete and you are ready to start using email.

●●●○○ AT&T 🛜   11:25 AM   ✈ ✳ 100% ▮

‹ Mail...   **Signature** — **32**

Best, — **31**
Brad

No Signatures, Please

If you don't want any text automatically appended to your messages, delete all the text in the signature box.

Email Notifications and Sounds

Because you will probably have a lot of email activity and will likely want to be aware of it, be sure you configure the notifications for the Mail app. These include whether unread messages are shown in the Notification Center, the type of alerts, whether the badge appears on the Mail icon, whether the preview is shown, alert sounds, and whether new messages are shown on the Lock screen. For a detailed explanation of configuring notifications, refer to Chapter 4, "Configuring an iPhone to Suit Your Preferences."

Working with Email

With your email account and settings configured, you're ready to start using your iPhone for email. To do this, you use the iPhone's Mail app, which offers lots of great features and is ideally suited for working with email on your iPhone. The Mail app organizes your email into threads (assuming you didn't disable this, of course), which makes following a conversation convenient.

You've got email

When you move to a Home screen, you see the number of new email messages you have in the badge on the Mail app's icon (if you haven't disabled it); tap the icon to move to the app. Even if you don't have any new email, the Mail icon still leads you to the Mail app. Other ways Mail notifies you of new messages include by displaying alerts and the new mail sound.

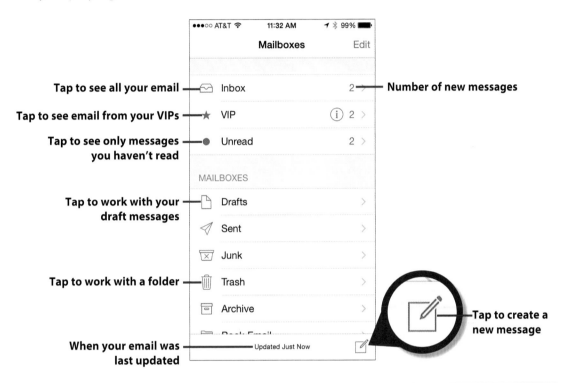

Tap to see all your email — Inbox — 2 — Number of new messages

Tap to see email from your VIPs — VIP — ⓘ 2 >

Tap to see only messages you haven't read — Unread — 2 >

Tap to work with your draft messages — Drafts >

Sent >

Junk >

Tap to work with a folder — Trash >

Archive >

When your email was last updated — Updated Just Now

Tap to create a new message

About Assumptions

The steps and figures in this section assume you have one email account configured on your iPhone. If you have multiple email accounts active on your iPhone, the Mailboxes screen shows an Inbox for each account, along with the one labeled Inbox that contains email to all your accounts in one place. Similarly, if you disable the Organize by Thread setting, you won't see messages in threads as these figures show. Instead, you work with each message individually.

The Mailboxes screen is the top-level screen in the app and is organized into two sections.

The Inboxes section shows the Inbox along with folders for email from people designated as VIPs (more on this later), your unread messages, and your draft (that you've started but haven't sent yet) messages; next to each Inbox or folder the number of new emails in that Inbox or folder is shown. (A new message is simply one you haven't viewed yet.)

The MAILBOXES section shows the folders for your account, such as Drafts, Sent, Junk, and Trash. You can tap one of these folders to see the messages it contains.

Receiving and Reading Email

To read email you have received, perform the following steps:

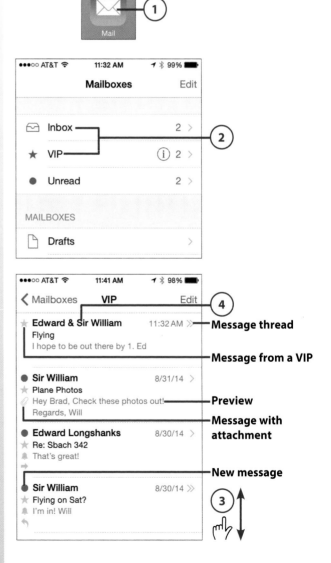

1. On the Home screen, tap Mail. The Mail application opens. If the Mailboxes screen isn't showing, tap the Back button in the upper-left corner of the screen until you reach the Mailboxes screen.

2. To read messages, tap the Inbox or the folder (such as the VIP folder) that contains messages you want to read.

3. Swipe up or down the screen to browse the messages. You can read the preview of each message to get an idea of its contents. Various icons indicate the status of each message, if it is part of a thread, if it has attachments, and so on.

4. If a message you are interested in is in a thread, tap it. You can tell a message is part of a thread by double right-facing arrows along the right side of the screen—single messages have only one arrow. (If it isn't part of a thread, skip to step 6.) A thread is a group

of emails that are related to the same subject. For example, if someone sends an email to you saying how wonderful the book *My iPhone* is, and you reply with a message saying how much you agree, those two messages would be grouped into one thread. Other messages with the same subject are also placed in the thread.

5. Swipe up or down the screen to browse the messages in the thread.

6. To read a message, tap it. As soon as you open a message (whether in a thread or not), it's marked as read and the new mail counter reduces by one. You see the message screen with the address information, including whom the message is from and whom it was sent to, at the top. Under that the message's subject along with time and date it was sent are displayed. Below that is the body of the message. If the message has an attachment or is a reply to another message, the attachment or quoted text appears toward the bottom of the screen.

7. Swipe up and down the screen to read the entire message, if it doesn't all fit on one screen.

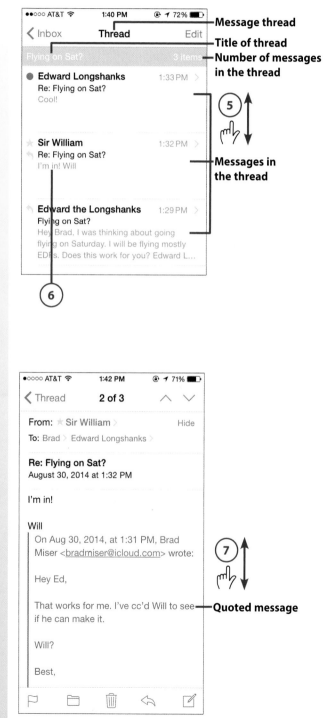

Message thread

Title of thread

Number of messages in the thread

Messages in the thread

Quoted message

Standard Motions Apply

You can use the standard finger motions on email messages, such as unpinching or tapping to zoom and swiping directions to scroll. You can also rotate the phone to change the orientation of messages from vertical to horizontal; this makes it easier to type for some people.

8 If the message contains an attachment, swipe up the screen to get to the end of the message. If an attachment hasn't been downloaded yet, it starts to download automatically (unless it is a large file). If the attachment hasn't been downloaded yet, which is indicated by a downward-facing arrow in the attachment icon, tap it to download it into the message. When an attachment finishes downloading, its icon changes to represent the type of file it is. If the icon remains generic, it might be of a type the iPhone can't display and you would need to open it on a computer or other device.

9 Tap the attachment icon to view it.

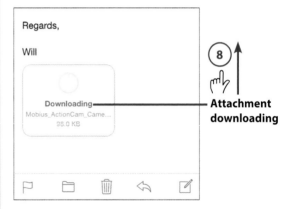

Attachment downloading

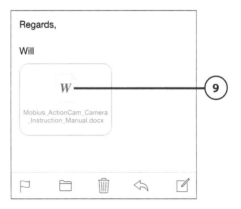

10. Scroll the document by swiping up, down, left, or right on the screen.

11. Unpinch or double-tap to zoom in.

12. Pinch or double-tap to zoom out.

13. To see the available actions for the attachment, tap the Share button.

14. Swipe to the left or right to see all the available actions.

15. Tap the action you want to take, such as opening the attachment in a different app, printing it, or sharing it via email. Tap Cancel to return to the attachment if you don't want to do any of these. If you open the attachment in an app, work with the attachment in that app. To return to the email, move back into the Mail app by tapping its icon on your home screen.

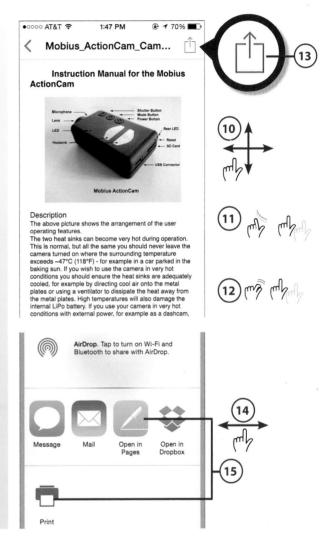

The Mail App on an iPhone 6 Plus

When you hold an iPhone 6 Plus horizontally and use the Mail app, its window splits into two panes. On the left side, you see the Navigation pane, in which you can select inboxes or folders containing messages you want to view. You can navigate within this pane just like you can on the Mailboxes screen when the iPhone is vertical. When you select an inbox or folder, its contents appear in the right pane. You can read messages in the right pane as you can when the iPhone is vertical. The nice thing about this is that you can easily select and read messages, because the two panes are independent, making it much faster to get to specific messages that you want to read.

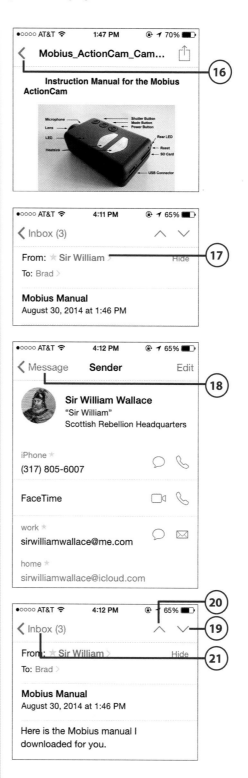

16 Tap the Back button.

17 To view information for an email address, such as who sent the message, tap it. The Info screen appears; its title tells you how the person relates to the message. For example, if you tapped the email address in the From field, the screen title is Sender. You see the person's email address along with actions you might want to perform, such as placing a call or FaceTime request, adding him to your VIP list (if he isn't already a VIP) if the person is in your Contacts app, or creating a contact if he isn't already one.

18 Tap Message to return to the message.

19 To read the next message in the current Inbox or thread, tap the down arrow.

20 To move to a previous message in the current Inbox, tap the up arrow.

21 To move back to see all the messages in the inbox you were viewing, tap the Back button, which is labeled with the inbox or thread whose messages you were viewing (such as Inbox or VIP).

Emailing by Speaking

Using Siri, you can speak to create new email messages and to reply to messages. You can also dictate into messages you are writing. See Chapter 12, "Working with Siri," for information on using Siri.

Sending Email

You can send email from most of the screens in the Mail app. Follow these steps for a basic walk-through of composing and sending a new email message:

1. Tap the Compose button on any Mail screen. A new email message is created.

2. To type a recipient's email address, tap the To field and type in the address. As you type, Mail attempts to find matching addresses in your Contacts list, or in emails you've sent or received, and displays the matches it finds. To select one of those addresses, tap it. Mail enters the rest of the address for you. Or, just keep entering information until the address is complete.

3. To address the email using your Contacts app, tap the Add button.

4. Use the Contacts app to find and select the contact to whom you want to address the message. (Refer to Chapter 7 for the details about working with contacts.) When you tap a contact with

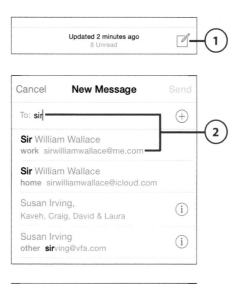

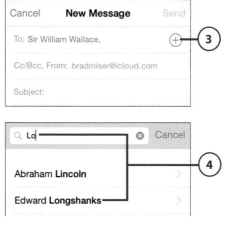

one email address, that address is pasted into the To field and you return to the New Message window. When you tap a contact with more than one email address, you move to the Info screen, which shows all available addresses; tap the address to which you want to send the message.

5 Repeat steps 2–4 to add all the recipients to the message.

6 Tap the Cc/Bcc, From line. The Cc and Bcc lines expand.

7 Follow the same procedures from steps 2–4 to add recipients to the Cc field.

8 Follow the same procedures from steps 2–4 to add recipients to the Bcc field.

Removing Addresses

To remove an address, tap it so it is highlighted in a darker shade of blue; then tap the Delete button on the iPhone's keyboard.

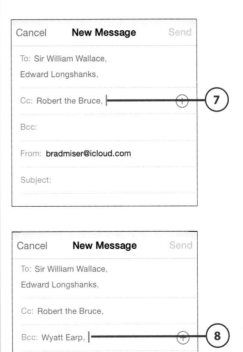

9 Type the subject of the message.

10 If you want to be notified when someone replies to the message you are creating, tap the bell; if not, skip to step 12.

11 Tap Notify Me. When anyone replies to the message, you are notified.

12 If you don't see the body of the message, swipe up the screen and it appears.

13 Tap in the body of the message, and type the message above your signature. Mail uses the iOS's text tools, attempts to correct spelling, and makes suggestions to complete words. To accept a proposed change, tap the spacebar when the suggestion appears on the screen; to ignore a correction, tap the *x* in the suggestion box. If the Predictive Text feature is enabled, you can tap the words shown above the keyboard that you want to enter. You can also use the copy and paste feature to move text around, and you can edit text using the spell checker and other text tools. (Refer to Chapter 1, "Getting Started with Your iPhone," for the details of working with text.)

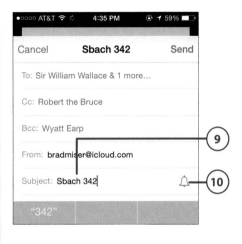

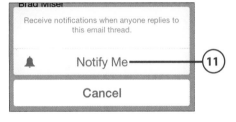

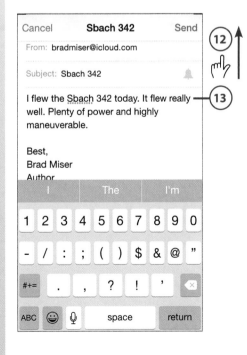

(14) When you finish the message and want to send it, tap Send. The progress of the send process is shown at the bottom of the screen; when the message has been sent, you hear the send mail sound you configured, which confirms that the message has been sent. If you enabled the reply notification for the message, you are notified when anyone replies to it.

Cancel   **Sbach 342**   Send (14)

From: bradmiser@icloud.com

Subject: Sbach 342

I flew the Sbach 342 today. It flew really well. Plenty of power and highly maneuverable.

Best,
Brad Miser
Author

Write Now, Send Later

If you want to save a message you are creating without sending it, tap Cancel. A prompt appears; select Save Draft to save the message; if you don't want the message, tap Delete Draft instead. When you want to work on a draft message again, tap and hold down the New Message button. After a moment, you see your most recent draft messages; tap the draft message you want to work on. You can make changes to the message and then send it or save it as a draft again. (You can also move into the Drafts folder to select and work with draft messages; moving to this folder is covered later in this chapter.)

Replying to Email

Email is all about communication, and Mail makes it simple to reply to messages.

(**1**) Open the message you want to reply to.

(**2**) Tap the Share button.

(**3**) Tap Reply to reply to only the sender or, if there was more than one recipient, tap Reply All to reply to everyone who received the original message. The Re: screen appears showing a new message. Mail pastes the contents of the original message at the bottom of the body of the new message below your signature. The original content is in blue and is marked with a vertical line along the left side of the screen.

Including a Photo or Video in a Message

To add a photo or video to a message, tap twice in the body. Tap the arrow pointing to the right on the right side of the resulting toolbar until you see the Insert Photo or Video command, and then tap Insert Photo or Video. Use the Photos app (see Chapter 15, "Working with Photos and Video You Take with Your iPhone," for information about this app) to move to and select the photo or video you want to attach. Tap Choose. The photo or video you selected is attached to the message.

(4) Use the message tools to add or change the To, Cc, or Bcc recipients.

(5) Write your response.

(6) Tap Send. Mail sends your reply.

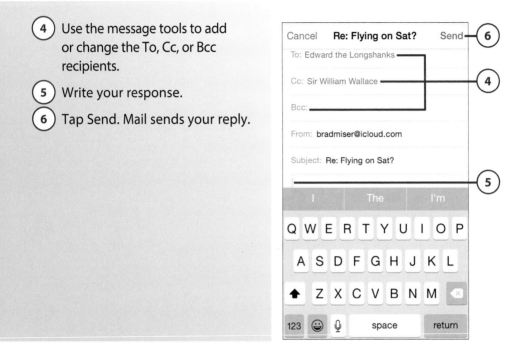

Sending Email from All the Right Places

You can send email from a number of places on your iPhone. For example, you can share a photo with someone by viewing the photo, tapping the Share button, and then tapping Mail. Or you can tap a contact's email address to send an email from your contacts list. For yet another example, you can share a YouTube video. In all cases, the iPhone uses Mail to create a new message that includes the appropriate content, such as a photo or link; you use Mail's tools to complete and send the email.

Print from Your iPhone

If you need to print a message, tap the Share button and tap Print. To learn about printing from your iPhone, refer to Chapter 1.

Forwarding Emails

When you receive an email you think others should see, you can forward it to them.

(1) Read the message you want to forward.

(2) If you want include only part of the current content in the message you forward, tap where you want the forwarded content to start. This is useful (and considerate!) when only a part of the message applies to the people to whom you are forwarding it. If you want to forward the entire content, skip to step 4.

(3) Use the text selection tools to select the content you want to include in your forwarded message.

(4) Tap the Share button.

(5) Tap Forward.

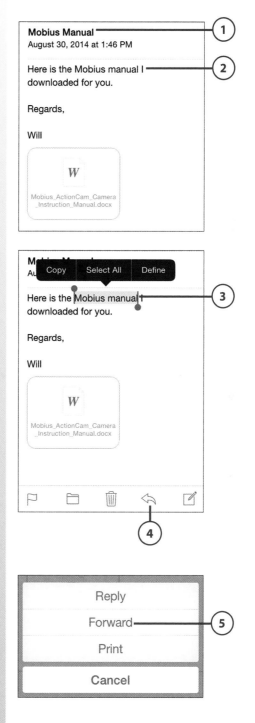

(6) If the message includes attachments, tap Include at the
prompt if you also want to forward the attachments, or tap
Don't Include if you don't want
them included. The Forward
screen appears. Mail pastes
the contents of the message
that you selected, or the entire
content if you didn't select anything, at the bottom of the message below your signature. Tap
Include or Don't Include when
prompted about an attached file
from the original message.

(7) Address the forwarded message
using the same tools you use
when you create a new message.

(8) Type your commentary about the
message above your signature.

(9) Tap Send. Mail forwards the
message.

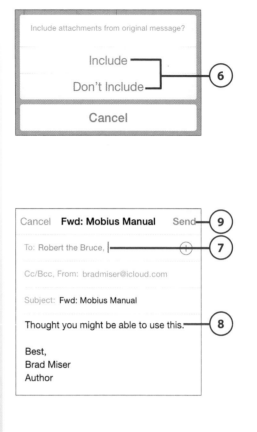

Large Messages

Some emails, especially HTML messages, are so large that they don't immediately download in their entirety. When you forward a message whose content or
attachments haven't fully downloaded, Mail prompts you to download the "missing" content before forwarding. If you choose not to download the content or
attachments, Mail forwards only the downloaded part of the message.

Managing Email

Following are some ways you can manage your email. You can check for new
messages, see the status of messages, delete messages, and organize messages
using the folders associated with your email accounts.

Checking for New Email

To manually retrieve messages, swipe down from the top of any Inbox or the Mailboxes screen. The screen "stretches" down and when you lift your finger, the Mail app checks for and downloads new messages.

Mail also retrieves messages whenever you move into the app or into any Inbox or all your Inboxes. Of course, it also retrieves messages according to the Fetch New Data option you selected. It downloads new messages immediately when they arrive in your account if Push is enabled or automatically at defined intervals if you've set Fetch to get new email periodically. (Refer to Chapter 3 for an explanation of these options and how to set them.)

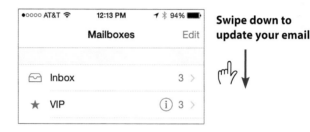

Swipe down to update your email

The bottom of the Mailboxes or Inbox screen always shows when email was most recently downloaded to your iPhone; on the bottom of Inbox screens, you also see the number of new email messages.

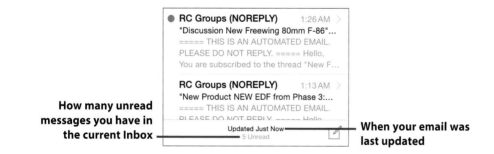

How many unread messages you have in the current Inbox

When your email was last updated

Understanding the Statuses of Email

When you view an Inbox or a message thread, you see icons next to each message to indicate its status (except for messages that you've read but not done anything else with, which aren't marked with any icon).

When the message is replied to, you receive a notification

Message you've forwarded

Unread message

Message with attachments

Message from a VIP

Message you've flagged

Message to which you've replied

Managing Email from the Message Screen

To delete a message while reading it, tap the Trash. If you enabled the warning preference, confirm the deletion and the message is deleted. If you disabled the confirmation prompt, the message is deleted immediately.

Tap to delete a message

Dumpster Diving

As long as an account's trash hasn't been emptied (for most types of accounts, this happens automatically after a specific period of time that a message has been in the trash), you can work with a message you've deleted by moving to the Mailboxes screen and tapping Trash. Then you can move the message back to the Inbox if you decide you want to keep it.

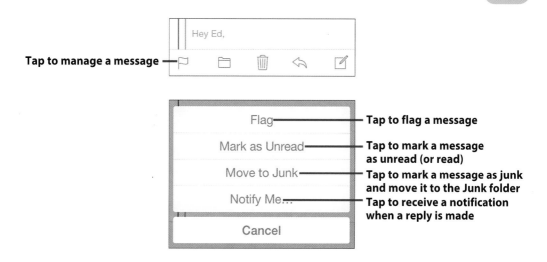

Tap to manage a message

Flag — Tap to flag a message

Mark as Unread — Tap to mark a message as unread (or read)

Move to Junk — Tap to mark a message as junk and move it to the Junk folder

Notify Me... — Tap to receive a notification when a reply is made

Cancel

To take other actions on a message you are reading, tap the Flag icon. On the menu that opens, you can do the following:

- Tap Flag to flag the message or Unflag to unflag it.

- Tap Mark as Unread or Mark as Read to change its read status.

- Tap Move to Junk to mark the message as junk and move it to the Junk folder.

- Tap Notify Me to receive a notification when there is a reply to the message or Stop Notifying to remove the notification.

Managing Email from an Inbox

NEW! Previously in this chapter, you saw how to configure swipe actions for email. You can determine how right and left swipes affect your email from an Inbox screen, such as archiving a message with a left swipe. The actions that become available are determined by the swipe settings you set in the "Setting Mail App Preferences" task at the beginning of this chapter. (Depending on the choices you set for the swipe preferences, the results you see when you swipe might be different than shown here. However, the swipe right or swipe left actions still reveal commands you can use unless you chose None in the settings, in which case nothing happens when you swipe on a message.)

Swipe to the right on a message to change its read status. If the message has been read, you can reset its status to unread or if it hasn't been read, you can mark it as read.

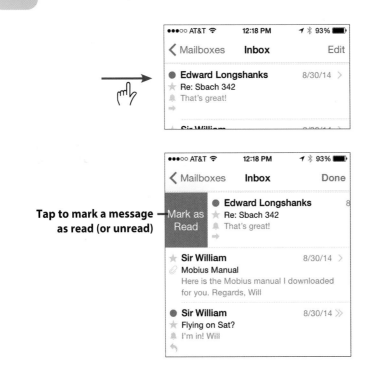

Tap to mark a message as read (or unread)

Swipe to the left on a message to see several other options. Tap Trash to delete the message or messages if you swiped on a thread (the number of messages that will be deleted is shown in parentheses). Tap Flag to flag the message or Unflag to remove the flag. Tap More to open a menu of additional commands.

Tap to see more commands

Tap to flag a message

Tap to delete a message or all the messages in a thread

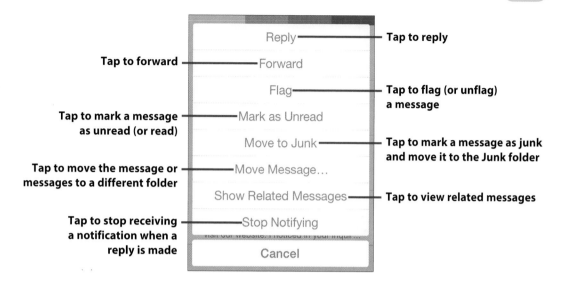

When you tap More, you see other commands for actions you can take on the message. These include:

- Tap Reply to reply to the message.

- Tap Forward to forward the message.

- Tap Flag to flag the message or Unflag to unflag it.

- Tap Mark as Unread or Mark as Read to change its read status.

- Tap Move to Junk to mark the message as junk and move it to the Junk folder.

- Tap Move Messages to move one or more messages to a different folder.

- Tap Show Related Messages to show messages related to the one on which you swiped.

- Tap Notify Me to receive a notification when there is a reply to the message or Stop Notifying to remove the notification.

Managing Multiple Emails at the Same Time

You can also manage email by selecting multiple messages on an Inbox screen, which is more efficient because you can take action on multiple messages at the same time.

1. Move to an Inbox screen showing messages you want to manage.

2. Tap Edit. A selection circle appears next to each message, and actions appear at the bottom of the screen.

3. Select the message(s) you want to manage by tapping their selection circles. As you select each message, its selection circle is marked with a check mark. At the top of the screen, you see how many messages you have selected.

4. To delete the selected messages, tap Trash. Mail deletes the selected messages and exits Edit mode. (If you enabled the warning prompt, you have to confirm the deletion.)

5. To change the status of the selected messages, tap Mark.

6. Tap the action you want to take on the selected messages. You return to the Inbox screen and exit Edit mode. To take more actions on multiple messages, tap Edit and repeat the steps in this task.

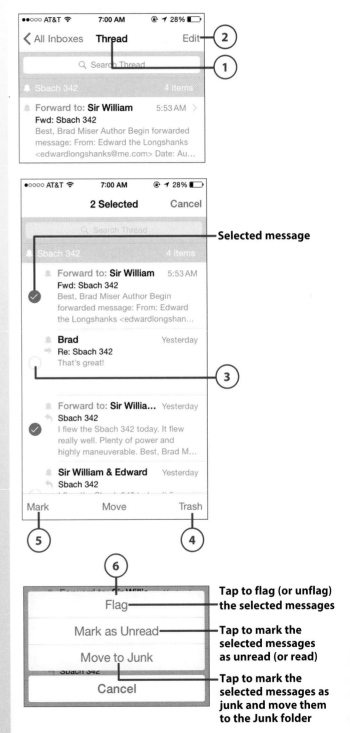

Selected message

Tap to flag (or unflag) the selected messages

Tap to mark the selected messages as unread (or read)

Tap to mark the selected messages as junk and move them to the Junk folder

Organizing Email from the Message Screen

You can have various folders to organize email, and you can move messages among these folders. For example, you can recover a message from the Trash by moving it from the Trash folder back to the Inbox.

1. Open a message you want to move to a different folder.

2. Tap the Mailboxes button. The Mailboxes screen appears. At the top of this screen is the message you are moving. Under that are the mailboxes available under the current account.

3. Swipe up and down the screen to browse the mailboxes available in the current account.

4. Tap the mailbox to which you want to move the message. The message moves to that mailbox, and you move to the next message in the list you were viewing.

Move to Other Accounts

If you want to move a message to a folder under a different account, tap Accounts in the upper-left corner of the screen. Tap the account to which you want to move the message (not all accounts will be available; if an account is grayed out, you can't move a message to it). Then tap the mailbox into which you want to move the message.

Makin' Mailboxes

You can create a new mailbox to organize your email. Move to the Mailboxes screen and tap the account on which you want to create a new mailbox. Tap Edit, and then tap New Mailbox. Type the name of the new mailbox. Tap the Mailbox Location and then choose where you want the new mailbox located (for example, you can place the new mailbox inside an existing one). Tap Save. You can then store messages in the new mailbox.

Organizing Email from the Inbox

Like deleting messages, organizing email from the Inbox can be made more efficient because you can move multiple messages at the same time.

1. Move to an Inbox screen showing messages you want to move to a folder.

2. Tap Edit. A selection circle appears next to each message. Options appear at the bottom of the screen.

3. Select the messages you want to move by tapping their selection circles. As you select each message, its selection circle is marked with a check mark.

4. Tap Move.

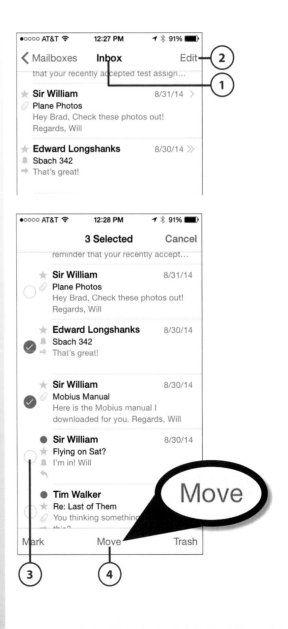

5 Swipe up and down the screen to browse the mailboxes available in the current account.

6 Tap the mailbox to which you want to move the selected messages. They are moved into that mailbox, and you return to the previous screen, which is no longer in Edit mode.

Picking at Threads
When you select a thread, you select all the messages in that thread. Whatever action you select is taken on all the thread's messages at the same time.

Viewing Messages in a Mailbox

You can open a mailbox within an account to work with the messages it contains. For example, you might want to open the Trash mailbox to recover a deleted message.

1 Move to the Mailboxes screen.

2 Tap the folder or mailbox containing the messages you want to view. You see the messages it contains. In some cases, this can take a few moments for the messages to be downloaded if that folder or mailbox hasn't been accessed recently.

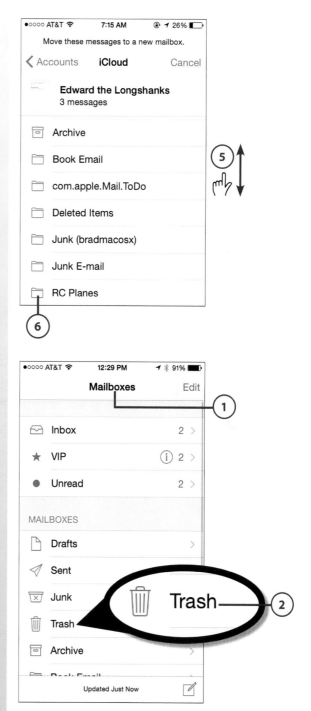

③ Tap a message or thread to view it. (If you want to move messages, such as to recover messages that are in the Trash, see "Organizing Email from the Inbox.")

Changing Mailboxes

You can change the mailboxes that appear on the Mailboxes screen. Move to the Mailboxes screen and tap Edit. To cause a mailbox to appear, tap it so that it has a check mark. To hide a mailbox, tap its check mark so that it just shows an empty circle. For example, you can show the Attachments mailbox to make messages with attachments easier to get to. Drag the Order button for mailboxes up or down the screen to change the order in which mailboxes appear. Tap Add Mailbox to add a mailbox not shown to the list. Tap Done to save your changes.

Saving Images Attached to Email

Email is a great way to share photos. When you receive a message that includes photos, you can save them on your iPhone.

① Move to the message screen of an email that contains one or more photos or images.

② Tap the Share button.

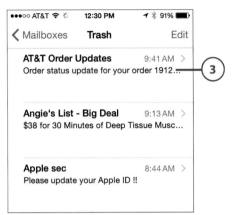

3 Tap Save *X* Images, where *X* is the number of images attached to the message. (If there is only one image, the command is just Save Image.) The images are saved in the Photos app on your iPhone. (See Chapter 15 for help working with the Photos app.)

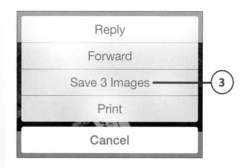

Searching Your Email

As you accumulate email, you might want to find specific messages. Mail's Search tool can help you do this.

1 Move to the screen you want to search, such as the Inbox or a folder's screen.

2 Swipe down to move to the top of the screen.

3 Tap in the Search tool.

4 Enter the text for which you want to search. As you type, Mail first searches the messages in the current location and then searches other mailboxes. The messages that meet your search are shown above the keyboard.

5 When you complete your search term, tap Search. The keyboard closes and you see all the messages that met your search.

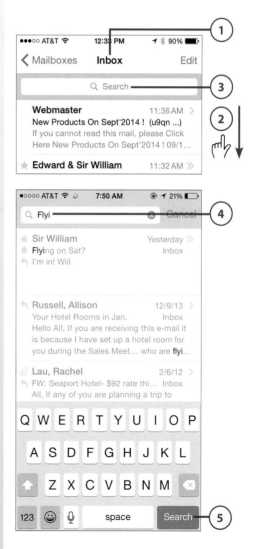

(6) Work with the messages you found, such as tapping a message to read it.

(7) To limit the results to only those messages in the current location, tap Current Mailbox.

(8) To show all messages that were found again, tap All Mailboxes.

(9) To clear a search and exit Search mode, tap Cancel.

(10) To clear a search but remain in Search mode, tap the Clear button (x).

Working with VIPs

The VIP feature enables you to indicate specific people as your VIPs. When a VIP sends you email, it is marked with a star icon and goes into the special VIP mailbox so you can access these important messages easily.

Designating VIPs

To designate someone as a VIP, perform the following steps:

1 View information about the
person you want to be a VIP by
tapping his name in the To or Cc
fields as you learned earlier in the
chapter.

2 On the Info screen, tap Add to
VIP. The person is designated
as a VIP and any email from
that person receives the VIP
treatment.

●○○○○ AT&T 📶 ◌ 7:53 AM ⊕ ⌁ 21% 🔋⚡

❮ Thread 1 of 2 ⌃ ⌄

From: Edward Longshanks ━━ Hide ◀ **1**

To: Brad ›

Re: Sbach 342 🔔
August 30, 2014 at 4:54 PM

●○○○○ AT&T 📶 ◌ 7:53 AM ⊕ ⌁ 21% 🔋⚡

❮ Message **Sender** Edit

Edward Longshanks
England

work
edwardlongshanks@me.com

AIM
edwardlongshanks@me.com

Jabber
edwardlongshanks@me.com

Notes

Add to VIP
2

Accessing VIP Email

To work with VIP email, do the following:

1 Move to the Mailboxes screen.

2 Tap VIP.

3 Work with the VIP messages you see.

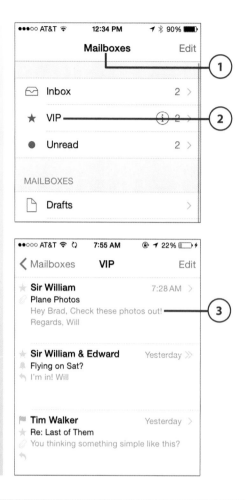

>>>Go Further

MORE ON VIPS

Here are a few more tidbits on VIPs:

- Messages from VIPs are marked with the star icon no matter in which mailbox you see the messages.

- To see the list of your current VIPs, move to the Mailboxes screen and tap the Info button (i) for the VIP mailbox. You see everyone currently designated as a VIP. Tap Add VIP to add more people to the list.

- You can configure specific notifications for email from your VIPs. See Chapter 4 for details.

- To return a VIP to normal status, view his information and tap Remove from VIP.

Managing Junk Email

Junk email, also known as spam, is an unfortunate reality of email. No matter what precautions you take, you are going to receive some spam emails. Of course, it is good practice to be careful about where you present your email address to limit the amount of spam you receive.

Consider using a "sacrificial" email account when you shop, post messages, and in the other places where you're likely to get spammed. If you do get spammed, you can stop using the sacrificial account and create another one to take its place. Or you can delete the sacrificial account from your iPhone and continue to use it on your computer where you likely have spam tools in place. If you have an iCloud account, you can set up and use email aliases for this purpose.

The Mail app on the iPhone doesn't include any spam or filtering tools. However, if you use an account or an email application on a computer that features a junk mail/spam tool, it acts on mail sent to your iPhone, too. For example, if you configure spam tools for a Gmail account, those tools act on email before it reaches your iPhone. Similarly, if you use the Mail app on a Mac, its rules and junk filter work on email as you receive it; the results of this are also reflected on your iPhone.

To change how you deal with junk email on your iPhone, change the junk email settings for your account online (such as for Gmail) or by changing how an email app on a computer deals with junk mail. The results of these changes are reflected in the Mail app on your iPhone.

Many email accounts, including iCloud and Google, have Junk folders; these folders are available in the Mail app on your iPhone. You can open the Junk folder under an account to see the messages that are placed there. As you saw earlier, you can also move a message to the Junk folder by swiping to the left on it, tapping More, and then tapping Move to Junk.

It's Not All Good

Unfortunately, while you can move email to a Junk folder in the Mail app, this really doesn't do any good because the Mail app doesn't use that action to be able to mark similar future email as junk like email apps on computers do. On an iPhone, there's really no difference between moving a message to a Junk folder and deleting it. Since it is faster to delete a message, that is a better way to get rid of junk email than moving it to a Junk folder.

Tap to send and receive text messages, photos, video, and more

Send messages from other apps too, such as to share photos

Tap to configure Messages

In this chapter, you'll explore the texting and messaging functionality your iPhone has to offer. The topics include the following:

→ Getting started
→ Preparing Messages for messaging
→ Sending messages
→ Receiving, reading, and replying to messages
→ Working with messages

Sending, Receiving, and Managing Texts and iMessages

You can use the iPhone's Messages app to send, receive, and converse; you can also send and receive images, videos, audio, and links with this app. You can maintain any number of conversations with other people at the same time, and your iPhone lets you know whenever you receive a new message via audible and visible notifications you configure. In addition to conversations with other people, many organizations use text messaging to send important updates, such as airlines communicating flight status changes. You might find messaging to be one of the most used functions of your iPhone.

Getting Started

Texting, also called messaging, is an especially great way to communicate with others when you have something quick you want to say, such as an update on your arrival time. It's much easier to send a quick text, "I'll be there in 10 minutes," than it is to make a phone call or send an email. Texting/messaging is designed for relatively short messages, and for that type of communication, it is perfect. It is also a great way to share photos and videos quickly and easily. And if you communicate with people in the "younger" generations, you'll find they tend to respond quite well since texting is a primary form of communication for them.

There are two types of messages that you can send with and receive on your iPhone in the Messages app.

The Messages app can send and receive text messages via your cell network based on telephone numbers—this is the texting function that almost all cell phones support. Using this option, you can send text messages to and receive messages from anyone who has a cell phone capable of text messaging.

You can also use iMessage within the Messages app to send and receive messages via an email account to and from other iOS devices (using iOS 5 or newer) or Macs (running OS X Lion or newer). This is especially useful when your cell phone account has a limit on the number of texts you can send via your cell account; when you use iMessage for texting, there is no limit on the amount of data you can send when you are connected to the Internet using a Wi-Fi network and so you incur no additional costs for your messages. This is also really useful because you can send messages to, and receive messages from, iPod touch, iPad, and Mac users since some of these devices don't have cell phone capability. The limitation to iMessage is that it only works on those supported devices and the people with whom you are messaging have to set up iMessage on their device (as you'll see shortly, this isn't difficult).

You don't need to be overly concerned about which type is which because the Messages app makes it clear which type a message is by color and text. It uses iMessage when available and automatically uses cellular texting when it isn't possible to use iMessage.

You can configure iMessage on multiple devices, such as an iPhone and an iPad. This means you have the same iMessages on each device. So, you can start a conversation on your iPhone, and then continue it on other devices.

Preparing Messages for Messaging

Like most of the apps described in this book, there are settings for the Messages app you can configure to choose how the app works for you. For example, you can configure iMessage so you can communicate via email addresses and configure how standard text messages are managed. You can also choose to block messages from specific people.

Setting Your Text and iMessage Preferences

Perform the following steps to set up Messages on your iPhone:

(1) Move to the Settings app and tap Messages.

(2) Set the iMessage switch to on (green).

(3) Tap Use your Apple ID for iMessage.

Already Signed In to an Apple ID?

If you have signed in to your Apple ID on your iPhone, such as to sign in to your iCloud account, you might move directly to the sign in screen, in which case you skip to step 8. If you want to change the Apple ID currently being used for iMessage, tap Send & Receive, tap the Apple ID shown at the top of the iMessage screen, and then tap Sign Out. You can then use the rest of these steps to sign into a different Apple ID.

(4) Type your Apple ID (if it isn't entered already or if you want to change the one shown) and associated password and tap Sign In.

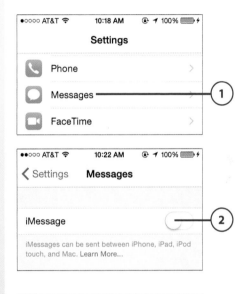

5 To prevent an email address from being available for messages, tap it so it doesn't have a check mark; to enable an address so it can be used for messages, tap it so it does have a check mark. If you only have one email address, you can skip this step.

6 Tap Next. The addresses you selected are activated for iMessage.

7 To notify others when you read their messages, slide the Send Read Receipts switch to on (green). Be aware that receipts apply only to iMessages (not texts sent over a cellular network).

8 To send texts via your cellular network when iMessage is unavailable, slide the Send as SMS switch to on (green). If your cellular account has a limit on the number of texts you can send, you might want to leave this set to off (white) so you use only iMessage when you are texting. If your account has unlimited texting, you should set this to on (green).

9 Tap Send & Receive. At the top of the iMessage screen, you see the Apple ID via which you'll send and receive iMessages. In the center part of the screen are the phone number and email addresses that can be used with the Messages app.

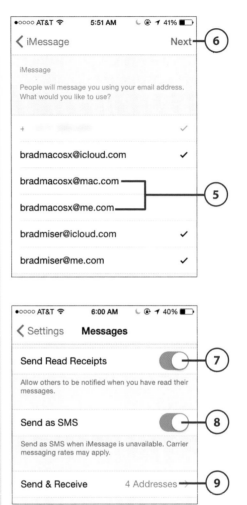

Verify and Notify

When you enable email addresses for iMessage, you might have to confirm the email addresses you enabled by responding to an email message to those addresses (the first time you enable them for iMessage). The message should only contain a link you click to verify the address you provided. If you receive an email asking for your Apple ID or other identifying information, this is not from Apple and you should delete it without responding to it. You also receive notifications on other devices on which the same Apple ID is configured informing you that the addresses have been enabled for iMessage on your iPhone.

10 Tap an address so it has a check mark to enable it for iMessage, or tap it so it doesn't have one to disable it. If you have only one email address, you can skip this step.

11 Swipe up the screen until you can see the START NEW CONVERSATIONS FROM section.

●○○○○ AT&T 🔆   6:02 AM   ☾ ⊕ ➹ 40% ▣▸

‹ Messages   **iMessage**

Apple ID: bradmacosx@mac.com

YOU CAN BE REACHED BY IMESSAGE AT

✓ +

✓ bradmacosx@icloud.com   ⓘ

bradmacosx@mac.com   ⓘ

bradmacosx@me.com   ⓘ

✓ bradmiser@icloud.com   ⓘ

✓ bradmiser@me.com   ⓘ

(12) Tap the phone number or email address you want to use by default when you start a new text conversation. In most cases, you should tap your email address so the Messages app always starts a new message using iMessage.

(13) Tap Messages.

(14) Swipe up the screen so you see the SMS/MMS section. This is where you configure settings for texts you send and receive via your cellular phone connection.

(15) If you don't want to allow photos and videos to be included in your messages, set the MMS Messaging switch to off (white). You won't be able to include images or videos with your messages sent using the cellular network. You might want to disable this option if your provider charges more for these types of messages—or if you simply don't want to deal with anything but text in your messages.

(16) To keep messages you send to a group of people organized by the group, set the Group Messaging switch to on (green). When enabled, replies you receive to messages you send to groups (meaning more than one person) are shown on a group message screen where each reply from everyone is included on the same screen. If this is off (white), when

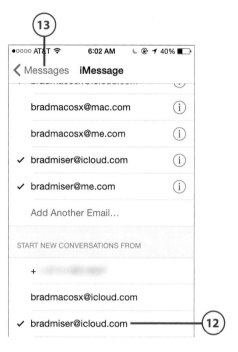

someone replies to a message sent to a group, the message is separated out as if the original message was just to that person. (The steps in this chapter assume Group Messaging is on.)

(17) To add a subject field to your messages, set the Show Subject Field switch to on (green). This divides text messages into two sections; the upper section is for a subject, and you type your message in the lower section. This is not a common way to text, so you can just leave this off. (The steps in this chapter assume this setting is off.)

(18) To display the number of characters you've written compared to the number allowed (such as 59/160), enable the Character Count setting by setting its switch to on (green). When it is off, you don't see a character count for messages you send. Technically, text messages you send via the cellular network are limited to 160 characters so showing the character count helps you see where you are relative to this limit (iMessages don't have this limit).

(19) Use the Blocked option to block people from texting you (see Chapter 17, "Maintaining and Protecting Your iPhone and Solving Problems," for detailed steps to using blocking).

(20) Tap Keep Messages.

●○○○○ AT&T 📶 6:06 AM 📞 @ ➤ 39% 🔋

❮ Settings **Messages**

SMS/MMS

MMS Messaging ⬤

Group Messaging ⬤ —(16)

Show Subject Field ○ —(17)

Character Count ○ —(18)

Blocked ──────────────➤ (19)

MESSAGE HISTORY

Keep Messages Forever ➤ (20)

21 Tap the length of time for which you want to keep messages.

22 If you tap something other than Forever, tap Delete. The messages on your iPhone older than the length of time you selected in step 21 are deleted.

23 Tap Messages.

24 Tap Expire in the AUDIO MESSAGES section.

●○○○○ AT&T 🤶 6:13 AM ◔ ⊕ ◀ 37% 🔋

❮ Messages **Keep Messages**

30 Days

1 Year ──────────────── **21**

Forever ✓

Delete Older Messages?

This will permanently delete all text messages and message attachments from your device that are older than 1 year.

Delete ───── **22**

Cancel

23

●○○○○ AT&T 🤶 6:13 AM ◔ ⊕ ◀ 37% 🔋

❮ Messages **Keep Messages**

30 Days

1 Year ✓

Forever

MESSAGE HISTORY

Keep Messages 1 Year ❯

AUDIO MESSAGES

Expire After 2 Minutes ─── **24**

25 Tap Never if you want to keep audio messages until you delete them or After 2 Minutes to have them deleted after two minutes. If you selected After 2 Minutes, audio messages are automatically deleted two minutes after you listen to them. This is good because audio messages require a lot of storage space and deleting them keeps that space available for other things.

26 Tap Messages.

27 If you want to be able to listen to audio messages by lifting the phone to your ear, set the Raise to Listen switch to on (green). If you set this to off (white), you need to manually start audio messages.

28 Tap Expire in the VIDEO MESSAGES section.

29 Tap Never if you want video messages included in an iMessage to be kept on your phone or After 2 Minutes to have them automatically deleted after two minutes. Video messages can take up a lot of storage space so it's usually a good idea to choose After 2 Minutes.

30 Tap Messages.

31 Tap Settings. You're ready to send and receive messages.

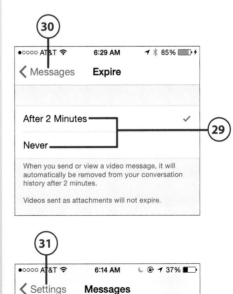

Audio and Video Messages

There are two types of audio and video messages you can send via the Messages app. Instant audio and video messages are embedded in the message itself. Audio and videos can also be attached to messages. The Expire settings only affect embedded audio or video messages. Audio or videos that are attached to messages are not deleted automatically.

Messages and Notifications

You should also configure the notifications the Messages app uses to communicate with you. You can configure the alert styles (none, banners, or alerts), badges on the icon to show you the number of new messages, and sounds and vibrations when you receive messages. Messages also supports repeated alerts, which by default is to send you two notifications for each message you receive but don't read. Configuring notifications is explained in detail in Chapter 4, "Configuring an iPhone to Suit Your Preferences."

Sending Messages

You can use the Messages app to send messages to people using a cell phone number (as long as the device receiving it can receive text messages) or an email address that has been registered for iMessage. If the recipient has both a cell number and iMessage-enabled email address, the Messages app assumes you want to use iMessage for the message.

When you send a message to more than one person and at least one of those people can use only the cellular network, all the messages are sent via the cellular network and not as an iMessage.

More on Mixed Recipients

If one of a message's recipients has an email address that isn't iMessage-enabled (and doesn't have a phone number), the Messages app attempts to send the message to that recipient as an email message. The recipient receives the email message in an email app on his phone or computer instead of through the Messages app.

Whether messages are sent via a cellular network or iMessage isn't terribly important, but there are some differences. If your cellular account has a limit on the number of texts you can send, you should use iMessage when you can because those messages won't count against your limit. Also, when you use iMessage, you don't have to worry about a limit on the number of characters in a message. When you send a message via a cellular network, your messages might be limited to 160 characters.

Siri is Messages' Best Friend

Using Siri, you can speak to text, and this is one of Siri's best uses. For example, you can start a new message by saying something like, "Send text to William Wallace." Siri then creates a new message and asks you what you would like the message to say. After you speak the message, you can review and send it. Using Siri text can be faster and easier than typing. See Chapter 12, "Working with Siri," for the details of using Siri for messaging and lots of other tasks.

Creating and Sending Messages

You can send text messages by entering a number or email address manually or by selecting a contact from your contacts list.

1. On the Home screen, tap Messages.

2. Tap New Message. If you haven't used the Messages app before, you skip this step and move directly to the compose message screen in the next step.

3. Type the recipient's name, email address, or phone number. As you type, the app attempts to match what you type with a saved contact or to someone you have messaged with before.

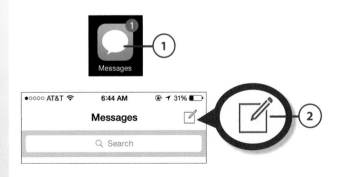

You see the available information, such as phone numbers and email addresses, for the contact. Phone numbers or addresses in blue indicate the recipient is registered for iMessage and your message will be sent via that means. When you see a phone number in green, the message will be sent as a text message over the cellular network. If a number or email address is black, you haven't sent any messages to it yet; you can tap it to attempt to send a message.

Tap to select a recipient from your contacts

iMessage-enabled email address

Phone number that hasn't been used for messaging

4 Tap the phone number or email address to which you want to send the message. The contact's name is inserted into the To field. Or, if the information you want to use doesn't appear, just type the complete phone number (as you would dial it to make a call to that number) or email address.

Straight to the Source

You can tap the Add button (+) in the To field to use the Contacts app to select a contact to whom you want to address the message.

Change Your Mind?

To remove a contact or phone number from the To box, tap it once so it becomes highlighted in blue and then tap the Delete key on the keyboard.

5 If you want to send the message to more than one recipient, tap in the space between the current recipient and the + button and use steps 3 and 4 to enter the other recipients' information, either by selecting contacts or by entering phone numbers or email addresses. As you add recipients, they appear in the To field. (If you addressed the message to a number or email address that matches a number in your contacts, the contact's name replaces the number in the To field. If not, the number or email address remains as you entered it.)

6. Tap in the Message bar, which is labeled iMessage if you entered iMessage addresses or Text Message if you entered a phone number. The cursor moves into the Message bar and you are ready to type your message.

7. Type the message you want to send in the Message bar.

8. Tap Send, which is blue if you are sending the message via iMessage or green if you are sending it via the cellular network. The Send status bar appears as the message is sent; when the process is complete, you hear the message sent sound and the status bar disappears.

If the message is addressed to iMessage recipients, your message appears in a blue bubble in a section labeled iMessage. If the person to whom you sent the message enabled his read receipt setting, you see when he reads your message.

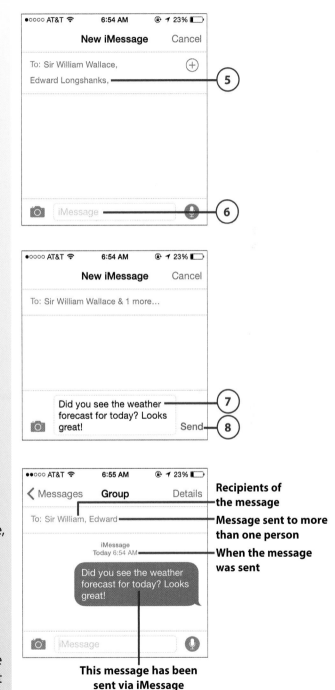

Recipients of the message

Message sent to more than one person

When the message was sent

This message has been sent via iMessage

If you sent the message to a cell phone, you see your message in a green bubble. If the message is sent to a cell phone or includes a cell phone recipient, it appears in a section labeled Text Message.

When you send a message, you see a new conversation screen if the message was not sent to someone or a group of people with whom you were previously messaging. If you have previously sent messages to the same recipient or recipients, you move back to the existing conversation screen and your new message is added to that conversation instead.

If you've addressed the message to only one person, that person's name appears at the top of the screen. If the message is going to more than one recipient, the title of the screen is Group MMS (assuming MMS is enabled) or just Group if it is an iMessage conversation.

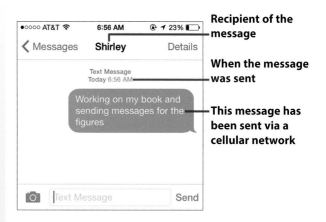

Recipient of the message

When the message was sent

This message has been sent via a cellular network

Speak Your Mind!

If you tap the Microphone icon, you can dictate text into a message. See Chapter 12 for details.

Receiving, Reading, and Replying to Messages

Text messaging is about communication, so when you send messages you expect to receive responses. People can also send new messages to you. The Messages app keeps messages grouped as a conversation consisting of messages you send and replies you receive.

Receiving Messages

Message alert notification on the Lock screen

Swipe to the right on the notification to move into the Messages app to read the entire message

When you aren't currently using the Messages screen in the Messages app and receive a new message (as a new conversation or as a new message in an ongoing conversation), you see, hear, and feel the notifications you have configured for the Messages app. (Refer to Chapter 4 to configure your message notifications.)

If you are on the Messages screen in the Messages app when a new message comes in, you hear and feel the new message notification but an alert does not appear.

If a message is from someone to whom you have previously sent a message or received a message from and you haven't deleted all the messages to or from those recipients (no matter how long it has been since a message was added to that conversation), the new message is appended to an ongoing conversation and that conversation moves to the top of the list of conversations on the Messages screen. If there isn't an existing message to or from the people involved in a new message, a new conversation is started and the message appears at the top of that list.

New message received while using the Messages app

Were We Speaking of Texting?

Using Siri to hear and speak text messages is extremely useful. Check out Chapter 12 for examples showing how you can take advantage of this great feature.

Reading Messages

You can get to new messages you receive by doing any of the following:

Tap an alert to read a new message in the Messages app

- Tap the banner alert notification. You move into the message's conversation in the Messages app.

- Swipe to the right on a message notification when it appears on the Lock screen.

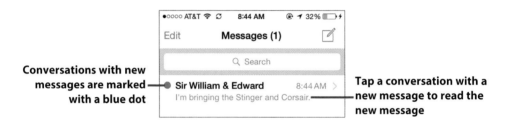

Conversations with new messages are marked with a blue dot

Tap a conversation with a new message to read the new message

- Open the Messages app and tap the conversation containing a new message; these conversations appear at the top of the Messages list and are marked with a blue circle. The conversation opens and you see the new message.

- If you receive a new message in a conversation that you are currently viewing, you immediately see the new message.

However you get to a message, you see the new message in either an existing conversation or a new conversation. The newest messages appear at the bottom of the screen.

Messages sent to you are on the left side of the screen and appear in a gray bubble. Just above the bubble is the name of the person sending the message; if you have an image for the contact, that image appears next to the bubble. The color of your bubbles indicates how the message is sent: blue indicates an iMessage while green indicates a cellular message.

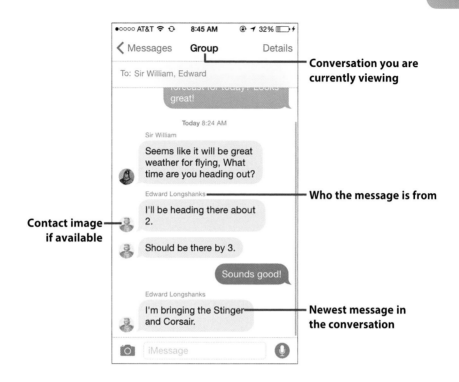

Conversation you are currently viewing

Who the message is from

Contact image if available

Newest message in the conversation

Viewing Images or Video You Receive in Messages

When you receive a photo or video, it appears in a thumbnail along with the accompanying message.

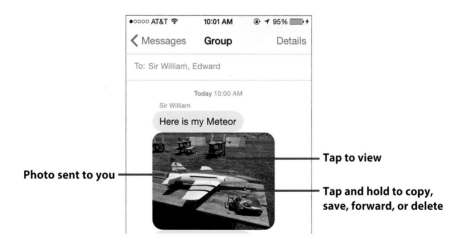

Photo sent to you

Tap to view

Tap and hold to copy, save, forward, or delete

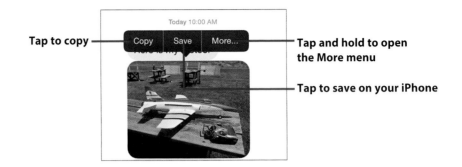

Tap to copy

Tap and hold to open the More menu

Tap to save on your iPhone

To copy the photo or video and paste it into another app, tap and hold on it; when the Copy command appears, tap it. To save the image on your iPhone, tap and hold on it until the menu appears; then tap Save. To forward it to someone else, tap and hold on the image. On the resulting menu, tap More. Tap the forward button located in the bottom-right corner of the screen. Complete the New Message that appears to send the photo along with a message. To delete the photo, tap and hold on the image. On the resulting menu, tap More. Then tap the Trash button.

To view a photo or video, tap it. You see the photo or video at a larger size.

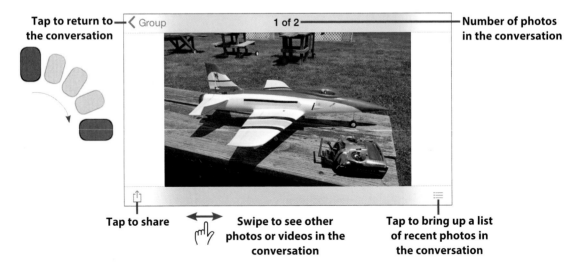

Tap to return to the conversation

Number of photos in the conversation

Tap to share   Swipe to see other photos or videos in the conversation   Tap to bring up a list of recent photos in the conversation

If there is more than one photo or video in the conversation, you see the number of them at the top of the screen. Swipe to the left or right to move through the available photos. You can rotate the phone, zoom, and swipe around the photo just like viewing photos in the Photos app. You can watch a video in the same way, too.

Tap the list button to see a list of the recent photos in the conversation (this only appears if there is more than one photo in the conversation). Tap a photo on the list to view it.

Tap the Share button to share the photo with others via a message, email, tweet, or Facebook.

To move back to the conversation, tap the Back button (which is labeled according to the title of the conversation).

Listening to Audio in Messages You Receive in Messages

NEW! Messages can include audio that is recorded and embedded in a conversation so you can hear it. You learn how to send your own audio shortly.

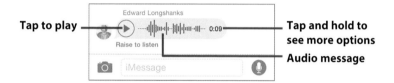

When you receive an embedded audio message, you can tap the Play button to play or if you enabled the Raise to Listen option in the Messages settings covered in a previous task, lift the phone to your ear and the message plays automatically.

While the message is playing you see its status along with the Pause button that you can tap to pause it. After the message finishes, you see a message saying that it expires in 2 minutes if you selected that setting. That message is quickly replaced by Keep.

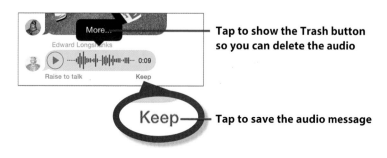

Tap Keep to save the message on your phone. To delete a message you have kept, tap and hold on it until you see More. Tap More and then tap the Trash button. (If you have chosen the setting to have the audio messages expire in 2 minutes in the Settings app, then you can just let it expire rather than deleting it. See, "Setting Your Text and iMessage Preferences," earlier in this chapter.)

Watching Video in Messages You Receive in Messages

NEW! Messages can include embedded video that is recorded and added to a conversation so you can watch it.

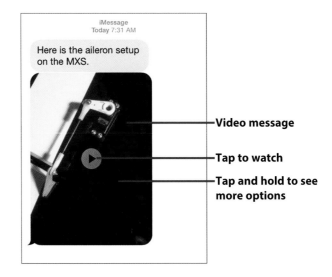

When you receive video embedded in a message, you can tap the Play button to watch it. The video plays. Tap it to stop the playback.

Assuming you left the Expire setting for videos at After 2 Minutes, the video is deleted automatically after two minutes.

To save a video message on your phone, tap and hold on it until the menu appears, and then tap Save. It is saved in the Photos app (see Chapter 15, "Working with Photos and Video You Take with Your iPhone" for information about using the Photos app).

If you want to delete a video before it expires or if you have the Expire setting on the Never option, tap and hold on the video to open the menu and then tap More. Tap the Trash icon and tap Delete Message at the prompt.

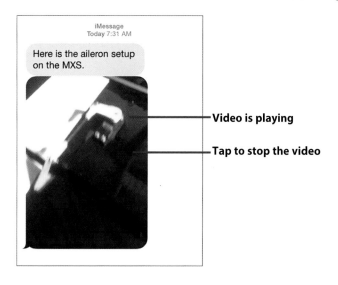

Video is playing

Tap to stop the video

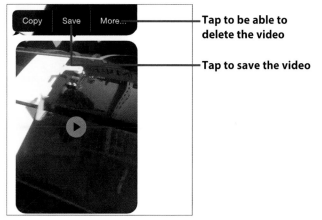

Tap to be able to delete the video

Tap to save the video

Replying to Messages from the Messages App

To reply to a message, read the message and do the following:

(1) Read, watch, or listen to the most recent message.

(2) Tap in the Message bar.

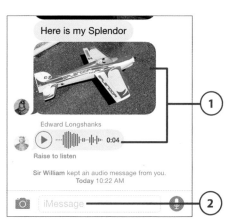

3. Type your reply or use the Dictation feature to speak your reply (this is translated to text unlike recording and embedding an audio message).

4. Tap Send. (If the message will be sent via the cellular network, the Send button is green; if it will be sent via iMessage, it is blue.) The message is sent, and your message is added to the conversation. Messages you send are on the right side of the screen in a blue bubble if they were sent via iMessage or a green bubble if they were sent via the cellular network.

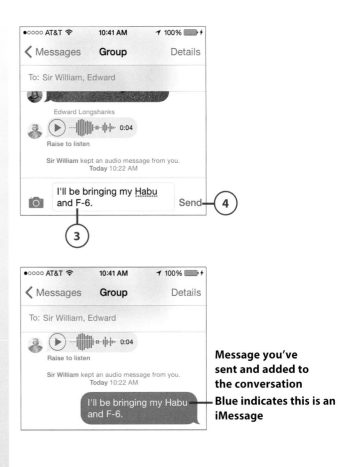

Message you've sent and added to the conversation

Blue indicates this is an iMessage

Mix and Match

The Messages app can switch between types of messages. For example, if you have an iMessage conversation going but can't access the iMessage service for some reason, the app can send messages as a cellular text. It can switch the other way, too. The app tries to send iMessages first if it can but chooses whichever method it can to get the messages through. (If you disabled the Send as SMS option, messages are only sent via iMessage.)

More Tricks of the Messaging Trade

My Acquisitions Editor Extraordinaire pointed out that when people have cellular data turned off, they can't receive messages. The sender doesn't see a warning in this case; you can only tell the message wasn't delivered because the "Delivered" status doesn't appear under the message. The message is delivered as soon as the other person's phone is connected to the Internet again, and its status is updated accordingly on your phone. Also, when an iMessage can't be delivered, you can tap and hold on it; then tap Send as Text Message. The app tries to send the message via SMS instead of iMessage.

Replying to Messages from a Banner Alert

NEW! If you have banner alerts configured for your messages, you can reply directly from the alert:

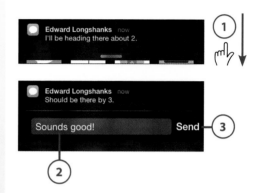

(**1**) Swipe down on the center of the banner alert notification. The reply box opens.

(**2**) Type your reply.

(**3**) Tap Send. Your message is added to the conversation.

Having a Messages Conversation

Messaging is all about the back-and-forth communication with one or more people. You've already learned the skills you need, so put them all together. You can start a new conversation by sending a message to one or more people with whom you don't have an ongoing conversation; or, you can add to a conversation already underway.

(**1**) Send a new message to a person or add a new message to an existing conversation. You see when your message has been delivered. If you sent the message to an individual person via iMessage and he has enabled his Read Receipt setting, you see when he has read your message and you see a bubble as he is composing a response. (If you are

Your message has been delivered

conversing with more than one person, the person doesn't have her Read Receipt setting enabled, or the conversation is happening via the cellular network, you don't see either of these.)

As the recipient composes a response, you see a bubble on the screen where the new message will appear when it is received (again, only if it is an iMessage with a single individual). Of course, you don't have to remain on the conversation's screen waiting for a response. You can move to a different conversation or a different app. When the response comes in, you are notified per your notification settings.

(2) Read the response.

(3) Type and send your next message.

(4) Repeat these steps as long as you want. Conversations remain in the Messages app until you remove them. Messages within conversations remain forever (unless you delete them), for one year, or for 30 days depending on your Keep Messages setting as shown earlier in this chapter.

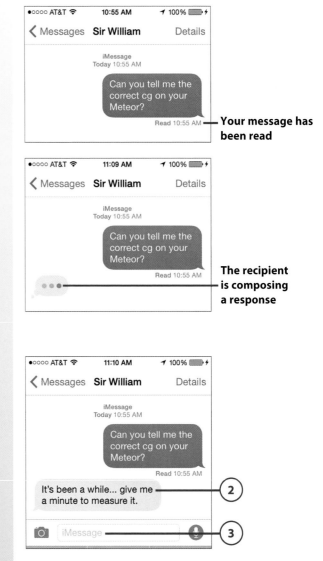

Your message has been read

The recipient is composing a response

Seen But Not Read

Don't take the Read status too literally. All it means is that the conversation to which your message was added has been viewed. Of course, the Messages app can't know whether the recipient actually read the message.

The iMessage Will Be With You...Always

Messages that are sent with iMessage move with you from device to device, so they appear on every device configured to use your iMessage account. Because of this, you can start a conversation on your iPhone while you are on the move and pick it up on your iPad or Mac later.

Working with Messages

As you send and receive messages, the interaction you have with each person or group becomes a separate conversation. A conversation consists of all the messages that have gone back and forth. You manage your conversations from the Messages screen.

Managing Messages Conversations

Use the Messages screen to manage your messages.

 On the Home screen, tap Messages.

The Messages screen showing conversations you have going appears. Conversations containing new messages appear at the top of the list. The name of the conversation is the name of the person or people associated with it, or it might be labeled as Group if the app can't display the names. If a contact can't be associated with the person, you see the phone number or email address you are conversing with instead of a name.

If you have the badge enabled, you see the number of new messages on the Messages icon

Information Messages

Many organizations use messages to keep you informed. Examples are airlines that send flight status information, and retailers that use messages to keep you informed about shipping. These messages are identified by a set of numbers that don't look like a phone number. You can't send a response to most of these messages; they are one-way only. In some cases, you can issue commands related to the texts from that organization, such as "Stop" to stop further texts from being sent.

(2) Swipe up and down the list to see all the conversations.

(3) Tap a conversation you want to read or reply to. The conversation screen appears; the name of the screen is the person with whom you are conversing, her number if she isn't in your contacts list, or Group if the message includes multiple recipients.

See the Time of Every Message

To see the time or date associated with every message in the conversation being displayed, swipe to the left and hold your finger down on the screen. The messages shift to the left and the time of each message appears along the right side of the screen. The date associated with each message appears right before the first message on that date.

(4) Read the new messages in the conversation. Your messages are on the right side of the screen in green (cell network) or blue (iMessage), whereas the other people's

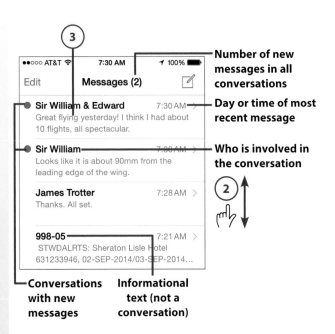

Number of new messages in all conversations

Day or time of most recent message

Who is involved in the conversation

Conversations with new messages

Informational text (not a conversation)

messages are on the left in gray. Messages are organized so the newest message is at the bottom of the screen.

5. Swipe up and down the conversation screen to see all the messages it contains.

6. To add a new message to the conversation, tap in the Message bar, type your message, and tap Send.

7. Swipe down the screen. As the screen scrolls down, you move back in time in the conversation.

8. To see details about the conversation, tap Details. The Details screen appears. At the top of the screen, you see location information for the people with whom you are texting if it is available (you learn more about locations in messages later in this chapter).

9. If you are working with a group message and want to give it a more meaningful name, swipe down the screen to reveal the Group Name field. If you are working with a conversation involving one other person, skip to step 11.

10. Tap in the Group Name field, enter the name of the group, and tap Done. The conversation is renamed with the name you entered.

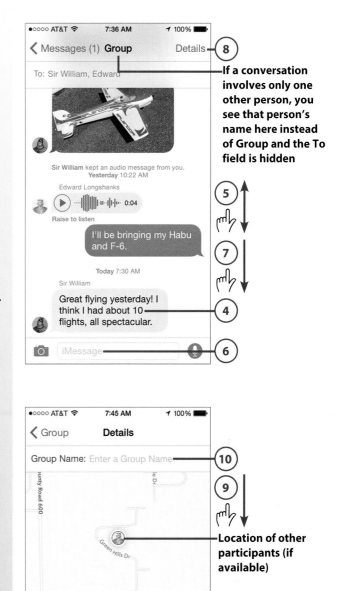

If a conversation involves only one other person, you see that person's name here instead of Group and the To field is hidden

Location of other participants (if available)

11 To place a voice call or audio-only FaceTime call to one of the participants in the conversation, tap the phone icon. If the person has a phone number configured, you're prompted to choose Voice Call or FaceTime Audio. When you make a choice, that call is placed. If the person only has an email address, an audio-only FaceTime call is placed over the Internet. You move into the Phone or FaceTime app and use that app to complete the call. Move to the Home screen and tap Messages or use the App Switcher to return to the Messages app. (See Chapter 8, "Communicating with the Phone and FaceTime Apps," for the details about those apps.)

12 To place a FaceTime call, tap the video camera icon. You move into the FaceTime app to complete the call. When you're done, move to the Home screen and tap Messages or use the App Switcher to return to the Messages app.

13 To send an email, tap the Email icon. Use the Mail app to compose and send the email (details are in Chapter 9, "Sending, Receiving, and Managing Email").

14 To view a participant's contact information, tap the info button.

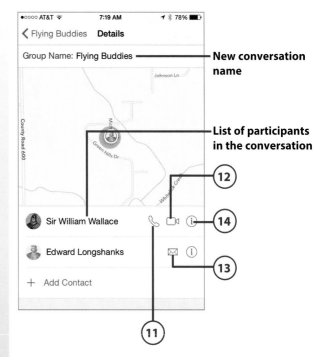

New conversation name

List of participants in the conversation

Receiving and Reading Messages on an iPhone 6 Plus

The iPhone 6 Plus' larger screen provides some additional functionality that is unique to it. You can access this by holding the iPhone 6 Plus horizontally when you use the Messages app.

1. Open the Mail app and hold the iPhone, so it is oriented horizontally. The window splits into two panes. On the left is the Navigation pane, where you can move to and select conversations you want to view. When you select a conversation in the left pane, its messages appear in the Content pane on the right.

2. Swipe up or down the Navigation pane to browse the conversations available to you. Notice that the two panes are independent. When you browse the left pane, the right pane doesn't change.

3. Tap the conversation containing messages you want to read. The messages in that conversation appear in the Content pane on the right.

4. Swipe up and down the Content pane to read the messages in the conversation.

5. Listen to embedded audio, watch embedded video, or work with attachments just like when you hold the iPhone vertically.

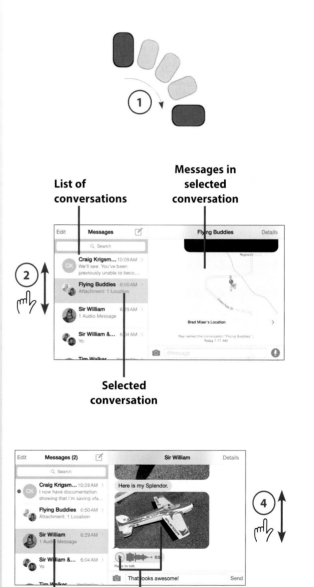

List of conversations

Messages in selected conversation

Selected conversation

(6) To add a message to the conversation, tap in the send bar, type your message, and tap Send. Of course, you can embed audio or video, attach photos or video, or send your location just as you can when using Messages when you hold the iPhone vertically.

(7) To work with the conversation's details, tap Details.

(8) To change conversations, tap the conversation you want to view.

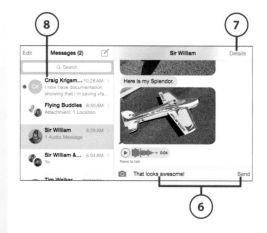

Adding Images and Video to Conversations

You can attach any image, photo, or video stored on your iPhone to a text conversation, or you can take a photo or video to include in a message. This is a great way to share photos and videos.

(1) Move into the conversation with the person to whom you want to send a photo, or start a new conversation with that person.

(2) Tap the Camera button. A dialog appears that enables you to add photos or videos in three ways. Perform steps 3 through 6 to send a photo you've recently taken. Perform steps 7 through 11 to send any photo or video stored on your iPhone. Start with step 12 to take a new photo or video to send.

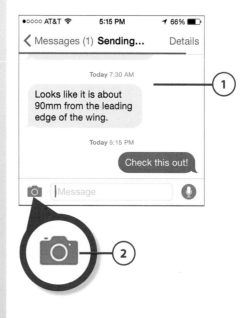

Limitations, Limitations

Not all cell carriers support MMS messages (the type that can contain images and video), and the size of messages can be limited. Check with your carrier for more information about what is supported and whether there are additional charges for using MMS messages. If you're using iMessage, you don't have this potential limit and are always able to include images and video in your texts. Also be sure your recipient can receive MMS messages before sending one.

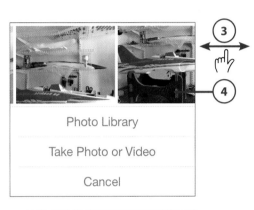

(3) If you have taken the photo recently, swipe to the left or right on the thumbnails you see above Photo Library to view the photos available to send.

(4) Tap the photo you want to send. The photo is marked with a check mark to show it is selected.

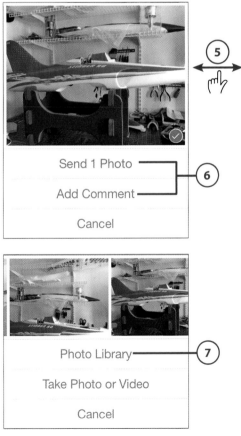

(5) To send more photos, swipe to the left and right on the photo to browse the others and then tap the photos you want to send.

(6) To send the photos without comment, tap Send *X* Photos, where *X* is the number of photos you selected; the photos send and you go back to the conversation and can skip to step 16. To send the photos and make a comment about them, tap Add Comment; the photos are added to the conversation and you are ready to type your comment; skip to step 15.

(7) Tap Photo Library.

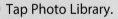

8 Browse the source containing the photos you want to send. (For more information about viewing sources of photos, see Chapter 15.

9 Swipe up or down the screen until you see the photo you want to send.

10 Tap the photo you want to send.

11 Tap Choose. You move back to the conversation and see the image in the Send box; move to step 15.

12 Tap Take Photo or Video.

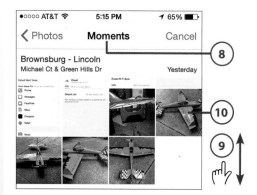

13) Take the photo or video you want to send. (For more information about taking photos or videos, see Chapter 15.)

14) Tap Use Photo or Use Video.

15) Type the message you want to send with the photo or video. (Or, you can just tap Send without adding a message.)

16) Tap Send. The message, and photo or video, is sent.

This Isn't Houston, but There Is a Problem

If a message you try to send is undeliverable or has some other problem, it is marked with an exclamation point inside a red circle. Tap that icon and tap Try Again to attempt to resend the message.

Sharing with Messages

You can share all sorts of information via Messages from many apps, such as Safari, Contacts, and Maps. From the app containing the information you want to share, tap the Share button. Then tap Messages. The information with which you are working is automatically added to a new message. Use the Messages app to complete and send the message.

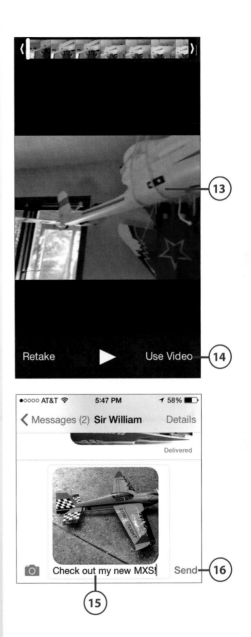

Adding Audio Recordings to Conversations

NEW! In a previous task you learned how to listen to embedded audio messages. Here's how to send your own audio messages:

1. Move to the conversation to which you want to add an audio message, or start a new conversation.

2. Tap and hold on the Microphone at the right edge of the screen (not the one on the keyboard). Recording starts.

3. Speak your message; keep your finger touching the Microphone while you speak.

4. When you are done recording, take your finger off the screen.

5. To replay your message, tap the Play button.

6. To delete your message, tap x.

7. To send the message, tap the upward-facing arrow. The audio message is added to the conversation and the recipients are able to listen to it.

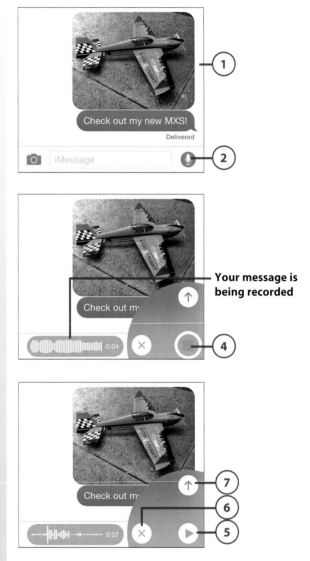

Your message is being recorded

Embedded vs. Attachments

When you record audio or video for a message, it is embedded in the message. When you use the steps in "Adding Images and Video to Conversations," the images or video are attachments to the conversation. You can view or watch these similarly, but attachments are not impacted by the Expire settings and you can do more actions with attachments than you can with embedded items, such as forwarding to others and viewing all the attachments to a conversation.

Adding Video to Conversations

NEW! Here's how to embed video into your conversations:

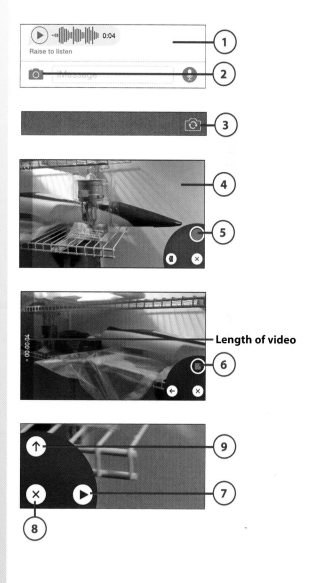

Length of video

(1) Move to the conversation to which you want to add video, or start a new conversation.

(2) Tap and hold the Camera icon until the video tool appears and the Messages screen is replaced by the video camera screen.

(3) If you don't want to take a "selfie" video (where the camera on the front side is used so your face is shown), tap the Switch Camera button to change to the backside camera.

(4) Adjust the image to what you want it to be when you start the video.

(5) Tap the Record button. The video starts recording.

(6) When you're done recording, tap the Stop button.

(7) To view the video, tap the Play button.

(8) To delete the video, tap the delete button.

(9) To send the video, tap the Send button. The video is added to the conversation and the recipients are able to view it.

Adding Locations to Conversations

NEW! Location information can be available for the participants in a conversation. You can add location information to a conversation as follows:

① Move to the conversation to which you want to add your location information.

② Tap Details.

③ To share your current location as a snapshot, tap Send My Current Location. Your current location is captured and sent to the recipients of the message. Skip the rest of these steps.

④ To share your location so that it updates as you move around, tap Share My Location.

⑤ Tap how long you want your location information to be shared. You location is shared with the participants in the conversation and can be viewed on the Details screen on their devices. A notification that you are sharing your location is added to the conversation.

⑥ To stop sharing your location, tap Stop Sharing My Location.

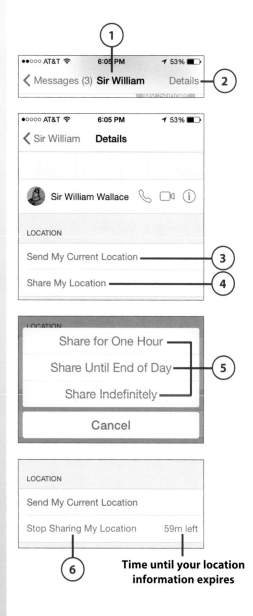

Time until your location information expires

Current Locations

When a current location is added to a conversation, it is static, meaning it is only the location at that point in time. It appears as a map thumbnail in the conversation. Recipients can tap it to zoom in on the location and then tap Directions to Here to generate directions from their location to the one sent as the current location.

Browsing Attachments to Conversations

NEW! As photos and videos are added to a conversation, they are collected so you can browse and view them at any time:

(1) Move to the conversation for which you want to browse attachments.

(2) Tap Details.

(3) Swipe up until you see the ATTACHMENTS section.

(4) Swipe up and down on the attachments until you see one you want to view.

(5) Tap the attachment you want to view.

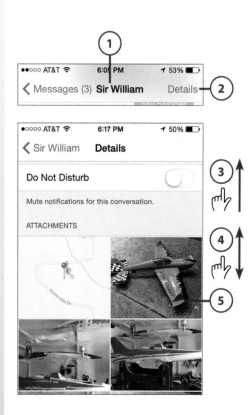

6 View the attachment.

7 Tap the attachment.

8 Tap the list button to see a list of all the attachments; tap an attachment to view it.

9 Tap the Share button to share the attachment via messages, email, etc. or to save it to your iPhone, add it to a contact, or take one of other available actions on it.

10 Tap Done to return to the Details screen.

Stop Bugging Me!

You can disable notifications for a specific conversation by moving to its Details screen and setting the Do Not Disturb switch to on (green). You no longer are notified when new messages arrive in that conversation. Set the switch to off (white) to have notifications resume.

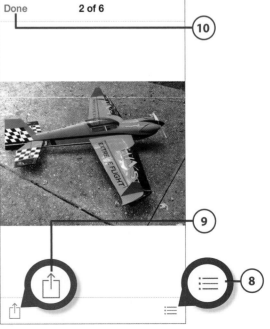

Deleting Messages and Conversations

Old text conversations never die, nor do they fade away (unless you have set the Keep Messages setting at 30 Days or 1 Year, in which case messages disappear from your iPhone when those respective times pass). All the messages you receive from a person or that involve the same group of people stay in the conversation. Over time, you can build up a lot of messages in one conversation; and, you can end up with lots of conversations. (If you set the Keep Messages setting to be 30 Days or 1 Year, messages older than the time you set are deleted automatically.)

When a conversation gets too long or if you just want to remove specific messages from a conversation, take these steps:

(1) Move to a conversation containing an abundance of messages.

(2) Tap and hold on a message you want to delete.

(3) Tap More. The message on which you tapped is marked with a check mark to show it is selected.

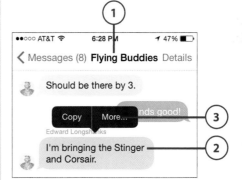

Long Conversation?

When a conversation gets very long, the Messages app won't display all its messages. It keeps the more current messages visible on the conversation screen. To see earlier messages, swipe down on the screen to move to the top and tap Load Earlier Messages.

(4) Tap other messages you want to delete. They are marked with a check mark to show you have selected them.

(5) Tap the Trash icon.

(6) Tap Delete X Messages, where X is the number of messages you have selected. The messages are deleted and you return to the conversation.

Delete Them All!

To delete the whole conversation, instead of performing step 4, tap Delete All, which appears in the upper-left corner of the screen. Tap Delete Conversation. The conversation and all its messages are deleted.

Pass It On

If you want to send one or more messages to someone else, perform steps 1–3. Tap the Forward button that appears in the lower-right corner of the screen. A new message is created and the messages you selected are pasted into it. Select or enter the recipients to whom you want to send the messages, and tap Send.

Deleting Conversations

If a conversation's time has come, you can delete it.

(1) Move to the Messages screen.

(2) Swipe to the left on the conversation you want to delete.

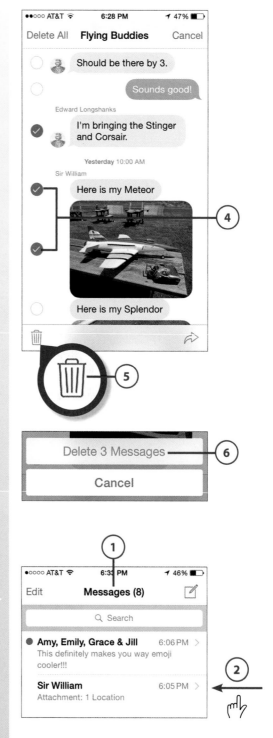

③ Tap Delete. The conversation and all the messages it contains are deleted.

●○○○○ AT&T 🛜   6:33 PM   ✈ 46% ▭

Done   **Messages (8)**

🔍 Search

● **Amy, Emily, Grace & Jill**   6:06 PM ›
This definitely makes you way emoji cooler!!!

am   6:05 PM ›
ent: 1 Location   Delete ──③

>>>*Go Further*

TEXTING LINGO

People frequently use shorthand when they text. Here is some of the more common shorthand you might see. This list is extremely short, but there are many websites dedicated to providing this type of information if you are interested. One that boasts of being the largest list of text message acronyms is www.netlingo.com/acronyms.php.

- FWIW—For What It's Worth
- LOL—Laughing Out Loud
- ROTFL—Rolling On the Floor Laughing
- CU—See You (later)
- PO—Peace Out
- IMHO—In My Humble Opinion
- TY—Thank You
- RU—Are You
- BRB—Be Right Back
- CM—Call Me
- DND—Do Not Disturb

- EOM—End of Message
- FSR—For Some Reason
- G2G—Got to Go
- IDK—I Don't Know
- IKR—I Know, Right?
- ILU—I Love You
- NM or NVM—Never Mind
- OMG—Oh My God
- OTP—On the Phone
- P911—Parent Alert
- PLZ—Please

Go here to figure
out where and
when you're
supposed to be

Tap here to use
your iPhone as a
clock

Use this app to
remind yourself
of…anything

In this chapter, you explore all the calendar and reminder functionality your iPhone has to offer. Topics include the following:

→ Getting started
→ Working with calendars
→ Working with reminders
→ Working with the clock

Managing Calendars, Reminders, and Clocks

When it comes to time, your iPhone is definitely your friend. Using the iPhone's Calendar app, you can view calendars that have been synchronized among all your devices, such as computers and iPads, using an online account, such as iCloud, or via the iTunes app on a computer. You can also make changes to your calendars on your iPhone and then sync them with your other devices so you have consistent information no matter which device you happen to be using at any time. The Reminders app ensures you don't forget tasks or anything else you want to remember. You can use the Clock app to set alarms, use as a stopwatch, and as a timer.

Getting Started

This chapter includes three different apps, because they are all related to managing your time.

The Calendar app does what it sounds like: it allows you to manage one or more calendars. This app has lots of features designed to help you work with multiple calendars and accounts, manage events that other people are invited to, and more. You don't have to use all these features, and you might just want to use its basic functionality, such as to record doctor appointments, dinner reservations, and similar events for which it is important to know the time and date (and be reminded when those time and dates are approaching).

The Reminders app can remind you about things you need to do at a specific time or it can be used to capture lists that don't have any specific time, such as things you need to buy the next time you go to a specific store.

The Clock app provides lots of very useful time functions, including an alarm, timer, and stopwatch.

It is likely that you can use the calendar, reminder, and time functions of your iPhone using their default settings. However, if you ever need to change those settings, you should know where they are.

To access the Calendar settings, open the Settings app; tap Mail, Contacts, Calendars; and swipe up until you see the CALENDARS section. Use the controls in this section to configure the Calendar app.

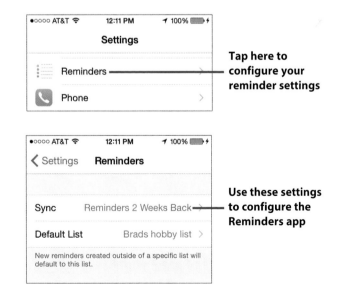

Use these settings to configure the Calendar app

Swipe up the Mail, Contacts, Calendars screen to see the CALENDARS section

To access the Reminders settings, open the Settings app and tap Reminders. Use the settings on the Reminders screen to configure the Reminders app.

Tap here to configure your reminder settings

Use these settings to configure the Reminders app

The Date & Time settings are the ones you are most likely to use. For example, if you prefer to use a 24-hour clock, set the 24-Hour Time switch to on (green). If you want to set your iPhone's time manually rather than having the server set the time according to your current time zone and location, set the Set Automatically switch to off (white) and use the resulting controls to set the time and date.

●●○○○ AT&T 📶   12:10 PM   ⬆ 100% ▭ ⚡

Settings

⚙️   General ———————————→ — **Tap here to get to the Date & Time settings**

●○○○○ AT&T 📶   12:11 PM   ⬆ 100% ▭ ⚡

‹ Settings   **General**

Swipe up the screen until you see Date & Time ↑

Auto-Lock   5 Minutes ›

Restrictions   Off ›

Date & Time ———————→ — **Tap to access to change date and time on your iPhone**

●○○○○ AT&T 📶   12:11 PM   ⬆ 100% ▭ ⚡

‹ General   **Date & Time** ———— **Use these settings to change your phone's date or time**

24-Hour Time   ⬜

Set Automatically   🟢

Time Zone   America/Indiana/Indianap…

Notifications

The Calendar and Reminders apps can communicate with you in various ways, such as displaying alerts or banners, and indicating when and how many invitations you've received. Configuring notifications to suit your preferences will make these apps even more valuable. Configuring notifications is explained in the section called "Setting Up Notifications and the Notification Center" in Chapter 4, "Configuring an iPhone to Suit Your Preferences."

Working with Calendars

The Calendar app helps you manage your calendars; you'll notice I wrote *calendars* rather than *calendar*. That's because you can have multiple calendars in the app at the same time. For example, you might have a calendar for your personal life, your work, and a particular club or group you belong to. Or, you might want a calendar for your travel plans.

In most cases, you start by adding existing calendar information from an iCloud, Google, or similar account or by using iTunes to sync your calendars with a calendar application on your computer. From there, you can view your calendars, add or change events, and much more directly in the Calendar app. Any changes you make in the Calendar app are automatically made in all the locations that use calendars from the same account, or you can manually sync calendar information via iTunes on your computer.

The best option for storing your calendar information is using online accounts (such as iCloud and Google) because you can easily access that information from many devices, and your calendars are kept in sync automatically. To learn how to configure an online account for calendar information, refer to Chapter 3, "Setting Up and Using iCloud and Other Online Accounts."

Viewing Calendars and Events

You use the Calendar app to view and work with your calendars, and you can choose how you view them, such as by month, week, or day.

To get into your calendars, move to the Home screen and tap the Calendar icon (which shows the current day and date in its icon). The most recent screen you were viewing appears. There are a couple of basic modes you use in the app. The one in which you'll spend most of your time in the app displays your calendars in various views, such as showing a month or a week and day. Another mode is the Calendars tool that enables you to choose and edit the calendar information that is displayed.

—**Tap to work with your calendars**

Configuring Calendars

If you only have one calendar and it's set up the way you want, you can skip this task. If you have more than one calendar and want to configure the calendar information you see in the app, perform the following steps:

(1) Open the Calendar app and tap Calendars. If you don't see this at the bottom of the screen, you are already on the Calendars screen (look for "Calendars" at the top of the screen), in which case you can skip this step. Or, you might have only one calendar on your iPhone and you don't need to set which calendar to display. In that case, you can skip to the next section.

The Calendars screen displays the calendars available, organized by the account from which they come, such as ICLOUD, GMAIL, or OTHER. Under each account, the individual calendars are provided by the account. By default, all your calendars are displayed, which is indicated by the check marks next to the calendars' names.

(2) Tap a calendar with a check mark to hide it. The check mark disappears and the calendar is hidden. (The calendar is still there, you just won't see it when you are viewing calendars.)

(3) To show a calendar again, tap its name. It is marked with a check mark and appears when you are viewing calendars.

(4) Tap the info button to see or change a calendar's information settings. Not all types of calendars support this function, and those that do can offer different settings. The following steps show an iCloud calendar; if you are working with a calendar of a different type, such as Google calendar, you might not have all or the same options as those shown here. In any case, the steps to make changes are similar across all available types of calendars.

(5) Change the name of the calendar by tapping it and then making changes on the keyboard; when you're done making changes, swipe down the screen to close the keyboard.

(6) To share the calendar with someone, tap Add Person, enter the email address of the person with whom you are sharing it, and tap Add.

(7) Tap the color in which you want events on the calendar to appear.

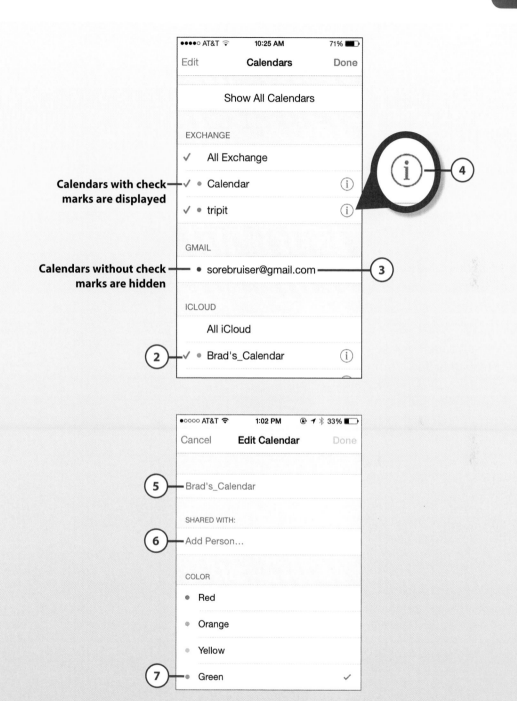

Calendars with check marks are displayed

Calendars without check marks are hidden

8 Swipe up the screen.

9 If you want alerts to be enabled (active) for the calendar, set the Event Alerts switch to on (green). If you set this to off, there won't be any alerts for events on the calendar.

10 To make the calendar public so that others can subscribe to a read-only version of it, set the Public Calendar switch to on (green), tap Share Link, and then use the resulting Share tools to invite others to subscribe to the calendar.

11 To remove the calendar entirely (instead of hiding it from view), tap Delete Calendar and then tap Delete Calendar at the prompt. The calendar and all its events are deleted. (It's usually better just to hide a calendar as described in step 2 so you don't lose its information.)

12 Assuming that you didn't delete the calendar, tap Done.

13 Edit other calendars as needed.

14 Tap Done. The app moves into viewing mode, and the calendars you enabled are displayed.

●○○○○ AT&T 📶   1:09 PM   @ ✓ ✳ 32% 🔋

Cancel   **Edit Calendar**   Done ── **12**

• Green ✓

• Blue

• Purple

8 ↑

• Brown 🖑

NOTIFICATIONS

Event Alerts ⬤━━ **9**

Allow events on this calendar to display alerts.

Public Calendar ◯── **10**

Allow anyone to subscribe to a read-only version of this calendar.

Delete Calendar ── **11**

●●●○○ AT&T 📶   5:18 PM   98% 🔋 ✦

Edit   **Calendars**   Done ── **14**

Show All Calendars

EXCHANGE

✓ All Exchange .

✓ • Calendar ⓘ

✓ • Travel (Tripit) ⓘ   ⓘ ── **13**

GMAIL

• sorebruiser@gmail.com

>>>Go Further
ALL OR NOTHING

You can make all your calendars visible by tapping the Show All Calendars button at the top of the screen; tap Hide All Calendars to do the opposite. After all the calendars are shown or hidden, you can tap individual calendars to show or hide them. You can show all the calendars from the same account by tapping the All command at the top of each account's calendar list, such as All iCloud to show all your iCloud calendars. Tap this again to hide all the account's calendars.

Navigating Calendars

The Calendar app uses a hierarchy of detail to display your calendars. The lowest level of detail, but longest timeframe displayed, is the year view. Next is the month view, which shows more detail but covers a shorter timeframe. This is followed by the week/day view; showing the highest level of detail is the event view.

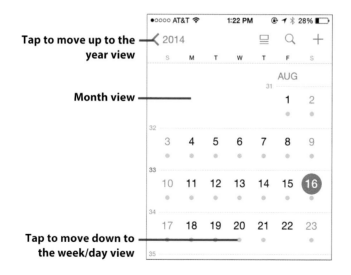

To move down in the hierarchy, you tap something on the view you are seeing. For example, to change from the month view to the week/day view, you tap the day in which you are interested. That day and the week it is in appear using the week/day view.

To move up in the hierarchy, you tap the Back button, which is always located in the upper-left corner of the screen. This is labeled to indicate where you will move when you tap it. For example, if you are in the month view, it is labeled with the month's year, indicating that when you tap it, you'll see that year. Likewise, when you are viewing the week/day view, the button has the name of the month that week is in.

To move to the year view so you are set up for the next task, keep tapping the Back button in the upper-left corner of the screen until it disappears (which happens when you are in the year view).

Viewing Calendars

You can view your calendars from the year level all the way down to the day/week view. It's easy to move among the levels to get to the time period you want to see. Here's how:

1. Starting at the year view, swipe up and down until you see the year in which you are interested. (If you aren't in the year view, keep tapping the Back button located in the upper-left corner of the screen until the button disappears.)

2. Tap the month in which you are interested. The days in that month display, and days with events are marked with a dot.

Today Is the Day

To quickly move to the current day, tap Today, located at the bottom of the screen. The current day is indicated by the date in the red circle.

(3) Swipe up and down the screen to view different months.

(4) To see the detail for a date, tap it. There are two ways to view the daily details: the Calendar view or the List view. Steps 5 through 8 show the Calendar view while steps 9 though 11 show the List view. Each of these views has benefits and as you can see, it is easy to switch between them.

(5) To see the Calendar view, ensure the List button is not selected (it isn't highlighted). On the resulting screen, just below the Back button, which is labeled with the month being displayed, are the days of the week you are viewing. The date in focus is highlighted with a black circle. Below this area is the detail for the day in focus showing the events on that date.

(6) Swipe to the left or right on the dates or date being displayed to change the date for which detailed information is being shown.

(7) Swipe up or down on the date detail to browse all its events.

(8) Tap an event to view its detail and skip to step 12.

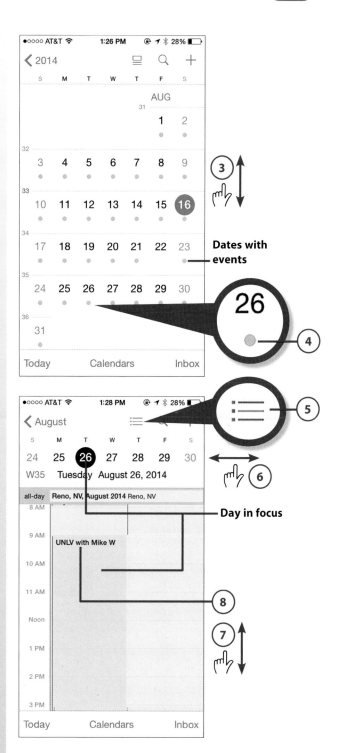

Dates with events

Day in focus

9 To see the events in List view, tap the List button so it is highlighted.

10 Swipe up and down to see the events for each day.

11 Tap on an event to view its detail.

12 Swipe up and down the screen to see all of the event's information.

13 Read information about the event.

14 Tap any links to move to information related to the event.

15 Tap the date to move back to the week/day view.

16 Tap the Back button (labeled with the month you are viewing) to move back to the month view.

17 To view your calendars in the multiday view, rotate your iPhone so it is horizontal. You can do this while in the week/day view or the month view.

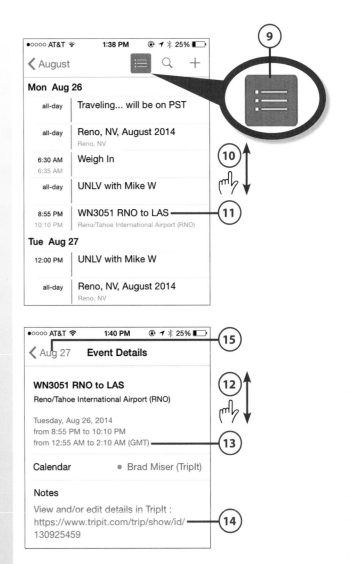

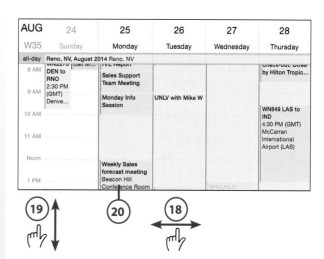

(18) Swipe left or right to change the dates being displayed.

(19) Swipe up or down to change the time of day being displayed.

(20) Tap an event to see its detail.

Adding Events to a Calendar

There are a number of ways you can add events to your calendar. You can create an event in an app on a computer, website, or other device and sync that event onto the iPhone through an online account or by syncing with iTunes on a computer. You can also manually create events in the Calendar app on the iPhone. Your events can include a lot of detail. You can choose to just create the basic information on your iPhone while you are on the move and complete it later from a computer or other device, or you can fill in all the details directly in the Calendar app.

(1) Tap the Add button, which appears in the upper-right corner of any of the views when your phone is vertical. The initial date information is taken from the date currently being displayed, so you can save a little time if you view the date of the event before tapping the Add button.

Location Prompt

The first time you create an event, you may be prompted to allow the Calendar app to access your location information. When you allow the app to use Location Services, you can search for and select the meeting location. The app can use this information to include an estimate of travel time for the event if that preference is turned on in the Settings app.

2 Tap in the Title field and type the title of the event.

3 Tap the Location bar and type the location of the event; if you allowed the app to use Location Services, you're prompted to find and select a location; if not, just type the location and skip to step 6.

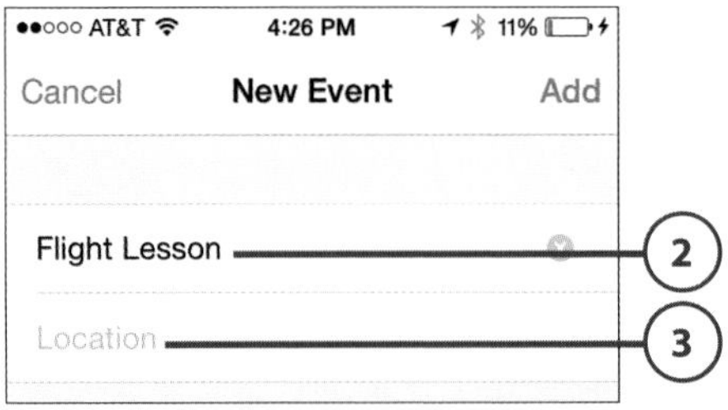

4 Type the location in the Search bar. Sites that meet your search are shown below.

5 Tap the location for the event.

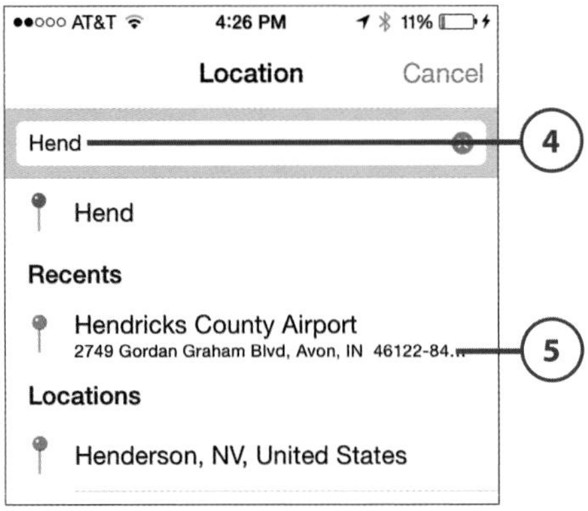

6 To set the event to last all day, set the All-day switch to the on position (green) and skip to step 17; to set a specific start and end time, leave this in the off (white) position.

7 To set a timeframe for the event, tap Starts. The date and time tool appears.

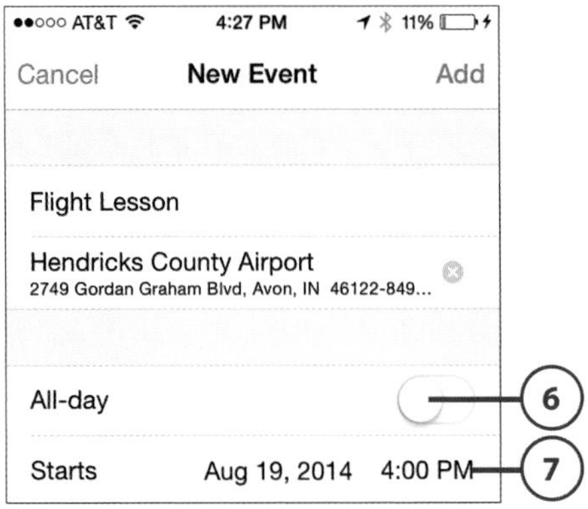

●●○○○ AT&T 📶 4:26 PM 🕐 ☀ 11% 🔋⚡

Cancel **New Event** Add

Flight Lesson — 2

Location — 3

●●○○○ AT&T 📶 4:26 PM 🕐 ☀ 11% 🔋⚡

Location Cancel

📍 Hend — 4

📍 Hend

Recents

📍 Hendricks County Airport
2749 Gordan Graham Blvd, Avon, IN 46122-84. — 5

Locations

📍 Henderson, NV, United States

●●○○○ AT&T 📶 4:27 PM 🕐 ☀ 11% 🔋⚡

Cancel **New Event** Add

Flight Lesson

Hendricks County Airport
2749 Gordan Graham Blvd, Avon, IN 46122-849...

All-day — 6

Starts Aug 19, 2014 4:00 PM — 7

8 Swipe up or down on the date wheel until the date on which the event starts appears in the center.

9 Swipe up or down on the hour wheel until the event's starting hour is shown.

10 Scroll and select the starting minute in the same way.

11 Swipe up or down on the hour wheel to select AM or PM.

12 If the time zone shown is correct, skip to step 14; if not, tap Time Zone. (Depending on your iPhone's settings and the type of calendar you are using, you might not see this field. If not, just skip to step 14.)

13 Search for and select the time zone with which the event should be associated.

14 Tap Ends.

15 Use the date and time tool to set the ending date and time for the event; these work the same way as for the start date and time.

16 Tap Ends. The date and time tool closes.

17 To make the event repeat, tap Repeat and follow steps 18–23. (For a nonrepeating event, skip to step 24.)

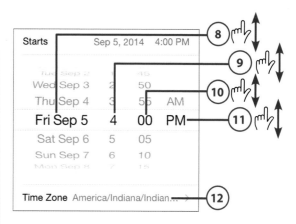

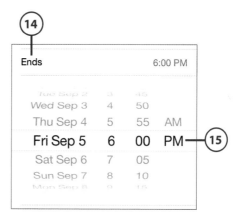

Custom Repeat

If one of the options listed on the Repeat screen isn't what you want, tap Custom and use the resulting tools to create a custom repeat frequency for the event. For example, you can use this to create an event that occurs on the first Monday of every month.

(18) Tap the frequency with which you want the event repeated, such as Every Day, Every Week, or Every Year; if you want to use a repeat cycle not shown, tap Custom and create the frequency with which you want the event to repeat.

(19) Tap End Repeat to set a time at which the event stops repeating.

(20) To have the event repeat ad infinitum, tap Never and skip to step 23.

(21) To set an end to the repetition, tap On Date.

(22) Use the date tool to set the date for the last repeated event.

(23) Tap New Event.

No Change Needed

If you don't make a change to one of the settings, such as on the Repeat screen, you need to tap New Event in the upper-left corner of the screen to get back to the New Event screen.

24 To configure travel time for the event, tap Travel Time; if you don't want to configure this, skip to step 31.

| End Repeat | Sun, Oct 5, 2014 > |
| Travel Time | None — **24** |

25 Set the Travel Time switch to on (green).

26 To manually add a travel time to the event, tap it and skip to step 30.

27 To build a travel time based on a starting location, tap Starting Location.

28 To use your current location as the starting point, tap Current Location. Alternatively, use the search tool to find a starting location, and then tap it to select that location.

●oooo AT&T 🤏 4:44 PM ✈ ✳ 28% 🔋✦

‹ New Event **Travel Time**

Travel Time ⚪ — **25**

Add travel time for this event to your calendar. Event alerts will take this time into account and your calendar will be blocked during this time.

●oooo AT&T 🤏 4:44 PM ✈ ✳ 28% 🔋✦

‹ New Event **Travel Time**

Travel Time 🔵

Starting Location — **27**
None

Select a starting location to automatically determine travel time, or select a time below.

5 minutes

15 minutes

✓ 30 minutes — **26**

●oooo AT&T 🤏 4:45 PM ✈ ✳ 28% 🔋✦

Location Cancel

Enter Location — **28**

✈ Current Location —

Recents

📍 Hendricks County Airport
2749 Gordan Graham Blvd, Avon, IN 46122-84...

(29) Tap the method you will use to travel to the location.

(30) Tap New Event.

(31) To change the calendar with which the event is associated, tap Calendar (if you only have one calendar or to leave the current calendar selected, skip to step 33).

(32) Tap the calendar with which the event should be associated.

(33) To set an alert for the event that is different than the default, tap Alert; if you want to use the default alert, skip to the step 37.

●○○○○ AT&T 📶   4:45 PM   🔋 ✳ 28% ▭ ⚡

❮ New Event **Travel Time** ─── **(30)**

Travel Time   ⬤

Starting Location   ❯
▮▮▮▮▮▮▮

Select a starting location to automatically determine travel time, or select a time below.

✓ 🚗 Based on location ── 25 min ── **(29)**

🚶 Based on location   3 hr, 10 min

5 minutes

Calendar   ● Brad's_Calendar → **(31)**

Invitees   None ❯

●●○○○ AT&T 📶   5:01 PM   🔋 ✳ 43% ▭ ⚡

❮ New Event **Calendar**

GMAIL

● sorebruiser@gmail.com

VFA

● Calendar

● Travel (Tripit)

ICLOUD

● Task Schedule

● Brad's_Calendar ───── ✓ ── **(32)**
Public and Shared with Sir William Wallace...

Invitees   2 ❯

Alert   15 minutes before travel time → **(33)**

34. Tap when you want to see an alert for the event.

35. To set a second alert that is different than the default, tap Second Alert; to use the default, skip to step 37.

36. Tap when you want to see a second alert for the event. If you have included travel time in the event, the Time to leave option is useful because it alerts you when your journey should begin.

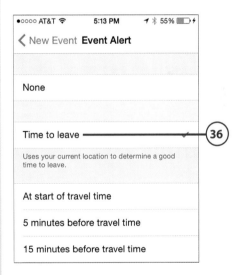

(37) To enter a URL associated with the event, tap in the URL field and type the URL.

(38) Tap Notes and type information you want to associate with the event.

(39) Tap Add. The event is added to the calendar you selected. Any alarms trigger according to your settings.

A Better Way to Create Events

Adding a lot of detail to an event in the Calendar app can be challenging. One effective and easy way to create events is to start with Siri. You can activate Siri and say something like "Create meeting with William Wallace in my office on November 15 at 10 AM." Siri creates the event with as much detail as you provided (and may prompt you to provide additional information, such as which email address to use to send invitations). When you get to a computer or iPad, edit the event to add more information, such as website links. When your calendar is updated on the iPhone, such as via iCloud syncing, the additional detail for the event appears in the Calendar app, too. (See Chapter 12, "Working with Siri," for detailed information about using Siri.)

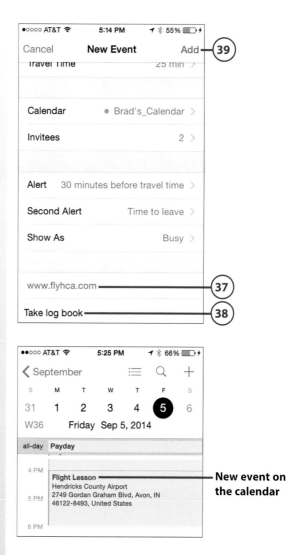

New event on the calendar

Searching Calendars

You can search for events to locate specific ones quickly and easily. Here's how:

1. Tap the Search tool. A list of all your events displays.

2. Tap in the Search box.

3. Type your search term. The events shown below the Search bar are those that contain your search term.

4. Swipe up or down the list to review the results.

5. Tap an event to see its detail.

6. Swipe up or down the event's screen to review its information.

7. Tap Back to return to the results.

8. Continue reviewing the results until you get the information for which you were searching.

9. Tap Cancel to exit the search mode or the Clear button (x) to clear the search but remain in search mode.

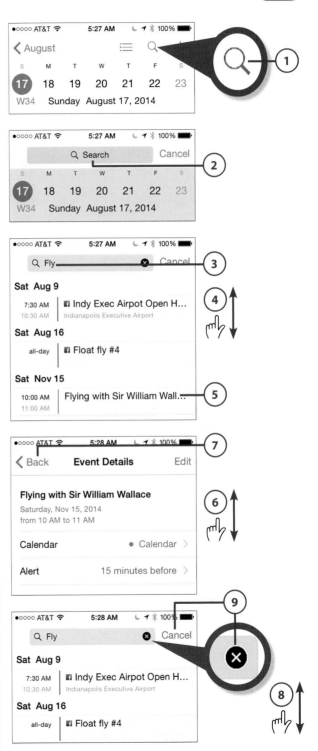

Managing Calendars, Events, and Invitations

Following are some more points about the Calendar app you might find helpful:

- When viewing the month view, the current date is highlighted in a red circle. When you are viewing the week/day view, the current day's date is in red. Remember that you can move to the current day by tapping Today at the bottom of the screen.

- You can also use the List view when you are viewing the calendar in month view. Tap the List button (just to the left of the Search button). The list opens at the bottom of the screen and shows the events on the day currently selected (indicated in the black circle unless the day selected is today in which case the circle is red).

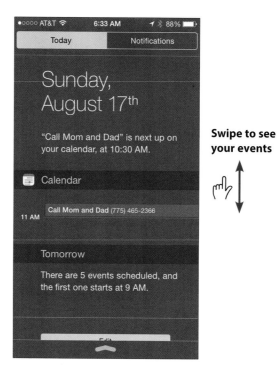

Swipe to see your events

- You can see today's events at any time by swiping down from the top of the screen to open the Notification Center. On the Today tab is a summary of your events for the day; your next event is shown just under the date at the top of the screen. Swipe up and down on the Calendar section to see the entire day's events.

Alert style event notification

- When an event's alarm goes off, an onscreen notification appears (according to the notification settings for the Calendar app) and the calendar event sound you've selected plays. When a banner notification appears, you see the event's name and location. You can tap the event to view its details or ignore it and it moves off the screen after a few moments. When an alert notification appears, the event's title, location (if one is set), and time appear. You have to take some action. You can tap Close to dismiss the alert or tap Options to see additional choices. On the Options dialog box, tap Snooze to snooze the alarm, View Event to see its details, or Close to dismiss the alarm.

- Siri is useful for working with calendars, especially for creating events. See Chapter 12 for detailed information about using Siri.

Working with Reminders

The Reminders app does just what it sounds like it does, which is to remind you about things. The things it reminds you about are up to you; these might be to-do items/tasks, thoughts you want to be reminded to follow up on later, or something to do when you return home. Reminders are also useful for lists of things you need to get or want to remember to think about later. Just as you can have multiple calendars to manage your events, you can have multiple lists for your reminders.

Tap to see what you want to be reminded about

When you open the Reminders app by tapping its icon on the Home screen, you might see the screen showing all the reminder lists you have available. To move to a specific list of reminders, tap it.

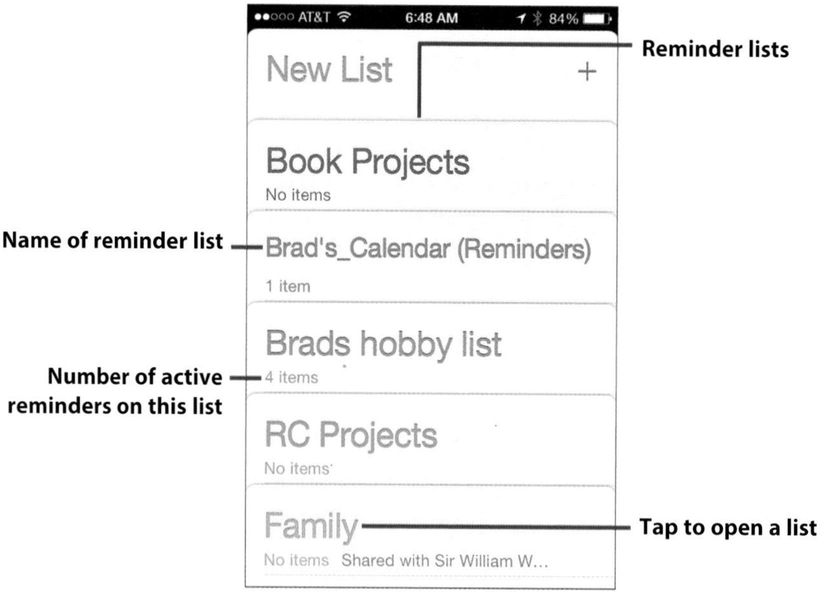

Reminder lists

New List +

Book Projects
No items

Name of reminder list — Brad's_Calendar (Reminders)
1 item

Brads hobby list

Number of active — 4 items
reminders on this list

RC Projects
No items

Family — Tap to open a list
No items Shared with Sir William W...

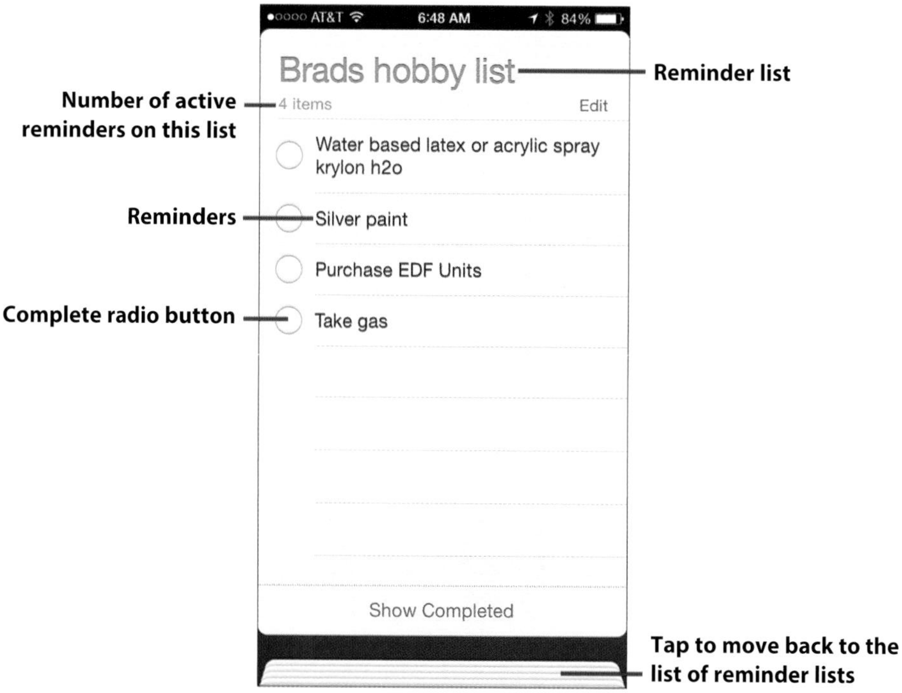

Brads hobby list — Reminder list

Number of active — 4 items   Edit
reminders on this list

Water based latex or acrylic spray
krylon h2o

Reminders — Silver paint

Purchase EDF Units

Complete radio button — Take gas

Show Completed

Tap to move back to the
list of reminder lists

When you open the Reminders app, you might see a specific list of reminders. To move from a reminder list to the screen showing the list of your reminder lists, tap the stack of lists at the bottom of the screen.

You can see how easily you can move between these two views. There are a couple of other views you can use, too (as you learn in a bit), but you'll likely spend most of your time on these two.

Creating Reminders

You can manually create reminders by performing the following steps:

1. Tap the Reminders icon on the Home screen.

2. If you see a reminder list instead of the list of reminder lists, skip this step. If you see the list of your reminders lists, tap the list on which you want to create a new reminder.

3. Tap in an open reminder space. The keyboard appears.

4 Type the reminder.

5 To create more reminders, tap the return button on the keyboard.

6 Create the next reminder.

7 Repeat steps 5 and 6 until you've created all the reminders you want.

8 Tap Done. You can stop here if you only want basic information in the reminder, which is just the reminder's text (the app won't actually remind you unless you configure the reminder for a specific date and time). Continue these steps to fully configure a reminder.

9 Tap the reminder you want to configure.

10 Tap the reminder's info button (i).

11 Slide the Remind me on a day switch to on (green) to set a specific date and time on which you want to be reminded; if you don't want the reminder to be time based, skip to step 16 instead.

12 Tap the default date and time below the switch to open the date and time tool.

13 Use the date and time tool to set a time for the reminder; these work just like they do when you create an event (see "Adding Events to a Calendar," earlier in this chapter).

14 To have the reminder repeated, tap Repeat, and on the resulting screen tap the repeat interval. This also works just like it does when you create an event.

15 If you configured the reminder to repeat, tap End Repeat (this appears only when you have set a reminder to repeat). Use the tools on the End Repeat screen to set the end of the repeating event, and tap Done (this works just like setting the Repeat).

16 Slide the Remind me at a location switch to on (green) to set the reminder to be activated based on you leaving or arriving at a location; if you don't want to set this, skip to step 20.

Remind me on a day	⬤
Sunday, Aug 17, 2014, 12:00 PM	**12**

Thu Aug 14	9	45	
Fri Aug 15	10	50	
Sat Aug 16	11	55	AM
Today	**12**	**00**	**PM** **13**
Mon Aug 18	1	05	
Tue Aug 19	2	10	
Wed Aug 20	3	15	

Repeat	Never **14**

Alarm	Sun, 8/17/14, 12:00 PM
Repeat	Never >
Remind me at a location	◯ **16**

Location Services Required

If you haven't enabled Location Services on your iPhone and for the Reminders app specifically, you're prompted to do so the first time you enable the Remind me at a location feature. You only have to do this the first time or after you disable the required Location Services.

---

(17) Tap Location.

(18) Tap Current Location, tap one of the addresses that appear on the list, or enter an address to associate the reminder with one of those locations and then select it on the list.

(19) Tap When I arrive to be reminded when you arrive at the location you selected, or tap When I leave to be reminded when you leave the location you selected.

(20) Drag the circle to be larger or smaller to change the distance from the location at which the reminder is triggered. As you drag, the distance appears.

(21) Tap Details.

(22) Tap the priority you want to associate with the reminder.

(23) Tap List.

Location and Time Interactions

If you set both a date/time reminder and a location reminder, you're reminded at the earliest event, such as the time passing or the change in location you set.

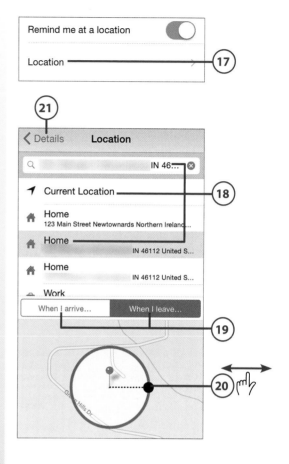

It's Not All Good

Priorities Really Don't Matter

Note that the priority rating is just a visual indication of the reminder's importance. Currently, there are no automatic actions that happen based on priority, such as the reminder list for a given day being sorted by priority by default or getting automatic alerts for high priority items. Hopefully, the priority setting will become more useful in future versions of the iOS software.

24 Tap the list on which you want to store the reminder (reminder lists are organized by the accounts from which they come).

25 Tap Notes.

26 Type notes you want to associate with the reminder.

27 Tap Done. The reminder is complete and you return to the reminder list, where you see the reminder you created including the alert time and location and notes.

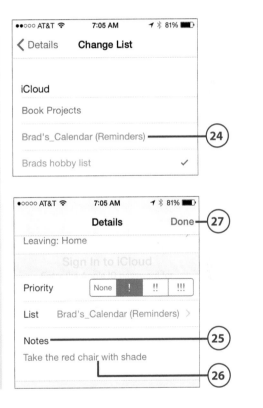

The Ultimate Assistant

Siri can handle reminders really well. Activate Siri and say something like "Remind me to take batteries to the field at 10 AM today." Siri creates the reminder for you. You can move to it in the Reminders app to add more detail if you wish, but using Siri makes creating reminders really fast and easy. See Chapter 12 for more on Siri.

Organizing Reminders with Lists

You can keep multiple lists of reminders for different purposes. Following are some tips to help you with your lists:

- The title of the current list is shown at the top of the list screen.
- To move between your lists, swipe down on the list title at the top of the screen. The list of your lists appears. Tap the list you want to view; the list and the reminders it contains appear.

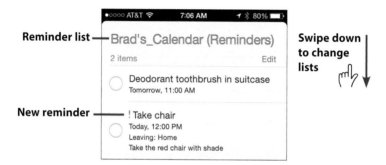

- To create a new list, tap New List. Type the new list's name. Tap the color you want to associate with the list, and then tap Done. You can then assign reminders to the new list.

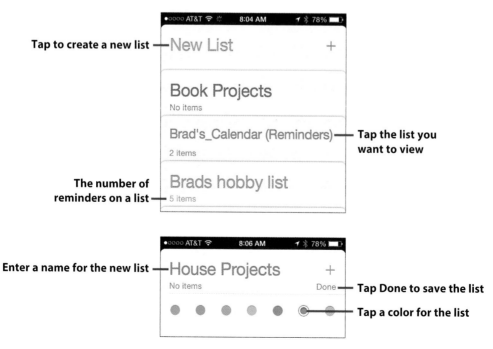

- To change a list, move to its screen and tap Edit. Change the list's name and color if needed and tap Done.

- You can share reminder lists just like sharing calendars. Tap Edit while viewing a list, and then tap Sharing. Tap Add person, configure the people with whom you want to share the list, and then tap Add. Tap Done. After the people you invite accept the invitation, they see the list in the Reminders app on their device.

- If you enable Family Sharing, a list called "Family" is created automatically and shared with everyone on your Family Sharing list. Family Sharing is covered in "Using Family Share to Share your iTunes Store Content," in Chapter 6, "Downloading Apps, Music, Movies, TV Shows, and More onto Your iPhone."

- To delete a list, tap Edit while viewing that list. Tap Delete List and confirm this is what you want to do at the prompt. The list and all the reminders it contains are deleted.

Managing Reminders

When you have reminders set up, you can manage them using some of the tips in the following list:

- When a reminder's Remind Me time or location event occurs, you see an alert according to the notification setting for the Reminders app. If it is a banner, you can tap it to view the reminder's details or ignore it. If it is an alert, you must dismiss it or view the reminder's details.

> ●○○○○ AT&T 🔅   8:17 AM   ✈ ✳ 77% ▭
>
> **Brad's_Calendar (Reminders)**
>
> 1 item   Edit
>
> ○ Deodorant toothbrush in suitcase
>   Tomorrow, 11:00 AM
>
> **Completed reminder** ⎯⎯⎯ ◉ ! Take chair
>   Today, 12:00 PM
>   Leaving: Home
>   Take the red chair with shade

- To mark a reminder as complete, tap its radio button. The next time you move back to the list, the reminder doesn't appear (it is moved onto your Completed list).

- To see your completed reminders, tap Show Completed, which is located at the bottom of the screen. All the reminders on the list appear. Those whose radio buttons are filled with the list's color are complete. Tap Hide Completed, also located at the bottom of the screen, to show only active reminders again.

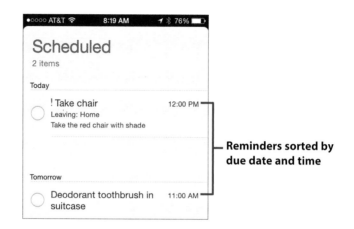

Reminders sorted by due date and time

- To see your reminders organized by date instead of by list, move to the Lists screen and tap the alarm clock icon located in the upper-right corner of the screen. The Scheduled screen shows your reminders based on the time and date with which they are associated. Swipe down on the word "Scheduled" to return to the List screen.

- To change or delete a reminder, tap it. Edit its text if needed. Tap the Information button to change its other details. Tap Done when you've made all the changes you want to make.

- To delete a reminder, swipe across it to the left and tap Delete.

Working with the Clock

Using the Clock app, you can configure alarms, such as to wake you up. The Clock also provides a nice stopwatch and surprisingly useful timer.

Telling Time

Your iPhone is also handy for knowing what time it is. The time is displayed at the top of many screens (although it is hidden when an app uses the full screen or when an app's controls are hidden). It also appears on the Lock screen. To get the time quickly while your iPhone is locked, just press the Home or Sleep/Wake button. The Lock screen appears and displays the time and date. Who needs a watch when you have an iPhone?

Setting and Using Alarms

Your iPhone is a handy alarm clock on which you can set and manage multiple alarms.

1. On the Home screen, tap Clock.

2. Tap Alarm. You see the currently set alarms, listed by their times, with the earlier alarms toward the top of the screen. Next to each alarm, you see its status switch. When the switch is off (white), the alarm is disabled. When it is on (green), the alarm is active.

3. To add an alarm, tap the Add button (+).

4 Swipe on the hour, minute, and AM/PM bars to set the time you want the alarm to activate.

5 To configure the alarm to repeat, tap Repeat; to set a one-time alarm, skip to step 9.

6 Tap the day of the week on which you want the alarm to repeat. It is marked with a check mark.

7 Repeat step 6 as many times as you need; however, the most frequently an alarm can repeat is once per day. Of course, you can create multiple alarms for the same day.

8 Tap Back. The Repeat option shows you the days you selected for the alarm to repeat.

9 To name the alarm, tap Label. The label is what appears on the screen when the alarm activates, so you might want to give it a meaningful title. (To leave the default label, which is "Alarm," skip to step 13.)

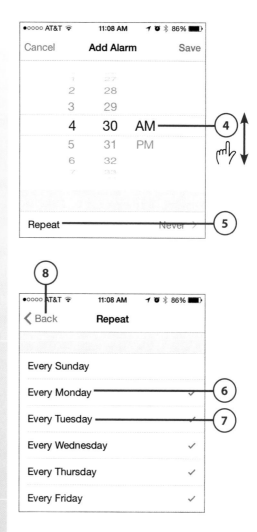

How iPhone Alarms Are Like Those on Bedside Clocks

You can't set an alarm for a specific date; they are set only by day of the week, just like a bedside alarm clock. To set an alarm for a specific date, configure an event using the Calendar app and associate an alarm with that event. Or, you can set a reminder as another way to be notified at a specific time and date.

10 To remove the current label, tap the Clear button (x).

11 Type a label for the alarm.

12 Tap Back.

13 To choose the alarm sound, tap Sound.

Silent Alarm

If you select the None sound, you won't hear anything when the alarm goes off, but a visual alarm displays.

14 Browse the list of available sounds.

15 Tap the sound you want to use for the alarm. You hear the sound, and it is marked with a check mark.

16 After you select the sound you want to use, tap Back.

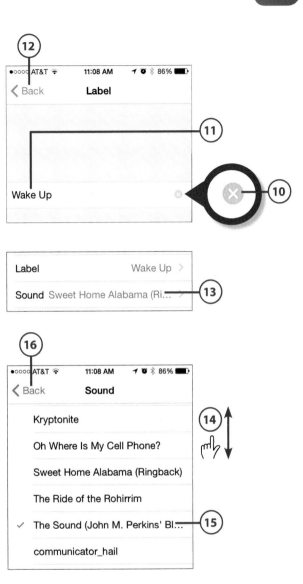

17 To disable the Snooze function, set the Snooze switch to off (white). When the alarm sounds and you dismiss it, it won't appear again. With Snooze set to on (green), you can tap Snooze to dismiss the alarm, and it returns at 10-minute increments until you dismiss it.

18 Tap Save. You return to the Alarm screen, which now shows the new alarm you set. When the appointed time arrives, the alarm sounds and displays on the screen (or just displays on the screen if it is a silent alarm).

●○○○○ AT&T 📶	11:08 AM	🡵 🔅 ⚡ 86% 🔋
Cancel	**Add Alarm**	Save ─ **18**

```
        1       27
        2       28
        3       29
        4       30   AM
        5       31   PM
        6       32
        7       33
```

Repeat	Weekdays >
Label	Wake Up >
Sound The Sound (John M. Perk...	>
Snooze	⬤ ─ **17**

World Clock

On the World Clock tab, you can configure clocks to display the times in different time zones around the world. Tap the Add button (+) and use the search tool to find and tap a city in the time zone in which you are interested. A clock for that city is added to the World Clock screen and you see the current time there. You can add multiple clocks to see the time in many times zones at once.

Managing Alarms

As you work with alarms, keep the following in mind:

- When at least one alarm is active, you see the Alarm Clock icon in the upper-right corner of the screen next to the Battery icon.

- You can enable or disable alarms by tapping their switches. Alarms showing green in their switches are enabled and sound when the time comes. Those with white are disabled and are ignored until you enable them.

Tap to change an alarm ——— Edit   Alarm   +

••••○○ AT&T 🛜   11:21 AM   ✦ ⊘ ✳ 85% ▰

At least one
alarm is active

4:30 AM
Wake Up, Weekdays

Tap to disable an alarm

5:05 AM
Alarm

Tap to enable an alarm

7:00 AM
Start Writing, Mon Tue Wed

10:00 AM
Parking, Thu Fri

3:45 PM
Alarm

World Clock   Alarm   Stopwatch   Timer

- To change an alarm, tap Edit, and then tap the alarm you want to change. You can change it using the same tools as when you create a new alarm. Tap Save when you're done making changes.

- To delete an alarm, tap Edit and then tap the Lock button (-) for the alarm you want to delete. Then tap Delete. Tap Done when you are done deleting alarms.

- When an alarm triggers, you see an alert and hear the sound associated with it. If the alarm is snooze-enabled, tap Snooze to dismiss it; it returns in 10 minutes. To dismiss the alarm completely, tap OK. You can also dismiss an alarm by pressing the Sleep/Wake button.

Not Dismissed So Easily

When you dismiss an alarm, it isn't deleted, but its status is set to off (unless it is set to repeat, in which case, it remains active and goes off at the next appointed time). To reenable the alarm, move to the Alarm screen and tap its switch. It turns on, and the alarm activates at the next appropriate time.

Using the Stopwatch

You can use the Stopwatch tab to record times for various things, such as walking laps.

1. On the Home screen, tap Clock.
2. Tap Stopwatch.
3. Tap the Start button to start the count.

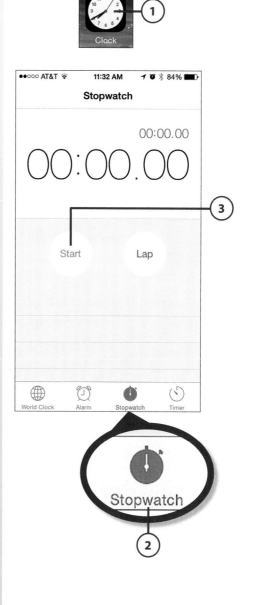

4 Tap Lap to set lap times. As you set lap times, they are recorded on a list on the app's screen along with the lap number.

5 Tap Stop to stop the stopwatch.

6 To start over, tap Reset.

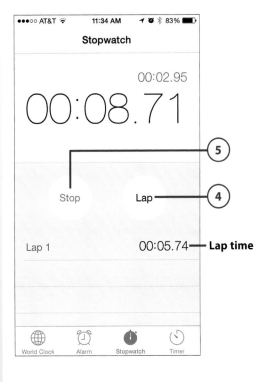

Using the Timer

The Timer is a handy way to count down from a stating time and see and hear an alarm when that time expires. Here's how to use it:

1. On the Home screen, tap Clock.
2. Tap Timer.
3. Use the hour and minute wheels to set the amount of time you want for the countdown.
4. Tap When Timer Ends.
5. Tap the sound you want to play when the timer expires.
6. Tap Set.

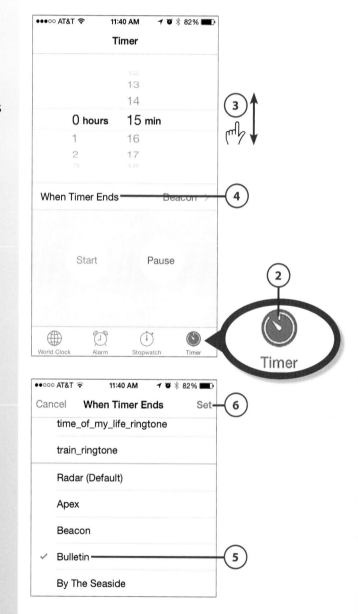

7 Tap Start. The timer begins counting down.

8 To pause the timer, tap Pause (tap Resume to restart it).

9 To cancel the timer before it finishes, tap Cancel. Otherwise, when the time you selected passes, you hear the end sound you selected in step 5 and see an onscreen message informing you that the time has expired.

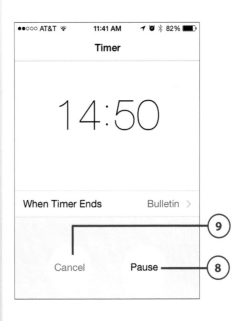

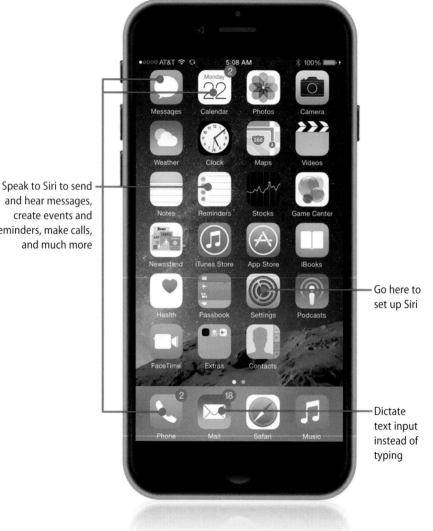

Speak to Siri to send and hear messages, create events and reminders, make calls, and much more

Go here to set up Siri

Dictate text input instead of typing

In this chapter, you'll learn about all the great things you can do with your iPhone by speaking to it. Topics include the following:

→ Getting started
→ Setting up Siri
→ Understanding Siri's personality
→ Learning how to use Siri by example

12

Working with Siri

Siri is Apple's name for the iPhone's and iPad's voice recognition feature. This technology enables your iPhone to "listen" to words you speak so that you can issue commands just by saying them, such as "Send text message to Sam," and the iPhone accomplishes the tasks you speak. This technology also enables the iPhone to take dictation; for example, you can speak words that you want to send in a text or email instead of typing them on the keyboard. Siri is pretty easy to use, but it can take a little practice to figure out the best ways to speak the commands you use most frequently. Fortunately, you can experiment with Siri and try new ways of speaking to it because you won't cause problems for yourself by doing so. That's because Siri always confirms the commands you speak so you are able to undo a command before it gets done.

Getting Started

Siri gives you the ability to talk to your iPhone to control it and to dictate text. Siri works with lots of iPhone apps—this feature enables you to accomplish many tasks by speaking instead of using your fingers on the iPhone's screen.

One particularly good thing about Siri is that you don't have to train it to work with your voice; you can speak to it normally and Siri does a great job understanding what you say. Also, you don't have to use any specific kind of phrases to have Siri do your bidding. Simply talk to Siri like you talk to people (well, you probably won't be ordering other people around like you do Siri, but you get the idea).

Because Siri works so well and quickly, you might not realize that your iPhone has to be connected to the Internet for Siri and dictation to work. That's because the words you speak are sent over the Internet, transcribed into text, and then sent back to your iPhone. If your iPhone isn't connected to the Internet, this can't happen, and if you try to use it, Siri reports that it can't complete its tasks. Because your iPhone is likely to be connected to the Internet most of the time (via Wi-Fi or a cellular network), this really isn't much of a limitation—but it is one of which you need to be aware.

Siri doesn't take much to set up either; most of the time, you don't need to do the steps in the next task as Siri is set up by default when you first turn on your iPhone. If you haven't made any changes to the Siri settings, skip ahead to "Understanding Siri's Personality." If you have made changes to Siri's settings, or just want to understand its options, proceed to the next section.

Setting Up Siri

Before you can speak to Siri, perform the following steps to configure it:

(**1**) Tap Settings.

(**2**) Tap General.

(**3**) Tap Siri.

(**4**) If the Siri switch is off (white), slide it to on (green). If the switch is already on, skip to step 6.

(**5**) Tap Enable Siri.

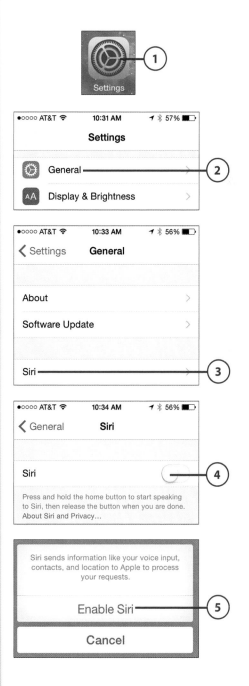

6 If you don't want to be able to activate Siri by saying, "Hey Siri" when your iPhone is connected to power (via its charger or when it is connected to a computer), set the Allow "Hey Siri" switch to off (white). In most cases, you should set this switch to on (green) until you figure out if you will use it.

7 Tap Language.

8 Swipe up and down the screen to see all the languages Siri can use.

9 Tap the language you want to use to speak to Siri.

10 Tap Siri.

11 Tap Voice Gender. Not all languages support this feature; if you don't see it, the language you selected in step 9 does not and you can skip to step 14.

12 Tap the gender of the voice you want Siri to use to speak to you.

13 Tap Siri.

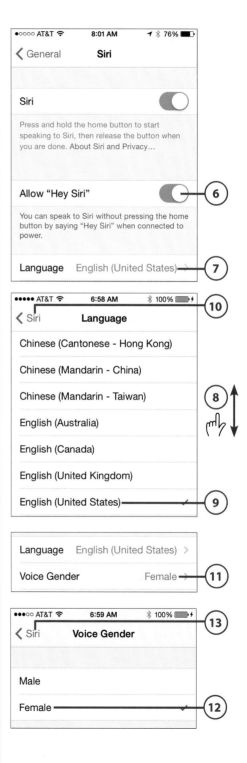

14 Tap Voice Feedback. Siri provides you with audible confirmation when you speak to it. For example, when you tell it to create a reminder, Siri speaks the reminder it thinks you told it to create so you know what it is doing without having to look at the screen.

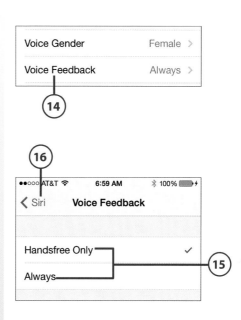

15 If you always want Siri to provide you with voice feedback, tap Always. If you only want voice feedback when you are operating in handsfree mode, such as when you are using the iPhone's EarPods or a Bluetooth headset, tap Handsfree Only. If you choose Handsfree Only, when you aren't using a headset, you will only see Siri's feedback on the screen, which is typically faster than the voice feedback.

16 Tap Siri.

17 Tap My Info.

18 Use the Contacts app to find and tap your information. Siri often uses your name when it speaks to you; this tells Siri what name to use when it addresses you, among other things. You're ready to meet Siri.

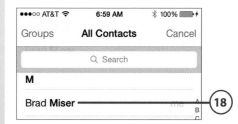

Understanding Siri's Personality

Siri's personality is pretty simple because it follows a consistent pattern when you use it, and it always prompts you for input and direction when needed.

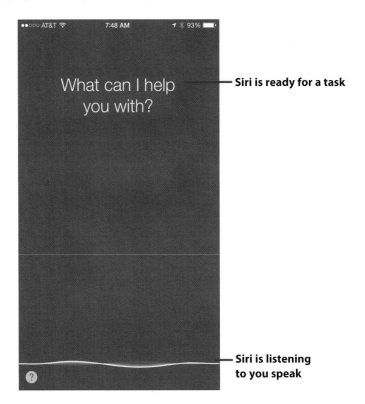

If Siri is already active, tap the Microphone icon at the bottom of the screen. If not, activate Siri using one of the following methods:

- Pressing and holding the Touch ID/Home button
- Pressing and holding the center part of the buttons on the EarPods
- Saying "Hey Siri" (if you've enabled that setting and your phone is connected to power)

After using one of the methods above, you hear the Siri chime. This puts Siri in "listening" mode and the "What can I help you with?" text appears along with a line at the bottom of the screen that shows when Siri is hearing you. This screen indicates Siri is ready for your command.

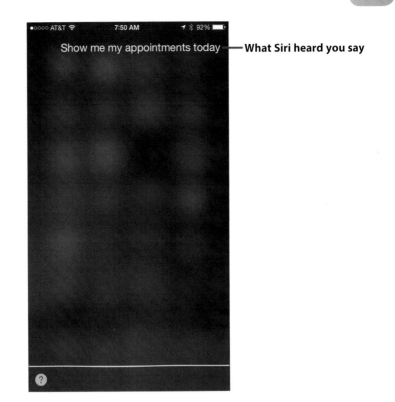

What Siri heard you say

Speak your command or ask a question. As you speak, the line at the bottom of the screen oscillates to show you that Siri is hearing your input, and Siri displays what it is hearing you say at the top of the screen. When you stop speaking, Siri goes into processing mode; the line is replaced by a rotating circle to show you that Siri is thinking.

After Siri interprets what you've said, it provides two kinds of feedback to confirm what it heard: it displays what it heard on the screen and provides audible feedback to you (unless you've set it for Handsfree Only and aren't using a headset). Siri then tries to do what it thinks you've asked and shows you the outcome.

If it needs more input from you, you're prompted to provide it and Siri moves into "listening" mode automatically. If Siri asks you to confirm what it is doing or to make a selection, do so. Siri completes the action and displays what it has done; it also audibly confirms the result unless you've selected Handsfree Only and aren't using a headset.

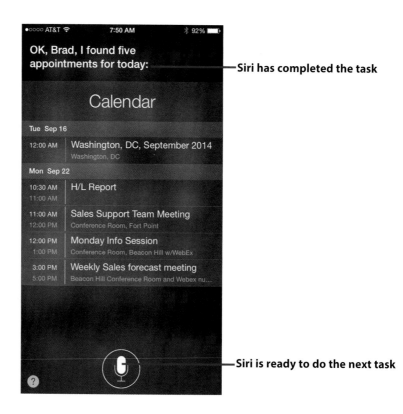

Siri has completed the task

Siri is ready to do the next task

If you want Siri to do more for you, tap the Microphone icon at the bottom of the screen and speak your command. If you want to work with the object Siri created for you in its associated app, tap the object Siri presents.

When you're done with Siri, you can lock the iPhone or tap the Touch ID/Home button to move back to the Home screen or to the app you were using.

Siri uses this pattern for all the tasks it does, but often Siri needs to get more information from you, such as when there are multiple contacts that match the command you've given. Siri prompts you for what it needs to complete the work. Generally, the more specific you make your initial command, the fewer steps you have to work through to complete it. For example, if you say "Meet Will at the park," Siri may require several prompts to get you to tell it who Will is and what time you want to meet him at the park. If you say "Meet William Wallace at the park on 10/17 at 10 am," Siri will likely be able to complete the task in one step.

Siri is amazingly flexible in how you can speak to it and the accuracy with which it interprets spoken input. However, using Siri effectively requires a bit of practice to learn the most efficient and effective ways to provide commands based on how you speak and what you want Siri to do. In many cases, Siri is a very good way to accomplish tasks, while for others, it might actually slow you down.

The best way to learn how and when Siri can help you is to try it—a lot. You find a number of examples in the rest of this chapter to get started. Don't be timid about trying Siri. You can't really hurt anything by trying it—as long as you pay attention to Siri's feedback so you can stop a task if it is going awry. For example, Siri might misinterpret a command and start doing something you don't want it to do, such as placing a call you didn't intend to make. You can always abort tasks Siri starts as long as you are paying attention and stop the task before it is completed.

Siri is amazing, but it does have some limitations, as all technology does. There are some things it seems like it should be able to do but might not be able to do. The list of what Siri can't do is getting shorter all the time, so make sure you try the tasks for which you might want to use Siri.

Following are some other Siri tidbits:

- If Siri doesn't automatically quit "listen" mode after you've finished speaking, tap the oscillating line. This stops "listen" mode and Siri starts processing your request. You need to do this more often when you are in a noisy environment because Siri might not be able to accurately discern the sound of you speaking versus the ambient background noise.

- If you are having trouble with Siri understanding commands, speak a bit more slowly and make sure you firmly enunciate and end your words. If you tend to have a very short pause between words, Siri might run them all together, making them into something that doesn't make sense or that you didn't intend.

- You can't pause too long between words or sentences because Siri interprets pauses of a certain length to mean that you are done speaking and goes into processing mode. Practicing with Siri will help you develop a good balance between speed and clarity.

- If Siri doesn't understand what you want, or if you ask it a general question, it often performs a web search for you. Siri takes what it thinks you are looking for and does a search. You then see the results page for the search Siri performed and you may have to manually open and read the results by tapping the listing you want to see. It opens in the Safari app. In some cases, Siri reads the results to you.

- When Siri presents information to you on the screen, such as events it has created, you can often tap that information to move into the app with which it is associated. For example, when you tap an event that Siri has created, you move into the Calendar app. For more complicated items, such as creating an event that has a lot of detail, use the following pattern to work with Siri. Use Siri to create the basic information, such as an event's title, time, and date, and when Siri creates it, tap it to move into the associated app to add more detail using that app's tools, such as inviting people to an event and changing the calendar it's associated with.

- When Siri needs direction from you, it presents your options on the screen, such as Yes, Cancel, Confirm, and lists of names. You can speak these items or tap them to select them.

- Siri is very useful for some tasks, such as creating reminders and responding to text messages, but not so useful for others, such as inputting search criteria, because it can take longer to use Siri than to just type your input.

- Siri is not very good at editing text you dictate. In many cases, your only option is to replace the text you've dictated to change it. For short text blocks, such as text messages or tweets, this can be fine, but for longer blocks of text, you have to use the virtual keyboard to make changes to just portions of text. You can use Siri to quickly dictate blocks of text and then edit the text using the iPhone's text editing tools.

- To use Siri effectively, you should experiment with it by trying to say different commands or similar commands in different ways. For example, when creating events, you can include more information in your initial command to reduce the number of steps because Siri doesn't have to ask you for more information. Saying "Meet with Wyatt Earp at 10am on 11/3 in my office" requires fewer steps than saying "Meet with Wyatt Earp" because you've given Siri all the information it needs to complete the task. How you speak impacts the sort of commands that will work best for you. It can take a little practice to make Siri work effectively for you and to learn when Siri actually helps you complete tasks you want to do versus just being a cool way to accomplish them. Sometimes, experimentation leads you to unexpected, but very useful, results.

- Lots of apps support Siri commands, but over time, we can expect even more apps to be able to accept Siri control. As the apps you use get updated, look for any that add Siri support so you can start speaking to them as well.

- When Siri can't complete a task that it thinks it should be able to do, it usually responds with the "I can't connect to the network right now," or "Sorry, I don't know what you mean." This indicates that your iPhone isn't connected to the Internet, the Siri server is not responding, or Siri just isn't able to complete the command for some other reason. If your iPhone is connected to the Internet, try the command again.

- When Siri can't complete a task that it knows it can't do, it will respond by telling you so. Occasionally, you can get Siri to complete the task by rephrasing it, but typically you have to use an app directly to get it done.

- If you have a passcode set to protect your iPhone's data (which you should), Siri might not be able to complete some tasks because the phone is locked. If that happens, simply unlock your phone and continue with what you were doing.

- Siri sees all and knows all (well, not really, but it sometimes seems that way). If you want to be enlightened, try asking Siri questions. Some examples are "What is the best phone?," "Will you marry me?," "What is the meaning of life?," or "Tell me a joke." Some of the answers are pretty funny, and you don't always get the same ones so Siri can keep amusing you. I've heard it even has responses if you curse at it, though I haven't tried that particular option.

Learning How to Use Siri by Example

As mentioned earlier in this chapter, the best way to learn about Siri is to use it. Following are a number of tasks for which Siri is really helpful. Try these to get some experience with Siri and then explore on your own to make Siri work at its best for you.

Using Siri to Make Voice Calls

You can use Siri to make calls by speaking. This is especially useful when you are using your iPhone in handsfree mode, such as in a vehicle.

(1) Activate Siri by pressing and holding the Touch ID/Home button.

(2) Say "Call *name numberlabel*," where *name* is the person you want to call and *number-label* is the label of the specific number you want to call, such as Home, Work, and iPhone. Siri identifies the contact you named. If the contact has only one number or you were specific about which number you want to call, Siri places the call and you move into the Phone app. If you weren't specific about the number you want to call (you simply said "Call *name*") and the person has multiple numbers, Siri lists the numbers available and asks you which number to use.

(3) Speak the label for the number you want to call, or tap it. Siri dials the number for you and you move to the Phone app as if you had dialed the number yourself.

Siri has found multiple numbers for William

Placing FaceTime Calls

You can also use Siri to make FaceTime calls by saying "FaceTime *name*."

Composing New Email with Siri

To create email with Siri, do the following:

(1) Activate Siri by pressing and holding the Touch ID/Home button.

(2) Say "Send email to *name*," where *name* is the person you want to email. Siri creates a new email addressed to the name you spoke. (If the recipient has more than one email address, Siri prompts you to choose the address you want to use.) Next, Siri asks you for the subject of the email.

3. Speak the subject of the email.

4. Siri inserts the subject, and then prompts you for the body of the message. Speak the body of the email. As you speak, you can include punctuation; for example, to end a sentence, say the word "period" or to end a question, say the words "question mark." As you speak, Siri displays the words it hears on the screen, which is useful if you are able to look at your phone while you dictate the message. When Siri completes the email, it displays the entire message on the screen and prompts you to send it.

5. Say "send" to send the email or "cancel" to delete it. If you say "send," Siri sends the message, confirms it will be sent, and plays the sent mail sound when it is.

More Than One Recipient?

To send an email to more than one recipient, say "and" between each name as in, "Send email to William Wallace and Edward Longshanks." Siri adds each address before and after the "and."

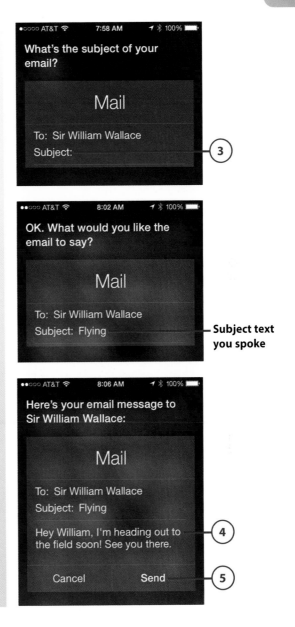

Subject text you spoke

Other Ways to Activate Siri

If you are using the iPhone's EarPods, you can activate Siri by pressing and holding the center button of the control on the right EarPod's wire. When you've held the button long enough, you hear Siri's activation chime and are ready to speak your command. If your iPhone is connected to power and you haven't disabled the related setting, you can also say "Hey Siri" to activate it.

Replying to Emails with Siri

You can also use Siri to speak replies to emails you've read. Here's how:

(1) Open the message to which you want to reply.

(2) Activate Siri by pressing and holding the Touch ID/Home button.

(3) Say "reply." Siri prompts you for what you want your reply to say.

(4) Complete and send the reply; this works just like when you create a new message.

●●○○○ AT&T 🔋   8:12 AM   ◀ ✳ 97% ▭

OK. What would you like the email to say? ───(4)

Mail

To: Wyatt Earp
Subject: Re: Doc

>>>Go Further
DOING MORE IN EMAIL WITH SIRI

Following are some other ways to use Siri for email:

• If you tell Siri to "Read email," Siri tells you how many emails are in your Inboxes and starts reading the time and date of the most recent email message followed by the subject and sender of the message. Siri then does the same for the next email until it has read through all of them. You can tap an email message to read it yourself, but Siri can't read the content of email messages to you.

• To edit an email Siri created, say "Change." Siri prompts you to change the subject, change the message, cancel it, or send it. If you choose one of the change options, you can replace the subject or the body of the message. To change just some of the subject or body or to change the recipients, tap the message and edit it in the Mail app.

• You can start a new and completely blank email by saying "New email." Siri prompts you for the recipients, subject, and body.

• You can address a new email and add the subject with one statement, such as "Send email to William Wallace about flying."

- You can retrieve your email at any time by activating Siri and saying "Check email." Siri checks for new email and then announces how many emails you have received since the oldest message in your Inboxes was received. If you don't have any new email messages, this does the same thing as "Read email."

- You can determine if you have emails from a specific person by asking something like, "Any email from William Wallace?" Siri's reply includes the number of emails in your Inboxes from William and displays them on the screen. Tap an email to read it.

- You can forward an email you are reading by saying "Forward this email" and then following Siri's lead to complete the process.

Having Messages Read to You

The Messages app is among the best to use with Siri because you can speak just about any task you would normally do with messages. Especially useful is Siri's ability to read new messages to you. When you receive new text messages, do the following to have Siri read them to you:

1. When you receive a text notification, activate Siri by pressing and holding the Touch ID/Home button.

2. Speak the command "Read text messages." Siri reads all the new text messages you've received, announcing the sender before reading each message. You have the option to reply (covered in the next task) or have Siri read the message again.

Siri reads each new message in turn until it has read all of them and then announces, "That's it" to let you know it has read all of them.

Siri only reads new text messages to you when you aren't on the Messages screen. If you've already read all your messages and you aren't in the Messages app, when you speak the command "Read text messages," Siri tells you that you have no new messages.

Reading Old Messages

To read an old message, move back to the conversation containing the message you want to hear. Activate Siri and say the command "Read text message." Siri reads the most recent text message to you.

Replying to Messages with Siri

You can also use Siri to speak replies to messages you've received. Here's how:

1. Listen to a message.

2. At the prompt, say "Reply." Siri prepares a reply to the message.

3. Speak your reply. Siri displays your reply.

4. At the prompt, say "Send" to send it, "Cancel" to delete it, or "Change" to replace it. If you tell Siri that you want to send the message, Siri sends it and then confirms that it was sent.

Sending New Messages with Siri

To send a new message to someone, do the following:

1. Activate Siri by pressing and holding the Touch ID/Home button.

2. Say "Send text to *name*," where *name* is the person you want to text. Siri confirms your command and prepares to hear your text message.

3) Speak your message. Siri listens and then prepares your message.

4) If you want to send the message, say "Send." Siri sends the message.

>>>*Go Further*
DOING MORE MESSAGING WITH SIRI

Following are some other ways to use Siri with messaging:

- If you say "Change" after you have created a new message, Siri prompts you to replace the message with a different one. If you say "Review" after creating a new message, Siri reads your message back to you. If you say "Cancel," Siri stops the process and deletes the message. If you don't respond to Siri's prompt, it prompts you with "Change, Review, or Cancel?" indicating the actions you can take.

- To send a text message to more than one recipient, say "and" between each name, as in, "Send text to William Wallace and Edward Longshanks."

- You can speak punctuation, such as "period" or "question mark" to add it to your message.

- You can tap buttons that Siri presents on the screen, such as Send or Cancel, to take those actions on the message on which you are working.

- Messages you receive or send via Siri are stored in the Messages app just like messages you receive or send by tapping and typing.

- You can dictate into a text message you start in the Messages app (you learn about dictating later in this chapter).

Using Siri to Create Events

Siri is useful for capturing meetings and other events you want to add to your calendars. To create an event by speaking, do the following steps:

(1) Activate Siri by pressing and holding the Touch ID/Home button.

(2) Speak the event you want to create. There are a number of variations in what you can say. Examples include "Set up a meeting with William Wallace on Friday at 10 am," "Doctor appointment on Thursday at 1 pm," "Meet Edward at 2 pm on October 20," and "Meet Tim at the park on Saturday at 3 pm." Siri is pretty flexible about what you say. Like all tasks, Siri provides a confirmation of what you asked. If you have any conflicts with the event you are setting up, Siri lets you know about them.

(3) Say "Confirm" if you don't have any conflicts or "Yes" if you do and you still want to have the appointment confirmed; you can also tap Confirm. Siri adds the event to your calendar. Say "Cancel" to cancel the event.

(4) To add more information to an event Siri has created for you, tap it on the confirmation screen. You move into the Calendar app and can edit the event just like events you create within that app.

Invitees

If you include the name of someone for whom you have an email address, Siri automatically sends invitations. If you include a name that matches more than one contact, Siri prompts you to choose the contact you want to invite. If the name doesn't match a contact, Siri enters the name but doesn't send an invitation.

Using Siri to Create Reminders

Using Siri to create reminders is one of the more useful things you can do with Siri, assuming you find reminders useful, of course. Here's how:

Here's your reminder for November 15, 2014. I'll remind you when you leave there, or by 11 am:

Reminder
Saturday, November 15, 2014

Take batteries
11:00 AM
Leaving: Flying's Home

Cancel   Confirm

1. Activate Siri by pressing and holding the Touch ID/Home button.

2. Speak the reminder you want to create. There are lots of ways to do this. Examples include "Remind me to buy the A-10 at Motion RC," "Remind me to finish chapter 10 at 10 am on Saturday," and "Remind me to buy milk when I leave work." Siri provides a confirmation of what you asked. If you didn't mention a time or date when you want to be reminded, Siri prompts you to provide the details of when you want to be reminded.

3. Speak the date and time when you want to be reminded. If you included a date and time in your original reminder request, you skip this step. Siri shows you the reminder it is going to create.

4. To create the reminder, say "Yes" or "Confirm," or to prevent it from being created, say "Cancel." If you confirmed the reminder, Siri adds it to your reminders.

5. To add detail to the reminder, tap it. You move into the Reminders app and can add more information to the reminder as you can when you create one manually.

>>>Go Further

GOING FURTHER WITH SIRI TO MANAGE TIME

Following are some other ways to use Siri with the Calendar, Reminders, and Clock apps:

- You can change events with Siri, too. For example, if you have a meeting at 3 p.m., you can move it by saying something like "Move my 3 pm meeting to Friday at 6 pm."

- You can get information about your events with Siri by saying things such as "Show me today's appointments," "Do I have meetings on November 3?," "What time is my first appointment tomorrow?," and "What are my appointments tomorrow?" Siri tells you about the events and shows you what they are on the screen. You can tap any event to view it in the Calendar app.

- You can speak to your iPhone to set alarms. Tell Siri what you want and when you want the alarm to be set. For example, you can say something like "New alarm *alarmname* 6 am tomorrow," where *alarmname* is the label of the alarm. Siri sets an alarm to go off at that time and gives it the label you speak. It displays the alarm on the screen along with a status button so you can turn it off if you change your mind. You don't have to label alarms, and you can just say something like "Set alarm 6 am tomorrow." However, a label can be useful to issue other commands. For example, if an alarm has a name, you can turn off an alarm by saying "Turn off *alarmname*." Any alarms you create with Siri can be managed just like alarms you create directly in the Clock app.

- To set a countdown timer, tell Siri to "Set timer for x minutes," where x is a number of minutes (you can do the same to set a timer for seconds or hours, too). Siri starts a countdown for you and presents it on the screen. You can continue to use the iPhone however you want. When the timer ends, you see and hear an alert. You can also reset the time and pause it by speaking.

- You can get information about time by asking questions, such as "What time is it?," or "What is the date?" You can add location information to the time information, too, as in "What time is it in London, England?"

- Tapping any confirmation Siri displays takes you back into the related app. For example, if you tap a clock that results from your asking what time it is, you can tap that clock to move into the Clock app. If you ask about your schedule today, you can tap any of the events Siri presents to move back into the Calendar app to work with them.

- When you use Siri to create events and reminders, they are created on your default calendar (events) or reminder list (reminders).

Using Siri to Get Information

There are lots of ways to use Siri to get information. There are lots of types information waiting for your command, such as topic information and places in your area. Just try speaking what you want to learn to best get the information you need. Here's an example looking for pizza places in my area:

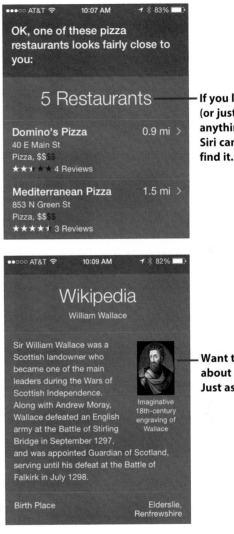

If you like pizza (or just about anything else), Siri can help you find it.

Want to learn about something? Just ask Siri.

(1) Activate Siri by pressing and holding the Touch ID/Home button.

(2) Say something like, "Show me pizza restaurants close to me." Siri presents a list of results that match your query. (You must have Location Services enabled for this to work. Refer to Chapter 4, "Configuring an iPhone to Suit Your Preferences," for information about configuring Location Services.)

You can also get information about topics. Siri responds by conducting a web search and showing you the result. For example, suppose you want to learn about William Wallace. Activate Siri and say, "Tell me about William Wallace." Siri responds with information about your topic. You can have Siri read the information by activating Siri and saying "Read." Siri reads the results (this doesn't always work; it works best when the results are presented via Wikipedia or something similar).

Using Siri to Play Music

You can also play music by telling Siri which music you want to hear.

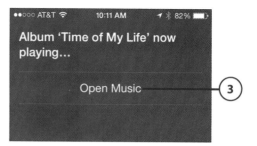

(1) Activate Siri by pressing and holding the Touch ID/Home button.

(2) Tell Siri the music you want to hear. There are a number of variations in what you can say. Examples include "Play album Time of My Life," "Play song Gone by Switchfoot," and "Play playlist Jon McLaughlin." Siri provides a confirmation of what you asked and begins playing the music.

(3) To move into the Music app to control the music with your fingers, tap Open Music.

>>>Go Further
MORE SPOKEN COMMANDS FOR MUSIC

There are a number of commands you can speak to find, play, and control music (and other audio). "Play *artist*" plays music by the artist you speak. "Play *album*" plays the album you name. In both cases, if the name includes the word "the," you need to include "the" when you speak the command. "Shuffle" plays a random song. "Play more like this" uses the Genius to find songs similar to the one playing and plays them. "Previous track" or "next track" does exactly what they sound like they do. To hear the name of the artist for the song currently playing, say "Who sings this song?" You can shuffle music in an album or playlist by saying "Shuffle playlist *playlistname*." You can stop the music, pause it, or play it by speaking those commands.

Using Siri to Get Directions

With Siri, it's easy to get directions—you don't even have to stop at a gas station to ask.

1. Activate Siri by pressing and holding the Touch ID/Home button.

2. Speak something like "Show me directions from Indianapolis Motor Speedway to Lucas Oil Stadium." If you don't include the "from" part, Siri assumes you want directions from your current location (as in "Show me directions to Lucas Oil Stadium").

3. If Siri needs you to confirm one or more of the locations, tap the correct one. Siri uses the Maps app to generate directions.

4. To start turn-by-turn instructions, tap Start.

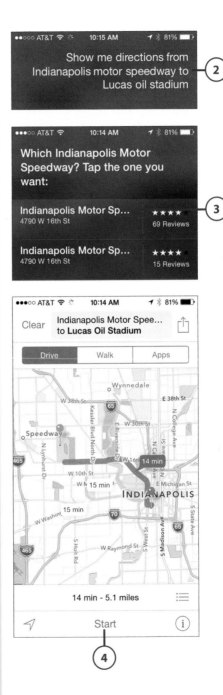

It's Not All Good

Voice commands to Siri work very well, but they aren't perfect. Make sure you confirm your commands by listening to the feedback Siri provides when it repeats them or reviewing the feedback Siri provides on the screen. Sometimes, a spoken command can have unexpected results, which can include making a phone call to someone in the Contacts app. If you don't catch such a mistake before the call is started, you might be surprised to hear someone answering your call instead of hearing music you intended to play. You can put Siri in listening mode by tapping the Microphone button and then saying "no" or "stop" to stop Siri should a verbal command go awry.

Using Dictation to Speak Text Instead of Typing

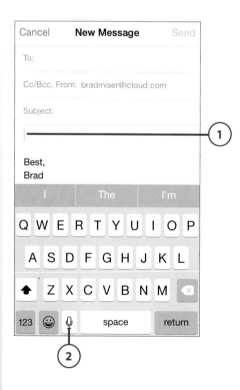

You can use the iPhone's dictation capability to speak text into any app, such as Mail or Messages. In fact, any time you see the Microphone button on the keyboard, dictation is available to you. Here's how this works:

(1) In the app you are using, put the cursor where you want the text you will dictate to start. For example, if you are creating an email, tap in the body.

(2) Tap the Microphone key.

(3) Speak the text you want to add.

For instance, when you create a new message, you can speak punctuation, but in this mode, you can create a new paragraph by saying "new paragraph." While you are speaking, you see the line that oscillates as you speak and the text you are speaking at the location of the cursor.

(4) Tap Done when you finish your dictation. The Dictation box closes, and the keyboard reappears. The text you spoke is part of the message. From there, you can edit it just like text you've typed.

The text you are dictating

4

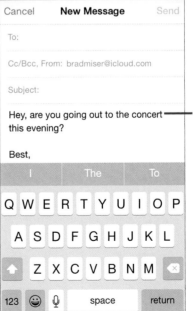

Dictating text is a great way to write without having to type

Tap to configure Safari

Tap to have the World Wide Web in the palm of your hand

In this chapter, you explore the amazing web browsing functionality your iPhone has to offer. Topics include the following:

→ Getting Started
→ Setting Safari preferences
→ Visiting websites
→ Viewing websites
→ Working with multiple websites at the same time
→ Searching the Web
→ Saving and organizing bookmarks
→ Sharing web pages
→ Completing forms on the Web
→ Signing into websites automatically
→ Using Safari's Reading List

Surfing the Web

The Web has become an integral part of most of our lives. It is often the first step to search for information, make plans (such as travel arrangements), conduct financial transactions, shop, and so much more. Fortunately, the Safari app on the iPhone puts the entire Web in the palm of your hand. Safari is a full-featured web browser; it doesn't need specially formatted, mobile websites to work (though it can certainly use those when available). Anything you can do on a website in a browser on a computer can be done with Safari on your iPhone.

Getting Started

The World Wide Web, more commonly called the Web, is a great resource for finding information, making travel arrangements, keeping up with the news, and just about anything else you want to do. Following are some of the more common terms you encounter as you use the Web:

- **Web page**—This is a collection of information (text and graphics) that is available on the Web. A web page is what you look at when you use the Web.

- **Website**—This is a collection of web pages that "go together." For example, most companies and other organizations have websites that contain information they use to help their customers or members, provide services, market and sell their products and services, and so on. A website organizes the web pages it contains and provides the structure you use to move among them.

- **Web browser**—This is the software you use to view web pages. There are many different web browsers available. Examples include Safari, Google Chrome, Internet Explorer, and Firefox. They all allow you to view and interact with web pages, and each has its own set of features. Some are available on just about every device there is, such as Safari and Google Chrome, while some are limited to certain devices, such as Internet Explorer that only runs on Windows computers.

- **Safari**—This is the default web browser on your iPhone; it is also the default web browser on Mac computers. You can download and install it on Windows computers, too.

- **URL.** A Uniform Resource Locator (URL) is a web page's or website's "address" on the Web. URLs allow you to direct your web browser to specific locations on the Web. Most URLs you deal with consist of text, such as www.apple.com or www.aarp.org. Some URLs are more complicated because they take you to specific web pages instead of a website. An example of this is: www.aarp.org/health, which takes you to the Health web page on the AARP website. You seldom have to type URLs because you usually access web pages by tapping on links or using a bookmark, but it's good to know what they are and how to use them.

- **Bookmark**—This is a saved location on the Web. When you visit a web page or website, you can save its URL as a bookmark so you can return to it with a just few taps instead of typing its URL. Safari allows you to save and organize your bookmarks on your iPhone.

- **Search engine or search page**—The Web contains virtually unlimited information on every topic under the sun. You can use a search engine/page to search for information in which you are interested. There are a number of search engines available, with Google being the most popular. You access a search engine through a web browser. Safari uses Google by default, but you can use any search engine you'd like, such as yahoo.com.

The Safari browser app on your iPhone is set up to work as soon as you turn your iPhone on and connect it to the Internet. You don't have to change anything in its settings, as explained in the next section, until you want to change the way Safari works. I recommend you skip ahead to "Visiting Websites" and get started browsing the Web on your iPhone. If you want to change how Safari works after you've started using it, you can come back to "Setting Safari Preferences" at a later time for the steps to follow.

Setting Safari Preferences

Like most apps, Safari offers settings you can use to adjust the way it works.

Configuring Safari's Search Settings

The settings that determine how you perform searches in Safari can be set as follows:

(1) On the Home screen, tap Settings.

(2) Swipe up on the screen until you see Safari.

(3) Tap Safari.

(4) To leave Google as the default search engine, skip to step 7. To change the default search engine, tap Search Engine.

5 Tap Yahoo!, Bing, or DuckDuckGo. The engine you selected is checked to show you that it is the search engine Safari will use by default.

6 Tap Safari.

7 If you want Safari to ask your default search engine for suggestions related to what you type in the Address/Search bar, leave the Search Engine Suggestions switch set to on (green). If you set this to off (white), Safari won't ask the search engine for suggestions, which limits the results of your search somewhat.

8 If you don't want Safari to send data about the Spotlight searches you perform in Safari (such as finding someone in your Contacts app when you search in Safari) to Apple, set the Spotlight Suggestions switch to off (white). If you leave this set to on, data about your Spotlight searches is sent to Apple to help it make Spotlight searches more relevant.

9 Tap Quick Website Search.

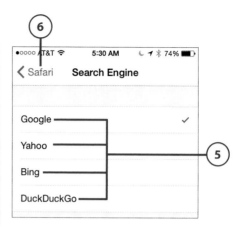

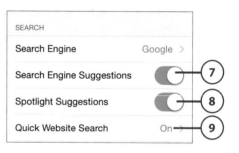

10 If you want to use Safari's Quick Website Search feature, set the Quick Website Search switch to on (green). When this is enabled, you can perform a search at a specific website by typing its name before your search term. For example, you can type "wiki william wallace" in the Address/ Search bar and the first section of the results will be entries in the Wikipedia related to William Wallace; this saves you the steps of moving to the search engine results and then tapping the articles you want to read because you can do this directly from the Search screen instead.

11 Tap Safari.

12 If you don't want Safari to automatically load web pages that are on your top hit list in the background, set the Preload Top Hit switch to off (white). If you leave this enabled, you may find accessing sites you search for to be quicker because the sites you move to or find more frequently are loaded while you search. Proceed to the next section to set Safari's General settings.

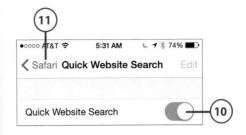

Configuring Safari's General Settings

To configure Safari's General settings, do the following:

1 On the Safari Settings screen, tap Passwords & AutoFill. These settings enable you to automatically log in to websites and to quickly complete forms on the Web by automatically filling in key information for you.

2 To use contact information stored on your iPhone to complete forms, set the Use Contact Info switch to on (green). If you don't want to allow this, leave it off and skip to step 17.

3 Tap My Info.

4 Find and tap your contact information. This tells Safari which information to fill in for you on forms, such as your name, address, etc. You move back to the Passwords & AutoFill screen and see the contact you selected (presumably your name) in the My Info section.

5 To enable Safari to remember usernames and passwords for websites you log in to, set the Names and Passwords switch to on (green). If you don't want to allow this, skip to step 18.

Passcode

If you don't have a passcode active when you perform step 5, you're prompted to create one. You should not allow Names and Passwords or Credit Cards to be saved without a passcode on your iPhone because that means anyone who can get to your phone can also get to your secured websites and credit card information. (Refer to Chapter 4, "Configuring an iPhone to Suit Your Preferences," for the details of setting passcodes.)

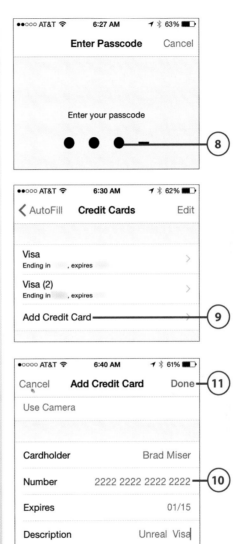

6. To allow credit card information to be saved on your iPhone, set the Credit Cards switch to on (green); if you don't want this information stored, skip to step 20.

7. Tap Saved Credit Cards.

8. Enter your passcode.

9. Tap Add Credit Card.

10. Complete the required credit card information.

11. Tap Done.

A Faster Way to Save Credit Card Information

Instead of manually typing the information in step 10, you can tap Use Camera. You're prompted to frame the credit card in the box on the camera screen. As you do, the information from the card is recorded and becomes highlighted in white text on the screen. When all of the information has been recorded, you return to the Add Credit Card screen. You can edit the information that was scanned if it isn't correct or tap Done if it was recorded correctly.

Removing Credit Card Information

To delete a credit card from your phone, move to the Credit Cards screen, tap Edit, tap the credit cards you want to remove, tap Delete at the top of the screen, and tap Delete again at the prompt.

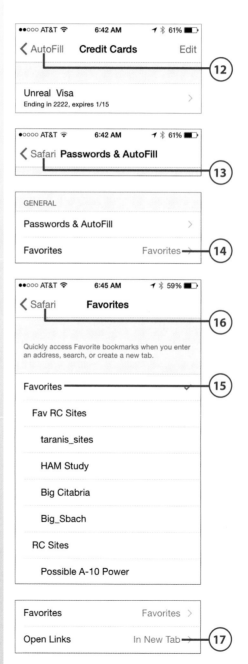

(12) Tap AutoFill.

(13) Tap Safari.

(14) Tap Favorites.

(15) Tap any folder of bookmarks that you want to be your Favorites (they do not have to be in the folder labeled Favorites). These are available when you enter a new URL, perform a search, or create new tabs so that you can get to them quickly and easily (you learn about creating and working with bookmarks later in this chapter).

(16) Tap Safari.

(17) Tap Open Links. This tells Safari the option you want to see when you tap and hold a link on a current web page to open a new web page.

18 Tap In New Tab to select the Open in New Tab option, which causes Safari to open and immediately take you to a new tab displaying the web page with which the link is associated. Tap In Background if you want Safari to display the Open in Background option, which opens pages in the background so you can view them later.

19 Tap Safari.

20 To enable pop-up blocking, slide the Block Pop-ups switch to on (green). Pop-ups are now blocked. Some websites won't work properly with pop-ups blocked, so you can also use this setting to temporarily enable pop-ups by sliding the switch to off (white). Proceed to the next task to complete the rest of Safari's settings.

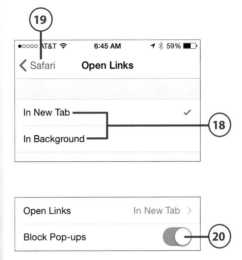

Revisiting Saved Passwords and Credit Cards

If you enable usernames and passwords to be stored on your iPhone, you can get information about them by moving to the Passwords & AutoFill settings page, tapping Saved Passwords, and entering your passcode. On the Passwords screen, you see a list of websites for which information is stored on your iPhone. Tap a website to view the details stored for it. To remove a saved password, tap Edit on the Passwords screen, tap the website associated with the passwords you want to remove, and tap Delete. The next time you visit that website, you'll need to reenter your account sign-in information.

You can take similar actions on credit cards you've saved from the Credit Cards screen. Tap a card to edit its information or use the Edit command to delete cards you no longer want to store on your iPhone.

Configuring Safari's Privacy & Security Settings

Configure Safari's Privacy & Security settings by performing the following steps:

(1) Swipe up the Safari Settings screen so you see the PRIVACY & SECURITY section.

(2) To enable private browsing, which means Safari doesn't track and keep a list of the sites you visit, set the Do Not Track switch to on (green). If you have open web pages, you are prompted to close all tabs in Safari; tap Close All to close them or Keep All to leave them open. From this point on, Safari doesn't keep a list of web pages you visit (which means you won't be able to use the History list to return to sites of interest).

(3) Tap Block Cookies.

(4) Tap the kind of cookies you want to allow. The Always Block option blocks all cookies. The Allow from Current Website Only setting allows cookies only from the website you are currently viewing to be stored on your phone. Allow from Websites I Visit blocks cookies from sites you didn't visit directly. This is the setting I recommend you choose because it enables websites you visit to store information on your iPhone while blocking cookies from sites you didn't visit. The Always Allow

option accepts all cookies; I don't recommend this option because if you get directed to a site by another site that you didn't intend to visit, its cookies can be stored on your iPhone.

(5) Tap Safari.

(6) If you don't want Safari to warn you when you visit websites that appear to be fraudulent, set the Fraudulent Website Warning switch to off (white). I recommend you leave this enabled.

(7) To clear the history of websites you have visited, tap Clear History and Website Data.

(8) Tap Clear History and Data at the prompt. This removes the websites you have visited from your history list. The list starts over, so the next site you visit is added to your history list again—unless you have enabled private browsing, in which case the sites you visit are not tracked. It also removes all cookies and other website data that have been stored on your iPhone.

●●○○○ AT&T 🔊	11:06 AM ✈ ✳ 43% ▮▮

❮ Safari   Block Cookies

COOKIES AND WEBSITE DATA

Always Block

Allow from Current Website Only

Allow from Websites I Visit   ✓

Always Allow

Block Cookies   Allow from Website... ❯

Fraudulent Website Warning   ⬤

About Safari & Privacy...

Clear History and Website Data

Clearing will remove history, cookies, and other browsing data.

History will be cleared from devices signed into your iCloud account.

Clear History and Data

Cancel

Making Cookies

Cookies are data that websites store on the device you use to browse them. Cookies can contain data about you, such as areas you last visited or things in which you are interested. Cookies are typically used to direct you back to these areas or point you to related areas. Most of the time, cookies are harmless and can even be helpful to you, at least from legitimate sites you intentionally visit.

⑨ Later, you'll learn about the Reading List that enables you to store web pages on your iPhone for offline reading; if you want to allow pages to be saved to your iPhone when you are using its cellular data connection, slide the Use Cellular Data switch to the on (green) position. Slide this switch to off (white) if you have a limited data plan and don't want to use it to store web pages (you can store them when you are using a Wi-Fi network). You're ready to browse the Web.

Clear History and Website Data

READING LIST

Use Cellular Data   ⑨

Use cellular network to save Reading List items from iCloud for offline reading.

Advanced   >

Advanced?

The Advanced option takes you to the Advanced screen. Here, you can tap Website Data to see the amount of data associated with websites you have visited; swipe up on the screen and tap Remove All Website Data to clear this data. You can disable JavaScript, which you aren't likely to want to do because many pages require this scripting language to work. You can also enable the Web Inspector. This enables website developers to check their websites on an iPhone for errors so that those sites can be updated to work properly. If you aren't a website developer, you probably won't need to use this tool. If you are a website developer, enable the tool when you evaluate your website using Safari on an iPhone.

Visiting Websites

If you've used a web browser on a computer before, using Safari on an iPhone is a familiar experience. If you've not used a web browser before, don't worry because using Safari on an iPhone is simple and intuitive.

Syncing Bookmarks

You can synchronize your Internet Explorer favorites or Safari bookmarks on a Windows PC—or Safari bookmarks on a Mac—to your iPhone so you have the same set of bookmarks available on your iPhone that you do on your computer and other devices, and vice versa. You can do this via the sync process or wirelessly using iCloud. Refer to Chapter 3, "Setting Up and Using iCloud and Other Online Accounts," for information about using iCloud to sync bookmarks or Chapter 5, "Working with iTunes on Your Computer," for details of syncing your iPhone using iTunes. If you use Internet Explorer or Safari on a computer, you should synchronize before you start browsing on your iPhone so you avoid typing URLs or re-creating bookmarks. When you enable Safari syncing via iCloud, you can also view tabs open in Safari on other devices, such as a Mac or an iPad.

Using Bookmarks to Move to Websites

Using bookmarks you've synced via iCloud, or from a computer or other device, onto your iPhone makes it easy to get to websites that are of interest to you. You can also create bookmarks on your iPhone (you learn how later in this chapter) and use them just like bookmarks you've synced onto the iPhone.

1. On the iPhone Home screen, tap Safari.

2. Tap the Bookmarks button.

Back to the Bookmarks

The most recent Bookmarks screen is retained when you move away from Bookmarks and then come back. Each time you open your Bookmarks, you're at the same place you were when you left it.

3 Tap the Bookmarks tab if it isn't selected already. (If you don't see this tab, tap the Back button in the upper-left corner of the screen until you do.)

4 Swipe up or down the list of bookmarks to browse the bookmarks and other folders of bookmarks available to you.

5 To move to a bookmark, skip to step 10; to open a folder of bookmarks, tap it.

6 Swipe up or down the folder's screen to browse the folders and bookmarks it contains.

7 You can tap a folder to see the bookmarks it contains.

8 To return to a previous screen, tap the Back button in the upper-left corner of the screen, which is labeled with the name of the folder you previously visited (the parent folder); this disappears when you are at the top-level Bookmarks screen.

9 Repeat steps 5–8 until you see a bookmark you want to visit.

Change Your Mind?
If you decide not to visit a bookmark, tap Done. You return to the page you were previously viewing.

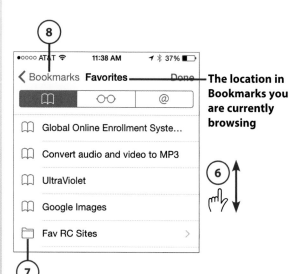

Your Favorites

Folder containing bookmarks

Bookmark

The location in Bookmarks you are currently browsing

10 Tap the bookmark you want to visit. Safari moves to that website.

11 Use the information in the section "Viewing Websites" later in this chapter to get information on viewing the web page.

Playing Favorites

You might see two Favorites folders on the Bookmarks screen. The folder marked with a star is the folder you designated, using the Safari settings described previously in this chapter, as the place to store Favorites on your iPhone. If you use Safari on a computer, you can also configure bookmarks and folders of bookmarks on its Bookmarks bar. When these bookmarks are synced from your computer to the iPhone, they might be stored in a folder of bookmarks also called Favorites and shown with the standard folder icon. If you set this synced folder in your iPhone's Safari settings to also be its Favorites folder, you won't have to deal with this potentially confusing situation of multiple Favorites folders.

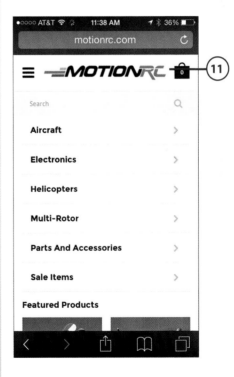

iPhone Web Pages

Some websites have been specially formatted for iPhones and other mobile devices. These typically have less complex information on each page, so they load faster. When you move to a site like this, you might be redirected to the mobile version automatically, or you might be prompted to choose which version of the site you want to visit. On the mobile version, there is typically a link that takes you to the "regular" version, too. (It's sometimes called the Desktop, Full, or Classic version.) Sometimes the version formatted for handheld devices offers less information or fewer tools than the regular version. Because Safari is a full-featured browser, you can use the version you prefer.

Using Your Favorites to Move to Websites

Using the Safari settings described earlier, you can designate a folder of bookmarks as your Favorites. You can get to the folders and bookmarks in your Favorites folder more quickly and easily than navigating to it as described in the previous section. (If you haven't set your Favorites yet, refer to the task "Configuring Safari's General Settings.") Here's how to use your Favorites:

(1) On the Home screen, tap Safari. (If you are in Safari and have the Bookmarks screen open, tap Done to close it.)

(2) Tap in the Address/Search bar (if you don't see the Address/Search bar, tap at the top of the screen to show it). Just below the Address/Search bar are your Favorites (bookmarks and folders of bookmarks). The keyboard opens at the bottom of the screen.

(**3**) Swipe up and down on your Favorites. The keyboard closes to give you more room to browse.

(**4**) To move to a bookmark, tap it and skip to step 8.

(**5**) To move into a folder, tap it.

More Commands

At the top of the Favorites screen, you might see two more commands. Tap Add to Favorites to add a bookmark to the current site to your Favorites folder. Tap Request Desktop Site if you are currently viewing the mobile version of a site and want to see the "full" version; you move to that version after you tap the command.

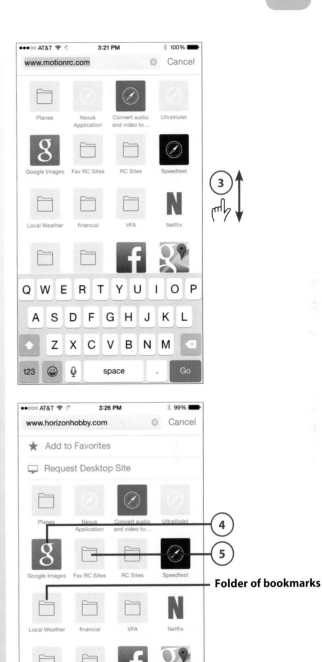

Folder of bookmarks

Bookmark

6 Continue browsing your Favorites until you find the bookmark you want to use. Like using the Bookmarks screen, you can tap a folder to move into it, tap a bookmark to move to its website, tap the Back button to move to the previous screen, and so on.

7 Tap the bookmark for the site you want to visit.

8 Use the information in the section "Viewing Websites" later in this chapter to view the web page.

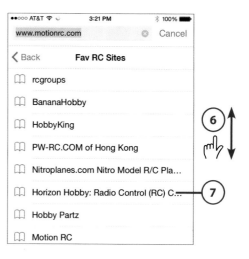

Typing URLs to Move to Websites

A Uniform Resource Locator (URL) is the Internet address of a web page. URLs can be relatively simple, such as www.apple.com, or they can be quite long and convoluted. The good news is that by using bookmarks, you can save a URL in Safari so you can get back to it using its bookmark (as you learned in the previous two tasks) and thus avoid typing URLs. Although it might not be fun to type URLs, sometimes that's the only way you have to get to a website.

1 On the Home screen, tap Safari. (If you are in Safari and have the Bookmarks screen open, tap Done to close it.)

2 Tap in the Address/Search bar (if you don't see the Address/Search bar, tap at the top of the screen). The URL of the current page becomes highlighted; if you haven't visited a page, the Address/Search bar is empty. Just below the Address/Search bar, your Favorites are displayed. The keyboard appears at the bottom of the screen.

3 If an address appears in the Address/Search bar, tap the clear button (x) to remove it.

4 Type the URL you want to visit. If it starts with www (which almost all URLs do), you don't have to type "www." As you type, Safari attempts to match what you are typing to a site you have visited previously and completes the URL for you if it can. Just below the Address/Search bar, Safari presents a list of sites that might be what you are looking for, organized into top hits, suggested sites, or a web search.

5 If one of the sites shown is the one you want to visit, tap it. You move to that web page; skip to step 8.

6 If Safari doesn't find a match, continue typing until you enter the entire URL.

7 Tap Go. You move to the web page.

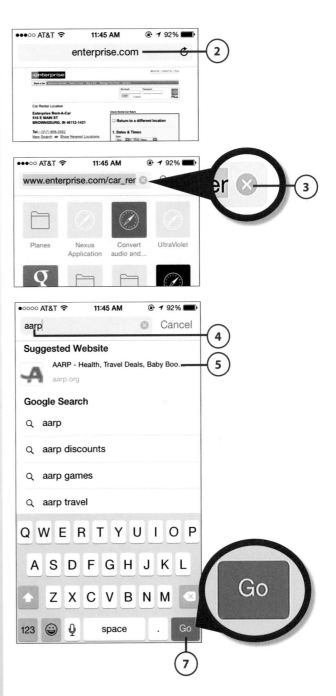

Shortcut for Typing URLs

URLs include a top-level domain code that represents the type of site (theoretically anyway) that URL leads to. Common examples are .com (commercial sites), .edu (educational sites), and so on. To quickly enter a URL's code, tap and hold the period key to see a menu from which you can select other options, such as .net, .edu, and so on. Tap the code you want on the keyboard, and it is entered in the Address/Search bar.

8 Use the information in the section "Viewing Websites" to view the web page.

Using Your Browsing History to Move to Websites

As you move about the Web, Safari tracks the sites you visit and builds a history list (unless you enabled the Do Not Track option, in which case this doesn't happen and you can't use History to return to previous sites). You can use your browsing history list to return to sites you've visited.

1 Tap the Bookmarks button.

2 If you aren't on the Bookmarks screen, tap the Back button until you move to the Bookmarks screen. (Safari remembers your last location, so if you were last on the Bookmarks screen, you don't need to tap any buttons to get back there.)

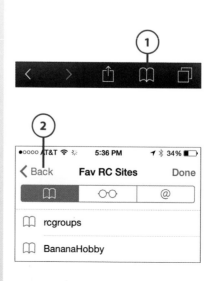

3 If necessary, swipe down the Bookmarks page until you see the History folder.

4 Tap History.

5 Swipe up and down the page to browse all the sites you've visited. The more recent sites appear at the top of the screen; the further you move down the screen, the further back in time you go. Earlier sites are collected in folders for various times, such as This Morning, Monday Afternoon, and so on.

6 Tap the site you want to visit. The site opens and you can use the information in the section "Viewing Websites" to view the web page.

Erasing the Past

To clear your browsing history, tap the Clear button at the bottom of the History screen. At the prompt, tap the timeframe that you want to clear; the options are The last hour, Today, Today and Yesterday, or All time. Your browsing history for the period of time you selected is erased. (Don't you wish it were this easy to erase the past in real life?)

Viewing Websites

Even though your iPhone is a small device, you'll be amazed at how well it displays web pages designed for larger screens.

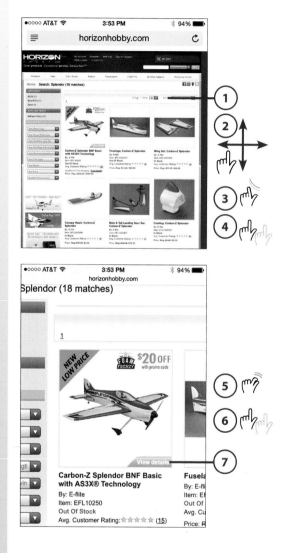

(1) Use Safari to move to a web page as described in the previous tasks.

(2) To browse around a web page, swipe your finger right or left, or up or down.

(3) To zoom in manually, unpinch your fingers.

(4) To zoom in automatically, tap your finger on the screen twice.

(5) To zoom out manually, pinch your fingers.

(6) To zoom on a column or a figure, tap it twice.

(7) To move to a link, tap it once. Links can come in many forms including text (most text that is a link is in color and underlined) or graphics. The web page to which the link points opens and replaces the page currently being displayed.

Where Did the URL Go?

When you first move to a URL, you see that URL in the Address/Search bar. After you work with a site, the URL is replaced with the high-level domain name for the site (such as sitename.com, sitename.edu, etc.). To see the full URL again, tap the Address/Search bar.

8 To view the web page in landscape orientation, rotate the iPhone so that it is horizontal.

9 Scroll, zoom in, and zoom out on the page to read it, as described in steps 2–7.

10 To refresh a page, tap Refresh. (Note: while a page is loading, this is the "x" button; tap it to stop the rest of the page from loading.)

11 To move to a previous page you've visited, tap Back.

12 To move to a subsequent page, tap Forward.

13 As you move around, the Address/Search bar at the top of the page and the toolbar at the bottom of the page are hidden automatically; to show them again, tap the top or bottom of the screen.

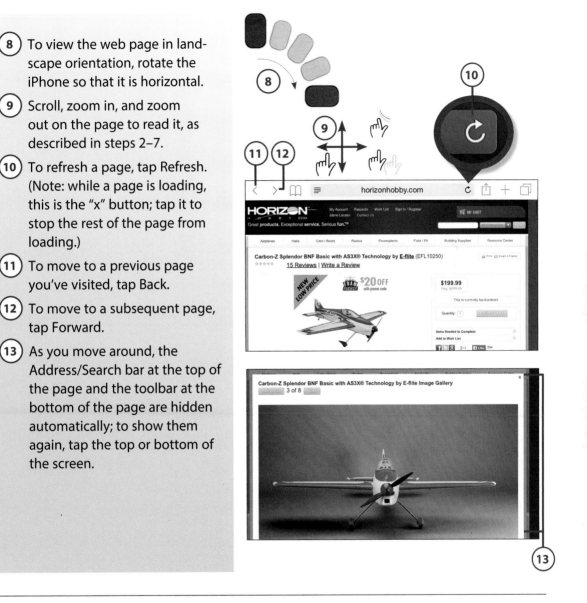

Different Phones Different Look

The type of iPhone you are using to browse the Web affects how pages look and where controls are located. For example, when you use an iPhone 5s, you see black at the top and bottom of the screen although you see white there on an iPhone 6. Also, when you rotate an iPhone 5s, the tools are at the top and bottom of the screen, while on an iPhone 6, the controls are all the top of the screen.

Do More with Links

To see options for a link, tap and hold your finger down for a second or so. When you lift your finger, a menu appears. Tap Open to open the page to replace the current page at which the link points (this is the same as tapping a link once). Tap Open in Background to open the page in a new Safari window that opens in the background, or tap Open in New Tab to open the new page in a new tab. The command that appears depends on the Open Links Safari setting. Tap Add to Reading List to add the page to your Reading List (which is explained in the tasks in the section "Using Safari's Reading List" later in this chapter). Tap Copy to copy the link's URL so that you can paste it elsewhere, such as in an email message. Tap Cancel to return to the current page and take no action.

Working with Multiple Websites at the Same Time

When you move to a web page by using a bookmark, typing a URL, tapping a link on the current web page, and so on, the new web page replaces the current one. However, you can also open and work with multiple web pages at the same time so that a new web page doesn't replace the current one.

When you work with multiple web pages, each open page appears in its own tab. You can use the tab view to easily move to and manage your open web pages. You can also close open tabs, and you can even open web pages that are open on other devices on which your iCloud account has been configured and Safari syncing enabled.

There are two ways to open a new web page in a new tab.

One is to tap and hold on a link on the current web page; you can use the resulting Open command to open the new page. There are two options for this approach; the one you use is determined by the Open Links preference set as described earlier in this chapter. The In Background option causes the new page to open and move to the background. This is most useful when you want to read the new page at a later time, such as when you are done with the current one. The In New Tab option causes the new page to open and move to the front so you see it instantly while moving the current page and its tab to the background.

The second way to open a new web page in a new tab is by using the Tab Manager.

All these options are described in the following tasks.

Tapping Without Holding

When you tap, but don't hold down, a link on a web page, the web page to which the link points opens and replaces the current web page—no new tab is created. When you tap and hold a link, the behavior is determined by the setting you chose in the preferences as covered in a task earlier in this chapter ("Configuring Safari's General Settings").

Opening New Pages in the Background

If you enabled the In Background option for the Open Links preference, you can open new web pages in new tabs by doing the following:

① Tap and hold on the link you want to open in the background.

② Tap Open in Background. The page to which the link points opens. The only result you see is the page "jumping" down to the Tab Manager button in the lower-right corner of the screen.

③ Continue opening pages in the background; see "Using Tab View to Manage Open Web Pages" to learn how to use the tab view to move to pages that are open in the background.

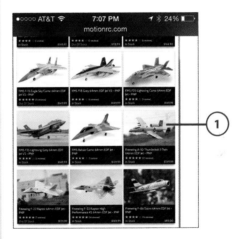

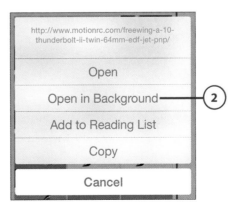

Opening New Pages in a New Tab

If you enabled the In New Tab option for the Open Links preference, you can open new pages by doing the following:

(1) Tap and hold on the link you want to open in the background.

(2) Tap Open in New Tab. A new tab opens and displays the page to which the link points. The web page from which you started moves into the background.

(3) Continue opening pages; see "Using Tab View to Manage Open Web Pages" to learn how to use the tab view to manage your open pages.

Just Open It

If you tap the Open command on the menu in step 2 of the previous tasks, the new web page replaces the one you were viewing on the current tab. This is the same as just tapping a link on the page.

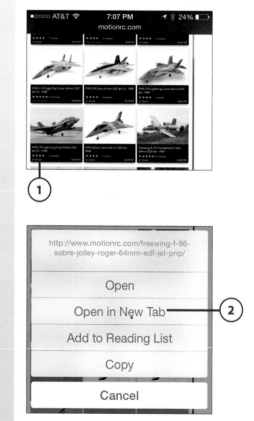

Using Tab View to Manage Open Web Pages

As you open new pages, whether in the background or not, new tabs are opened. Safari's tab view enables you to view and work with your open pages/tabs. Here's how:

1. Tap the tab view button. Each open page appears on its own tab.

2. Swipe up or down on the open tabs to browse them.

3. Tap a tab/page to move into it. The page opens and fills the Safari window.

4. Work with the web page.

5. Tap the tab view button.

Open web pages/tabs

6 To close a tab, click its close button or swipe to the left on the tab you want to close. That page/tab closes.

7 To open a new tab, tap the Add button to create new tab that shows your Favorites screen; navigate to a new page in that tab using the tools you've already learned in other tasks (bookmarks or typing a URL).

8 To close the tab view, tap Done. The tab view closes, and the page you were most recently viewing is shown.

Tabs Are Independent

Each tab is independent. So, when you are working with a tab and use the back/forward buttons to move among its pages, you are just moving among the pages open under that tab. Pages open in other tabs are not affected.

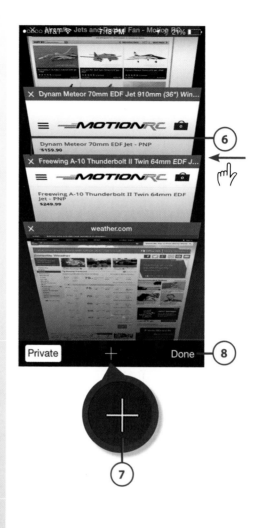

Opening Web Pages That Are Open on Other Devices

When you enable iCloud Safari syncing, iCloud tracks the websites you have open on all the devices on which you have Safari syncing enabled, including your iPhone, iPads, Macs, and so on. This is really handy when you have pages open on another device and want to view them on your iPhone. (Pages open on your iPhone are available on your other devices, too.) To view a page you have open on another device, do the following:

A Mac with open web pages

(1) Open the tab view.

(2) Swipe up the screen until you see the pages open on other devices. There is a section for each device; sections are labeled with the device's name. In each device's section, you see the pages open in Safari on those devices.

(3) Tap the page you want to view. The page opens on the iPhone and becomes a new tab.

Keep Private Things Private

If you aren't browsing in Private mode and tap the Private button at the bottom of the tab view, you see two options. Tap Close Private Tabs to close all the tabs you are viewing privately. Tap Keep Private Tabs to keep them open but hide them in the tab view. Tap the button again to return to the previous state. If you are browsing in Private mode, tapping the Private button shows or hides the tabs in the tab view.

Searching the Web

In the first task of this chapter, you learned that you can set Safari to search the Web using Google, Yahoo!, Bing, or DuckDuckGo. No matter which search engine you chose, you search the Web in the same way.

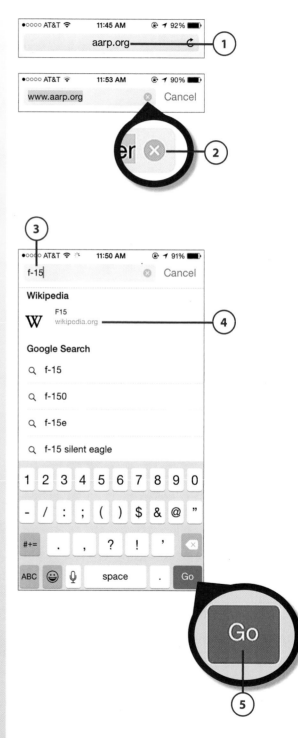

1. Tap in the Address/Search bar. The keyboard appears along with your Favorites.

2. If there is any text in the Address/Search bar, tap the clear button.

3. Type your search word(s). As you type, Safari attempts to find a search that matches what you typed. The list of suggestions is organized in sections, which depend on what you are searching for and the search options you configured through Safari settings. One section, labeled with the search engine you are using (such as Google Search), contains the search results from that source. Other sections can include Bookmarks and History, Apps (from the App Store), etc. At the bottom of the list is the On This Page section, which shows the terms that match your search on the page you are browsing.

Quick Website Search

If you enabled the Quick Website Search feature, you can include the site you want to search in the Address/Search bar, such as "Wiki F-15." When you do this, the results from the site you entered appear at the top of the list and you can access them directly by tapping the information that appears (as opposed to having to move to the search engine site first as in these steps).

④ To perform the search using one of the suggestions provided, tap the suggestion you want to use. The search is performed and you can skip to step 6.

⑤ If none of the suggestions are what you want, keep typing until you have entered the entire search term and tap Go. The search engine you use performs the search and displays the results on the search results page.

⑥ Use the search results page to view the results of your search. These pages work just like other web pages. You can zoom, scroll, and click links to explore results.

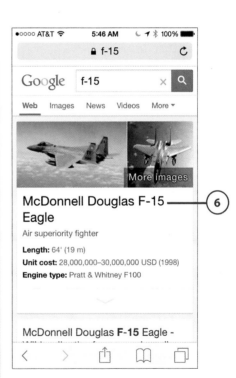

Searching on a Web Page

To search for words or phrases on a web page you are viewing, perform these steps, except in step 4, tap the word or phrase for which you want to search in the On This Page section. You return to the page you are browsing and each occurrence of your search term on the page is highlighted.

Saving and Organizing Bookmarks

In addition to moving bookmarks from a computer or iCloud onto your iPhone, you can save new bookmarks directly in your iPhone (they are synced onto other devices, too). You can also organize bookmarks on your iPhone to make them easier and faster to access.

Creating Bookmarks

When you want to make it easy to return to a website, create a bookmark. Do the following to create a new bookmark:

(1) Move to a web page you want to save as a bookmark.

(2) Tap the Share button.

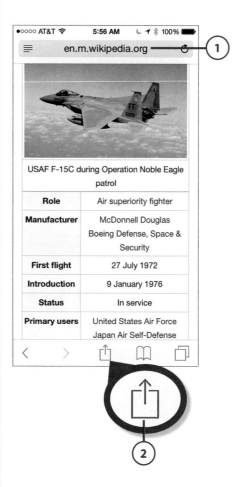

(3) Tap Add Bookmark. The Add Bookmark screen appears, showing the title of the web page you are viewing, which will also be the name of the bookmark initially; its URL; and the Location field, which shows where the bookmark will be stored when you create it.

(4) Edit the bookmark's name as needed, or tap the Clear button (x) to erase the current name and then type the new name of the bookmark. The titles of some web pages are quite long, so it's a good idea to shorten them so the bookmark's name is easier to read on the iPhone's screen and you can fit more bookmarks on the screen.

(5) Tap Location. The Choose a Folder screen appears. The folder that is currently selected is marked with a check mark.

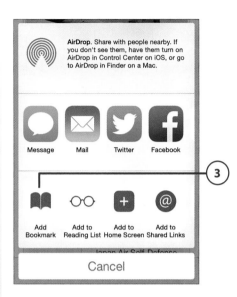

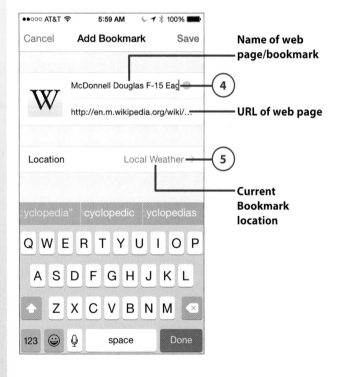

Name of web page/bookmark

URL of web page

Current Bookmark location

6 Swipe up and down the screen to find the folder in which you want to place the new bookmark. You can choose any folder on the screen; folders are indented when they are contained within other folders.

7 To choose a folder in which to store the new bookmark, tap it. You return to the Add Bookmark screen, which shows the location you selected.

8 Tap Save. The bookmark is created and saved in the location you specified. You can use the bookmark to return to the website at any time.

●oooo AT&T 🔹	6:05 AM	🔹 ⚡ 99% ▬
‹ Back	**Choose a Folder**	

☆ Favorites

📁 Fav Planes ────────── **7**

📁 Fav RC Sites ───────── **6**

   📁 taranis_sites

   📁 HAM Study

   📁 Big Citabria

   📁 Big_Sbach

📁 RC Sites

●oooo AT&T 🔹	6:05 AM	🔹 ⚡ 99% ▬
Cancel	**Add Bookmark**	Save ── **8**

W   F-15 ⊗

http://en.m.wikipedia.org/wiki/...

Location   Fav Planes ›

It's Not All Good

Unfortunately, bookmarks that you create on the iPhone are useful on the computer to which they are synced only if you use Internet Explorer or Safari (Windows PC) or Safari (Mac). If you use Firefox, Chrome, or another web browser, the bookmarks moved onto the computer from the iPhone are of little value to you because they appear in only one of the supported browsers (Internet Explorer or Safari). You can make them available in other browsers, but that requires going through extra gyrations, which can negate the value of syncing.

Organizing Bookmarks

You've seen how bookmarks can be contained in folders, which is a good thing because you're likely to have a lot of them. You can change the names and locations of your existing bookmarks and folders as follows:

(1) Move to the Bookmarks screen showing the bookmarks and folders you want to change. (You can't move among the Bookmarks screens while you are in Edit mode so you need to start at the location where the items you want to change are located.)

(2) Tap Edit. Unlock buttons appear next to the folders and bookmarks you can change; some folders, such as the History folder, can't be changed. The order icons also appear on the right side of the screen, again only for folders or bookmarks you can change.

(3) Tap the order icon next to the bookmark or folder you want to move and drag it up or down the screen to change the order in which it appears on the screen. When you drag a folder or bookmark between other items, they slide apart to make room for the folder or bookmark you are dragging. The order of the items in the list is the order in which they appear on the Bookmarks screen.

(4) To change the name or location of a folder, tap it.

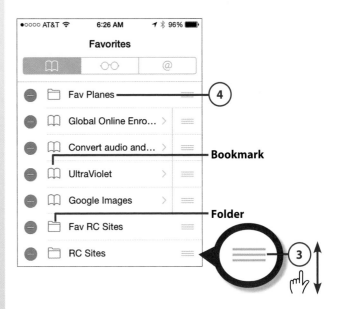

Can't Move?

If you have only one bookmark you've added, you can't move them around as described here because Safari won't let you "disturb" the default bookmarks and folders (such as Favorites and History). You can only delete default bookmarks.

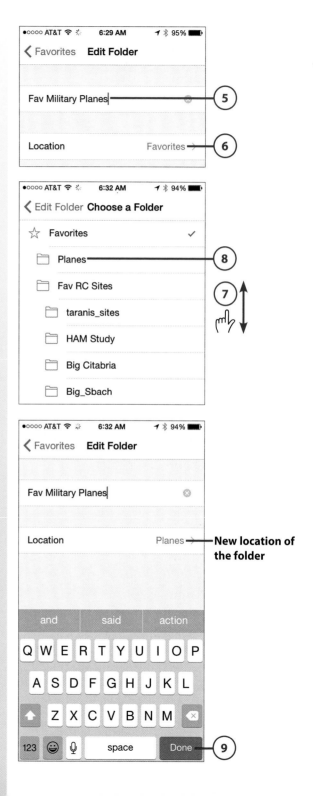

New location of the folder

5 Change the name in the Name bar.

6 To change the location of the folder, tap the Location bar, which shows the folder's current location.

7 Swipe up and down the list of folders until you see the folder in which you want to place the folder you are working with.

8 Tap the folder into which you want to move the folder you are editing. You move back to the Edit Folder screen.

9 Tap Done. You move back to the Bookmarks screen, which reflects any changes you made.

10 Tap a bookmark you want to change.

11 Change the bookmark's name in the Name bar.

12 If you want to change a bookmark's URL, tap the URL bar and make changes to the current URL. For example, you might want to change it to have the bookmark point to a site's home page rather than the page you are viewing.

13 To change the location of the folder or bookmark, tap the Location bar and follow steps 7 and 8.

14 Tap Done. You move back to the previous screen, and any changes you made—such as changing the name or location of a bookmark—are reflected.

Editing a Bookmark

If the bookmark you want to change isn't on the Bookmarks screen you are currently viewing, tap Done to exit Edit mode. Then open the folder containing the bookmark you want to change and tap Edit. You are able to change the bookmark.

Can't Change?

You can't change default bookmarks, you can only delete them.

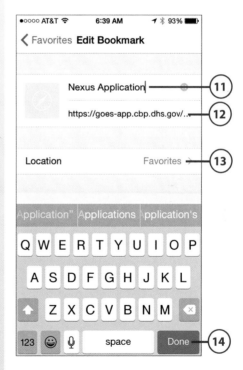

15 To create a new folder, tap New Folder.

16 Enter the name of the folder.

17 Follow steps 6–8 to choose the location in which you want to save the new folder.

18 Tap Done. The new folder is created in the location you selected. You can place folders and bookmarks into it by using the Location bar to navigate to it.

19 Tap Done. Your changes are saved and you exit Edit mode.

Deleting Bookmarks or Folders of Bookmarks

You can get rid of bookmarks or folders of bookmarks you don't want any more by deleting them:

1. Move to the screen containing the folder or bookmark you want to delete.

2. Swipe to the left on the folder or bookmark you want to delete.

3. Tap Delete. The folder or bookmark is deleted. Note that when you delete a folder, all the bookmarks it contains are deleted, too.

Creating Bookmarks on the Home Screens

You can add a bookmark icon to a Home screen so that you can visit a web page from there; this handy trick saves you several navigation moves that would be required to move into Safari and type the URL or use a bookmark to get the page you want to see.

1. Use Safari to move to a web page to which you want to have easy access from the Home screen.

2. Tap the Share button.

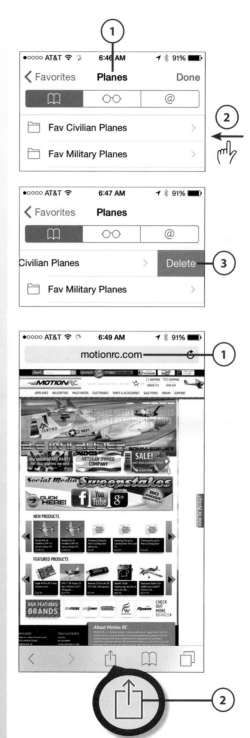

③ Tap Add to Home Screen.

④ If needed, edit the name of the icon that will appear on the Home screen. The default name is the name of the web page. It's best to edit it to a shorter name because it has a small amount of room on its icon on the Home screen.

⑤ Tap Add. You move to the Home screen and see the icon you added. You can return to the site at any time by tapping this button.

Location Is Everything

You can organize the buttons on the pages of the Home screen so that you can place your web page buttons in convenient locations, and you can create folders on your Home screens to keep your web page icons neat and tidy there, too. Refer to Chapter 4 for details.

Sharing Web Pages

Safari makes it easy to share web pages that you think will be valuable to others. There are many ways to share, including AirDrop, Message, Mail, Twitter, and Facebook. A couple of examples will prepare you to use any of them.

Emailing a Link to a Web Page

You can quickly email links to web pages you visit.

1. Use Safari to navigate to a web page whose link you want to email to someone.

2. Tap the Share button.

3. Tap Mail. A new email message is created, and the link to the web page is inserted into the body. The subject of the message is the title of the web page.

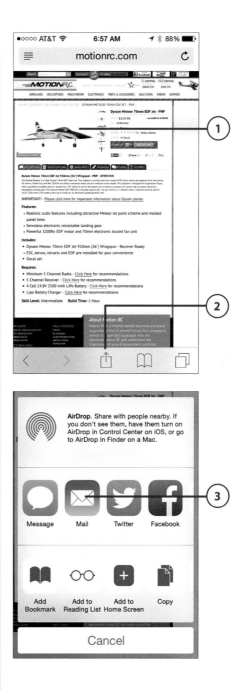

4 Complete and send the email message. (Refer to Chapter 9, "Sending, Receiving, and Managing Email," for information about the Mail app.) When the recipient receives your message, he can visit the website by clicking the link included in the email message.

Messaging a Web Page

If you come across a page that you want to share with someone via Messages, Safari makes it easy.

1 Use Safari to navigate to a web page whose link you want to message to someone.

2 Tap the Share button.

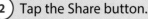

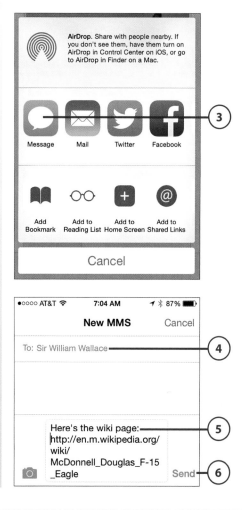

3. Tap Message. A new message is created, and the link to the web page is inserted.

4. Address the message.

5. Enter text you want to send along with the link to the web page.

6. Tap Send. Your message is sent. The recipients can visit the web page by tapping the link included in the message.

>>>Go Further
MORE WAYS TO SHARE THE WEB

If you want to share a web page in the old-fashioned way, you can print it by opening the Share menu and tapping Print (assuming you have your iPhone set up to print, as explained in Chapter 1, "Getting Started with Your iPhone"). If you tap Copy, the web page's address is copied to the clipboard, from where you can paste it into documents, emails, notes, or messages. You can also share via Twitter and Facebook.

Completing Forms on the Web

Just like web browsers on a computer, you often have to complete forms on your iPhone, such as to log in to your account on a website or request information about something. You can manually enter information or use AutoFill to have Safari add the information for you. (AutoFill must be enabled using Safari settings, as explained at the beginning of this chapter.)

Manually Completing Forms

To manually fill in a form, do the following:

1. Open Safari and move to a website containing a form.

2. Zoom in on the fields you need to complete.

3. Tap in a field. If you tapped a text field, the keyboard appears.

4. Enter the information in the field. (If the site suggests information you want to enter, just tap it to enter it. You might have to tap Done to temporarily hide the keyboard to see all the suggestions. If a suggestion isn't the information you want to enter, just keep typing.)

5. Tap the Next button. If there isn't another field on the form, this button is disabled, so skip this step. If it is enabled, you move to the next field on the form.

Selecting Data

You can select, instead of type, some types of information. For example, when you are entering an address, you usually choose a state or province from a list. And you often choose dates rather than typing them. When you see a downward-facing arrow in a field, tap it to choose that information or just move into a field that you select like any other. The selection tool replaces the keyboard at the bottom of the screen. Swipe on the wheels or use the other tools in this area to select the data you want to enter.

(6) Repeat steps 4 and 5 to complete all the fields on the form.

(7) Tap Done. If it's open, the keyboard closes and you move back to the web page.

(8) Tap Continue, Submit, Go, Login, or whatever button is provided to send the form's information to the website.

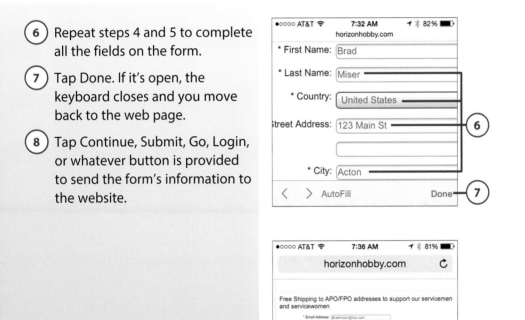

Using AutoFill to Complete Forms

AutoFill makes completing forms faster and easier because Safari can enter information for you with the tap of a button.

(1) Open Safari and move to a website containing a form. Zoom in on the fields you need to complete, and tap in a field. If you tapped a text field, the keyboard appears.

(2) Tap AutoFill. Safari fills any fields it can, based on the information you designated when you configured AutoFill to use your contact information. Any fields that Safari tries to complete are highlighted in yellow.

(3) Use the steps shown in the preceding task to review all the fields and to type in what AutoFill wasn't able to complete or edit those that AutoFill completed but that need to be changed.

AutoFillin'

For AutoFill to work, it must be enabled in the Safari settings as described at the beginning of the chapter. If the data AutoFill enters is not correct, use the Safari settings to choose your correct contact info or, if the correct info is selected in Safari settings, update it in the Contacts app.

Signing In to Websites Automatically

If you enable Safari to remember usernames and passwords, it can enter this information for you automatically. When Safari encounters a site for which it recognizes and can save login information, you are prompted to allow Safari to save that information. This doesn't work with all sites; if you aren't prompted to allow Safari to save login information, you can't use this feature with that site. When saved, this information can be entered for you automatically.

(1) Move to a web page that requires you to log in to an account.

(2) Enter your account's username and password.

(3) Tap the button to log in to your account, such as Continue, Sign In, Submit, Login, and such. You are prompted to save the login information.

(4) To save the information, tap Save Password. The next time you move to the login page, your username and password are entered for you automatically. Tap Never for This Website if you don't want the information to be saved and you don't want to be prompted again. Tap Not Now if you don't want the information saved but do want to be prompted again later to save it.

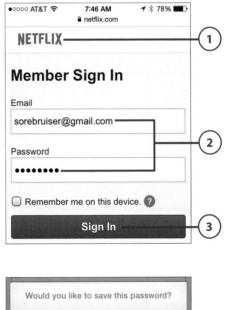

LETTING SAFARI CREATE PASSWORDS FOR YOU

If you have enabled the Names and Passwords setting, Safari can create passwords for you. Go to a website that requires you to create a password, such as when you register for a new account. When you tap in a field that Safari recognizes as requiring a password, tap Suggest Password. Safari presents a password for you; most of these will not be easy to remember, but that doesn't matter because it is saved for you automatically so you won't have to enter it manually. If you want to use the recommended password, tap Use Suggested Password; Safari enters the password in the password and verify password fields.

Using Safari's Reading List

The Reading List is a way to save pages you want to read at a later time. You can collect the pages you want to read on your Reading List as you browse. When you want to read the pages you have collected, open the Reading List and see the pages you have added there. The Reading List is useful to store pages that you do not necessarily want to bookmark because your use of them is temporary.

Reader View

Safari offers the Reader View that reformats web pages so they are oriented vertically, making them easy to read because you just have to scroll up and down the page and everything fits on the screen's width. If a site has a Reader View available, you will see a message saying so in the Address/Search bar when you move to that site. When the page has loaded, tap the button located at the left edge of the Address/ Search bar to move into Reader View. Tap it again to switch back to regular view.

Adding Pages to Your Reading List

To add pages to your Reading List:

1. Using Safari, open a web page.
2. Tap the Share button.
3. Tap Add to Reading List.

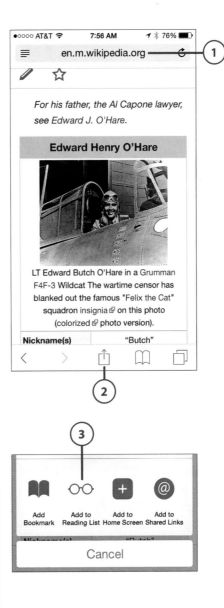

(4) Repeat steps 1–3 to add more pages to your Reading List.

Connection Not Always Required

To read the pages currently on the Reading List, your iPhone doesn't have to be connected to the Internet, which is what makes this feature particularly useful. However, to move to any links on a page on the Reading List, the iPhone does have to be connected to the Internet.

Using Your Reading List

To use your Reading List, do the following:

(1) Open the Bookmarks page and tap the Reading List tab. You see the pages on your Reading List.

(2) To see only pages you haven't read yet, tap Show Unread. The list is narrowed accordingly.

(3) Swipe up or down to browse the pages you see.

(4) Tap the page you want to view. It opens.

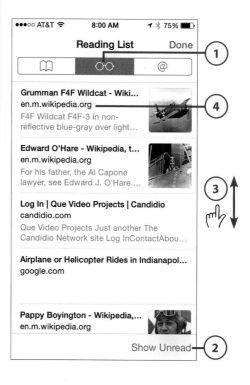

⑤ Read the page.

⑥ Tap the Bookmarks button to return to your Reading List, so you can choose a different page to read.

Whittle Down the List

To remove a page from your Reading List, swipe to the left across the page you want to remove and tap the Delete button that appears.

Tap here to configure your iPhone for music

Tap here to enjoy musical bliss

In this chapter, you explore how you can use the Music app to enjoy all sorts of music. The topics include the following:

→ Getting started
→ Stocking your iPhone with music
→ Configuring Music settings
→ Using the Cover Browser to find and listen to music
→ Finding music
→ Playing music
→ Creating and using Genius playlists
→ Using AirPlay to listen to your iPhone's music on other devices
→ Listening to iTunes Radio

Finding and Listening to Music

The very first portable "i" device, the original iPod, did only one thing—though it did that one thing better than any other device ever—which was to enable people to take their music with them and enjoy it anywhere. While the iPhone has evolved way beyond anything the first iPod could do, one of the best reasons to have an iPhone is that it continues to be an amazing device for listening to all kinds of music and audiobooks. The Music app enables you to quickly move to and play any music in your personal music library. Using its iTunes Radio feature, you can also listen to music that is not in your library (kind of like listening to music on an old-fashioned radio only much better).

Getting Started

Listening to music with the Music app on your iPhone is very convenient because you can carry an entire music collection in the palm of your hand. The Music app offers lots of great tools you can use to find, play, and control your tunes. As you use the Music app, you'll encounter the following terms:

- **iTunes Radio**—This service provides radio-like "stations" to which you can listen. These are better than traditional radio stations because you can create your own stations. iTunes Radio is free to use.

- **Playlist**—A playlist is a collection of songs to which you can listen. You can create your own playlists, which are similar to albums or CDs except that you can determine exactly which songs are in your playlists and the order in which those songs play.

- **Genius**—This is a feature that chooses music you are likely to enjoy based on music you select; it builds collections of songs that "go with" a song you choose. The genius makes music more interesting because you can quickly and easily create playlists that present your music in new and exciting ways.

- **AirPlay**—This technology allows you to play music on your iPhone on other devices, such as AirPlay speakers. If you have an Apple TV connected to your home theater system, you can use AirPlay to play your music over that system.

Stocking Your iPhone with Music

There are a couple of primary ways to make music in your music library available in the Music app on your iPhone:

- Add music to your iTunes Library on your computer and then sync that music onto your iPhone (refer to Chapter 5, "Working with iTunes on Your Computer"). This is often the easiest way to determine the music you have available on your phone.

- Download music directly from the iTunes Store onto your iPhone using the iTunes app (refer to Chapter 6, "Downloading Apps, Music, Movies, TV Shows, and More onto Your iPhone").

Yet Another Way to Listen

You can use iTunes Radio to listen to music that isn't stored on your iPhone. This is a great way to sample lots of music, some of which you might choose to add to your music collection. iTunes Radio is explained in the section "Listening to iTunes Radio," at the end of this chapter.

Configuring Music Settings

You can use an iPhone for music just fine without performing any of the steps in this section. However, because this book is named *My iPhone*, you should explore these options to make an iPhone your own for audio playback.

Available But Not Required

Most of the time, you'll be able to enjoy music without changing any of the Music app's settings. Skip ahead to "Using the Cover Browser to Find and Listen to Music" to start playing music. When you are comfortable using the Music app, come back here to see if you want to make any changes to its settings.

You can use the Music settings to configure various aspects of iPhone's music functionality.

1. Tap to open the Settings app.

2. Swipe up the screen.

3. Tap Music.

4. If you don't want the Music app to shuffle to the next song when you shake the iPhone, slide the Shake to Shuffle switch to off (white). Slide the switch to on (green) to enable shuffling by shaking again. (Shuffling causes music to play randomly instead of in sequential order.)

5. Slide the Sound Check switch to on (green), if you want the Music app to attempt to even the volume of the music you play, so that all the songs play at about the same relative volume level.

6. To set an equalizer, tap the EQ bar.

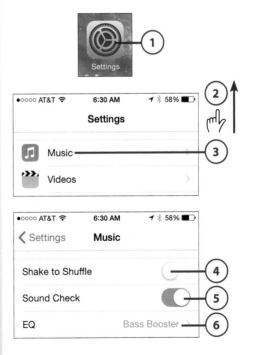

7 Swipe up and down the screen to see all the equalizers available to you.

8 Tap the equalizer you want; the current equalizer is indicated by the check mark. To turn off the equalizer, tap Off at the top of the list.

9 Tap Music.

10 To set a limit to the volume level on your iPhone, tap Volume Limit.

11 Drag the volume slider to the point that you want the maximum volume level to be.

12 Tap Music.

13 To hide lyrics and podcast information on the Now Playing screen, slide the Lyrics & Podcast Info switch to off (white). When disabled, you always see only the album art for whatever is playing.

14 If you want music to always be grouped by the artist associated with its album, set Group By Album Artist to on (green). If you want music to be grouped by the artist performing it instead, set this to off. This impacts how you see compilation albums that contain music from different artists.

15 Set the Show All Music switch to on (green) so that all the music you have purchased from the iTunes Store is shown—even if it is not currently stored on your iPhone. If this switch is off, only music currently stored on the iPhone appears in the Music app.

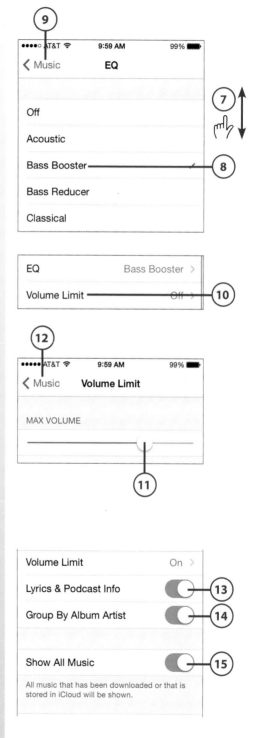

16. To use the Genius feature, which can find music for you, set the Genius switch to on (green).

17. Swipe up and down the screen to read about the Genius feature.

18. Tap Accept.

19. Swipe up the screen.

20. To enable streaming content from iTunes libraries and other sources, tap Apple ID in the HOME SHARING section.

21. Enter the Apple ID and password associated with the music you want to share; in most cases, this should be your Apple ID.

22. Tap Done. You move back to the Music screen and your iPhone is able to stream music from shared sources.

23. Tap Settings (not shown, this is located in the upper-left corner of the screen). You're ready for some tunes.

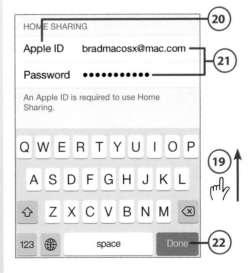

Genius — 16

Turning on Genius will share information about your music library anonymously with Apple. Learn More

No Service 📶   5:36 PM   ✈ ＊ 100% 🔋⚡

Cancel   **Genius**   Accept — 18

When you opt-in to the Genius feature, Apple will, from time to time, automatically collect information that can be used to identify media in your iTunes library on this computer, such as your play history and play lists. This includes media purchased through iTunes and media obtained from other sources. This information will be stored anonymously and not associated with your name or iTunes account. When you use the Genius feature, Apple will use this information and the contents of your iTunes library, as well as other information, to give personalized recommendations to you.

Apple may only use this information and combine it with aggregated information from the iTunes libraries of other users who also opt-in to this feature, your iTunes Store purchase history data,

— 17

HOME SHARING — 20

Apple ID   bradmacosx@mac.com — 21

Password   ●●●●●●●●●●

An Apple ID is required to use Home Sharing.

Q W E R T Y U I O P

A S D F G H J K L

⇧ Z X C V B N M ⌫

123 🌐   space   Done — 22

— 19

Using the Cover Browser to Find and Listen to Music

The Cover Browser shows you your music by its cover art; you can quickly peruse your entire music collection to get to and play the right music for your current mood.

To use the Cover Browser, perform these steps:

(1) On the Home screen, tap Music.

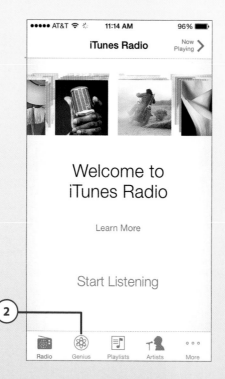

(2) If the Music app opens to any screen other than iTunes Radio, you can skip to step 3. If you see the iTunes Radio screen, tap one of the other buttons on the toolbar at the bottom of the screen. It doesn't matter which one. You learn what these buttons do and how to use iTunes Radio later in this chapter.

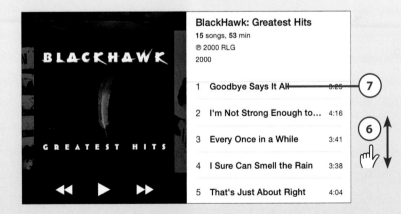

3 Rotate your iPhone so it is horizontal. The Cover Browser appears. Each cover represents an album from which you have at least one song stored on your iPhone.

4 To browse your music, swipe a finger to the right to move ahead in the albums or to the left to move back; the faster you swipe, the faster you scroll through the albums.

5 To see the songs on an album, tap its cover. The album "opens." On the left side of the screen are the album art and the playback controls. On the right side of the screen is a list of all the songs from that album that are available to you.

6 To browse the list of songs, swipe your finger up or down the list of songs.

7 To play a song, tap it. The song plays and is marked with a red "graphic equalizer" icon on the list of songs.

Turn It Up! (Or Down!)

No matter which technique you use to find and play music, you can control the volume using the Volume buttons on the left side of iPhone. Press the upper button to increase volume or the lower one to decrease it. While you are pressing a button, a volume indicator appears on the screen to show you the relative volume level as you press the buttons. When you are on the Now Playing screen or viewing the Music control bar (both of these are covered later in this chapter), you can also use the Volume slider to set the sound level. And, if you listen with the EarPods included with your iPhone, you can use the buttons on the right EarPod's wire to crank it up (press and hold the top button) or down (press and hold the bottom button).

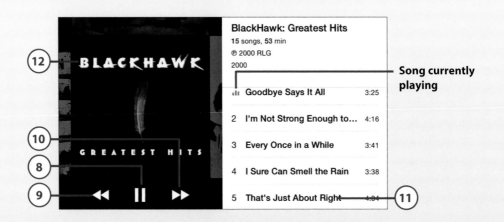

8. To pause a song, tap the Pause button. The music pauses, and the Play button replaces the Pause button; tap Play to start the music again.

9. To jump to the previous song on the list, tap the Previous button.

10. To jump to the next song on the list, tap the Next button.

11. To play a different song on the list, tap it.

12. To return to the browser, tap the album cover. The music continues to play.

Shuffle Off (But Not to Buffalo)

If the Shuffle setting is active (you learn how to set this later), when you tap the Previous or Next button, the song that plays is random rather than being the previous or next one on the list. Unfortunately, there's no way to tell whether Shuffle is active from the Cover Browser. You have to move to the Now Playing screen for that (you'll get to that shortly).

13 While you're listening, you can continue browsing to find more music you want to listen to. When you select more music to play, it replaces the music currently playing.

14 Rotate the iPhone to be vertical to see the Now Playing screen.

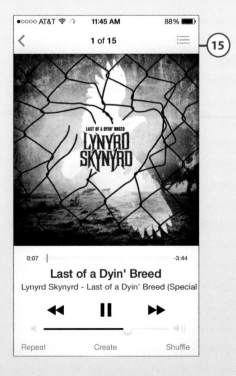

15 Use the Now Playing screen to control the music (covered in detail in the "Playing Music on the Now Playing Screen" task later in this section).

What to Listen On?

You can play music through the iPhone's speakers. Although you can hear the music, its quality isn't so good on these speakers. A good option is the EarPods headphones that came with your iPhone or, if you don't find those comfortable, you can use an over-the-ear set of headphones instead. You can also connect your iPhone to external speakers using a cable that plugs into the Headphone port or wirelessly via AirPlay or Bluetooth.

Finding Music

Before you can listen to music, you need to find the music you want to listen to by using one of the many browsing and searching features the Music app offers. These include the Cover Browser you learned about in the previous section, working with playlists, browsing your music by artist, and searching.

Finding Music by Playlist

Playlists are collections of music you create in iTunes on a computer or directly on the iPhone. A playlist can include music grouped for any reason, such as being from the same artist or your favorite songs by different artists. Finding and listening to music in your iTunes playlists that you have moved onto your iPhone is simple.

(1) On the Home screen, tap Music.

I See Music

If music is already playing when you open the Music app, you automatically move to the Now Playing screen. Tap the Back button, which is located in the upper-left corner of the screen, and you see the Playlists button at the bottom of the screen.

2. Tap the Playlists button. The playlists available on your iPhone appear. If you use folders to organize your playlists, you see those folders on the Playlists screen. For example, if you have a folder called "Best Rock" in iTunes, a playlist called "Best Rock" appears on the Playlists screen and contains all the playlists in the Best Rock folder. Playlists marked with the "nuclear" symbol were created by the iTunes Genius (you learn all about this feature later in this chapter).

3. Swipe your finger up and down the list to browse your playlists.

4. Tap a playlist or folder you'd like to explore. The list of songs in that playlist or the list of playlists within the folder appears with the title of the playlist or folder at the top of the screen.

5. If you moved into a folder containing playlists, swipe up and down the screen to browse the playlists in that folder; if you moved into a playlist, skip to step 7.

6. Tap the playlist you want to see.

7 Swipe your finger up and down to browse the songs the playlist contains. (You can also search a playlist by swiping down from the top of the screen until you see the Search bar; learn how in the section "Finding Music by Searching" later in this chapter.)

8 When you find a song you want to listen to, tap it. The song begins to play, and the Now Playing screen appears.

9 Use the Now Playing screen to control the music (covered in detail in the "Playing Music on the Now Playing Screen" section later in this chapter).

10 Tap the Back button to move back to the playlist's screen. (When you view a playlist's screen, the song currently playing is marked with the red graphic equalizer icon.)

Finding Music by Artist

You can find music by browsing artists whose music is stored on your iPhone. You can then see all the music by a specific artist and select the music you want to play.

(1) On the Home screen, tap Music.

(2) Tap Artists. (If you don't see the Artists button, tap the Back button located in the upper-left corner of the screen until you do.) The list of all artists whose music is available to the Music app appears. Artists are grouped by the first letter of their first name or by the first letter of the group's name (not counting *the* as the first word in a name).

(3) Swipe your finger up and down the list to browse all available artists.

(4) To jump to a specific artist, tap the letter along the right side of the screen for the artist's or group's first name; to jump to an artist or a group whose name starts with a number, tap # at the bottom of the screen. For each artist, you see album art associated with the artist's music along with the number of albums and songs available to you.

(5) Tap an artist whose music you'd like to explore. A list of songs by that artist appears. If you have more than one album by that artist, the songs are organized by album.

Browse with Speed

If you swipe on top of the index, you can browse screens at a very fast speed. This is especially useful when you are browsing very long lists.

(6) Swipe your finger up and down the screen to browse the artist's albums. As you swipe up or down, you see the next album on the list. Each album's cover continues to appear on the screen as long as at least one of its songs remains on the screen; when you scroll past the last song on the album, the next album's art "bumps" the first album's art off the screen.

(7) When you find the song you want to listen to, tap it. The song begins to play, and the Now Playing screen appears.

	••○○○ AT&T 🛜	6:16 PM	@ ⬈ 67% 🔋
‹ Artists	**Frank Sinatra**	Now Playing ›	

Nothing But the Best - The Frank Sinatra Colle...
22 songs, 75 min
℗ 2008 Frank Sinatra Enterpri...
2008

19	All My Tomorrows	4:36
20	My Way	4:37
21	Theme from New York, New York	3:25
22	Body and Soul	4:20

Frank Sinatra: Classic Sinatra - His Great Perf...
1 song, 3 min
℗ 2000 Capitol
2000

16	Come Fly With Me	3:19

Holiday Classics

Radio   Genius   Playlists   Artists   More

6 ↕ 🖑

●○○○○ AT&T 🛜	6:17 PM	@ ⬈ 67% 🔋
‹ Artists	**Frank Sinatra**	Now Playing ›

The Best Of Frank Sinatra
12 songs, 44 min

5	What Now My Love	3:59
6	That's Life	4:02
7	My Way	3:57
8	Somethin' Stupid	4:23
9	September In The Rain	3:18
10	I Only Have Eyes For You	3:18
11	High Hopes	3:10
12	It Was A Very Good Year	4:14

(7)

8. Use the Now Playing screen to control the music (covered in detail in the "Playing Music on the Now Playing Screen" task later in this section).

9. Tap the Back button to move back to the artist's screen to find and play more music by the current artist.

To Now Playing and Back

Whenever music is playing or paused, the Now Playing screen is active even when it isn't visible. You can move to the Now Playing screen by tapping Now Playing located in the upper-right corner of the screen. You can return from the Now Playing screen back to where you were by tapping the Back button, which is always located in the upper-left corner of the Now Playing screen.

10. Tap Artists to move back to the Artists screen to browse music by other artists.

Shuffling an Artist's Music

If you tap the Shuffle button next to any album on an artist's screen, music by that artist is randomly selected and begins to play. When the first song finishes, another is selected at random from that artist's music and it plays. This continues until you stop playing music or until all the artist's songs are played.

Shuffle

Finding Music in Other Ways

On the Music toolbar at the bottom of the screen are five buttons. The first four are ways you can select music in which you are interested. (You've already learned how to use two of these: Playlists and Artists.) The More button takes you to the More screen that shows you all the content categories available in the Music app. (You see only categories that apply to you—for example, if you don't have any audiobooks in your collection, you won't see the Audiobooks category.) You can use this screen to access content when it can't be found by one of the category buttons on the toolbar at the bottom of the screen.

Tap to see music organized by a category

Tap to see a list of other categories

Open the Music app and tap More. The More screen appears. You see the categories that aren't currently on the toolbar (in a later note, you learn how to configure the toolbar's contents), including:

- **Songs**—This option shows you a list of all the songs available to you. The list is organized alphabetically; you can browse it or tap a letter on the index to jump to songs starting with that letter. Tap a song to play it.

- **Albums**—This view is similar to Songs and Artists except music is organized by album. You can browse albums. Tap an album to which you want to listen. You see a list of songs on that album and can tap a song to play it.

- **Audiobooks**—This takes you to a list of the audiobooks available to you. Browse the books and then tap a book to which you want to listen. Listening to audiobooks is similar to listening to music.

- **Genres**—This list shows you music by the genre with which it is associated, such as Rock, Country, etc.

- **Compilations**—This is similar to albums except a compilation can contain songs from multiple artists, such as greatest hits of the '70s, or a collection of songs grouped in other ways.

- **Composers**—Songs can have composers associated with them (composers are responsible for writing the music while the artist is responsible for playing it). Sometimes these are the same people, but sometimes they aren't, especially for classical music. This shows you music organized by composer rather than artist.

- **Shared**—The Shared source shows you music being shared via the Home Sharing feature. When you tap this, you see a list of all the iTunes Libraries being shared. Tap a library to see the music available to you. Browse, select, and play shared music as you do with music in your iPhone's music library. (If a shared library requires a password, you have to enter that to be able to access its music.)

Finding Music by Searching

Browsing is a useful way to find music, but it can be faster to search for specific music in which you are interested. You can search most of the screens you browse. When a category, such as Songs, contains many items, searching can get you where you want to go more quickly than browsing. Here's how:

1. Move to a screen you can browse; this example uses the Songs screen, but you can search most screens similarly.

2. Swipe down to move to the top of the screen where you see the Search tool, or tap the magnifying glass icon at the top of the screen's index to expose the Search tool.

3. Tap in the Search tool.

4. Type the text or numbers for which you want to search. As you type, the items that meet your search criterion are shown; the more you type, the more specific your search becomes. Below the Search tool, the results are organized into categories, such as Albums and Songs.

5. When you think you've typed enough to find what you're looking for, tap Search. The keyboard disappears.

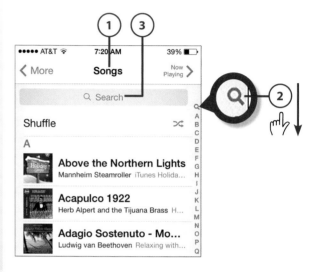

Browse the results.

 Tap a song or album to get to the music you want to play.

Clearing a Search

You can clear a search by tapping the "x" that appears on the right end of the Search tool. Tapping Cancel also clears the search, and also closes the Search screen.

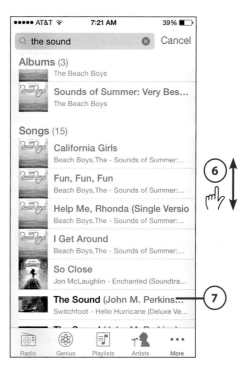

Playing Music

After you find and select what you want to hear, use the iPhone's music playback controls to listen to your heart's content. You can control music playback from a number of places.

Playing Music on the Now Playing Screen

As you have seen in this chapter already, the Now Playing screen appears when you play music and the iPhone is in vertical orientation. (If it is in horizontal orientation, you see the Cover Browser instead.) In the upper part of the screen the cover art for the current song (for the album from which the song comes) is shown. In the lower part of the screen are controls for the music and information about it. The Now Playing screen has many features, including:

- **Timeline**—Just below the art, you see the timeline. The elapsed time is on the left side, and the remaining time is on the right. The red line is the Playhead that shows you where you are in the song. You can drag this to the left to move back in the song or to the right to move ahead.

- **Song information**—Below the Timeline is the song's name (in larger, bold font). Under that is the artist and album title. If any of this information is too large to fit on the screen, it scrolls across the screen to display it all.

- **Previous/Rewind**—If the current song has been playing for more than a second or two, tap this button once to move to the beginning of the current song. If you are at the beginning of the current song, tap it to move to the previous song in the current source (such as album or artist). Tap and hold to rewind in the current song.

- **Pause/Play**—Tap Pause to pause the song. Tap Play to play it again.

- **Next/Fast-Forward**—Tap once to move to the next song on the list (or the next randomly selected song if you are shuffling). Tap and hold to fast-forward in the current song.

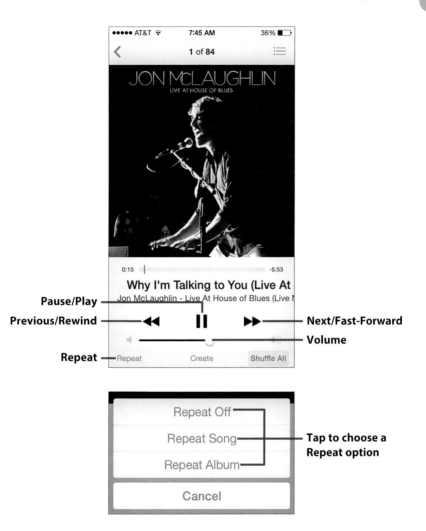

- **Volume**—Drag the slider to the left to lower the volume or to the right to increase it.

- **Repeat**—Tap Repeat to make the Repeat menu appear. Tap Repeat Song to repeat the current song. Tap Repeat [*context*] to repeat everything currently selected, where [*context*] is how you got to the music to which you are listening. For example, if you came to the Now Playing screen from the Artists screen, Repeat Artist causes all the artist's songs to be repeated. If you came from an album, Repeat Songs causes the songs on the album to be repeated. Tap Repeat Off to stop repeating. The Repeat button changes to reflect the current state. For example, when Repeat Artist is selected, the button becomes Repeat Artist.

- **Create**—This creates a new genius playlist. The Genius feature is covered in detail later in this chapter.

- **Shuffle**—Tap Shuffle, which becomes Shuffle All, indicating that all the music in the current selection will be played randomly. When the current song finishes, another one from the group is selected randomly and played. Tap Shuffle All to turn off Shuffle so that songs play in the order in which they appear (top to bottom) on the screen from where you came to get to the Now Playing screen (such as an album's screen). (See the "Shuffling Music" section for more information.)

- **Track List**—Tap the Track List button. The contents of the current source are shown. Depending on the source of music you are playing, you might see two tabs. For example, if you are playing a playlist, the Playlist tab shows the contents of the playlist while the Album tab shows the contents of the album that contains the song currently playing. Tap the tab for the contents you want to see. Swipe up or down the list to browse the songs. Tap a song to play it.

  To rate a song, tap Rating, tap the song you want to rate, and then tap the number of stars you want to give the song (between one and five). (Of course, the song plays when you tap it if it is not currently playing.) The ratings you apply to songs can be used to give you information about how much you like the song, and they can be used in smart playlists, such as to play songs in the Rock genre you have rated at four starts or higher.

To return to the prior screen, tap Done. You see the album art and playback controls again.

Back to the Album

If you tap the Album tab and then tap a song on that album that isn't in the current playlist, you change the source of music from the playlist to the album. The Playlist tab closes and from that point on, you work with the album as the source.

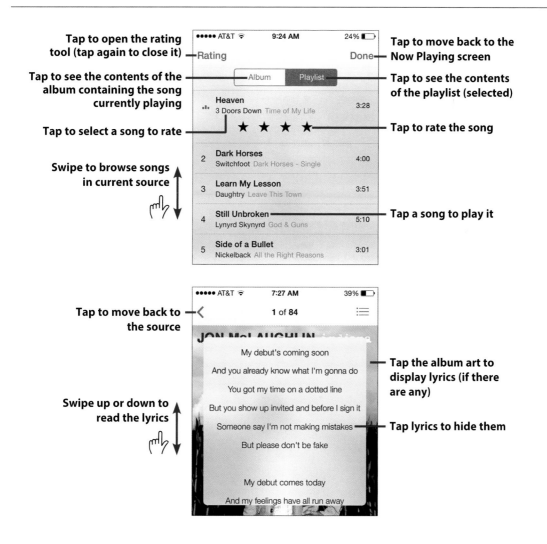

Tap to open the rating tool (tap again to close it) — Rating

Tap to see the contents of the album containing the song currently playing — Album

Tap to select a song to rate

Swipe to browse songs in current source

Tap to move back to the Now Playing screen — Done

Tap to see the contents of the playlist (selected) — Playlist

Tap to rate the song — ★ ★ ★ ★

Tap a song to play it — Still Unbroken

Heaven
3 Doors Down Time of My Life   3:28

2 Dark Horses
Switchfoot Dark Horses - Single   4:00

3 Learn My Lesson
Daughtry Leave This Town   3:51

4 Still Unbroken
Lynyrd Skynyrd God & Guns   5:10

5 Side of a Bullet
Nickelback All the Right Reasons   3:01

Tap to move back to the source — 1 of 84

Swipe up or down to read the lyrics

Tap the album art to display lyrics (if there are any)

Tap lyrics to hide them — Someone say I'm not making mistakes

My debut's coming soon
And you already know what I'm gonna do
You got my time on a dotted line
But you show up invited and before I sign it
Someone say I'm not making mistakes
But please don't be fake

My debut comes today
And my feelings have all run away

- **Lyrics**—In iTunes, you can associate lyrics with songs. Assuming you haven't disabled the Lyrics & Podcast Info setting (see "Configuring Music Settings"), tap the art to display the song's lyrics. Swipe up and down on the lyrics to read them all. Tap the lyrics to hide them again.

  If a song doesn't have lyrics, when you tap it, the Rating tool replaces the song information (see the following note).

- **Back**—Tap the Back button to move to the current source's screen.

Another Way to Rate

If you tap the song information just below the Timeline on the Now Playing screen, the song information is replaced by the rating tool. Tap the number of stars with which you want to rate the song. Tap outside the rating tool to display the song information again.

>>>Go Further

COMPLETING ALBUMS

If you don't have all the songs on an album that is available in the iTunes Store, when you browse its contents, you see the Show Complete Album link. Tap this to see all the songs on the album. Tap a song's price button to buy and download it. Tap the Complete my album button, which shows the price to add all the songs on the album, to buy and download all the songs on the album that aren't currently in your library.

Playing Music from the Control Center

As you've seen, the Now Playing screen provides lots of control for your music. However, it can take several taps to get back to that screen if you are using your iPhone for something else while you listen to music. To get to most of the music controls quickly, swipe up from the bottom of the screen to open the Control Center. Just above the AirDrop and AirPlay buttons is the Music section. Here you see some of the controls you can use for music playback; the controls here work the same as on the Now Playing screen.

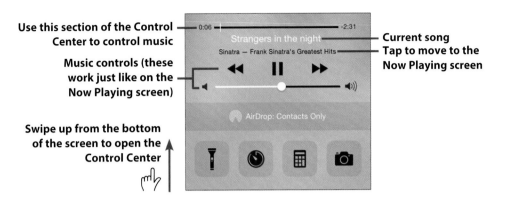

Use this section of the Control Center to control music

Music controls (these work just like on the Now Playing screen)

Swipe up from the bottom of the screen to open the Control Center

Current song
Tap to move to the Now Playing screen

Use the controls you see; then close the Control Center by swiping down from its top and continue what you were doing. Or, tap the artist—title information to jump to the Now Playing screen (the Control Center closes when you do this).

More than Just Music

What I've called the Music section of Control Center is more accurately called the Audio Controls section because it changes based on the app you are using to play audio. For example, when you are using the Podcasts app to play a podcast, these tools control the podcast playback. Likewise, if you play audio with a different app, these controls work for that app. In other words, this section reflects the app currently playing audio.

Playing Music from the Lock Screen

When audio is playing and your iPhone is locked, it would be a hassle to move back to the Music app to control that audio; you'd have to tap the Touch ID/ Home button or Sleep/Wake button to wake the iPhone up, unlock the phone, and then move to the Music app (which can require several steps depending on what you were last doing). Fortunately, you can control music playback right from the Lock screen.

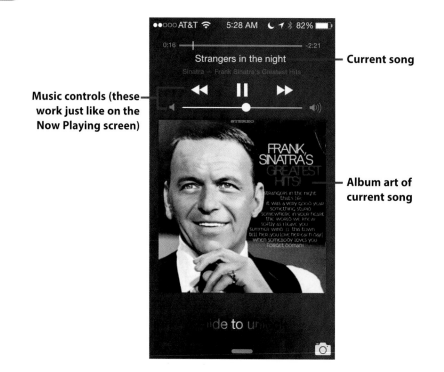

Music controls (these work just like on the Now Playing screen)

Current song

Album art of current song

Press the Sleep/Wake or Touch ID/Home button. Your iPhone wakes up and you see the Lock screen, which displays information about and controls for the music currently playing. Use the controls you see; these work like they do on the Now Playing screen (of course, there are more controls on that screen).

When you're done controlling the tunes, tap the Sleep/Wake button again to prevent the controls from being on the screen (so that they don't accidentally get activated if you put your iPhone back in your pocket, for example).

The Music Plays On

However you play music, it continues to play even when you move into a different app. For example, you can start a song playing and then use the App Switcher to move into Messages so you can send a text. Music continues to play in the background.

Shuffling Music

Shuffling music is a good way to keep your music fresh because you don't know which song will be played next. As you learned earlier, you can shuffle music from the Now Playing screen by tapping the Shuffle button. There are a couple of other ways to shuffle, too:

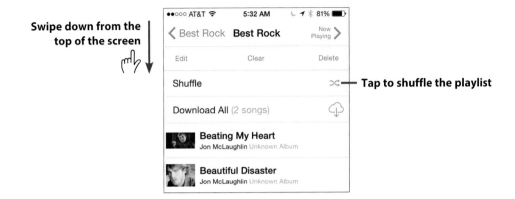

• When browsing a source of music, such as a playlist, an artist, or an album, tap the Shuffle button (you may need to swipe down from the top of the screen to reveal the Shuffle section). A song is randomly selected from the source and begins to play. You move to the Now Playing screen where you see the Shuffle All button is active. The first song plays; when it finishes, the next song is selected at random from the current source and plays.

• Start music playing and gently shake your iPhone in a back-and-forth motion. A song is selected at random and begins to play. You can shake your iPhone at any time to move to the next randomly selected song. (This requires the Shake to Shuffle setting to be enabled, as explained in "Configuring Music Settings.") (If you are carrying your iPhone around in a pocket or bag, it's a good idea to leave this setting disabled; otherwise, you might find your music shuffling in the middle of songs.)

Controlling Music from the EarPods

You have basic controls over music by using the switch on the EarPods that came with your iPhone. Press the upper part of the switch to increase volume or the lower part to decrease it. Press the center part to play or pause music.

Creating and Using Genius Playlists

The Genius feature finds music and builds playlists based on songs that "go with" a specific song. How the Genius selects songs that "sound good" with other songs is a bit of a secret, but it works amazingly well. You can have the Genius build a playlist for you in a couple of ways and then listen to or update it.

To create a Genius playlist based on the song currently playing, do the following:

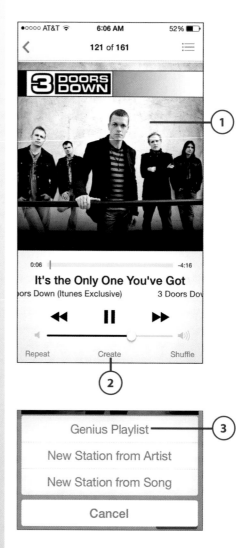

1 Find and play a song using any of the techniques you learned earlier in this chapter; you see the Now Playing screen.

2 Tap Create.

Create Station?

The New Station commands create iTunes Radio stations based on the current artist or song. You learn about iTunes Radio later in this chapter.

3 Tap Genius Playlist. The Genius playlist is created, and you move to the Genius screen where you see the songs the Genius selected. The song that is currently playing is at the top of the list and is marked with the Genius and red graphic equalizer icons.

4 Swipe up and down the list to browse the songs the Genius included.

5 To save the playlist, tap Save. The name of the playlist changes from Genius Playlist to be the name of the song on which the playlist was based. At the top of the screen, you see the Refresh and Delete buttons.

Song the Genius playlist is based on

>>>Go Further

BECOMING A GENIUS WITH THE GENIUS

The Genius can be really useful. Check out these other genius tips:

- If you have only a few songs on your iPhone, the Genius won't work.

- Here's another way to have the Genius create a playlist for you; with this method, you don't have to play the song you want to use first. Move to the Playlists screen. Swipe down the screen so you see the top of it. Tap Genius Playlist. You see the Songs screen on which all the songs available to you are displayed. Browse the list, use the index, or search to find the song on which you want the Genius to base the new playlist. Tap that song. The Genius creates the playlist, and you move back to the Playlists screen. Tap the new playlist, which is called Genius Playlist. You see the songs it contains. If you want to save the playlist, tap Save.

- Genius playlists appear on the Playlists screen like other playlists you have created, except they are marked with the Genius icon. You can play Genius playlists just like others on the Playlists screen.

- Genius playlists are also moved into your iTunes Library on your computer the next time you sync your iPhone.

- The Genius can change the songs in a Genius playlist for you so it becomes a new, fresh playlist. To do this, view the Genius playlist and tap Refresh. The Genius selects a new set of songs based on the playlist's title song.

- To delete a Genius playlist you have saved, open its screen and tap Delete. Tap Delete Playlist at the prompt. The playlist is deleted. (If you have synced your iPhone since you saved the playlist, you won't see the Delete button because the playlist has been saved to your iTunes Library. To delete a playlist after you've synced your iPhone, delete it from your iTunes Library or remove it from the sync settings and then re-sync the iPhone.)

- You can also delete a Genius playlist by opening the Playlists screen and swiping to the left on the playlist you want to delete. Tap Delete. The playlist is deleted.

Siri and Music

You can use Siri to select, play, and control music, too. For example, you can activate Siri and say "Play album Frank Sinatra's Greatest Hits" to play that album or "Play song Free Bird" to play that song. Refer to Chapter 12, "Working with Siri," for details.

Using AirPlay to Listen to Your iPhone's Music on Other Devices

With AirPlay, you can stream your music and other audio to other devices so you can hear it using a sound system instead of the iPhone's speakers or EarPods. For example, if you have an Apple TV connected to a home theater system, you can stream your audio to the Apple TV so it will play via the home theater's audio system. You can also stream to an AirPort Express base station to which you've connected speakers; or, you can stream to AirPlay-compatible speakers that are designed to receive AirPlay signals directly.

Bluetooth Speakers

You can also use Bluetooth to stream music from your iPhone to Bluetooth speakers. Just pair and connect the iPhone to the speakers; the music plays through the speakers. This is a great way to make your music sound better when you are out and about because there are lots of great Bluetooth speakers that you can carry with you. See Chapter 2, "Connecting Your iPhone to the Internet, Bluetooth Devices, and iPhones/iPods/iPads," for the details about using Bluetooth devices.

To use AirPlay, your iPhone needs to be on the same Wi-Fi network as the devices to which you are going to stream the music.

After you have set up the devices you are going to use, such as an AirPort Express base station and speakers, you can stream to them using the following steps:

1. Play the music or audio you want to stream.

2. Swipe up from the bottom of the screen to open the Control Center.

3. Tap AirPlay. (Note that this only appears if there is at least one AirPlay-compatible device with which your iPhone can currently communicate.)

(4) Tap the device to which you want to stream the music. It is marked with a check mark to show it is the active device.

(5) Tap Done.

(6) Use the playback controls you learned about earlier to control the music. If you are using an AppleTV, use the controls on the audio system to which it is connected to control the volume.

(7) To return the sound control to your iPhone, perform steps 2 and 3, tap iPhone, and then tap Done.

	AirPlay	Done (5)
◀))	iPhone	
💻	Apple TV	(4)
	Mirroring	⚪
◎	Brad's AirPort Express	
◎	Extender Express Base Station	

With AirPlay Mirroring you can send everything on your iPhone's display to an Apple TV, wirelessly.

It's Not All Good

Unfortunately, you can only select and stream to one AirPlay device at a time.

Downloading Songs

If there are songs that you've previously downloaded from the iTunes Store but aren't currently stored on your iPhone, you see the Download button, which is a cloud with a downward-pointing arrow. Tap this button to download the song to your iPhone. You also see the Download All command at the top of lists (such as the Artists screen) when there are multiple items that aren't downloaded. Tap Download All to download all the items on the list to your iPhone.

Listening to iTunes Radio

iTunes Radio streams music from the Internet onto your iPhone, much like listening to radio on a car or home stereo. However, with iTunes Radio you can create your own stations. The stations you create can be based on types of music you like or based on music that is similar to music you know you like. (If you've used Pandora, iHeart Radio, or similar services, you'll understand how to use iTunes Radio right away because it is similar to those services.)

In iTunes Radio, there are two basic types of stations. Featured Stations are those that are "default" and to which you can immediately listen. My Stations are stations you create.

When you listen to iTunes Radio and discover music you'd like to have in your collection, it's simple to buy and download that music from the iTunes Store so you have it permanently.

You can also indicate music you like; over time, iTunes Radio tailors the music it selects and plays for you based on music you like. (This is kind of like the Genius you learned about earlier.)

Listening to a Featured Station

To listen to a featured station, do the following:

1. On the Home screen, tap Music.

2. Tap Radio.

3. Swipe to the left and right on the Featured Stations to browse the stations available to you. (You might find the selection of music on the Featured Stations to be limited; most of the time, you'll probably listen to stations you create anyway.)

4. Tap the station you want to hear. The first song starts to play and you move to iTunes Radio's Now Playing screen, which is similar to the Now Playing screen you see when you are listening to your own music collection.

The First Time

The first time you select Radio, you see the Welcome screen. Tap Start Listening to, well, start listening.

⑤ Use the controls you see to play the music; see "Playing iTunes Radio Music" for details.

Creating Your Own iTunes Radio Stations Based on an Artist, a Genre, or a Song

To create your own stations, do the following:

① On the Home screen, tap Music.

② Tap Radio.

③ Tap New.

New to iTunes Radio?

If you haven't created any iTunes Radio stations yet, the My Stations section will be empty except for the New Station icon. Tap the "+" to create your first station and move to step 4.

4 Enter an artist, a genre, or a song in the bar at the top of the screen. As you type, the app presents a list of possible matches.

5 If you want to use one of the matches, tap it. The station is created and it starts to play; skip to step 9.

6 Tap Search to see the full list of results.

7 Swipe up and down the screen to browse the results. The results are grouped by type, such as Top Hit, Songs, and Artists. The type you select determines what the new station is based on. For example, if you tap an artist, the new station has music made by "similar" artists. If you tap a song, the new station is based on similar songs.

8 Tap the song, artist, or other result on which you want your new station based. The new station is created and you move back to the iTunes Radio screen briefly where you see your new station. The station starts playing and you move to iTunes Radio's Now Playing screen.

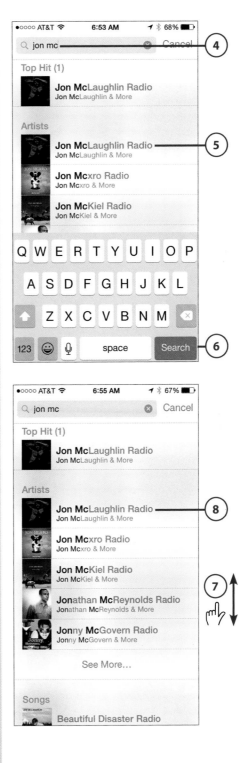

9 Use the controls you see to play the music; see "Playing iTunes Radio Music" for details.

10 Tap the Back button. You move to the iTunes Radio screen and see the stations you have created.

11 Tap New and repeat steps 4–8 to create more stations.

Creating Stations from the Defaults

When you tap New Station, the Search bar that you use in step 4 appears at the top of the screen. If you wait for a few moments before entering a search term, you see a list of genres that you can use to create a station, too. Swipe up and down to browse the list. Tap a genre of interest. You see a list of stations that belong to that genre. Tap a station to sample the music it contains. Tap the Add button (+) to add the station to your stations.

You briefly see your new station before it starts to play

Creating an iTunes Radio Station Based on Music in Your iTunes Library

NEW! You can also create an iTunes Radio station based on music in your library. Here's how:

1. Play a song on which you want to base a new station, or play music from an artist from which you want to create a new station.

2. Tap Create.

3. Tap New Station from Artist to create a station based on the artist whose music is currently playing, or New Station from Song to base the new station on the song currently playing. The station is created, you see it briefly on the iTunes Radio screen, and it begins to play.

4. Use the controls you see to play the music; see the task, "Playing iTunes Radio Music," for details.

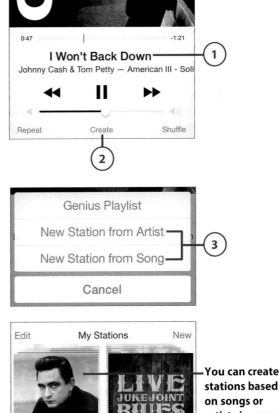

You can create stations based on songs or artists in your iTunes Library

Listening to Your iTunes Radio Stations

To listen to one of your stations, do the following:

1. Tap Radio.

2. Swipe up and down to browse your stations. (The current station's name is in red.)

3. Tap the station to which you want to listen.

4. Use the controls you see to play the music; see "Playing iTunes Radio Music" for details.

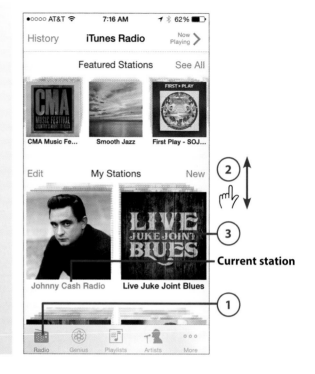

Current station

Playing iTunes Radio Music

Many of the controls you see on iTunes Radio's Now Playing screen are the same as on the Now Playing screen you learned about earlier. These include the Back button, the Timeline (although you can't drag the Playhead on this Timeline), Pause/Play, Next, and the Volume slider. Following are the controls unique to iTunes Radio you see and how you can use them:

- **Rate song**—Tap the star on the Now Playing screen. Tap Play More Like This to indicate you like the song so iTunes Radio should choose more songs like it; over time, the selection of songs you hear should get better as you "like" more songs. Tap Never Play This Song if you don't like the song and never want to hear it again. Tap Add to iTunes Wish List to add the song to your Wish List; you can go into the iTunes Store and buy the song from your Wish List at a later time.

  After you make a selection, the menu closes. If you tapped Play More Like This, the star becomes red to show you have "liked" the song. If you tapped Never Play This Song, the next song plays immediately. If you tapped Add to iTunes Wish List, the star is unchanged.

If you tap the star again, you can undo your "like" (by tapping Play More Like This again) or remove the song from your Wish List. However, once you've "disliked" a song, it is gone forever (from your iTunes Radio playlist at any rate).

Info button — Tap to buy the song

- **Buy song**—To buy and download a song, tap the button showing the song's price. Then tap BUY SONG. If you're prompted to sign into your Apple ID, touch the Touch ID/Home button if you are using an iPhone 5s or later or enter your Apple ID password and tap OK if you are using a different model. The song is added to your Music Library.

Tap to create a new station based on the current artist or song

Drag to change how songs are selected for the station

Tap to share the station

Tap to return to the Now Playing screen

Tap to buy the song

Tap to see the full album in the iTunes Store

Set to on (green) if you don't want explicit content to be blocked

- **Info**—Tap the Info button to see a menu with a number of options. You can buy the song by tapping its price. You can see the full album containing the song in the iTunes Store by tapping the List button. You create another station based on the artist or song, and you can even prevent or allow explicit content. Use the slider to choose how the songs in the station are selected: Hits causes songs to be played by their popularity, Variety causes a broader range of songs to play, and Discovery stretches the songs the station includes to help you discover more music. You can also share the station with others. Tap Done to return to the iTunes Radio Now Playing screen.

>>>*Go Further*

TURNING iTUNES RADIO UP

Here are a few more things you can do with iTunes Radio:

- To change one of your stations, tap Edit on the iTunes Radio screen (or if you are on the Now Playing screen, tap the Back button to move there). You see the My Station screen. Tap the station you want to edit. On the resulting screen, you can change the station's name and add more artists, songs, or genres that should be included in the station. You can also select songs, artists, or genres you don't want to play with the station. You can also share or delete the station.

- Be aware that not all stations and songs support all the iTunes Radio features. For example, you may run across songs you can't rate or stations you can't rename or edit in any way.

- At the top of the iTunes Radio screen, tap History. On the Played tab, you see a list of songs you have played, grouped by the station that played them. You can browse the list and tap a song to play it again. Tap the price button to buy a song, or tap Wish List to see songs on your iTunes Wish List. You can buy a song on your Wish List by tapping its price button. To clear either list, tap the Clear button and then confirm that you want to clear it. Tap Done to close the History screen.

View, edit, and share photos, slideshows, and video

Take photos and video

Configure photo and camera settings

15

Working with Photos and Video You Take with Your iPhone

The iPhone's Camera app takes very good quality photos and video. Because you'll likely have your iPhone with you at all times, it's handy to capture photos with it whenever and wherever you are. And, you can capture video just as easily.

Whether you've taken photos and video on your iPhone or added them from another source, the Photos app enables you to edit, view, organize, and share your photos. You'll likely find that taking and working with photos and videos are among the most useful things your iPhone can do.

Each generation of iPhone has had different photo and video capabilities and features. The current versions sport high-quality cameras, and in fact, there is a camera on each side of the iPhone. One takes photos of what you are looking at while one takes photos of what the screen is facing (for example, when you are taking selfies or using FaceTime). Current generations also have a flash; the ability to zoom; take burst, panoramic, and time-lapse photos; and other features you expect from a quality digital camera.

The iPhone's photo and video capabilities and features are probably the largest area of differences among the various models. This chapter focuses on the iPhone 6 and iPhone 6 Plus, because they are the most advanced models. If you have a different model, some of the tasks described might not be applicable to you or some of the details in this chapter might be different than what you see on your iPhone.

Additionally, the iPhone's photo and video capabilities have been increasingly tied into iCloud. For example, you can store your entire photo library under your iCloud account; this offers many benefits including backing up all your photos, making it easy to access your photos from any device, and being able to quickly share your photos with others. Therefore, I've assumed you are using iCloud and have configured it to work with photos as described in Chapter 3, "Setting Up and Using iCloud and Other Online Accounts." Like differences in iPhone camera capabilities, if you don't use iCloud with your photos, some of the information in this chapter doesn't apply to you and what you see on your phone might look different than what you see in this chapter.

Getting Started

An iPhone has lots of capabilities when it comes to taking and working with photos and videos. In fact, there are so many capabilities, they can seem overwhelming. The good news is that you can do basic things such as taking photos or videos very simply and learn to use the more advanced features, such as editing and sharing your photos, over time.

Setting Your Photos & Camera Preferences

There are a number of settings related to the Photos and Camera app that you can set with the following steps (this chapter assumes you configure your settings as shown in these steps):

1. On the Home screen, tap Settings.

2. Swipe up until you see Photos & Camera.

3. Tap Photos & Camera.

4. Set the set the iCloud Photo Library switch to on (green) to have all of the photos and videos you take with your iPhone uploaded to and stored on the Internet under your iCloud account. This is useful for several reasons. One is that your photos are automatically backed up in the event something happens to your iPhone. Another is that you can access your entire library from other devices, such as an iPad or a Mac. When you set the switch to on, photos and videos on your iPhone are immediately uploaded to the cloud and accessible from any device you are logged into your iCloud account with your Apple ID.

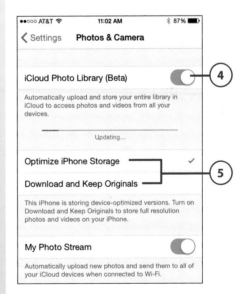

5. Tap Optimize iPhone Storage if you want to keep only versions of your photos that are optimized for the iPhone stored on your phone; this saves space so that you can keep more photos and videos (and other content, such as music) on your iPhone while providing images whose quality is perfect for displaying on the iPhone's screen. With this

option selected, full resolution photos are uploaded to the cloud so you can still use them with devices that are capable of displaying them in all their glory.

Tap Download and Keep Originals if you prefer to store full resolution versions of your photos and videos on your iPhone. They consume more space than optimized versions and you aren't likely to be able to tell the difference when viewing them on your iPhone.

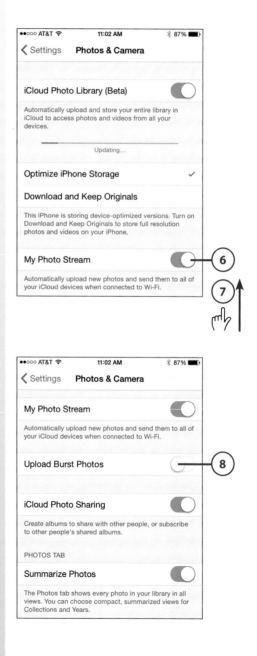

6) To have your photos automatically uploaded and sent to all your devices configured to use your iCloud account, set My Photo Stream to on (green). With this switch off, photos aren't available to other iCloud devices automatically.

7) Swipe up the screen.

8) To upload all of the photos in a burst (which is a series of photos that the iPhone takes in rapid succession), set the Upload Burst Photos switch to on (green). To save storage space, it's usually better to leave this switch off (white). You typically only want to save a small number of the photos in a burst and you will learn how to work with burst photos later in this chapter.

9 To share your photos with others and to subscribe to other people's shared albums, slide the iCloud Photo Sharing switch to on (green).

10 Set the Summarize Photos switch to on (green) to see a more compact view of your photo collections in the Photos app; you see thumbnails for only some of the photos in a collection and the timeframe of each group is larger. If you set this to off (white) instead, you see a thumbnail of every photo in your collections, which takes up much more screen space and you have to scroll more to move among your collections. This setting impacts how you see Collections view and Years view only.

11 Swipe up the screen.

12 To display a grid when you are taking photos, set the Grid switch to on (green). This can be helpful to keep your photos aligned vertically and horizontally. If you don't want to see this grid, set Grid to off (white).

13 To record video at a higher frame rate, set the Record Video at 60 FPS switch to on (green). This results in higher quality video, but also much larger file sizes. (Only available on the iPhone 6 and iPhone 6 Plus.)

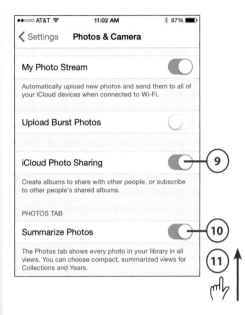

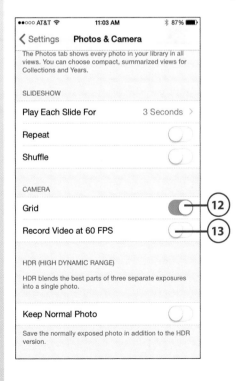

(14) If you want only the HDR version of photos (see the note following these steps for more on HDR) to be saved, set Keep Normal Photo to off (white). If you want both the HDR version and the normal version to be saved, set Keep Normal Photo to on (green); note that this creates two versions of every photo you take, which takes up more space on your phone and causes you more work because you have to deal with duplicate photos.

(15) Tap Settings.

(15)

●●○○○ AT&T 🛜	11:03 AM	⚡ 87% ▬

‹ Settings   **Photos & Camera**

The Photos tab shows every photo in your library in all views. You can choose compact, summarized views for Collections and Years.

SLIDESHOW

Play Each Slide For   3 Seconds ›

Repeat

Shuffle

CAMERA

Grid   🔵

Record Video at 60 FPS

HDR (HIGH DYNAMIC RANGE)

HDR blends the best parts of three separate exposures into a single photo.

Keep Normal Photo   ──**(14)**

Save the normally exposed photo in addition to the HDR version.

HDR

The High Dynamic Range (HDR) feature causes the iPhone to take three shots of each image with each shot having a different exposure level. It then combines the three images into one higher-quality image. You can choose to use HDR for specific photos when you take them or let the Camera app choose when to use HDR automatically. HDR works best for photos that have good lighting and no motion. (You can't use the iPhone's flash with HDR images.) Also, HDR photos take longer to capture so you need to allow more time between taking photos when you use it. (This only matters if you are taking a series of images quickly.) When you use HDR for a photo and save the normal photo, too (step 14 in the previous task), you see two versions of each photo in the Photos app: One is the HDR version, and the other is the normal version. You might want to do this to see the difference between the two types. If you prefer the HDR versions, set the Keep Normal Photo to off so that your photos don't use as much space on your iPhone and you don't have twice as many photos to deal with.

Taking Photos and Video with Your iPhone

You use the Camera app to take photos and video with your iPhone. This app has a number of controls and features. Some features are easy to spot while others aren't so obvious. By the end of this section, you'll know how to use all these features to take great photos and video with your iPhone.

Taking Photos

You can use the Camera app to capture your photos, like so:

1 On the Home screen, tap Camera.

2 To capture a horizontal photo , rotate your iPhone so that it's horizontal; of course, you can use either orientation to take photos just as you can with any other camera.

3 Swipe up or down (right or left if the phone is vertical) on the screen just above the Capture button to choose the type of photo or video you want to take; as you swipe, the tool currently selected is shown in yellow. Choose TIME-LAPSE to take a time-lapse photo, SLO-MO to take slow motion video, VIDEO to take standard speed video, PHOTO to take a full-frame image, SQUARE to capture a square image, or PANO to take a panoramic image (steps to do this are in a later task). This task's steps cover the PHOTO and SQUARE options, for which the only difference is the shape and proportion of the resulting photos. (The rest of the options are coved in later tasks.)

4 Tap the lightning bolt to set the flash. The flash menu appears.

Location, Location!

If you allow the Camera app to use Location Services (you're prompted to allow this the first time you use the Camera app), the app uses the iPhone's GPS to tag the location where photos and video were captured. (You have to be in a location where the iPhone can receive the GPS signal.) Some apps can use this information, such as the Photos app on your iPhone, to locate your photos on maps, find photos by their locations, and organize Collections by location.

⑤ Tap Auto to have the flash set automatically, depending on the lighting conditions for the photo you are taking. Tap On to have it on for every photo, or Off to disable the flash. After you make a choice or after a few seconds of inactivity, the Flash menu closes.

⑥ Tap HDR to configure HDR for the photo you are taking. The HDR menu appears.

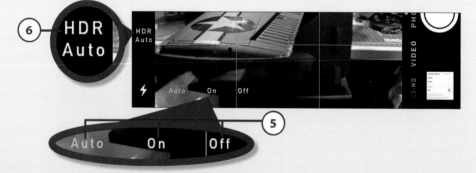

⑦ Tap Auto to have the HDR set automatically depending on the lighting and other conditions for the photo you are taking, tap On to have it on for every photo, or Off to disable HDR. After you make a choice or after a few seconds of inactivity, the HDR menu closes. (HDR is not always available, for example, when the flash is used, HDR is not.)

Auto Flash

When you have the flash set to Auto, a lighting bolt inside a yellow box appears on the screen when you are setting up a photo to indicate that the flash will be used. If you position the shot so the flash won't be used, this box doesn't display.

Set Once

You only need to set the Flash, HDR, and other options when you want to change the current settings, which are retained even after you move out of the Camera app and back into it. The current status of the Flash and HDR options are indicated next to their icons; for example when the flash is set to Auto, you see Auto next to the lightning bolt.

8 Tap the Lens Change button to switch the camera being used for the photo. When you change the lens, the image briefly freezes, and then the view changes to the other lens. The front lens (the one facing you when you look at the screen) has fewer features than the back lens. For example, you can't zoom when using the front lens nor does it use the flash. (The front lens is used most frequently for FaceTime and other video communication and for taking selfies.) When you are using the front lens, some of the details in these steps won't apply, but the general process is the same.

9 Frame the image by moving and adjusting the iPhone's distance and angle to the image; if you have the Grid turned on, you can use its lines to help you frame the image way you want it. As you move the phone, the app indicates the part of the image that is used to set focus, brightness, and exposure with a yellow box. If this is the most important part of the image, you are good to go. If not, you can set this point manually.

The yellow box indicates the part of the image being used to set brightness, focus, and exposure

10 To zoom in, unpinch on the image. The camera zooms in on the subject and the Zoom slider appears. (Reminder: You can't use zoom when taking photos with the frontside camera.)

11 Unpinch on the image or drag the slider toward the + to zoom in or pinch on the image or drag the slider toward the – to zoom out to change the level of zoom until you get it the way you want it to be in the photo.

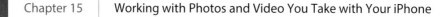

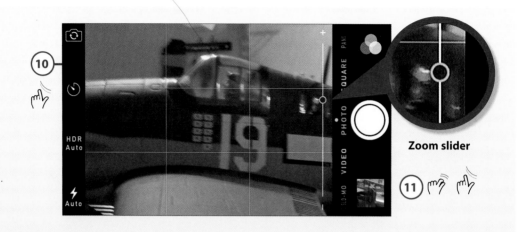

Zoom slider

Zoom, Zoom

The iPhone uses a digital zoom rather than a lens-based zoom. That means the quality of a zoomed photo isn't quite as good as a non-zoomed one. For best results, move closer to the subject of the photo if you can.

(12) Tap the screen to manually set the area of the image to be used for setting the focus, brightness, and exposure. The yellow focus box appears where you tapped. This indicates where the focus and exposure are set.

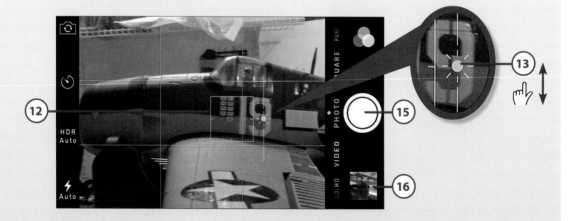

(13) To change the brightness, swipe up on the sun icon to increase the brightness or down to decrease it. Note that the sun slides up and down on the slider, and you can see the brightness difference in the photo image as you change it.

14 Continue making adjustments in the framing of the image, the zoom, focus point, and brightness until it is the image you want to take.

15 Tap the Capture button on the screen, or either Volume button on the side of the iPhone. The Photo app captures the photo, and the shutter closes briefly while the photo is recorded. When the shutter opens again, you're ready to take the next photo. The process takes longer when HDR is on because the camera has to save three versions of the image and blend them together.

16 To see the photo you most recently captured, tap the Thumbnail button. The photo appears on the screen with iPhone's photo-viewing controls.

Lock It In

If you want to lock in the exposure and focus location, tap and hold your finger on the screen until the AE/AF Lock indicator appears on the screen. When you move the camera or the subject, the exposure and focus area remains locked in its position. Tap and hold on the screen until the indicator disappears to unlock it again.

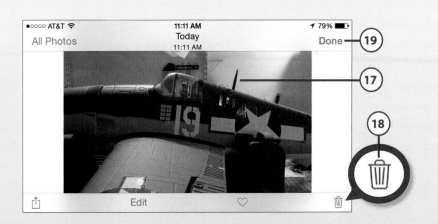

17 Use the photo-viewing tools to view the photo (see "Viewing, Editing, and Working with Photos on Your iPhone" later in this chapter for the details).

18 To delete a photo, tap the trashcan icon, and then tap Delete Photo. The app deletes the photo, and you see the next photo in the All Photos album.

19 Tap Done. You move back into the Camera app, and you can take more photos.

Sensitive, Isn't It!

The iPhone's camera is sensitive to movement, so if your hand moves while you are taking a photo, it's likely to be blurry. Sometimes, part of the image will be in focus while part of it isn't, so be sure to check the view before you capture a photo. This is especially true when you zoom in. If you are getting blurry photos, the problem is probably your hand moving while you are taking them. Of course, since it's digital, you can take as many photos as you need to get it right; you'll want to delete the rejects (you learn how later) periodically, so you don't have to waste storage room or clutter up the Photos app with them.

Applying Filters to Your Photos

You can apply filters to photos as you take them as follows:

(1) Use the skills you learned in the previous task to set up the photo you want to take.

(2) Tap the Filters button. The Filters palette appears. You see a preview of the image as it would look with each filter applied to it.

(3) Tap the filter you want to apply. You return to the image you are capturing and see the filter applied to it. The Filters button is highlighted with color to show a filter is applied, in case you can't tell just by looking!

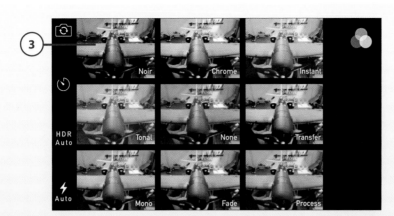

④ Tap the Capture button to take the photo with the filter applied.

⑤ To remove the current filter, tap the Filters button, and then tap None.

More on Filtering

When you set a filter, it remains on until you choose another one; choose the None filter to remove all filters. Also, you can apply a filter to a photo after you've taken it as you learn later in this chapter. In fact, that is a better way because you can then apply easily apply different filters to the same photo to see which filter you prefer.

Taking Panoramic Photos

The Camera app can take panoramic photos by capturing a series of images as you pan the camera across a screen, and then "stitching" those images together into one panoramic image. To take a panoramic photo, perform the following steps:

(1) Open the Camera app and hold the iPhone vertically (it can't take panoramic photos horizontally, though you can view them that way).

(2) Swipe on the toolbar or screen until PANO is selected. The app moves into Panorama mode. On the screen, you see a box representing the entire image and a smaller box representing the current photo.

(3) Tap the Capture button. The app begins capturing images.

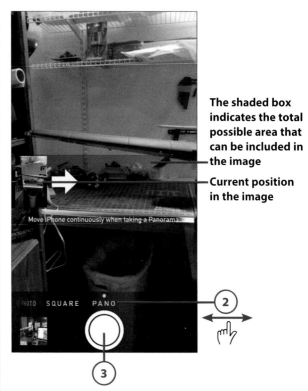

The shaded box indicates the total possible area that can be included in the image

Current position in the image

4 Slowly sweep the iPhone to the right while keeping the arrow centered on the line on the screen (if you move the phone too fast, you see a message on the screen telling you to slow down). This keeps the center-line consistent through all the images; the better you keep the arrow on the line, the better the photo will be.

5 When you've moved to the "end" of the image, tap the Stop button or when you reach the limit of what you can capture, the process stops automatically. You move back to the starting point and the panoramic photo is created.

6 Preview the image by tapping the preview icon. You see the image in the Photos app.

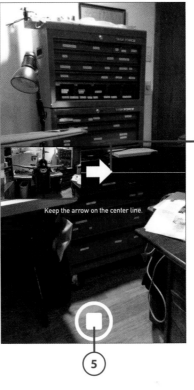

As you move the iPhone from the start of the image to the end, keep the arrow centered on the line

(7) Use the photo-viewing tools to view the panoramic photo. (See "Viewing, Editing, and Working with Photos on Your iPhone" later in this chapter for the details.)

(8) To delete a panoramic photo, tap the trashcan and tap Delete Photo. The app deletes the photo, and you see the next photo in the All Photos album.

(9) Tap Done. You move back into the Camera app, and you can take more panoramic photos.

Taking Photos in Burst Mode

Use can use the Burst mode to rapidly take a series of photos, such as to capture action.

(1) Open the Camera app and set the photo as you normally would.

(2) When you are ready to start taking photos, tap and hold on the Capture button or either of the Volume buttons on the side of the phone. The Camera app rapidly takes a series of photos. As it captures images, you see the number of photos captured on the screen.

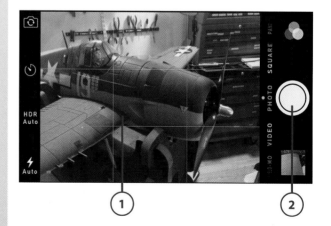

3 When you're done taking photos, lift your finger off the Capture button. (Later in this chapter, you learn how to work with Burst mode photos.)

Number of photos you have taken in the series   **3**

>>>Go Further
TAKING IPHONE SCREENSHOTS

There are times when it is useful to capture screen images of the iPhone's screen (such as when you are writing a book about your iPhone). The iPhone includes a screen capture utility you can use to take a picture of whatever is on iPhone's screen at any point in time. This is particularly helpful when you need to get help with a problem. Capture a screenshot showing the problem you are having and send it to whomever is trying to help you.

When the screen you want to capture appears, press the Home and Wake/Sleep buttons at the same time. The screen flashes white and the shutter sound plays to indicate the capture has been taken. The resulting image is stored in the All Photos album. You can view the screen captures you take, email them, send them via Messages, or other tasks as you can with photos you take with the iPhone's camera.

Camera Roll vs All Photos

If you are not using the iCloud Photo Library, your album might be labeled Camera Roll instead of All Photos. This label doesn't really matter. Just know that it is the location where all of your pictures taken on your phone can be found.

Taking Photos Using the Timer

NEW! You can use the Camera app's timer to take a photo after either a three- or ten-second delay.

(1) Move into the Camera app.

(2) Tap the Timer button.

(3) Tap 3s or 10s to set a three- or ten-second delay, respectively.

(4) Set up the photo as you want it to be by framing it, and setting the zoom.

(5) Tap the Capture button. The timer starts to countdown, which you see on the screen. When it reaches 0, the photo is taken.

(6) When you are done with the timer, tap it and set it to Off again. Like the other settings, the timer persists so unless you turn it off, it is active the next time you take a photo.

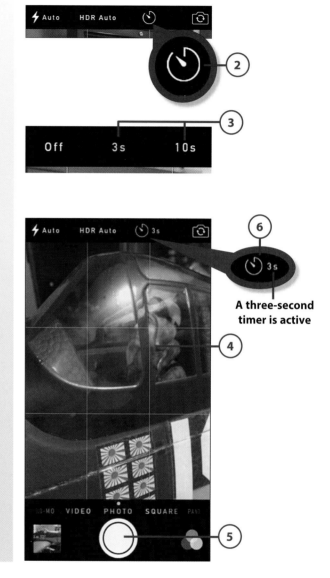

A three-second timer is active

Timer and Burst

If you set the timer, and then tap and hold on the Capture button for a second or so, a burst of ten photos is captured when the timer expires. If you just tap the Capture button quickly, only one photo is taken when the timer expires.

Taking Video

You can capture video as easily as you can still images. Here's how.

1. Move into the Camera app.

2. To capture horizontal video, rotate the iPhone so that it's horizontal; of course, you can use either orientation to take video just as you can with any other video camera.

3. Swipe on the toolbar until VIDEO is selected.

4. Choose the camera on the back of the iPhone or the one facing you, configure the flash, or zoom in, just like setting up a still image. (The grid and HDR mode are not available when taking video.)

5. Tap on the screen where you want to focus. The yellow box indicates where you tapped.

6. If needed, adjust the brightness just like for a still photo.

7. To start recording, tap the Record button. The Camera app starts capturing video; you see a counter on the screen showing how long you've been recording.

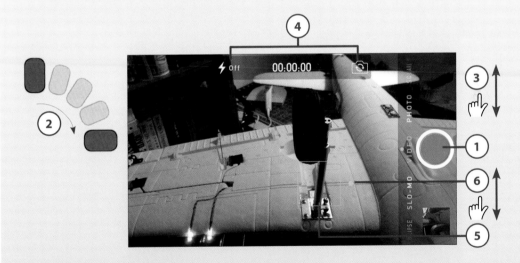

You Are Recording

When you tap the Record button, you hear the start/stop recording tone. When you stop recording, you hear the same tone. That's assuming you don't have the iPhone muted.

8 To take still images while you take video, tap the Capture button.

9 To stop recording, tap Stop. Also, like still images, you can then tap the video's thumbnail to preview it. You can use the Photos app's video tools to view or edit the clip. (See "Viewing, Editing, and Working with Video on Your iPhone" later in this chapter for the details.)

00:00:07 — **Length of video**

9

8

Slow-Motion Video

You can also take slow-motion video. Choose SLO-MO on the toolbar; you see 120 FPS or 240 FPS (Frames Per Second), depending on the model of iPhone you are using, on the screen indicating you are taking slow-motion video. Set up the shoot and take the video as you do with normal speed video. When you play it back, you can select the part you want to see in slow motion (see "Watching Slow-Motion Video" later in this chapter).

Taking Time-Lapse Video

NEW! No doubt you've seen a documentary with time-lapse photography showing something that usually takes a long time in just a few seconds, such as a plant growing. It's not likely you'll leave your iPhone in place long enough to photograph something like that, but even so you might find its ability to take time-lapse photos interesting.

1. Move into the Camera app.

2. Swipe on the toolbar or screen until TIME-LAPSE is selected.

3. Set up the shot you want to start with and tap to set the focus and brightness.

4. Tap the Record button. The tick marks around the Stop button rotate. The large marks indicate when a frame is captured.

5. When you are done recording, tap the Stop button. You can then tap the video's thumbnail to preview it. Because it is a time-lapse video, the time shown in the video is accelerated so the clip plays very quickly.

The large tick marks indicate when a frame is captured

Taking Photos and Video from the Lock Screen

Because it is likely to be with you constantly, your iPhone is a great camera of opportunity. You can use its Quick Access feature to quickly take photos when your iPhone is asleep/locked. Here's how:

1. Press the Touch ID/Home button. The Lock screen appears.

2. Swipe up on the camera icon. The Camera app opens. (If you don't swipe far enough up the screen, the Lock screen "drops" down again. Swipe almost all the way up the screen to open the Camera app.)

3. Use the Camera app to frame and zoom the photo and set its options and filters as needed; these work just like when you start with the Camera app as described in the previous tasks, except that you can only view the most recent photo you captured.

4. Press either Volume button on the side of the iPhone, or tap the Capture button icon to take the photo. If you selected VIDEO, tap the Record button to start capturing video.

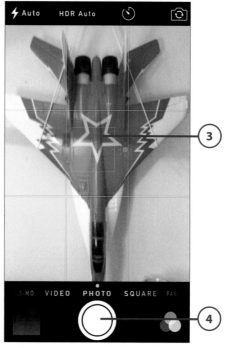

Bypass the Passcode

If you have a passcode set on your iPhone, you can use the Quick Access feature without tapping the Touch ID/Home button or entering your passcode. You can also view the photos you have taken since you started using Quick Access. To do anything else, you need to unlock your phone by using Touch ID or entering your passcode.

Taking Photos and Video from the Control Center

You can get to the camera quickly using the Control Center too.

(1) Swipe up from the bottom of the screen to open the Control Center.

(2) Tap the Camera button. The Camera app opens.

(3) Use the Camera app to take photos or video as you've learned in the previous tasks.

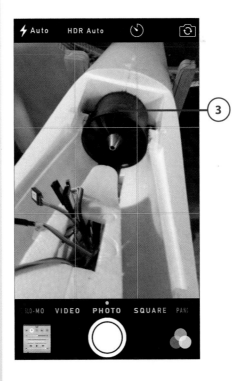

Viewing, Editing, and Working with Photos on Your iPhone

After you've loaded your iPhone with photos, you can use the Photos app to view and work with them individually. You can also edit your photos and use them in a number of tasks, such as sharing your photos via AirDrop or email.

Finding Photos to Work With by Browsing

The first step in viewing, editing, or doing other tasks with photos is finding the photos you want to work with. When you open the Photos app, you see three ways to access your photos: Photos, Shared, and Albums. You can browse these sources to find photos in which you are interested.

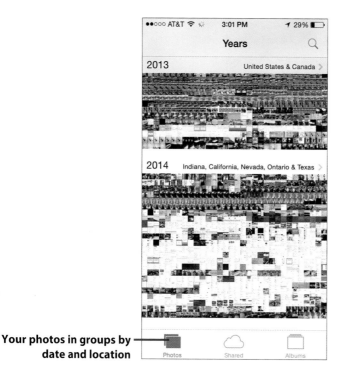

Your photos in groups by date and location

The Photos source organizes your photos with groupings of photos by date and location. (This is done automatically based on the data associated with your photos.) The top level is Years, which show your photos grouped by the year in which they were taken. You can then "drill down" into a year where you find collections, under which photos are organized by location and date ranges, which are determined according to the time, date, and location information on your photos. When you tap one of these collections, you drill down and see moments, which show you the detail of a collection. At the moment level, you see and can work with the individual photos in the collection.

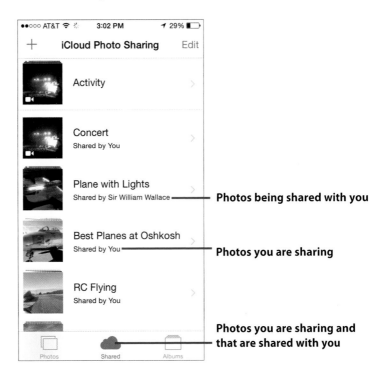

Shared shows photos you are sharing with other people and photos other people are sharing with you. For each group of photos being shared, you see the name of the group and who is sharing it (you, for photos you are sharing, or the name of the person sharing with you). When you tap a shared group, you see the photos it contains and can work with them. (Working with photo sharing is covered in detail in "Using iCloud with Your Photos" later in this chapter.)

Albums allow you to organize your photos in a number of ways. Following are some of the albums or types of albums you see:

- **All Photos**. This album contains photos and videos you've taken with the iPhone's camera.

- **Videos**. Videos you've taken with your iPhone are collected here.

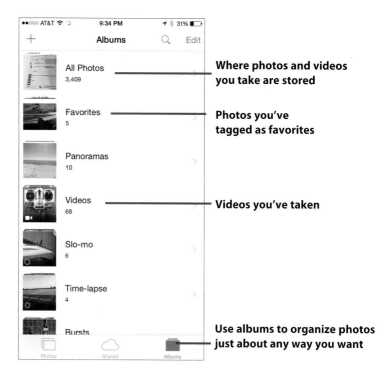

- **Albums synced from computers**. In Chapter 5, "Working with iTunes on Your Computer," you learned about syncing your iPhone with a computer. Photos can be included in the sync process, and you see any albums on a computer that you've included in the sync. These are identified by the source, such as "From My Mac," which indicates a folder synced from a Mac computer.

- **Albums you create**. Later in this chapter, you learn how to create albums for your photos. Albums that you've created on your iPhone are indicated by just having the name you give them (no "From" text).

Your Albums May Vary

Some apps, such as Instagram, might add albums to the Albums tab.

While each of these sources looks a bit different, the steps to browse them to find the photos you want to work with are similar for all three sources; this example shows using the Photos source to browse for photos:

1. On the Home screen, tap Photos.

2. Tap Photos. On the Years screen, you see photos collected by the year in which they were taken. Next to the year, you see a summary of the various locations where the photos were taken.

3. Swipe up and down the screen to browse all the years.

4. Tap the year that contains photos you want to work with. You move to the Collections screen that groups the selected year's photos based on locations and time periods.

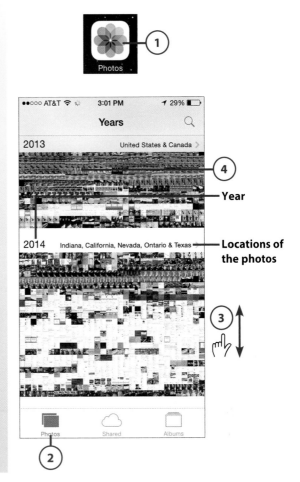

Start at the Beginning

If the title at the top of the screen isn't "Years," tap the Back button located in the upper-left corner of the screen until it is.

(5) Swipe up and down the screen to browse all the collections in the year you selected.

(6) Tap the collection that contains photos you want to see. Doing so opens the Moments screen, which breaks out the photos in the collection by location and date.

(7) Swipe up and down the screen to browse all the moments in the collection you selected.

(8) To see the photos in the moment based on their location, tap the moment's title. You see a map with photos collected at the various locations.

No Map Required

If you don't want to see photos in a moment shown on the map, just tap any photo in the moment to return to browsing that moment's photos as one group of photos.

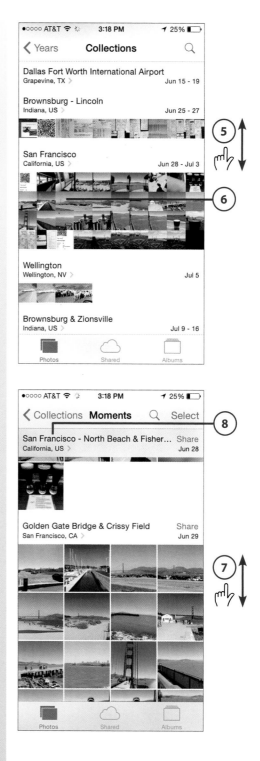

9 Zoom in by unpinching your fingers on the map to get more detail. As you zoom, the locations of photos become more specific.

10 Tap the location that contains photos you want to see. You see a thumbnail of each photo at that location.

11 You're ready to view the photos in the group and can move to the next task.

Go Back

You can move back to the screens from where you came by tapping the Back button, which is always located in the upper-left corner of the screen; this button is named with the screen it takes you back to. To choose a different source, you might have to tap the Back button several times as the Photos, Shared, and Albums buttons at the bottom of the screen are only visible on the opening screen of the Photos app.

Finding Photos to Work With by Searching

NEW! Browsing photos can be a fun way to find photos, but at times you might want to get specific photos more quickly. You can use the Search tool to get to photos quickly.

1 Continuing in the Photos app, tap the magnifying glass. The Search bar opens.

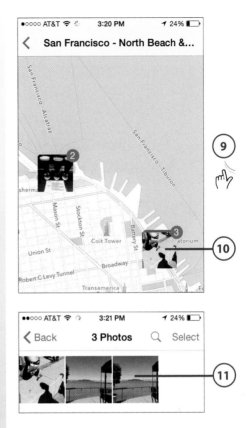

(**2**) Type your search term. This can be any information associated with your photos, such as a date or location. As you type, collections of photos that match your search criteria are listed under the Search bar. The more specific you make your search term, the smaller the set of photos that will be found.

(**3**) Tap the results you want to explore.

(**4**) Browse the results to find the photo you want.

(**5**) Tap Cancel to clear the search.

Viewing Photos Individually

The Photos app enables you to view your photos individually. Here's how:

(**1**) Using the skills you learned in the previous tasks, open the group of photos that you want to view.

(**2**) Swipe up and down to browse all the photos in the group.

(**3**) Tap the photo you want to view. The photo display screen appears.

Orientation Doesn't Matter

Zooming, unzooming, and browsing photos works in the same way whether you hold your iPhone horizontally or vertically.

(**4**) To see the photo without the app's toolbars, tap the screen. The toolbars are hidden.

(**5**) Rotate the phone horizontally if you are viewing a horizontal photo.

(**6**) Unpinch or double-tap on the photo to zoom in.

(**7**) When you are zoomed in, drag on the photo to move it around.

(**8**) Pinch or double-tap on the photo to zoom out.

(**9**) Swipe to the left to view the next photo in the group.

No Zooming Please

You can't have any zoom when you swipe to move to the next or previous photo so make sure you are zoomed out all the way before performing step 9 or 10.

10 Swipe to the right to view the previous photo in the group.

11 When you're done viewing photos in the group, tap the screen to show the toolbars again.

12 Tap the Back button. You move back to the group's screen where you see the thumbnails of the photos it contains.

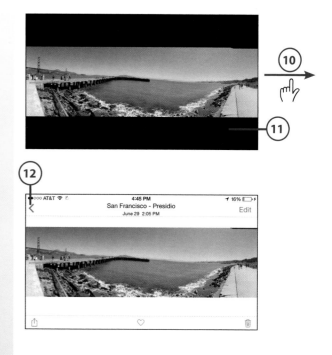

Working with Burst Mode Photos

When you use the Burst mode to take photos, the Camera app rapidly takes a series of photos. (Typically, you use Burst mode to capture motion, where the action is happening too quickly to be able to frame and take individual photos.) You can review the photos taken in Burst mode and save any you want to keep as favorites; your favorites become separate photos just like those you take one at a time. Here's how:

1 View a Burst mode photo. Burst mode photos are indicated by the word Burst and the number of photos in the burst.

2 Tap Select. The burst is expanded. At the bottom of the screen, you see thumbnails for the photos in the burst. At the top part of the screen, you see previews of the photos; the photo in the center of the previews is marked with a downward-facing arrow. Photos

Burst mode photo

Number of photos in the series

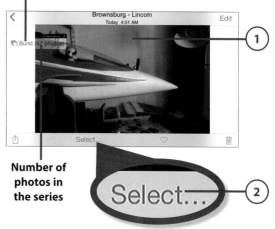

marked with a dot are "suggested photos," meaning the best ones in the series according to the Camera app.

3 Swipe all the way to the right to move to the first photo in the series; swiping on the thumbnails at the bottom flips through them move faster.

4 Tap a photo that you want to save. It is marked with a check mark.

5 Swipe to the left to move through the series.

6 Tap each photo you want to save.

7 Continue reviewing and selecting photos until you've gone through the entire series.

8 Tap Done.

9 Tap Keep Only *X* Favorites, where *X* is the number of photos you selected or tap Keep Everything to keep all the photos in the burst. Each photo you kept becomes a separate, individual photo; you can work with these just like photos you take individually.

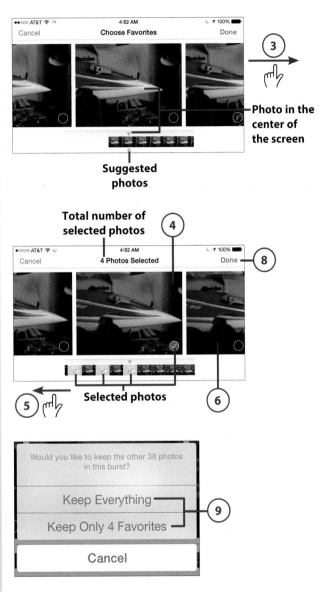

Burst Mode Photos and Uploads to the Cloud

If the Upload Burst Photos switch is set to off, burst photos are not uploaded to the cloud until you go through the steps to select and save photos from a burst. The photos you keep are uploaded to the cloud just like individual photos you take.

Editing Photos

Even though the iPhone has great photo-taking capabilities, not all the photos you take are perfect from the start. Fortunately, you can use the Photos app to edit your photos. The following tools are available to you:

- **Enhance.** This tool attempts to adjust the colors and other properties of the photos to make them better.

- **Straighten, rotate, and crop.** You can rotate your photos to change their orientation and crop out the parts of photos you don't want to keep. You can also have the Photos app do this with the tap of a button.

- **Filters.** You can apply different filters to your photos for artistic or other purposes.

- **Remove red-eye.** This one helps you remove that certain demon-possessed look from the eyes of people in your photos.

- **Smart adjustments.** You can adjust the light, color, and even the black and white properties of your photos.

Enhancing Photos

To improve the quality of a photo, use the Enhance tool.

 View the image you want to enhance.

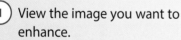 Tap Edit.

(3) Tap the Enhance button. The image is enhanced and the Enhance button turns blue.

(4) If you don't like the enhancements, tap the Enhance button again to remove the enhancements.

(5) To save the enhanced image, tap Done.

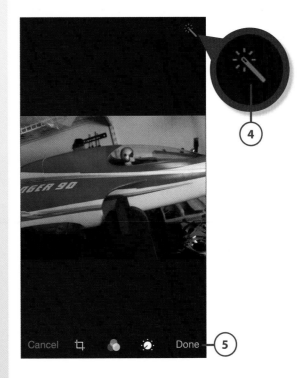

Straightening, Rotating, and Cropping Photos

NEW! To change the orientation of a photo and how it is cropped, use the Straighten, Rotate, and Crop tool.

1. View the image you want to rotate.

2. Tap Edit.

3. Tap the Crop button. The Photos app attempts to straighten and crop the photo automatically.

4. If you are satisfied with how the photo is straightened and cropped, tap Done and skip the rest of these steps. If not, continue to the next step.

5. To undo the automatic straighten and crop, tap RESET.

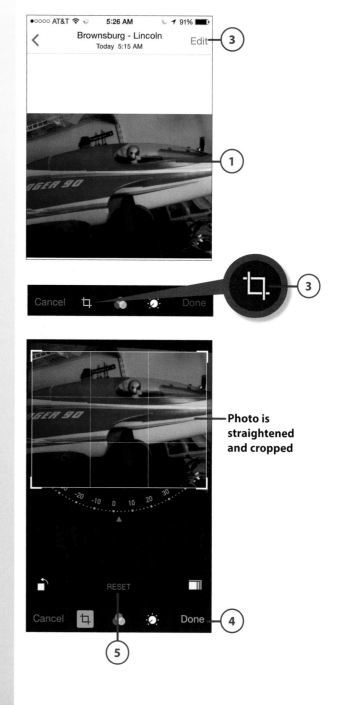

Photo is straightened and cropped

6 To rotate the image, tap the Rotate button. Each time you tap this button, the image rotates 90 degrees.

7 To straighten the image, drag the triangle to the left or right to rotate the image.

8 When the image is straightened, remove your finger. The dial shows how much you've rotated the image.

9 To crop the image proportionally, tap the Constrain button; to crop the image without staying to a specific proportion, skip to step 11.

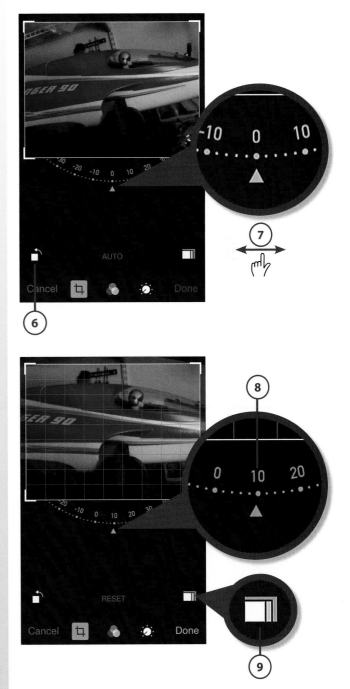

(10) Tap the proportion with which you want to crop the image. You use this to configure the image for how you intend to display it. For example, if you want to display it on a 16:9 TV, you might want to constrain the cropping to that proportion so the images matches the display device.

(11) Drag the corners of the crop box until the part of the image you want to keep is shown in the box.

(12) Drag on the image to move it around inside the crop box.

(13) When the image is cropped and position as you want it to be, tap Done. The edited image is saved.

More on Straightening and Cropping Photos

To undo changes you've made, tap the RESET button and the photo returns to the state is was before you started editing it. To have the app automatically straighten and crop the photo again, tap AUTO. To exit the Edit mode without saving your changes, tap Cancel.

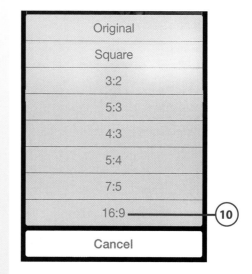

Applying Filters to Photos

To apply filters to photos, do the following:

1. View the image to which you want to apply filters.

2. Tap Edit.

3. Tap the Filters button. The palette of filters appears.

4. Swipe to the left or right on the palette to browse all of the filters.

5. Tap the filter you want to apply. The filter is applied to the image and you see a preview of the image as it will be with the filter; the filter currently applied is highlighted with a blue box. Keeping trying filters until the image is what you want it to be.

6. Tap Done. The photo with the filter applied is saved.

Undoing What You've Done

To restore a photo to its unedited state, tap Revert, which appears when you edit a photo that you previously edited and saved. At the prompt, tap Revert to Original and the photo is restored to its "like new" condition.

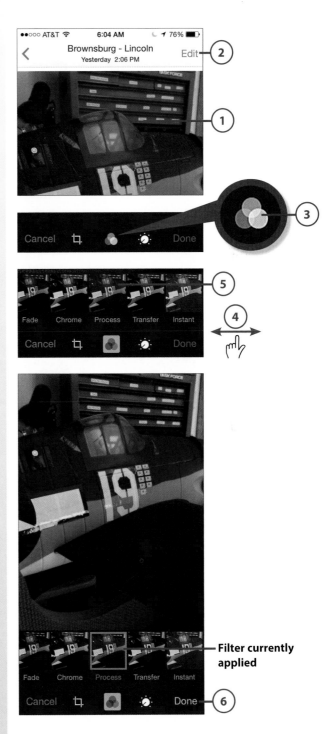

Filter currently applied

Removing Red-Eye from Photos

When you edit a photo with people in it, the red-eye tool becomes available (if no faces are recognized, this tool is hidden). To remove red-eye, perform the following steps:

1. View an image with people that have red-eye.

2. Tap Edit.

3. Tap the Red-eye button.

4. Zoom in on the eyes from which you want to remove red-eye.

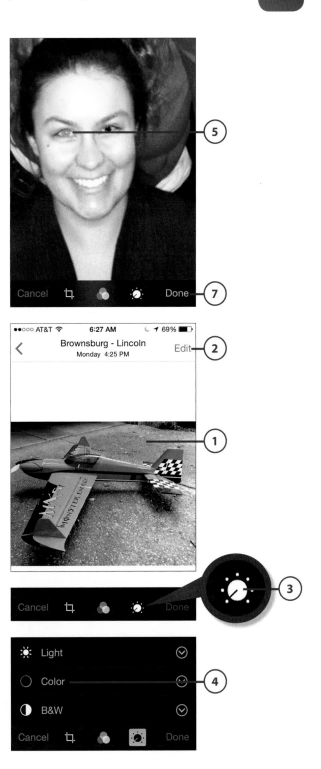

5. Tap each eye containing red-eye. The red in the eyes you tap is removed.

6. Repeat steps 4 and 5 until you've removed all the red-eye.

7. Tap Done.

Making Smart Adjustments to Photos

NEW! You can edit your photos using the Photo app's Smart Adjustment tools. Using these tools, you can change various characteristics related to light, color, and black and white aspects of your photos.

1. View the image you want to adjust.

2. Tap Edit.

3. Tap the Smart Adjust button.

4. Tap the area you want to adjust, such as Color.

Get Straight to the Point

To jump directly to a specific aspect of the area you are adjusting, tap the downward-facing arrow along the right side of the screen. On the resulting menu, tap the aspect you want to adjust. For example, if you open this menu for Color, you tap Saturation, Contrast, or Cast to adjust those factors.

---

5 Swipe to the left or right to change the level of the parameter you are adjusting. As you make changes, you see the results of the change on the image.

6 When you're done adjusting the first attribute you selected, tap the List button.

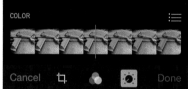

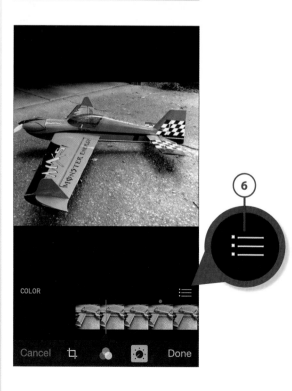

(7) Tap one of the options under the attribute you are already working with to adjust it; or tap the downward-facing arrow under one of the other attributes, and then tap the characteristic you want to change.

(8) Swipe to the left or right to change the level of the parameter you are adjusting. As you make changes, you see the results of the change on the image.

(9) Repeat steps 6 though 8 until you've made all the adjustments you want to make.

(10) Tap Done to save the adjusted image.

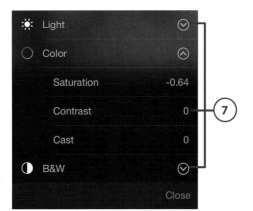

Working with Photos

Once you have photos on your iPhone, there are a lot of things you can do with them, including:

- Emailing one or more photos to one or more people (see the next task).
- Sending a photo via a text message (see Chapter 10, "Sending, Receiving, and Managing Texts and iMessages").
- Sharing photos via AirDrop.
- Sharing photos with others via iCloud (covered later in this chapter).
- Posting your photos on your Facebook wall or timeline.
- Assigning photos to contacts (see Chapter 7, "Managing Contacts").
- Using photos as wallpaper (see Chapter 4, "Configuring an iPhone to Suit Your Preferences").
- Sharing photos via tweets.
- Printing photos (see Chapter 1, "Getting Started with Your iPhone").
- Deleting photos (covered later).
- Organizing photos in albums (also covered later).

Copy 'Em

If you select one or more photos and tap the Copy button, the images you selected are copied to the iPhone's clipboard. You can then move into another application and paste them in.

You'll easily be able to accomplish any actions on your own that are not covered in detail here once you've performed a couple of those that are demonstrated in the following tasks.

Individual versus Groups

Some actions are only available when you are working with an individual photo. For example, you can send only a single photo via Twitter whereas you can email multiple photos at the same time. Any commands that aren't applicable to the photos that are selected won't appear on the screen.

Sharing Photos via Email

You can email photos via iPhone's Mail application starting from the Photos app.

1. View the source containing one or more images that you want to share.

2. Tap Select.

3. Select the photos you want to send by tapping them. When you tap a photo, it is marked with a check mark to show you that it is selected.

4. Tap the Share button.

Too Many?

If the total size of photos you have selected is too large to send via email, the Mail button won't appear. You need to select fewer photos to attach to an email message.

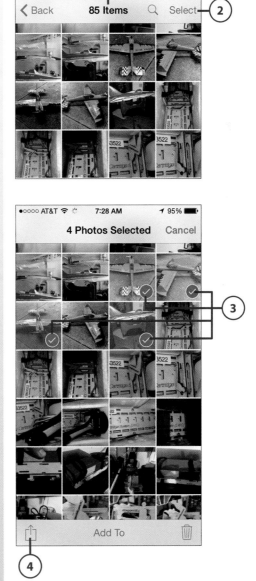

5 Tap Mail. A new email message is created, and the photos you selected are added as attachments.

6 Use the email tools to address the email, add a subject, type the body, and send it. (See Chapter 9, "Sending, Receiving, and Managing Email," for detailed information about using your iPhone's email tools.)

Images from Email

As you learned in Chapter 9, when you save images attached to email that you receive, they are stored in the All Photos album just like photos you take with your iPhone.

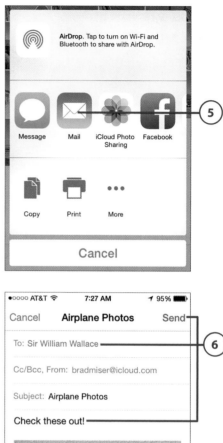

⑦ Tap the size of the images you want to send. Choosing a smaller size makes the files smaller and reduces the quality of the photos. You should generally try to keep the size of emails to 5MB or less to ensure the message makes it to the recipient. (Some email servers block larger messages.) After you send the email, you move back to the photos you were browsing.

Organizing Photos in a New Album

You can create photo albums and store photos in them to keep your photos organized.

To create a new album, perform these steps:

① Move to the Albums screen by tapping Albums on the toolbar.

② Tap the Add button.

③ Type the name of the new album.

④ Tap Save. You're prompted to select photos to add to the new album.

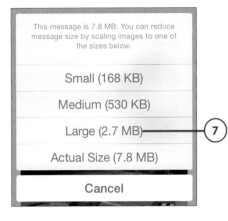

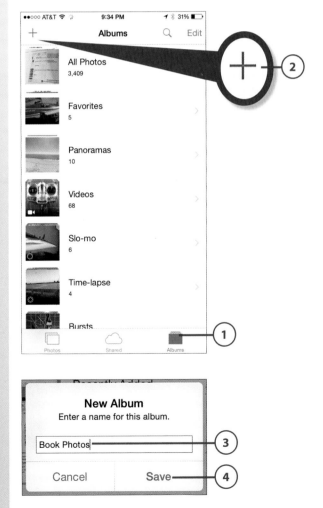

5 Move to the source of the photos you want to add to the new album.

6 Swipe up and down to browse the source and tap the photos you want to add to the album. They are marked with a check mark to show that they are selected. The number of photos selected is shown at the top of the screen.

7 Tap Done. The photos are added to the new album and you move back to the Albums screen. The new album is shown on the list, and you can work with it just like the other albums you see.

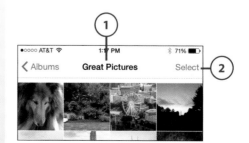

Playing Favorites

To mark any photo or video as a favorite, tap the Heart button. It fills in with blue to show you that item you are viewing is a favorite. Favorites are automatically collected in the Favorites album so this is an easy way to collect photos and videos you want to be able to easily find again without having to create a new album or even put them in an album. You can unmark a photo or video as a favorite by tapping the Heart button again.

Adding Photos to an Existing Album

To add photos to an existing album, do these steps:

1 Move to the source containing the photos you want to add to an album.

2 Tap Select.

3 Tap the photos you want to add to the album.

4 Tap Add To. You move to the Albums screen.

5 Swipe up and down the list to find the album to which you want to add the photos.

6 Tap the album; if an album is grayed out and you can't tap it, that album was not created on the iPhone and so you can't change its contents. The selected photos are added to the album.

More Album Fun

You can change the order in which albums are listed on the Albums screen. Move to the Albums screen and tap Edit. Tap the Unlock button next to the albums you want to move, and then drag albums up or down by their List buttons. Likewise, you can delete an album that you created in the Photos app. Move to the Albums screen and tap Edit. Tap the Unlock button for the album you want to delete, tap Delete, and then tap Delete Album. When you're done making changes to your Albums, tap Done. To remove a photo from an album, view the photo, tap the trash can button, and then tap Remove from Album. Photos you remove from an album remain in the All Photos album and in your library; they are only deleted from the album.

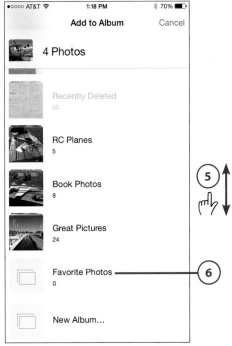

Deleting Photos

You can delete photos and videos that were taken with the iPhone's camera or have stored on it from another app on the phone. (To remove photos that are loaded onto iPhone via syncing with a computer, you must change the sync settings so those photos are excluded, and then resync.) To delete photos or videos you've taken with iPhone's camera, captured as a screenshot, or downloaded from email, take the following steps.

1. Open the source containing photos you want to delete.

2. Tap Select.

3. Tap the photos you want to delete. Each item you select is marked with a check mark.

4. Tap the trashcan button.

5. Tap Delete *X* Photos, where *X* is the number of photos you selected. The photos you selected are deleted.

Deleting Individual Photos

It's a good idea to delete photos and video you don't want anymore to free up space on your iPhone. You can delete individual photos that you are viewing by tapping the trashcan button, and then tapping Delete Photo.

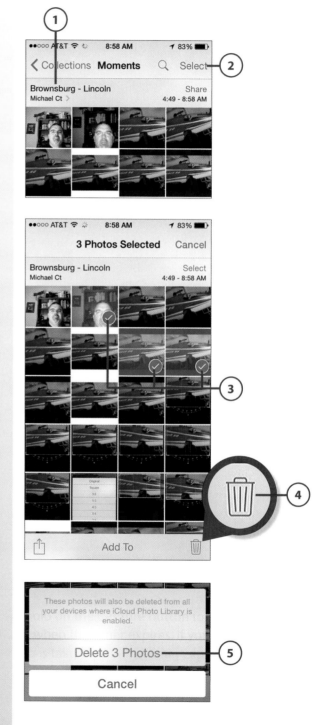

Viewing, Editing, and Working with Video on Your iPhone

As shown previously in this chapter, you can capture video clips with your iPhone. Once captured, you can view clips on your iPhone, edit them, and share them.

Finding and Watching Videos

Watching videos you've captured with your iPhone is simple.

1. Move to the Albums screen.

2. Tap the Videos album. You see the videos you've taken on your iPhone. Video clips have a camera icon and running time at the bottom of their icons.

3. Swipe up and down the screen to browse your videos.

4. Tap the video you want to watch.

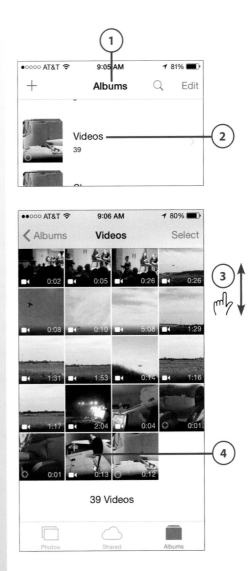

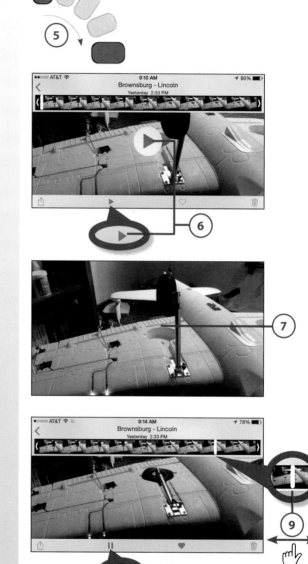

5 Rotate the phone to change its orientation if necessary.

6 Tap either Play button. The video plays. After a few moments, the toolbars disappears.

7 Tap the video. The toolbars reappear.

8 To pause the video, tap Pause.

9 To jump to a specific point in a video, drag the playhead to where you want to start playing it; if you hold your finger in one place for a few seconds, the thumbnails expand so your placement of the playhead can be more precise. When you lift your finger, the playhead remains at its current location; if the clip is playing, it resumes playing from that point or you can tap the Play button to start it playing again.

Deleting Video

To remove a video clip from your iPhone, view it, tap the trashcan icon, and then tap Delete Video at the prompt.

Watching Slow-Motion Video

Watching slow-motion video is slightly different than watching regular speed video. You have to set the part of the video that you want to play in slow motion, and then watch it to see the action slowed down.

1. Open a slow-motion video to view it.

2. Drag the left marker to where you want the slow motion to start; if you want the entire clip to play in slow motion, drag the marker all the way to the left.

3. Drag the right marker to where you want slow motion to end; if you want the entire clip to play in slow motion, drag the marker all the way to the right. When you play the video, the section between the markers plays in slow motion.

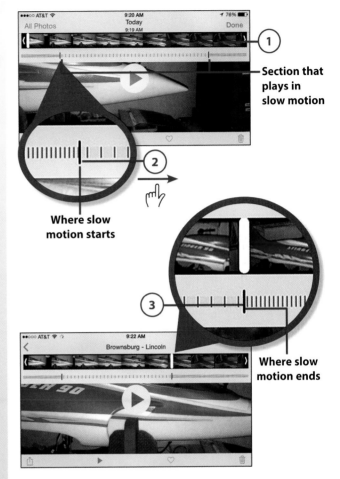

Section that plays in slow motion

Where slow motion starts

Where slow motion ends

Slow Motion and Only the Slow Motion

If you want the video to contain only the slow-motion section, trim it so the trim starts and ends where the slow motion does. (Trimming is described in the next task.)

Watching Time-Lapse Video

Watching time-lapse videos is just like watching a normal video except the playback occurs at a very rapid speed.

Editing Video

You can trim a video clip to remove unwanted parts. Here's how you do it.

(1) View the video you want to edit.

(2) Drag the left trim marker to where you want the edited clip to start; the trim marker is the left-facing arrow at the left end of the time-line. If you hold your finger in one place for a few seconds, the thumbnails expand so your placement of the crop marker can be more precise. As soon as you move the trim marker, the part of the clip that is inside the selection is highlighted in the yellow box; the Trim button also appears.

(3) Drag the right trim marker to where you want the edited clip to end.

(4) Tap Trim.

(5) Tap Save as New Clip to save the trimmed clip as a new clip or Cancel to leave the clip as it was. When you save it as a new clip, the frames outside the crop markers are removed from the clip and it is added to your library as a new clip.

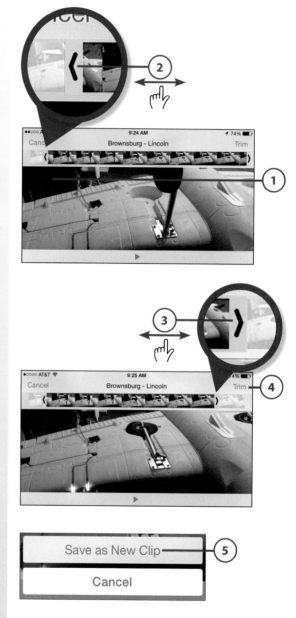

Trim from the Right

Some people I know find it easier to start trimming from the right side first as it makes it less likely you'll grab the playhead instead of the trim marker.

There's an App for That

For more powerful video editing on your iPhone, download the iMovie app. This app provides a much more powerful video editor. You can use themes to design a video, add music, include titles and photos, and much more.

Using iCloud with Your Photos

With iCloud, your devices can automatically upload photos to your iCloud account on the Internet. Other devices can automatically download photos from iCloud, so you have your photos available on all your devices at the same time. Using iCloud with your photos has two sides: a sender and receiver. Your iPhone can be both. Photo applications, such as Photos, iPhoto, or Aperture on a Mac, can also access your photos and download them to your computer automatically. Windows PCs can also be configured to automatically download photos from the cloud.

The most important aspect of using iCloud with your photos is that it stores all of the photos and video you take (assuming you configure it as described in the first part of this chapter) on the cloud. This means that should something happen to your iPhone, you don't lose your photos and video. You can use another device, such as an iPad, to access them. Even if you don't use sharing and other great features, you should use iCloud to protect your photos and video.

In addition to backing up your photos and having all your photos available to you, you can also share your photos and videos with others and view photos and videos being shared with you.

>>>Go Further

AUTOMATIC DOWNLOADS FROM YOUR ICLOUD ACCOUNT TO A COMPUTER

One of the best things about storing photos on the cloud is that photos you take on your iPhone are automatically uploaded to your iCloud account from where they are downloaded to a computer and permanently saved there. So, you don't need to worry about losing your photos, because they are saved on a computer automatically, giving you at least two copies of every photo you take.

On a Mac, iPhoto, Aperture, and Photos apps running on OX Mavericks or on OS X Yosemite can automatically download your Photo Stream photos. Configure this in the Preferences for the app you are using. Photos you take on the iPhone are automatically added to your photo library on your computer. Any photos you add directly to the application are uploaded to your iCloud account and available on your iPhone too.

On a Windows PC, open the iCloud control panel (you need to download and install the iCloud control panel first; to do that, open a web browser and go to www.apple.com/icloud/setup/pc.html). Check the Photo Stream check box. Click Options. Use the upper Change button to choose the location in which you want your photos to be downloaded automatically. Check the My Photo Stream and Shared Photo Streams check boxes. Use the Change button to choose the location where you want Photo Steam photos to be stored. Click OK to close the choose folder dialog box, click OK to close the Photo Stream Options dialog box, and then click Close or Apply. You can move photos from the download folder into a photo application or work with them directly on the desktop. Any image files you place in the upload folder are added to your Photo Stream automatically.

Sharing Your Photos

You can share your photos with others by creating a shared album. This is a great way to share photos, because others can subscribe to your shared albums to view and work with the photos you share. When you share photos, you can add them to an album that's already being shared or create a new shared album.

To create a new, empty, shared album, do the following:

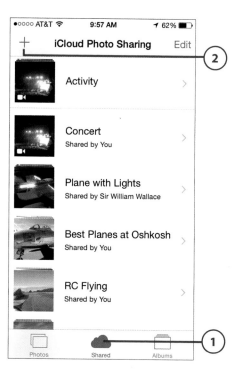

1. Open the Shared source. You see all the iCloud Photo Sharing screen that lists the shared albums in which you are currently participating (as either the person sharing them or subscribed to them).

2. Tap the add (+) button.

(3) Type the title of the new album.

(4) Tap Next.

(5) Enter or select the email address of the first person with whom you want to share the photos.

(6) Add other recipients until you've added everyone you want to access the photos.

(7) Tap Create. The shared album is created and is ready for you to add photos. The recipients you included in the new album receive notifications that invite them to join the album.

| Cancel | iCloud | Next —(4) |

RC Planes ——(3)

For example: "Cars", "Trip to Hawaii" or "Wedding"

| Cancel | iCloud | Create |

To: si (+)

iPhone (317) 805-6007

Sir William Wallace ——(5)
work sirwilliamwallace@me.com

Sir William Wallace
home sirwilliamwallace@icloud.com

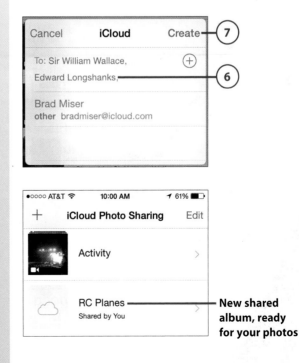

| Cancel | iCloud | Create —(7) |

To: Sir William Wallace,   (+)
Edward Longshanks, ——(6)

Brad Miser
other bradmiser@icloud.com

●○○○○ AT&T 🔗   10:00 AM   🔒 61% ▭

\+   **iCloud Photo Sharing**   Edit

Activity   >

RC Planes —— **New shared**
Shared by You   **album, ready**
for your photos

Adding Photos to a Shared Album

To add photos to an album you are sharing, perform the following steps:

1. Move to the source containing photos you want to add to a shared album.

2. Tap Select.

3. Tap the photos you want to share.

4. Tap the Share button.

5. Tap iCloud Photo Sharing.

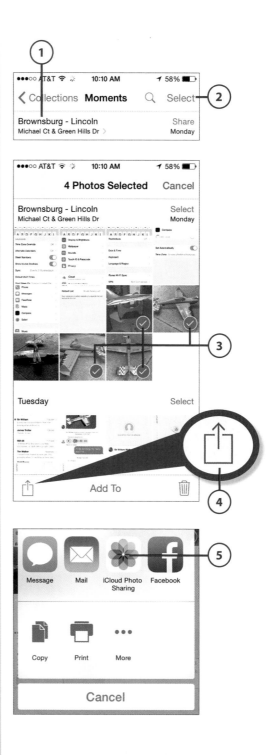

6 Enter your commentary about the photos you are sharing. (Note, this commentary is associated only with the first photo.)

7 Tap Shared Album.

8 Swipe up and down to browse the list of shared albums available.

9 Tap the album to which you want to add the photos.

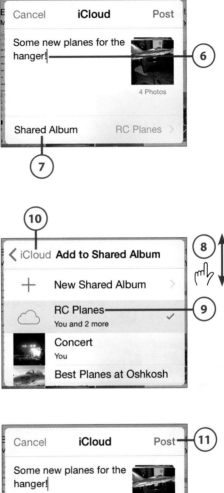

New Shared Album with Photos

You can create a new shared album with the selected photos by tapping New Shared Album.

10 Tap iCloud.

11 Tap Post. The photos you selected are added to the shared album. People who are subscribed to the album receive a notification that photos have been added and can view the new photos along with your commentary.

iCloud Account Required

The people with whom you share photos must have an iCloud account.

Adding Comments to Shared Album

To add commentary to photos or to add more photos to an album you are sharing, do the following:

 Open the Shared source.

② Tap the shared album you want to work with. You see the photos it contains.

③ Tap the photo to which you want to add commentary.

④ Tap Add a comment.

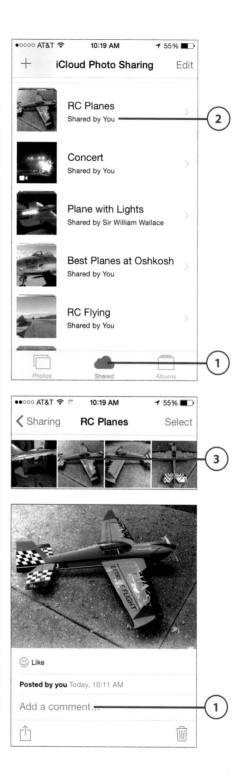

5 Enter your comments.

6 Tap Send. People who are subscribed to the album can read your comments.

7 To indicate you like a photo (though why you would share a photo you don't like I don't know!), tap the Like button.

8 Tap the Back button.

9 To add more photos, tap the add (+) button. You are prompted to select the photos you want to add. Use the app's tools to open the source containing the photos you want to add, select them, and tap Done. Enter your commentary and then tap Post.

Photo Sharing and Family Sharing

If you have Family Sharing set up, an album called Family is created automatically and shared with everyone in your sharing group automatically.

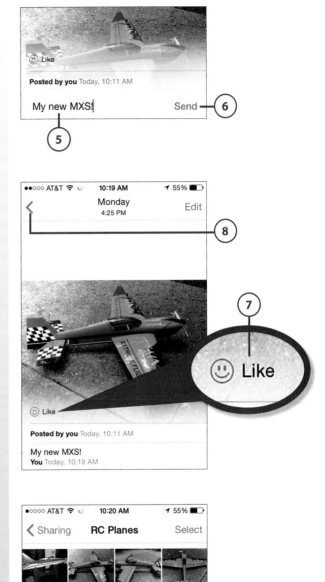

Inviting People to a Shared Photo Album

To invite people to an album you are sharing, perform the following tasks:

(1) Open the shared album to which you want to invite more people to share.

(2) Tap People. At the top of the resulting screen, you see the people you invited to share the album. If they haven't accepted yet, you see Invited as their status.

(3) To invite more people to share the album, tap Invite People, and use the resulting Invite People screen to add people to the album (type or select the person's email address and tap Add).

(4) To allow others to add their photos and videos to the album, set the Subscribers Can Post switch to on (green).

(5) To enable anyone to see the album by clicking a link you provide to them, set the Public Website switch to on (green).

(6) If you enabled the Public Website setting, tap Share Link to share a link to the site.

(7) To receive notifications when others post photos, add comments, or like the album's photos, set the Notifications switch to on (Green).

(8) To delete the album, tap Delete Shared Album and tap Delete at the prompt.

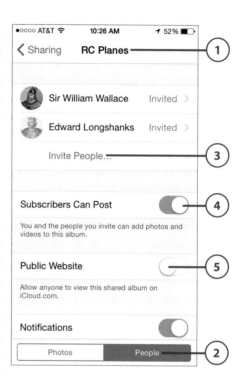

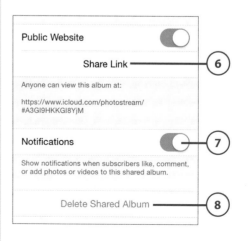

Working with Photo Albums Shared with You

You can work with albums people share with you as follows:

① Tap the notification you received, or tap the Shared source when you see a badge indicating you have activity.

② Tap Accept. The shared album becomes available on your Shared tab.

③ Tap Sharing.

④ Tap the new shared album.

⑤ Tap a photo in the album.

(6) Tap Like to indicate you like the photo.

(7) Tap Add a comment.

(8) Type your comment.

(9) Tap Send. Your comments are added to the album.

(10) Tap the Back button.

(11) If allowed, tap the add (+) button and post your own photos to the album you are sharing. This works just like posting to your own albums.

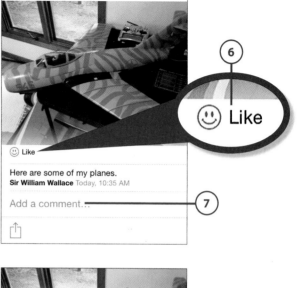

More on Shared Photos

You can do most of the tasks with shared photos that you can with your own, such as emailing them, using them as wallpaper, and posting them to Facebook.

To unsubscribe from an album, move to its People screen and tap Unsubscribe and confirm that is what you want to do. The shared album is removed from your iPhone.

To see the activity associated with albums being shared with you, and those you are sharing, open the Activity Album on the iCloud Photo Sharing screen. You see new postings to the albums when someone comments, and when someone joins the album.

>>>Go Further

IMPORTING YOUR PHOTOS ONTO A COMPUTER

If you don't use iCloud to automatically save your photos on a computer, you can manually import them from the iPhone onto a computer. When you connect your iPhone to a computer, you are usually prompted to import the photos into a photo application. For example, on a Mac, you can import photos directly from the iPhone into Photos. On a Windows PC, when you connect your iPhone to the computer, you should be prompted to choose how you want photos on your iPhone to be handled. From that point on, you should be prompted to import new photos from the iPhone to the computer each time you connect it to the computer.

Find your way

Keep yourself healthy

Listen to or watch podcasts

Maximize your AARP benefits

Manage your travel more easily

Take phone calls on Macs and iPads, too

Use Handoff to work seamlessly across devices

Using Other Cool iPhone Apps and Features

In previous chapters, you learned a lot about a number of great apps, such as Mail, Messages, Safari, and Calendar. In this chapter, you learn about some other very useful apps. You also learn how to use your iPhone with Macs and iPads using the new iOS 8 Handoff feature.

The iPhone universe is in a constant state of growth; at the end of this chapter, you learn about two very exciting developments that weren't quite done when this book was produced, but you'll find a good preview of what's to come from Apple.

Getting Started

An iPhone can truly become *your* iPhone over time as you customize it with the apps that you find to be useful for living your daily life, traveling, managing your health, and communicating. The great thing about iPhone apps is that there are so many to choose from, and because many of them are free, you can try lots of apps. Keep and use the ones you like, delete the ones you don't. Over time, you'll develop a group of core apps that you use constantly and a few that you use just occasionally. The rest you can just delete to get rid of them or move them out of the way (see Chapter 4, "Configuring an iPhone to Suit Your Preferences" for details on deleting and organizing apps).

In previous chapters, you learned about many of the core apps that come pre-installed on your iPhone. In this chapter, you learn about a few more of the pre-installed apps and get an overview of a number of apps that you might want to download onto your iPhone so you can give them a try.

Don't be hesitant to try apps. Apple maintains extremely tight control over the apps that make it into the App Store so there's virtually no chance that an app you download and install can put you or your information at any risk. It usually only takes a few minutes using an app to determine if it is useful to you, so you're not risking much of your time either.

Listening to Podcasts with the Podcasts App

Podcasts are episodic audio or video programs that are available on many, many topics. Using the Podcasts app, you can subscribe to and manage lots of podcasts so that you always have something of interest available to you.

Using the Podcasts App to Subscribe to Podcasts

When you subscribe to a podcast, new episodes are downloaded to your iPhone automatically so the current content is always ready for you. Here's how:

(1) On the Home screen, tap Podcasts.

2. Tap My Podcasts. You see any podcasts to which you are subscribed in the center part of the screen. At the top, you see the Search bar and other tools. You can use three of the buttons at the bottom of the screen to choose how you want to look for podcasts to which to subscribe. The options are Featured, Top Charts, and Search. The rest of these steps show using the Top Charts option; using Featured to browse for podcasts it similar. Search is described in the Go Further box at the end of this task.

3. Tap Top Charts.

4. Tap Categories.

5 Swipe up and down to browse the available categories. Some categories have sub-categories, indicated by the right-facing arrow along the right side of the screen.

6 Tap the category you want to browse. If you tapped a category with sub-categories, you see a list of those sub-categories. If the category didn't have sub-categories, you see the podcast's screen and can skip to step 8.

7 Tap the sub-category in which you are interested. You see the podcasts in that category.

8 Tap Audio to browse audio podcasts or Video to see video podcasts.

9 Swipe up and down the screen to see the available podcasts.

10 Tap a podcast that you want to explore. At the top of the podcast's screen, you see its image, title, and other information. Below the SUBSCRIBE button, you see the podcast's description.

11 Read the description.

12 Tap More if the entire description isn't displayed (not shown in the figure).

13 To subscribe to the podcast, tap SUBSCRIBE. You are subscribed to the podcast and episodes are downloaded according to the Podcast settings in the Settings app. For example, if you choose the 1 Month Limit Episodes setting, only the episodes released within the past month are downloaded.

14 Tap My Podcasts. You move back to your podcast library where you see the podcast to which you subscribed and it is ready for you to listen to it.

15 Tap the podcast to play it (details about finding and playing podcasts are in the following tasks).

Podcasts you've subscribed to

>>>*Go Further*

MORE ON FINDING PODCASTS TO WHICH TO SUBSCRIBE

As you ponder podcasts, consider the following:

• Searching can be the fastest way to get to a specific podcast. Tap the Search button, tap in the Search bar at the top of the screen, type text or numbers associated with the podcast (such as its name, producer, or topic), and tap Search. Podcasts that meet your search criteria are listed. You can swipe around the screen to browse the results. Tap a podcast to move to it. If you want to subscribe to it, read step 13 of the preceding task.

• To unsubscribe from a podcast without deleting all the episodes you've downloaded, go back to the podcast's screen and tap UNSUBSCRIBE.

• To unsubscribe from a podcast and delete all the episodes you've downloaded, tap My Podcasts. Tap the Edit button in the upper-left corner of the screen. Tap the delete button (x) in the upper-left corner of the podcast's thumbnail. The podcast is deleted from your library.

Choosing a Podcast

When you're ready to listen, open the Podcasts app and tap My Podcasts. You can use the My Podcasts screen to quickly find the podcast you want to hear or see.

• Swipe up and down the My Podcasts screen to browse all the podcasts to which you are subscribed. You see a thumbnail for each podcast. Tap a thumbnail to see a podcast's page so you can select and play episodes (covered in the next task).

• You search for podcasts in your library or in the Store using the Search bar. Tap in the Search bar and type your search term. The podcasts and episodes of podcasts that meet your search criteria appear in the list of results. Tap a podcast to view and play its episodes, or tap an episode to play it. Tap Search iTunes Store to search there for podcasts related to your search.

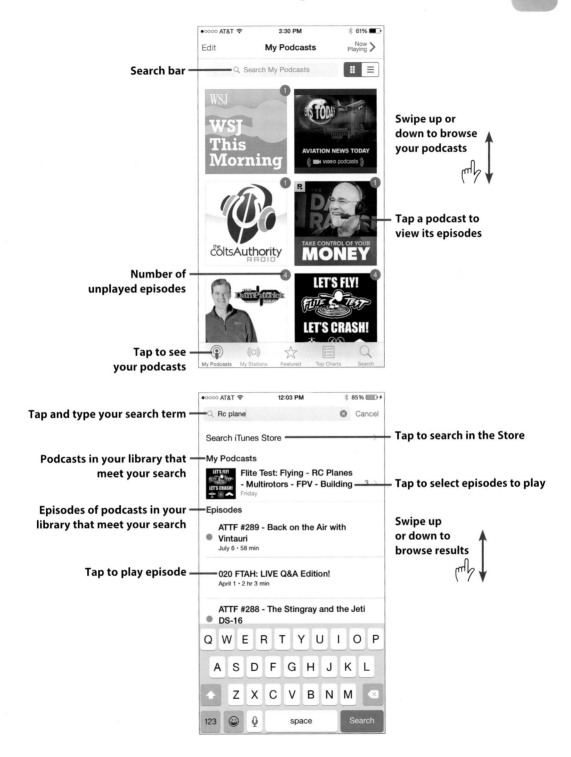

Search bar

Swipe up or down to browse your podcasts

Tap a podcast to view its episodes

Number of unplayed episodes

Tap to see your podcasts

Tap and type your search term

Tap to search in the Store

Podcasts in your library that meet your search

Tap to select episodes to play

Episodes of podcasts in your library that meet your search

Swipe up or down to browse results

Tap to play episode

Search results in the iTunes Store

Tap to explore a podcast

Tap to play an episode

Tap to clear search

Swipe to browse results

- Browse the results in the iTunes Store to find podcasts, or episodes of podcasts, to which you want to subscribe or listen.

Listening to Podcasts

The first step in listening to a podcast is to find the episode you want to listen to.

As you learned in the previous task, one way to do this is by tapping the podcast on the My Podcasts screen to open it. When you open a podcast, you see the podcast's screen, an example of which is shown in the figure at the top of the following page. At the top of a podcast's screen, you see general information about the podcast. Below that is the list of episodes for the podcast. What you see on this screen depends on the settings for the podcast, such as how long you keep episodes. Episodes are grouped in various ways, depending on the Podcasts app's settings in the Settings app. You can browse the list of episodes by swiping up and down on it.

Tap the episode you want to listen to. If it is not currently downloaded, it downloads and starts to play as soon as enough of it has been downloaded that it can play without stopping. If it is already stored on your phone, it starts playing immediately. You move to the Now Playing screen, which you see in the bottom figure on the following page.

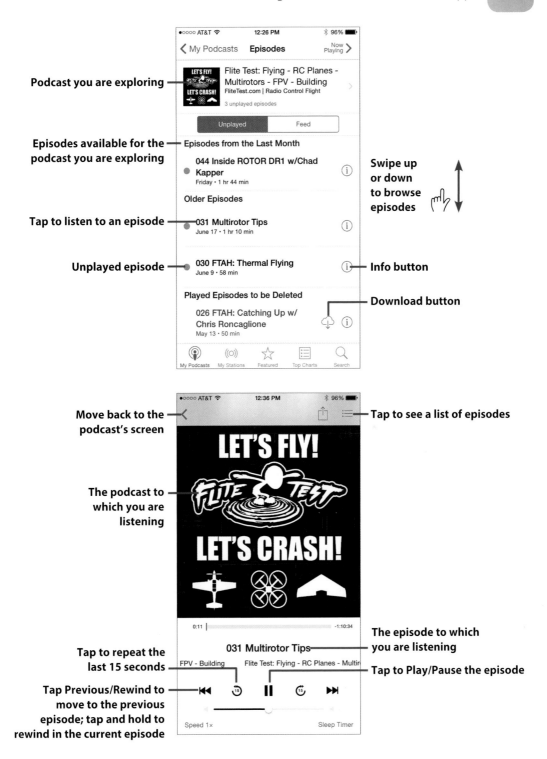

Podcast you are exploring

Episodes available for the podcast you are exploring

Swipe up or down to browse episodes

Tap to listen to an episode

Unplayed episode — Info button

Download button

Move back to the podcast's screen

Tap to see a list of episodes

The podcast to which you are listening

The episode to which you are listening

Tap to repeat the last 15 seconds

Tap to Play/Pause the episode

Tap Previous/Rewind to move to the previous episode; tap and hold to rewind in the current episode

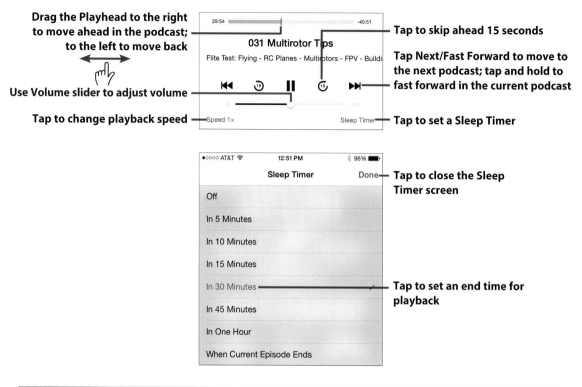

Drag the Playhead to the right to move ahead in the podcast; to the left to move back

Use Volume slider to adjust volume

Tap to change playback speed

Tap to skip ahead 15 seconds

Tap Next/Fast Forward to move to the next podcast; tap and hold to fast forward in the current podcast

Tap to set a Sleep Timer

Tap to close the Sleep Timer screen

Tap to set an end time for playback

Play vs. Download

If an episode hasn't been downloaded to your iPhone, the Download icon appears along the right side of the screen. You can tap the episode itself to stream it (download as well as play it while it downloads), or you can tap the download button to download it to your iPhone to play at a different time. (You might want to do this if you aren't going to be able to connect to the Internet later and want to be able to listen to the episode.)

Managing Podcasts and Episodes of Podcasts

When you are viewing the episode list for a podcast, you can use the controls shown in the following figure:

Tap to manage episodes

Tap to manage the podcast

Swipe down to reveal options

To manage a podcast and its episodes, move to its screen and swipe down to reveal options at the top of the screen. Tap Settings to move to the Settings screen for that podcast. Here, you can mange its settings; for example, to determine how long you keep its episodes on your iPhone.

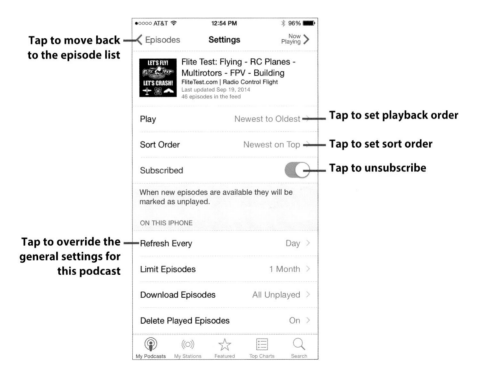

Tap to move back to the episode list

Tap to set playback order

Tap to set sort order

Tap to unsubscribe

Tap to override the general settings for this podcast

To manage a podcast's episodes, move to its screen and tap Edit (shown in an earlier figure). Selection circles appear next to each episode and you can do the following:

Tap to delete the selected episodes — Delete (2)

Tap to exit Edit mode

Tap to see options

If you tap More, you have the following options:

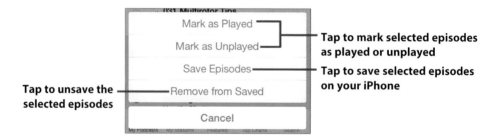

Tap to mark selected episodes as played or unplayed

Tap to save selected episodes on your iPhone

Tap to unsave the selected episodes

You can manage individual episodes by tapping their info button (i):

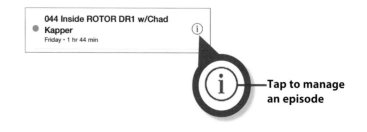

Tap to manage an episode

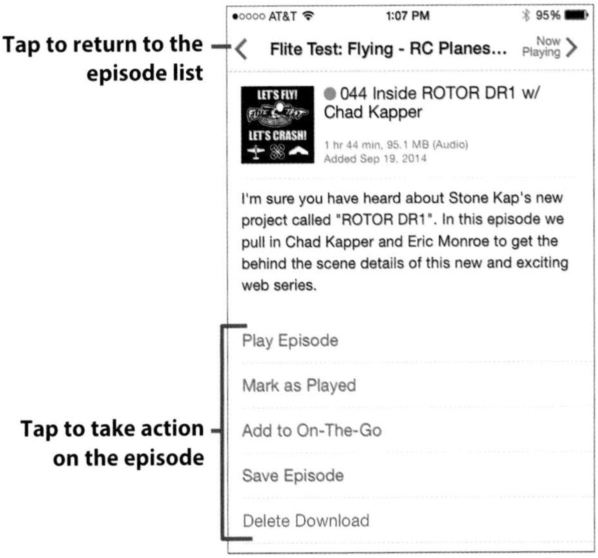

Tap to return to the episode list —

Tap to take action on the episode —

(screenshot content:)

●○○○ AT&T 🛜   1:07 PM   ⚡ 95% 🔋

< Flite Test: Flying - RC Planes...   Now Playing >

● 044 Inside ROTOR DR1 w/ Chad Kapper

1 hr 44 min, 95.1 MB (Audio)
Added Sep 19, 2014

I'm sure you have heard about Stone Kap's new project called "ROTOR DR1". In this episode we pull in Chad Kapper and Eric Monroe to get the behind the scene details of this new and exciting web series.

Play Episode

Mark as Played

Add to On-The-Go

Save Episode

Delete Download

Here are a few more podcast pointers to keep in mind:

- To delete individual episodes of a podcast, swipe to the left on the episode you want to delete and tap Delete. Tap More to see commands similar to those you see after you tap the info button.

- When a podcast is marked with an exclamation point badge, it has a problem. Tap the podcast to see an explanation of the problem at the top of the screen. Most commonly, it is that the app has stopped downloading the podcast because you haven't listened to any episodes in a while. Tap the message to refresh the podcast.

- You can also refresh all your podcasts by swiping down from the top of the My Podcasts screen or refresh a specific podcast by swiping down from the top of its screen.

Podcast Settings

If you decide you like the Podcasts app and want to keep using it, check out its settings by opening the Settings app and tapping Podcasts. You can configure how the app downloads and manages all of your podcasts (you can override these settings for individual podcasts as you saw earlier in this section).

Finding Your Way with the Maps App

The Maps app enables you to find locations and view them on the map. However, the real power of the Maps app is that you can then get detailed, turn-by-turn directions to those places. You can use these directions to drive, or walk, to the places you find. Following are some pointers to help you get started with this great app:

1. Tap the Maps icon to open the app.

2. Tap in the Search bar, and type in the location you want to find. You can type in an address, a place name (such as Lucas Oil Stadium), or even a description of what you are looking for (e.g., Starbucks near me). As you type, the app presents a list of locations that meet your search. Tap the location you want to see on the map. The location or locations (if you do a more general search) are marked with a pushpin.

3. If there is more than one, tap the pushpin to see the summary of the location you selected, including an estimated time to go there.

4. Tap the right-facing arrow to view information about the location and to get directions. On the location's info screen, you see a variety of information about it, such as phone number, website, physical address, and so on (the information provided varies).

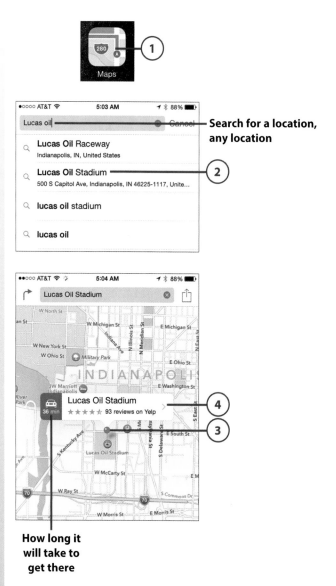

Search for a location, any location

How long it will take to get there

5 To start navigation to the location, tap Directions to Here.

6 If you want directions from your current location, you are ready to go because the app enters your current location by default; tap Route to start the directions. When the app determines the route you selected, you see it in dark blue on the map; alternate routes are shown in other colors (you can tap an alternate route to use it).

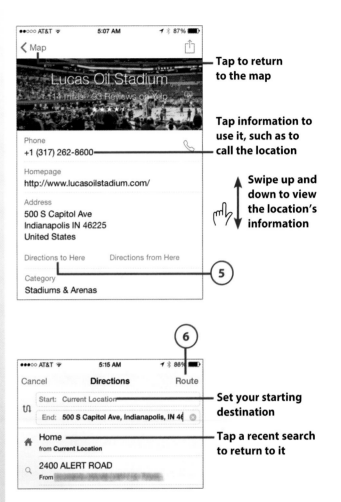

Tap to return to the map

Tap information to use it, such as to call the location

Swipe up and down to view the location's information

Set your starting destination

Tap a recent search to return to it

(7) Tap Drive to get driving directions or Walk to get walking directions, and then tap Start to have the app start navigating for you.

(8) Follow the instructions the app provides. It shows you the part of the route you are on and announces when you need to do something else, such as when and where you need to turn. It gives you a "heads-up" warning when a change is coming up, such as a notice you will be exiting a highway 2 miles before the exit. The app guides you until you reach the destination. If you get off course, it recalculates the route for you automatically. This continues until you arrive at your destination.

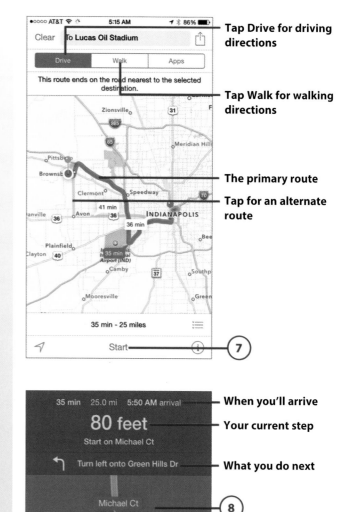

Tap Drive for driving directions

Tap Walk for walking directions

The primary route

Tap for an alternate route

When you'll arrive

Your current step

What you do next

9 As you navigate, you can tap the screen to show its controls.

10 Tap End to end the navigation before you reach the destination or Overview to see an overview of your route.

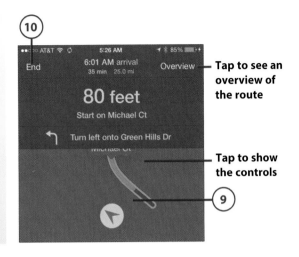

Tap to see an overview of the route

Tap to show the controls

Settings, Settings Everywhere

Make sure you check out the settings for the apps you use. Tap Settings and swipe up the screen until you see the app whose settings you want to configure. Tap the app and use its settings screen to configure it.

Managing Your Health with the Health App

NEW! Apple's Health app, which is installed for you automatically, does two things. One is that you can use it to store your medical information in one place for easy access, for your reference or for the reference of others during an emergency. The other is that it can be a dashboard for other health-related apps you use. For example, if you use an app to help you lose weight, that app can provide information to the Health app. Likewise, apps you use to monitor your exercise can feed their results to the Health app so you can get all your health information in one place.

1 Tap Health to open the app.

(2) To create a Medical ID, which stores vital medical information about you, tap the Medical ID button.

(3) Tap Create Medical ID.

(4) Set the Show When Locked switch to on (green) so that you or others can access your medical information when your iPhone is locked. For example, if someone needs to provide you with medical treatment, they can get to this information on the Lock screen.

(5) Tap and complete each section of information to add it to your Medical ID. This information includes your birthdate, medical conditions, medical notes, allergies, medications, emergency contacts, blood type, and other important information.

(6) Tap Done to save the updated information.

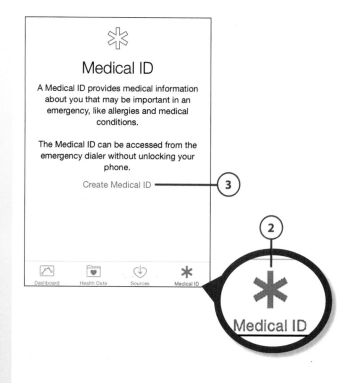

You can view your Medical ID information at any time by returning to the Medical ID screen. To update your information, tap Edit and change or add information.

If you enabled the Show When Locked feature in step 4, your medical information can be accessed while your iPhone is locked. This is especially useful for situations in which you are incapacitated and others need this information to treat you. To access this information while the phone is locked, wake the phone up, swipe to the right on the slider to move to the Enter Passcode screen. Tap Emergency. Then tap Medical ID.

Enter passcode to unlock the phone

Tap to access the Emergency screen without unlocking the phone

Tap to access your Medical ID

Using the other options at the bottom of the Health app's screen, you can also do the following:

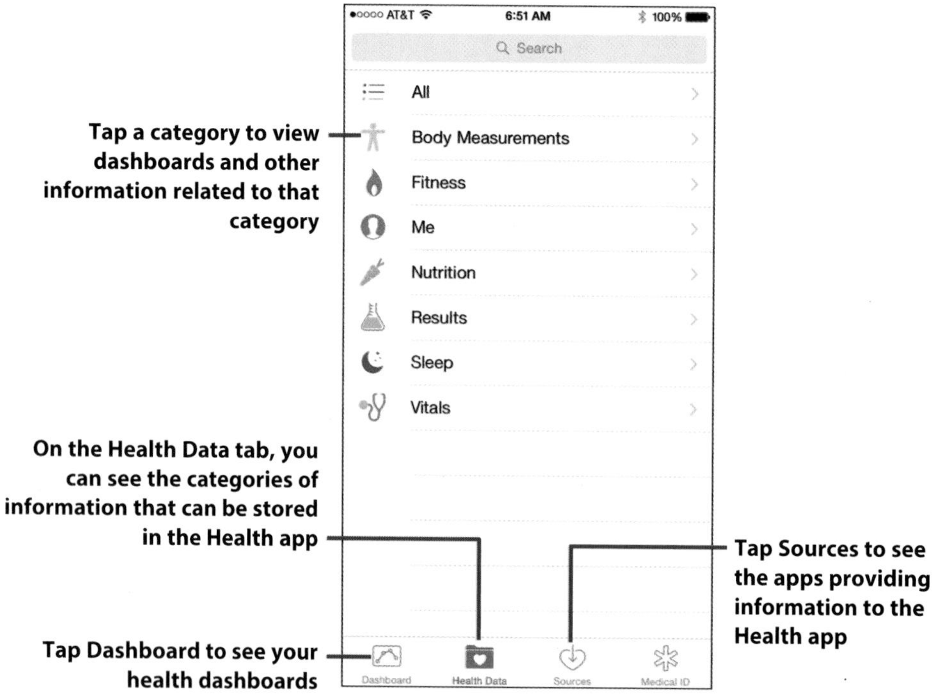

Tap a category to view dashboards and other information related to that category
On the Health Data tab, you can see the categories of information that can be stored in the Health app
Tap Dashboard to see your health dashboards
Tap Sources to see the apps providing information to the Health app
AT&T
6:51 AM
100%
Search
All
Body Measurements
Fitness
Me
Nutrition
Results
Sleep
Vitals
Dashboard
Health Data
Sources
Medical ID

Nobody's Perfect

At press time, Apple was still going through some development on the Health app. Check this book's website (see the back cover for details) for updated information on the Health app as it becomes available.

Working Seamlessly Across Your Devices

With iOS 8, your iPhone can work seamlessly with other iOS devices (such as iPads) and Macs running OS X Yosemite. This enables you to change devices and keep working on the same tasks. For example, you can start an email on your iPhone and then continue it on your Mac without missing a beat.

You can also take phone calls on iPads or Macs.

Working with Handoff

NEW! Handoff enables you to work seamlessly between iOS devices (for example, an iPad), as well as Macs running OS X Yosemite. Each device needs to be signed into the same iCloud account and to have Handoff enabled. If you do not have multiple iOS devices, or a Mac running Yosemite, then there is no need to turn on this feature.

1. To turn Handoff on, open the Settings app. Tap General, and then tap Handoff & Suggested Apps. Set the Handoff switch to on (green).

2. Start an email on your iPhone (note this only works for iCloud email).

3. Swipe up on the Mail icon on an iPad 's Lock screen and unlock the iPad.

(4) Finish the email on the iPad

(5) When your Mac detects activity associated with Handoff, an icon on the Dock appears. Click that icon to open the activity, such as an email, web page, Pages document, or other iCloud-based activity.

Handoff on a Mac

To enable Handoff on a Mac running OS X Yosemite, open the Settings app, and then open the General pane. Ensure that the Allow Handoff between this Mac and your iCloud devices check box is checked.

(6) Finish the activity, such as completing and sending an email message, on the Mac.

This works in the other direction, too. For example, if you open a web page on your Mac, you see the Safari icon on your iPhone's Lock screen. Swipe up on it and unlock your iPhone and the web page on your Mac opens on your iPhone.

Most Apple apps support Handoff and Apple has made it available to other software developers so they can add Handoff to their apps, too.

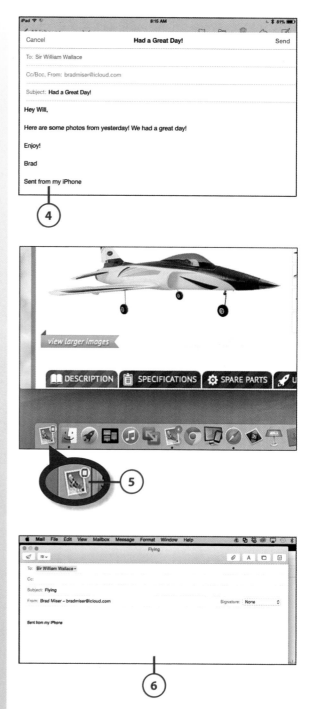

Taking Phone Calls on Macs or iPads

NEW! When your iPhone is on the same Wi-Fi network as an iPad running iOS 8, or a Mac running OS X Yosemite, you can take phone calls on those devices even if they don't offer a cellular connection because Wi-Fi is used instead. When a call comes in to your iPhone, you see the call screen on the other devices and can take the call on that other device (see Chapter 8, "Communicating with the Phone and FaceTime Apps").

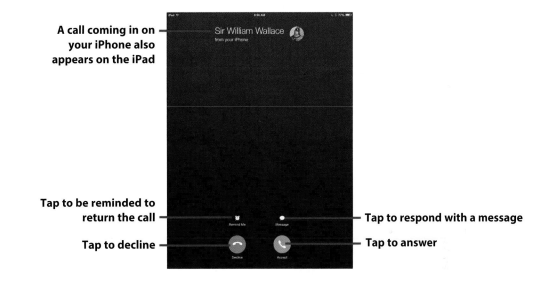

A call coming in on your iPhone also appears on the iPad

Tap to be reminded to return the call

Tap to decline

Tap to respond with a message

Tap to answer

Disabling Calls on Other Devices

Note that this feature is not controlled by the Handoff setting as you might expect. If you don't want calls to your iPhone to come to other devices, open the FaceTime screen in the Settings app and set the iPhone Cellular Calls switch to off (white). This prevents calls coming to your iPhone from being received on your other devices.

Using Even More Great Apps

The following table provides "mini-reviews" of some apps you might find useful. (Chapter 6, "Downloading Apps, Music, Movies, TV Shows, and More onto Your iPhone," explains how to find and download apps.)

Table 16-1 Other Useful Apps

	App	Description
	AARP	You can get information provided by AARP by reading articles and watching videos. You can also get information about your AARP benefits and access your AARP account.
	Airline apps	All the major airlines have apps you can use to make reservations, check flight status, and more. The best of these apps also enable you to check in for flights and provide an electronic boarding pass through the Passbook app.
	AroundMe	Use the app to locate "things" that are around you. You can find hospitals, restaurants, gas stations, hotels, and much more. This app is really useful when you are in a new area because you can quickly find and get to places of interest.
	First Aid	This handy app provides first aid information for a wide variety of situations, including emergencies. It provides examples, and then leads you through how to deal with them in a step-by-step format.
	Foodler	Foodler is a service that collects information about restaurants in a specific area. You can view menus and make orders for delivery in many cases. When you are in a populated area that Foodler services, this app gives you lots of dining choices that you can access quickly and easily.
	GateGuru	This one helps you make airline travel better by providing information about the airports you visit along the way. You can find amenities, see maps, and get flight information.
	iBooks	This app enables you to read ebooks and PDF documents. You can access the iTunes Store to buy and download books to your iPhone. iBooks provides lots of nice tools that make reading better, such as the ability to configure the book's format, change font size and background. You can use its library to carry lots of books with you so you are never without something to read.

	App	Description
	Notes	The Notes app, which is installed by default, enables you to create text notes to record any type of information, such as instructions to a caregiver or shopping lists. If you set the Notes switch to on (green) on the iCloud Settings screen, your notes are stored on the cloud so that they are available on all your iCloud-enabled devices. You can also share notes with others by opening a note, tapping the Share button, and then tapping how you want to share it (for example, tap Mail to send the note via an email message).
	Passbook	Passbook collects different kinds of information for you. For example, if you check into a flight using an airline's app, you can tap the Add to Passbook button to add the boarding pass to the Passbook app. When the time for your flight approaches, Passbook puts a notification for the flight on the iPhone's Lock screen. When you swipe it, you see the boarding pass that you can then use to board the plane by placing your phone's screen under the scanner. It works similarly for gift cards.
	TripAdvisor	You can use this handy app to access TripAdvisor services to plan your travel by accessing reviews of hotels, restaurants, and attractions posted by other travelers who use Trip Advisor.
	TripIt	This is a great app if you travel frequently because it consolidates your travel plans in one place. When you book a trip, you email your itinerary to the TripIt address. The details are extracted and a TripIt itinerary is created. The app then tracks the status of flights and other information and it keeps you informed of any changes. For example, if a flight gets delayed, you see a notification and your itinerary is automatically updated.
	Urban Spoon	This app provides information about restaurants and enables you to book reservations in many of them. You can find restaurants by category, such as pizza, or based on reviews or location.
	WebMD	You can use this one to look up symptoms of health problems to help you identify potential causes and treatment. You can also look up medical terms, get information about tests and treatments, and access other medical information.

Table 16-1 continued

	App	Description
	Yelp	This is another app you can use to find places of interest to you, including shopping, restaurants, gas stations, and more. You can also get deals at participating organizations and read reviews posted by other Yelp users.

Looking into the Future

With the announcement of the iPhone 6 and iPhone 6 Plus, Apple also announced two other major developments to come in the near future. While these weren't far enough along to cover in detail in this book, you should be aware of them.

Apple Pay

NEW! Apple Pay enables you to pay for things more easily and securely than with physical credit cards. (Note: Apple Pay requires an iPhone 6 or iPhone 6 Plus, or later.) When you are making a purchase in a physical store, you can simply hold your iPhone up to a contactless reader connected to the cash register and tap your finger on the Touch ID button. The iPhone communicates the information required to complete the purchase.

Apple Pay also simplifies purchases made in online stores.

Apple Pay is actually more secure than using a credit card because your credit card information is not passed to the device; instead a unique code is passed that ties back to your card, but that can't be used again. And, you never present your credit card so the number is not visible to anyone, either visually or digitally.

When Apple Pay is released, you can store your credit cards in the Passbook app, and they are instantly available to make purchases.

To Come

At press time, Apple was still going through some development of Apple Pay. Check on this book's website (see the back cover for details) for updated information on this capability.

Apple Watch

NEW! Apple's Watch is well, a watch. Except Apple's Watch is a sophisticated piece of technology that enables you to use apps just like those you use on your iPhone (an iPhone 5 or newer is required to use the Apple Watch). You can take phone calls, send and receive messages and emails, use Apple Pay, and much more just from a small device on your wrist.

To keep tabs on the developments of the Apple Watch, check out http://www. apple.com/watch.

Index